Foreign Exchange Option Pricing

For other titles in the Wiley Finance series
please see www.wiley.com/finance

Foreign Exchange Option Pricing

A Practitioner's Guide

Iain J. Clark

A John Wiley and Sons, Ltd., Publication

This edition first published 2011
© 2011 Iain J. Clark

Registered office

John Wiley & Sons Ltd, The Atrium, Southern Gate, Chichester, West Sussex, PO19 8SQ, United Kingdom

For details of our global editorial offices, for customer services and for information about how to apply for permission to reuse the copyright material in this book please see our website at www.wiley.com.

Library of Congress Cataloging-in-Publication Data

Clark, Iain J.
Foreign exchange option pricing : a practitioner's guide / Iain J. Clark.
    p. cm.
ISBN 978-0-470-68368-2
1. Options (Finance)–Prices.   2. Stock options.   3. Foreign exchange rates.   I. Title.
HG6024.A3C563   2011
332.4′5–dc22

                                                            2010030438

A catalogue record for this book is available from the British Library.

ISBN 978-0-470-68368-2
Typeset in 10/12pt Times by Aptara Inc., New Delhi, India
Printed in Great Britain by Antony Rowe Ltd, Chippenham, Wiltshire

For Isabel

Contents

Acknowledgements

I would like to thank everyone at Standard Bank, particularly Peter Glancey and Marcelo Labre, for their patience during the execution of this work. This is an industry book and it would not have happened without the help and encouragement of everyone I've worked with, most recently at Standard Bank and in previous years at JP Morgan, BNP Paribas, Lehman Brothers, Dresdner Kleinwort and Commerzbank. As such, special thanks are due to David Kitson, Jérôme Lebuchoux, Marek Musiela, Nicolas Jackson, Robert Campbell, Dominic O'Kane, Ronan Dowling, Tim Sharp, Ian Robertson, Alex Langnau and John Juer.

A special debt of gratitude to Messaoud Chibane, outstanding quant and very good friend, who has encouraged me every step of the way over the years.

For parts of Chapter 11, I am indebted to the excellent work on longdated modelling of my former team members at Dresdner Kleinwort: Andrey Gal, Chia Tan, Olivier Taghi and Lars Schouw.

I must also thank Pete Baker, Aimee Dibbens, Karen Weller and Lori Boulton at Wiley Finance for their help and patience with me during the completion and production of this work, as well as all the rest of the Wiley team who have done such an excellent job to bring this book to publication. While I take sole responsibility for any errors that remain in this work, I am very grateful to Pat Bateson and Rachael Wilkie for their thoroughness in checking the manuscript. Thanks are due to my literary agent Isabel White for seeing the potential for me to write a book on this topic.

I would also like to thank my amazing wife, to whom I owe more than I can possibly say. I am as always grateful to my parents John and Joan for their love, support and tolerance of my difficult questions and interest in science and mathematics – I'm glad to say some things haven't changed so much! Also to my extended family, whom I don't get to see as often as I would like, thanks for keeping us in your thoughts and all your messages of encouragement. They mean a lot to an author.

Finally, to my young nieces and nephews in Canada – Andrew, Bradley, Isabel, Mackenzie and William – who asked me if my mathematics book for grown-ups was going to have 'very hard sums' like $1\,000\,010 - 1\,000\,000\,012$, I have a *very* hard sum just for you:

$$
\begin{array}{r}
101\,598\,490 \\
+ \quad \underline{21\,858\,299}
\end{array}
$$

This book is for you and for all students, young and old, of the mathematical arts. I wish you all the very best with your studies and your work.

Web page for this book

www.fxoptionpricing.com

List of Tables

List of Figures

1
Introduction

This book covers foreign exchange (FX) options from the point of view of a practitioner in the area. With content developed with input from industry professionals and with examples using real-world data, this book introduces many of the more commonly requested products from FX options trading desks, together with the models that capture the risk characteristics necessary to price these products accurately, an area often neglected in the literature, which is nevertheless of paramount importance in the real financial marketplace. Essentially this is a mathematical practitioner's cookbook that contains all the information necessary to price both vanilla and exotic FX options in a professional context.

Connecting mathematically rigorous theory with practice, and inspired by the questions asked daily by junior quantitative analysts (quants) and other colleagues (both from FX and other asset classes) this book is aimed at quants, quant developers, traders, structurers and anyone who works with them. Basically, this is the book I wish I'd had when I started in the industry. This book will also be of real benefit to academics, students of mathematical finance across all asset classes and anyone wishing to enter this area of finance.

The level of knowledge assumed is about at the level of Hull (1997) and Baxter and Rennie (1996) – both excellent introductory works. This work extends that knowledge base specifically into FX and I hope will be useful to those joining (or hoping to join) the finance industry, to industry practitioners who wish to learn more about FX as an asset class or the numerical techniques used in FX, and last but not least to academics – both in regard to their own work and as a reference for their students.

1.1 A GENTLE INTRODUCTION TO FX MARKETS

The simplest foreign exchange transaction one can imagine is going to a *bureau de change*, such as one might find in an airport, and exchanging a certain number of banknotes or coins of one currency for a certain amount of notes and coins of another realm. For example, on 24 September 2009, the currency converter at www.oanda.com was quoting a GBPUSD rate of 1.63935 US dollars per pound sterling (or conversely, 0.6100 pounds sterling per US dollar). Thus, neglecting two-sided bid–offer pricing and commissions, a holidaymaker at Heathrow seeking to buy $100.00 for his/her holiday in Miami should expect to pay £61.00.

This transaction is, to within a minute or two, immediate. Now let us suppose instead that the transaction is larger in notional by a factor of 1000 – perhaps motivated by investment purposes. Suppose that our traveller is seeking to transfer pounds sterling into a US account as a deposit on the purchase of a condo in Miami. The traveller is clearly not going to pull out £61 000.00 in the Heathrow departures hall and expect to collect $100 000.00 in crisp unmarked US dollar bills. A trade of this size will be executed in the FX spot market, and instead of the US dollar funds being available in a minute or two (and the UK pound funds being transferred away from the client), the exchange of funds happens at the spot date, which is generally in a couple of days (this is vague; see Section 1.4 for exact details). This lag is largely for historical reasons. On that day, the US dollar funds appear in the client's US account

Figure 1.1   Dates of importance for FX trading

and the UK pound sterling funds are transferred out of the client's UK account. This process is referred to as *settlement*. The risk that one of these payments goes through but the other does not is referred to as foreign exchange settlement risk or Herstatt risk (after the famous example of Herstatt bank defaulting on dollar payments on 26 June 1974).

Another possibility is that perhaps the traveller is flying to Miami to see a new build apartment building being built, and he/she knows that the $100 000.00 will be needed in six months' time. To lock in the currency rate today and protect against currency risk, he/she could enter into an FX forward, which fixes the rate today and requires the funds to be transferred in six months. The date in the future when the settlement must take place is called the *delivery date*.

A third possibility is that the traveller, being structurally long in pounds sterling, could buy an option to protect against depreciation of the sterling amount over the six month interval – in other words, an option to buy USD (and, equivalently, sell GBP) – i.e. a put on the GBPUSD exchange rate, at a prearranged strike price. This removes any downside risk, at the cost of the option premium. Since the transaction is deferred into the future, we have the delivery date (just as for the forward) but also an *expiry date* when the option holder must decide whether or not to exercise the option.

There are, therefore, as many as four dates of importance: today (sometimes called the *horizon date*), spot, expiry and delivery (see Figure 1.1).

Being a practitioner's guide, this chapter seeks to describe exactly how all these important dates are determined, and the next chapter describes how they impact the price of foreign currency options. A good introductory discussion can be found in Section 3.3 of Wystup (2006), but the devil is very much in the detail.

1.2   QUOTATION STYLES

Unlike other asset classes, in FX there is no natural numeraire currency. While no sensible investor would denominate his or her wealth in the actual number of IBM or Lehman Brothers stocks he or she owns, it is perfectly natural for investors to measure their wealth in US dollars, euros, Aussie dollars, etc. As a result, there is no special reason to quote spot or forward rates for foreign currency in any particular order. The choice of which way around they are quoted is purely market convention.

For British pounds against the US dollar, with ISO codes[1] of GBP and USD respectively, the market standard quote could be GBPUSD (the price of 1 GBP in USD) or USDGBP (the price of 1 USD in GBP). For this particular currency pair, it is the former – GBPUSD.

Note that the mainstream financial press, such as the *Financial Times* and the *Economist* (in the tables inside the back cover), report the values of all currencies in the same quote terms – for example, the value of one US dollar in each of AUD, CAD, EUR, MXN, . . . , ZAR. While easier to understand, this is *not* the way spot rates are quoted in FX markets.

---

[1] ISO 4217 code, from the International Organization for Standardization; www.iso.org.

Table 1.1 Currency pair quotation conventions and market terminology

Currency pair	Common trading floor jargon
EURUSD	Euro-dollar
USDJPY	Dollar-yen
EURJPY	Euro-yen
GBPUSD	Cable (from the late 1800s transatlantic telegraph cables)
EURGBP	Euro-sterling
USDCHF	Dollar-swiss
AUDUSD	Aussie-dollar
NZDUSD	Kiwi-dollar
USDCAD	Dollar-cad (or dollar-canada or, less commonly, dollar-loonie)
EURNOK	Euro-nokkie
EURSEK	Euro-stockie (from Stockholm)
EURDKK	Euro-danish
EURHUF	Euro-huff ('huff', not H-U-F)
EURPLN	Euro-polish
USDTRY	Dollar-turkey (or dollar-try, pron. 'try')
USDZAR	Dollar-rand (or dollar-zar, pron. 'zar')
USDMXN	Dollar-mex ('mex', not M-E-X)
USDBRL	Dollar-brazil
USDSGD	Dollar-sing

For a currency pair quoted[2] as ccy1ccy2, the spot rate S_t at time t is the number of units of ccy2 (also known as the domestic currency, the terms currency or the quote currency) required to buy one unit of ccy1 (the foreign currency or sometimes the base currency) – the spot rate being fixed today and with settlement occurring on the spot date. The spot rate is therefore dimensionally equal to units of ccy2 per ccy1 – this is why pedantic quants such as myself tend to discourage currency pairs from being written with a slash ('/') between the currency ISO codes. It's all too easy to read 'GBP/USD' as 'GBP per USD', which is *not* what the market quotes. The GBPUSD quote is for US dollars per pound sterling, so if GBPUSD is 1.63935, then one British pound can be bought for $1.63935 in the spot market. It's a USD per GBP price. It's the cost of one pound, in dollars.

Note that on FX trading floors, the spot rate S_t is invariably read aloud with the word 'spot' used to indicate the decimal place, e.g. 'one **spot** six three nine three five' in the GBPUSD example above. The exception is where there are no digits trailing the decimal place; e.g. if the spot rate for USDJPY was 92.00, we would read this out as '92 **the figure**'.

When I was first learning this, I found it convenient to remember that precious metals are quoted in the same way as currencies (gold has the ISO code XAU, silver has the ISO code XAG and similarly we have XPT and XPD) and are quoted, for example, as 'currency' pair XAUUSD, with spot rate close to 1000.00 (in September 2009). That number means $1000 per ounce – 1000 USD per XAU. Having a physical ounce of gold to think about may help you keep your bearings where this whole currency 1/currency 2 thing is concerned.

In fact, to sound the part on a trading floor, the names in Table 1.1 above are recommended (FX practitioners rarely refer to a currency pair by spelling out the three-letter currency

---

[2] The use of monikers such as ccy1 and ccy2 is standard among FX market practitioners. It is also very confusing when one gets into the world of quantos and multicurrency options and therefore is generally avoided in that context.

ISO code if they can possibly avoid it – though you may hear it for some emerging market currencies).

So how do we know which way round a particular currency pair should be quoted? Regrettably, it's purely market convention and seems to be quite arbitrary, as the examples shown in the first column of Table 1.1 demonstrate. There are, however, a few guidelines that hint at which ordering is more likely.

Currency quote styles – heuristic rules

1. Precious metals are always ccy1 against *any* currency, e.g. XAGUSD.
2. Euro is always ccy1, unless rule (1) takes precedence, e.g. EURCHF.
3. Emerging market (EM) currencies strongly tend to be ccy2, e.g. USDBRL, USDMXN, USDZAR, EURTRY, etc., as EM currencies are very often weaker than the majors and this quote style gives a spot rate greater than unity, which is easier for bookkeeping. The same heuristic holds even if the currency is revalued, as in the revaluation of the Turkish currency from TRL to TRY in 2005.
4. Currencies that historically[3] were subdivided into nondecimal units (e.g. pounds, shillings and pence[4]), such as GBP, AUD and NZD, tend to be ccy1 for ease of accounting. To give an example, it was much easier back in the late 1940s to quote GBPUSD as \$4.03 per pound sterling than to quote USDGBP as 4 shillings and $11\frac{1}{2}$ pence per US dollar.[5] For INR (and presumably PKR), heuristic (3) takes precedence.
5. For currency pairs where the spot rate would be either markedly greater than or markedly less than unity, the quote style tends to end up being the quote style that gives a spot rate significantly greater than unity, once again for ease of bookkeeping – e.g. USDJPY, with spot levels around 100.0 rather than JPYUSD, which would have spot levels around 0.01. Similarly USDNOK would be around 5.8.

Counterexamples to the above heuristic rules exist with probability one, but the general pattern holds surprisingly often. What I hope to convey above is that while the market conventions are arbitrary, there is at least *some* underlying logic.

A useful hierarchy of which of the major currencies dominate in their propensity to be ccy1 can be written:

$$\text{EUR} > \text{GBP} > \text{AUD} > \text{NZD} > \text{USD} > \text{CAD} > \text{CHF} > \text{JPY}.$$

As spot rates are quoted to finite precision, the least significant digit in the spot rate is called a pip. It represents the smallest usual price increment possible in the FX spot market (though half-pips are becoming more common with tighter spreads). A big figure is invariably 100 pips and is often tacitly assumed when quoting a rate. A few examples are: if the spot rate for EURUSD is 1.4591, the big figure is 1.45 and there are 91 additional pips in the price.

---

[3] In the 20th century, anyway.

[4] An interesting historical note is that the florin, a very early precursor to decimal coinage worth 2 shillings, was introduced in Britain in 1849 bearing the inscription 'one tenth of a pound', to test whether the public would be comfortable with the idea of decimal coinage. They weren't – the coin stayed, but the inscription was dropped.

[5] There are only two currencies in the world that still have nondecimal currency subunits – those of Mauritania and Madagascar, with ISO codes of MRO and MGA respectively.

If the spot rate for EURJPY is 131.25, the big figure is 131 and there are 25 additional pips. Finally, to return to our earlier example, if the spot rate for GBPUSD is 1.63935, the big figure is 1.63 and there are $93\frac{1}{2}$ additional pips.

Most currency pairs are quoted to five significant figures, except for those currencies that fall through a particular level and lose a digit – e.g. USDJPY used to trade at levels well above 100.00 and had a pip value of 0.01, but in late 2009, with the currency pair trading closer to 90.00, only four significant figures remain. Many currency pairs have a pip value of 0.0001, with some exceptions. A couple of examples are: majors against the Japanese yen, which have a pip value of 0.01, and majors against the Korean won, with a pip value of 0.1. Other exceptions are easy to find.

1.3 RISK CONSIDERATIONS

In equities, it should be pretty clear whether one is considering upside or downside risk. Downside risk is if the value of the stock goes down and upside risk is if the stock appreciates dramatically. Further, if one is long the stock, then upside risk is positive to the stockholder and downside risk is negative.

In FX, the complexity of having two currencies to consider makes this more subtle. Perhaps one is a euro based investor who is long USD dollars. In that case the investor, regarding this particular exposure, is long US dollars and commensurately short euros. More complicated situations arise when options are introduced: if the euro based investor above attempts to hedge his or her long USD/short EUR position by buying a USD put/EUR call option. Since the premium for such an option is generally quoted in USD (see Section 3.3.1), purchasing the FX option hedge will make the option holder's position somewhat shorter US dollars (as intended) and longer euros from holding the option – and additionally, short the number of USD required to purchase the option.

1.4 SPOT SETTLEMENT RULES

A foreign currency spot transaction, if entered into today with spot reference S_0, will involve the exchange of N_d units of domestic currency for N_f units of foreign currency, where the two notionals are related by the spot rate S_0, i.e. $N_d = S_0 \cdot N_f$. However, these two payments are in general *not* made on the day the transaction is agreed. The day on which the two payments, in domestic and foreign currency, are made is known as the *value date*. For conventional spot trades, which are almost always the case, it is known as the *spot date*. So we have two dates of special interest: today and spot.

It is often believed that FX trades settle two business days (2bd) after the trade date, known as T+2 settlement, so that the spot date is obtained by counting forward to the second good business day after today. This is mostly correct, but with some notable exceptions and with the specific handling of holidays requiring some further explanation.

The first point to make is that not all currency pairs trade with T+2 settlement. The most commonly cited exception is USDCAD which trades with T+1 settlement; i.e. the currencies are exchanged one good business day after today. Eventually we shall probably see some currency pairs trading with T+0 settlement. In the meantime, at the time of compilation of this work, the exceptions to T+2 settlement I could find are listed in Table 1.2. For notational

Table 1.2   Currency pair exceptions to T+2 settlement

ccy1	ccy2				
	USD	EUR	CAD	TRY	RUB
USD			T+1	T+1	T+1
EUR	T+2		T+2	T+1	T+1
CAD				T+1	T+1
TRY					T+1
RUB					

ease, we shall refer to T+x settlement. Now we need to define the concept of a good business day for currency pairs.

Definition: A day is a good business day for a currency ccy if it is not a weekend (Saturday and Sunday for most currencies, but not always for Islamic countries). For currency pairs ccy1ccy2, a day is only a good business day if it is a good business day for both ccy1 and ccy2.

The situation with respect to currencies in the Islamic world is complicated, and appears to vary by institution and country. The reason for this is that Friday is a particularly holy day for Jumu'ah prayers in the Muslim faith, influencing trading calendars similarly to Sunday in the Christian faith.

Weekends in Islamic countries are generally constructed with this in mind. For some countries such as Saudi Arabia, the weekend is taken on Thursday and Friday. It is, however, becoming more common for Islamic countries to change to observing weekends on Friday and Saturday – such as is the case in Algeria, Bahrain, Egypt, Iraq, Jordan, Kuwait, Oman, Qatar, Syria and the UAE – in an effort to harmonise business arrangements with the rest of the world and their neighbours.

Since readers with a special geographic interest in this trading region very likely have colleagues with local experience they can refer questions to directly, I refer the reader to the section 'Arab currencies' of the web page http://www.londonfx.co.uk/valdates.html for further details.

To give an idea of the sort of potential complexity one may encounter, a T+2 spot FX transaction in a currency pair such as USDSAR effected on a Wednesday may well have a spot date of Monday the next week (the two business days counting forward from Wednesday being Thursday and Friday in the USA and Saturday and Sunday in Saudi Arabia), but one may even have split settlement where the dollars are settled on Friday and the Saudi Arabian riyal are settled separately on Monday.

The determination of the *spot date* for currency pair ccy1ccy2, from the *today date*, is best described by the following algorithm. Note that settlement can neither be on a USD holiday nor a holiday in either of the currencies in the currency pair – this arises when constructing such a spot trade via the crosses of ccy1 and ccy2 versus USD. For currency pairs with T+2 settlement, the interim date *can* be a USD holiday so long as it is not a holiday in any non-USD currencies in the currency pair – except for currency pairs involving 'special' Latin American currencies such as MXN, ARS and CLP, which impose the same restrictions for the interim date as the settlement date itself.

Spot settlement rules – algorithm

function SpotFromHorizonDate(horizonDate)

```
if T+2 settlement   // Step 1
{
if CCY1 or CCY2 is a ''special'' LatAm currency // MXN, ARS,
CLP (not BRL)
{
advance forward one good business day, skipping CCY1, CCY2
and USD holidays
}
else
{
advance forward one good business day, skipping holidays in
CCY1 (unless CCY1=USD) and similarly skipping holidays in
CCY2 (unless CCY2=USD)
}
}

// step 2
if T+1 or T+2 settlement, or T+0 settlement and today is either
not a good business day or a holiday in CCY1, CCY2 or USD
{
advance forward one good business day, skipping holidays in
CCY1, CCY2 and USD
}
```

Spot settlement rules – examples

(a) EURUSD: Today: Mon 28Sep09, Spot: Wed 30Sep09 // T+2
(b) USDTRY: Today: Thu 12Feb09, Spot: Fri 13Feb09 // T+1
(c) GBPUSD: Today: Sat 20Jun09, Spot: Tue 23Jun09 // T+2 from a weekend
(d) EURUSD: Today: Wed 29Apr09, Spot: Mon 04May09 // 01May09 = EUR holiday
(e) USDCAD: Today: Fri 31Jul09, Spot: Tue 04Aug09 // 03Aug09 = CAD holiday
(f) AUDNZD: Today: Thu 08Oct09, Spot: Tue 13Oct09 // 12Oct09 = USD holiday
(g) USDBRL: Today: Tue 10Nov09, Spot: Thu 12Nov09 // 11Nov09 = USD holiday
(h) USDMXN: Today: Tue 10Nov09, Spot: Fri 13Nov09 // 11Nov09 = USD holiday

The spot date for today and the spot date relative to any expiry date (see Section 1.5 below) are known as *value dates*, and are by convention rolled forward to the next applicable value date at 5 pm New York time – with the exception of NZDUSD, which rolls forward at 7 am Auckland time. Note that these times are fixed in local time, and depending on whether the USA or New Zealand are currently observing daylight savings time, this will affect the exact time of the value date rollover in other financial centres, or even relative to UTC.

1.5   EXPIRY AND DELIVERY RULES

If we have an FX option that expires on a particular date (the expiry date), then, if exercised, it will (generally) be exercised as a spot FX transaction at the prearranged strike K. Consequently, the delivery date bears the same $T + x$ relationship to the expiry date that the spot date bears to today – though it can be later, in which case the option is said to have a delayed delivery feature.

If an option is specified with a concrete expiry date, e.g. 22Sep09, then the determination of the delivery date follows from Section 1.4 above. However, it is more common for options to be quoted for a specific term, e.g. 9D, 2W, 3M or 1Y (days, weeks, months and years respectively). How do we interpret this?

The devil is once again in the detail. For terms expressed as n months or n years, we count forward from the spot date by n or $12n$ calendar months respectively to obtain the delivery date, making sure that we don't inadvertently roll over the end of a month (i.e. using the *modified forward* convention, which is explained properly in Section 1.5.2 below). This aligns the delivery date for a 1M, 2M, . . . , 1Y, . . . FX option with the settlement date for an FX forward of the same tenor. We then count backwards to obtain the expiry date, which has *that* date as its value date. A simple example of this is given in Section II.B of the Master Agreement in ICOM (1997).

However, for terms expressed as n days or n weeks, as there is no liquid FX forwards market quoted with respect to tenors measured in an integral number of days or weeks, we count forward from today by n or $7n$ calendar days respectively to determine the expiry date (if the date arrived at isn't a good expiry date, we adjust that expiry date forward if required so that it is a good business day). Finally, the delivery date is given by obtaining the spot date corresponding to that expiry date using the procedure described in Section 1.4 above.

In short, for expiries measured in days or weeks, we count forward from today to the expiry date and then forward to the delivery date – but for expiries measured in months or years, we count forward from the spot date to the delivery date and then back to the expiry date.

1.5.1   Expiry and delivery rules – days or weeks

The prescription here is to count forward n or $7n$ calendar days from today to obtain the expiry date. If the candidate for the expiry date arrived at is a holiday in whichever of ccy1 and ccy2 is not USD (or both, if ccy1ccy2 is a cross), then we keep counting forward (going over the end of a month into the next month is perfectly permissible) until we have a good business day that is not a holiday in whichever of ccy1 and ccy2 is not USD. Note that USD holidays are completely disregarded for determination of the expiry date.

Expiry rule – days or weeks – algorithm

function ExpiryFromToday(today,term,units)

```
if units = 'D'   // Step 1 - obtain candidate expiry date
d = today + term
else if units = 'W'
d = today + 7*term
else
throw error
```

```
// Step 2 - obtain actual expiry date by avoiding impermissible
holidays
x1 = false
x2 = false
x1 = isCcy1Holiday(d)
x2 = isCcy2Holiday(d)
while (IsWeekend(d) or x1 or x2)
{
d = d + 1
x1 = isCcy1Holiday(d)
x2 = isCcy2Holiday(d)
}
expiry = d
delivery = SpotFromHorizonDate(expiry)
```

1.5.2   Expiry and delivery rules – months or years

The prescription for inferring the expiry and delivery dates when the tenor is provided in units of months or years is the following. We roll forward from today's spot date by that number of months or years, making sure that we don't inadvertently move over the end of a month end boundary. For example, if the spot date is Mon 31 Jan 2011, then the 1M delivery date obviously cannot be 31 February (February only has 29 days at most!) and commonsense requires that it be set to Monday 28 Feb 2011, and not roll over into any date in March.

Markets generally implement this using what is referred to as the *modified following* convention. Suppose the spot date is the ith day of month X and we need to calculate the delivery date n months forward from the spot date.

If this spot date is the last good business day of month X, then the delivery date is the last good business day of month $X + n$. Additionally, if month $X + n$ has less than i days or the ith day of month $X + n$ is beyond the last good business day in that month, the delivery date is the last good business day in month $X + n$.

If none of these conditions hold, then the delivery date is set to the jth day of month $X + n$, where $j \geq i$ is the first good business day in month $X + n$, obtained by counting forward from the ith day of month $X + n$ until a good business day (possibly even the ith day itself) is found.

Expiry rule – months or years – algorithm

function DeliveryFromSpot(spotDate,term,units)

```
m = (units = 'Y') ? 12 : 1 // should allow only units of 'M' or 'Y'
convertDateToYearMonthDay(spotDate, theYear, theMonth, theDay)
theMonth = theMonth + m * term
while (theMonth > 12)
{
theMonth = theMonth - 12
theYear = theYear + 1
```

```
}
numberOfDaysInMonth = LastDayOfMonth(theMonth, theYear)
if spotDate is the last good business day in the month for
CCY1CCY2 (excluding holidays in CCY1 and CCY2)
{
theDay = numberOfDaysInMonth // ensure that month end sticks
to month end
}
if (theDay > numberOfDaysInMonth) theDay = numberOfDaysInMonth

d = DateSerial(theYear, theMonth, theDay)

switch (theDay)
case numberOfDaysInMonth:
while (!isValidFXDeliveryDay(d, ccy1, ccy2)) { d = d - 1 }
return d

default:   // i.e. theDay < numberOfDaysInMonth
while (!isValidFXDeliveryDay(d, ccy1, ccy2)) { d = d + 1 }
if (d.month() <> theMonth)
{
d = d - 1
while (!isValidFXDeliveryDay(d, ccy1, ccy2)) { d = d - 1 }
}
return d
```

Once we have the delivery date, we find the expiry date by selecting the furthest horizon date in the future, subject to being a good business day and a trading day in at least one centre, which has a spot date corresponding to the given delivery date.

function ExpiryFromDelivery(deliveryDate)


```
d = deliveryDate
while (d is a weekend or 01JAN or a CCY1 holiday (unless CCY1=USD)
or a CCY2 holiday (unless CCY2=USD) or SpotFromHorizonDate(d) >
deliveryDate) { d = d - 1 }
return d
```

1.6   CUTOFF TIMES

From Section 1.5 above, we are able to determine the expiry date. However, at what *time* on that date should the option be understood to expire? This is a particularly relevant question given the international 24-hour markets that FX trades in.

There are, in practice, only a few possibilities that arise – these are known as *cutoff times*. As a rule, the cutoff is 3 pm local time in the trading centre in question, with the exception of New York, for which it is 10 am local time. However, as Hicks (2000) describes, 10 am New York time usually coincides with 3 pm London time, except when one centre is on daylight saving time (DST) and the other is not. As a result, the London cutoff is extremely rarely used – the most common cutoff by far, and the one that is implicitly meant when a particular cutoff is not

Table 1.3 Cutoff times

Cutoff	Fixing centre	Local time	UTC time
NYO	New York	10 am EST (10 am EDT)	3 pm (2 pm)
TOK	Tokyo	3 pm JST	6 am
ECB	Frankfurt	2:15 pm CET (2:15 pm CEST)	1:15 pm (12:15 pm)
LON	London	3 pm GMT (3 pm BST)	3 pm (2 pm)
SYD	Sydney	3 pm AEST (3 pm AEDT)	5 am (4 am)

specified, is the New York cutoff (NYO). This is typically used for trades originating out of Europe or the Americas: 10 am New York time, which in London is usually 3 pm local time, but is actually 2 pm for two weeks in late March and one in early November (this overlap last changed in 2005 and may change again in the future).

The most commonly encountered alternative is the Tokyo cutoff (TOK), which is used in the Asia-Pacific region. Another possibility, used more commonly with regard to fixing rates in structured products marketed to corporate customers, is the ECB cutoff, corresponding to the European Central Bank fixings published on Reuters page ECB37. An interesting feature of the ECB cutoff, as discussed by Becker and Wystup (2005) and Castagna (2010), is that the actual spot fixing at 2:15 pm Frankfurt time is not known with certainty until the page is electronically published 5–10 minutes later.

There are certainly other much less commonly used fixings that are occasionally encountered.

Table 1.3 shows some frequently encountered cutoffs,[6] both in local time and UTC time.

Note that while daylight savings time is in effect in the UK, local time there is British Summer Time (BST) – one hour ahead of UTC. For the remainder of the year, it is Greenwich Mean Time (GMT), which is basically equivalent to UTC for everyday applications.

Useful further references are http://www.newyorkfed.org/fxc/tokyo.pdf (page 34) and Section III.A.9 of ICOM (1997).

---

[6] Times shown in parentheses are the fixing times when daylight savings time is in effect in the fixing centre; e.g. 10 am EDT in NY corresponds to 2 pm UTC, etc. Note that Japan does not observe daylight savings time.

2
Mathematical Preliminaries

2.1 THE BLACK–SCHOLES MODEL

We require a model for FX spot rates that allows them to experience stochastic behaviour and strict positivity. These are the same requirements as for equities, in which the Black–Scholes model is applicable. We therefore follow Black and Scholes (1973) and the associated work of Garman and Kohlhagen (1983) as applied to foreign currency options, and describe the spot rate by a geometric Brownian motion

$$dS_t = \mu S_t\, dt + \sigma S_t\, dW_t. \tag{2.1}$$

Note that this is far from the only choice for a simple one-factor asset price process – Bachelier (1900) used an arithmetic Brownian motion

$$dS_t = \mu\, dt + \sigma\, dW_t$$

to derive closed-form pricing formulae for European options. Though of extremely limited practical use as it doesn't impose positivity of asset prices,[1] Crack (2001) poses this as a three-star exercise (Question 3.20) and provides a comprehensive worked solution in Appendix B.

Other more complex models for the FX spot process can be introduced. We will see more of these in Section 2.10 and subsequent chapters. For now, we introduce the Black–Scholes model.

2.1.1 Assumptions of the Black–Scholes model

The analysis of this chapter presupposes the standard Black–Scholes assumptions, as stated in Section 11.4 of Hull (1997):

1. The spot price S_t (in domestic currency) of one unit of foreign currency follows lognormal process (2.1), driven by constant volatility σ.
2. Short selling is permissible.
3. No transaction costs or taxes (i.e. frictionless trading).
4. Domestic and foreign currencies have risk-free rates r^d and r^f, constant across all maturities.
5. No riskless arbitrage.
6. Trading is continuous between now ($t = 0$) and expiry ($t = T$).

2.2 RISK NEUTRALITY

The analysis in this section relies on the presumption of risk neutrality. In its simplest form, this means that all risk-free portfolios can be assumed to earn the same risk-free rate. If this

---

[1] One could sensibly use it, however, as a one-factor model for spread options.

were not the case, then there would be an immediate arbitrage opportunity – one could borrow at the lowest risk-free rate and invest at the highest risk-free rate, locking in an instantaneous risk-free profit. Clear and thorough descriptions of the risk-neutral approach to option pricing can be found in Sundaram (1997) and Bingham and Kiesel (1998).

The crucial point for risk-neutral valuation of derivatives is that while the underlying asset is risky, and therefore derivatives on such a financial asset are also risky, a risk-free portfolio consisting of a combination of underlying assets and derivatives can be constructed that is instantaneously risk free. The proportions of the asset and the derivative do, however, vary with time, which is why the procedure is often referred to as *dynamic hedging* (Taleb, 1997).

In Section 2.3, we shall see that by exactly this principle of risk neutrality, the expected drift of the stochastic process (whether describing an equity price or an FX spot rate) does not enter into the partial differential equation governing the price of derivatives on the process. Consequently, the drift can be assumed to be the risk-neutral drift, i.e. the drift, which means that two tradeables have the same expected growth.

2.3 DERIVATION OF THE BLACK–SCHOLES EQUATION

The Black–Scholes analysis for obtaining a partial differential equation (PDE) governing the price of equity derivatives in the absence of dividends on the underlying equity is standard – see Black and Scholes (1973) and Chapter 11 of Hull (1997). The case of derivatives on foreign currencies (or, for that matter, on equities with continuous dividends) is slightly different, as discussed in Garman and Kohlhagen (1983). In this section, we present both.

2.3.1 Equity derivatives (without dividends)

Suppose that the price of a contingent claim $V(S_t, t)$, which derives its value from the performance of a tradeable equity security with asset price S_t, is known. How can we obtain any information about this? Let $V_t = V(S_t, t)$ denote[2] the value of the contingent claim at time t, conditional on the equity price being S_t at that time. Applying Itô, we have

$$dV_t = \frac{\partial V}{\partial t}dt + \frac{\partial V}{\partial S}dS_t + \frac{1}{2}\frac{\partial^2 V}{\partial S^2}dS_t^2. \qquad (2.2)$$

where dS_t^2 denotes the quadratic variation of S_t, not to be confused with differential increments in the second asset price process $S_t^{(2)}$, such as encountered in Chapter 10. However, we know from (2.1) that $dS_t^2 = \sigma^2 S_t^2\, dt$ and consequently at time t we have

$$dV_t = \left[\frac{\partial V}{\partial t} + \frac{1}{2}\sigma^2 S^2 \frac{\partial^2 V}{\partial S^2}\right]dt + \frac{\partial V}{\partial S}dS_t. \qquad (2.3)$$

The term inside the square brackets above is deterministic, whereas the term appearing in front of dS_t is the only stochastic term. We remove the stochastic term by construction of a portfolio Π_t, which is long one unit of the contingent claim (with value V_t) and short $\partial V/\partial S$ units of the underlying asset

$$\Pi_t = V_t - \frac{\partial V}{\partial S}S_t. \qquad (2.4)$$

---

[2] Note that the subscript does *not* denote $\partial V/\partial t$.

This has the stochastic differential equation (SDE)

$$d\Pi_t = dV_t - \frac{\partial V}{\partial S} dS_t \tag{2.5}$$

and from (2.3) we have

$$d\Pi_t = \left[\frac{\partial V}{\partial t} + \frac{1}{2}\sigma^2 S^2 \frac{\partial^2 V}{\partial S^2}\right] dt. \tag{2.6}$$

As the growth of Π_t is riskless, we can appeal to risk neutrality and equate the expected growth of Π_t to that of the domestic risk-free bond B_t^d, which is described by

$$dB_t^d = r^d B_t^d\, dt. \tag{2.7}$$

We therefore put

$$d\Pi_t = r^d \Pi_t\, dt, \tag{2.8}$$

where r^d denotes the domestic interest rate. Equating terms in (2.6) and (2.8) we have

$$\frac{\partial V}{\partial t} + \frac{1}{2}\sigma^2 S^2 \frac{\partial^2 V}{\partial S^2} = r^d \Pi_t$$

$$= r^d \left[V_t - \frac{\partial V}{\partial S} S\right], \tag{2.9}$$

leading to the familiar Black–Scholes equation

$$\frac{\partial V}{\partial t} + \frac{1}{2}\sigma^2 S^2 \frac{\partial^2 V}{\partial S^2} + r^d S \frac{\partial V}{\partial S} - r^d V_t = 0. \tag{2.10}$$

It is standard, and important, at this point to note that the real-world growth rate μ does not appear in the Black–Scholes equation in any form.

2.3.2 FX derivatives

The situation in FX is slightly more complicated in that the FX spot rate S_t is not a natural store of wealth and cannot be regarded as a tradeable as in the analysis above. One should instead think of it as the exchange rate as a stochastic conversion rate relating two numeraires, each of which has its *own* natural store of wealth – the money market account in either currency.

As in Section 2.3.1 we suppose that the price of a contingent claim $V(S_t, t)$ is known, which derives its value from the performance of an FX rate S_t. Note that the tradeable asset in this case is not the FX rate S_t; it is instead the foreign bond valued in units of the domestic currency, i.e. $S_t B_t^f$.

Once again using V_t to denote the price of the contingent claim at time t, we still have

$$dV_t = \left[\frac{\partial V}{\partial t} + \frac{1}{2}\sigma^2 S^2 \frac{\partial^2 V}{\partial S^2}\right] dt + \frac{\partial V}{\partial S} dS_t, \tag{2.11}$$

but the construction of the delta-hedged portfolio is somewhat different. As remarked above, we cannot buy and sell units of the FX spot rate – the construction of the hedged portfolio Π_t is obtained by going long one unit of the contingent claim (with value V_t) and short Δ_t units of the underlying foreign bond:

$$\Pi_t = V_t - \Delta_t S_t B_t^f. \tag{2.12}$$

The question is what value of Δ_t makes Π_t riskless. We have

$$
\begin{aligned}
d\Pi_t &= dV_t - \Delta_t d(S_t B_t^f) \\
&= dV_t - \Delta_t B_t^f dS_t - \Delta_t S_t dB_t^f \\
&= dV_t - \Delta_t B_t^f dS_t - \Delta_t S_t r^f B_t^f dt \\
&= dV_t - \Delta_t B_t^f \left[(r^d - r^f)S_t\, dt + \sigma S_t\, dW_t \right] - \Delta_t S_t r^f B_t^f\, dt \\
&= dV_t - \Delta_t B_t^f \left[r^d S_t\, dt + \sigma S_t\, dW_t \right] \\
&= \frac{\partial V}{\partial t} dt + \frac{1}{2}\sigma^2 S^2 \frac{\partial^2 V}{\partial S^2} dt + \frac{\partial V}{\partial S} dS_t - \Delta_t B_t^f \left[r^d S_t\, dt + \sigma S_t\, dW_t \right] \\
&= \frac{\partial V}{\partial t} dt + \frac{1}{2}\sigma^2 S^2 \frac{\partial^2 V}{\partial S^2} dt + \frac{\partial V}{\partial S} dS_t - \Delta_t B_t^f r^d S_t\, dt - \Delta_t B_t^f \sigma S_t\, dW_t \\
&= \left[\frac{\partial V}{\partial t} + \frac{1}{2}\sigma^2 S^2 \frac{\partial^2 V}{\partial S^2} - \Delta_t B_t^f r^d S_t \right] dt + \frac{\partial V}{\partial S} dS_t - \Delta_t B_t^f \sigma S_t\, dW_t \\
&= \left[\frac{\partial V}{\partial t} + \frac{1}{2}\sigma^2 S^2 \frac{\partial^2 V}{\partial S^2} - \Delta_t B_t^f r^d S_t \right] dt + \frac{\partial V}{\partial S} \left[(r^d - r^f)S_t\, dt + \sigma S_t\, dW_t \right] \\
&\quad - \Delta_t B_t^f \sigma S_t\, dW_t \\
&= \left[\frac{\partial V}{\partial t} + \frac{1}{2}\sigma^2 S^2 \frac{\partial^2 V}{\partial S^2} - \Delta_t B_t^f r^d S_t + \frac{\partial V}{\partial S}(r^d - r^f)S_t \right] dt \\
&\quad + \left[\frac{\partial V}{\partial S} - \Delta_t B_t^f \right] \sigma S_t dW_t.
\end{aligned}
\tag{2.13}
$$

From this we see that in order to cancel the dW_t term, we require Δ_t to satisfy $\Delta_t B_t^f = \partial V/\partial S$, i.e.

$$
\Delta_t = \frac{1}{B_t^f} \frac{\partial V}{\partial S}.
\tag{2.14}
$$

Substituting (2.14) into (2.13) we obtain

$$
d\Pi_t = \left[\frac{\partial V}{\partial t} + \frac{1}{2}\sigma^2 S^2 \frac{\partial^2 V}{\partial S^2} - r^d S_t \frac{\partial V}{\partial S} + \frac{\partial V}{\partial S}(r^d - r^f)S_t \right] dt.
\tag{2.15}
$$

Once again as in Section 2.3.1 we appeal to domestic risk neutrality and put $d\Pi_t = r^d \Pi_t\, dt$, where, in the FX context, from (2.12) and the analysis above,

$$
\Pi_t = V_t - \frac{\partial V}{\partial S} S_t.
\tag{2.16}
$$

We therefore have

$$
\left[\frac{\partial V}{\partial t} + \frac{1}{2}\sigma^2 S^2 \frac{\partial^2 V}{\partial S^2} - r^d S_t \frac{\partial V}{\partial S} + \frac{\partial V}{\partial S}(r^d - r^f)S_t \right] dt = r^d \left[V_t - \frac{\partial V}{\partial S} S_t \right] dt,
$$

which reduces to

$$
\frac{\partial V}{\partial t} + \frac{1}{2}\sigma^2 S^2 \frac{\partial^2 V}{\partial S^2} + (r^d - r^f)S\frac{\partial V}{\partial S} - r^d V = 0.
\tag{2.17}
$$

Note the appearance of the foreign interest rate r^f in the convection term (the term containing a multiple of $\partial V / \partial S$) but not in the forcing term (the term containing a multiple of V), and the absence of any μ term.

2.3.3   Terminal conditions and present value

Black–Scholes type PDEs such as (2.10) or (2.17) are able to describe the value of a derivative contract (we shall see examples of more complicated option pricing PDEs in subsequent chapters). Basically, these equations describe how the value of a derivative contract at a continuum of potential future scenarios diffuses backwards in time towards today. If the contract depends only upon the value of the tradeable process S_T at expiry T, i.e. $V_T = V_T(S_T)$, then we immediately have the terminal condition

$$V(S_T, T) = V_T(S_T)$$

and the value of the derivative contract today (the 'present value', or PV) can be directly read off from the $t = 0$ time slice:

$$PV = V(S_0, 0).$$

Note that in contrast to most partial differential equations encountered in engineering or physics, where the initial conditions are specified and the solution is sought at some future time, the option pricing PDEs encountered in finance are solved *backwards* in time – the terminal conditions are specified and the solution *today* is sought.

2.4   INTEGRATING THE SDE FOR S_T

From (2.1), let $dS_t = \mu S_t \, dt + \sigma S_t \, dW_t$. We can write this more simply as

$$\frac{dS_t}{S_t} = \mu \, dt + \sigma \, dW_t, \quad \text{noting that} \quad \frac{dS_t^2}{S_t^2} = \sigma^2 \, dt. \tag{2.18}$$

Consider the process $X_t = f(S_t)$ defined by $f(x) = \ln(x)$. We have $f'(x) = 1/x$ and $f''(x) = -x^{-2}$. A simple application of Itô's lemma gives

$$dX_t = f'(S_t) \, dS_t + \frac{1}{2} f''(S_t) \, dS_t^2$$

$$= \frac{dS_t}{S_t} - \frac{1}{2} \frac{dS_t^2}{S_t^2} \tag{2.19a}$$

$$= \mu \, dt + \sigma \, dW_t - \frac{1}{2}\sigma^2 \, dt. \tag{2.19b}$$

This can be immediately integrated to give

$$X_t = X_0 + \left(\mu - \frac{1}{2}\sigma^2 \right) t + \sigma [W_t - W_0]. \tag{2.20}$$

Since W_t is assumed to be a standardised Brownian motion with $W_0 = 0$, one obtains

$$X_T = X_0 + \left(\mu - \frac{1}{2}\sigma^2 \right) T + \sigma W_T \tag{2.21}$$

and since $X_t = \ln(S_t) \Leftrightarrow S_t = \exp(X_t)$, one obtains the desired result

$$S_T = S_0 \exp\left(\left(\mu - \frac{1}{2}\sigma^2\right)T + \sigma W_T\right). \tag{2.22}$$

Note that (2.21) can be written as

$$X_T = X_0 + \left(\mu - \frac{1}{2}\sigma^2\right)T + \sigma\sqrt{T}\xi, \tag{2.23}$$

where $\xi \sim N(0, 1)$.

2.5 BLACK–SCHOLES PDEs EXPRESSED IN LOGSPOT

The algebra of Section 2.4 shows that, under the assumption of geometric Brownian motion for the traded asset, it is easier to deal with the stochastic differential equation for logspot X_t than the equivalent stochastic differential equation for spot S_t, as the drift and volatility terms for X_t are homogeneous while those for S_t depend on the level of the traded asset. In the same manner, the Black–Scholes PDEs (2.10) and (2.17) are simpler when expressed in terms of spatial derivatives with respect to logspot x, as opposed to derivatives with respect to spot S. We obtain, for $V = V(X_t, t)$, with a slight abuse of notation as this should be $\hat{V} = \hat{V}(X_t, t)$:

$$\frac{\partial V}{\partial t} + \frac{1}{2}\sigma^2\frac{\partial^2 V}{\partial x^2} + \left(r^d - r^f - \frac{1}{2}\sigma^2\right)\frac{\partial V}{\partial x} - r^d V = 0. \tag{2.24}$$

2.6 FEYNMAN–KAC AND RISK-NEUTRAL EXPECTATION

From Section 2.3 above, we have a backward parabolic partial differential equation such as (2.10) or (2.17), which the price $V(S_t, t)$ of a derivative security must obey, as measured in units of the domestic currency. We make the observation that the drift μ of the underlying process for S_t does not enter into the partial differential equation.

The Feynman–Kac formula makes the connection between solution of such a partial differential equation and the expectation of the terminal value of the derivative under an artificial measure – i.e. *not* the real-world measure. If we have a backward Kolmogorov equation of the form

$$\frac{\partial g}{\partial t} + a(x, t)\frac{\partial g}{\partial x} + \frac{1}{2}b^2(x, t)\frac{\partial^2 g}{\partial x^2} = 0, \tag{2.25}$$

with terminal condition $g(x, T) = h(x)$, then the solution of (2.25) can be expressed as an expectation[3]

$$g(x, 0) = E^d\left[h(X_T)|X_0 = x\right], \tag{2.26}$$

where X_t is described by the diffusion[4]

$$dX_t = a(X_t, t)\,dt + b(X_t, t)\,dW_t^d. \tag{2.27}$$

---

[3] We use the notation $E^d[\cdot]$ as we shall identify this as expectation with respect to the domestic risk-neutral measure in Section 2.7 below.

[4] A similar notation is used for the driving Brownian motion W_t^d.

The Feynman–Kac result can be verified by considering the process $g_t = g(X_t, t)$ and constructing the stochastic differential for $\mathrm{d}g_t$:

$$\mathrm{d}g_t = \frac{\partial g}{\partial t}\mathrm{d}t + \frac{\partial g}{\partial x}\mathrm{d}X_t + \frac{1}{2}\frac{\partial^2 g}{\partial x^2}\mathrm{d}X_t^2. \tag{2.28}$$

Substituting (2.27) into (2.28), we have

$$\mathrm{d}g_t = \left[a(X_t, t)\frac{\partial g}{\partial x} + \frac{1}{2}b^2(X_t, t)\frac{\partial^2 g}{\partial x^2} + \frac{\partial g}{\partial t}\right]\mathrm{d}t + b(X_t, t)\frac{\partial g}{\partial x}\mathrm{d}W_t^d. \tag{2.29}$$

The term in square brackets above vanishes due to (2.25), and so

$$\mathrm{d}g_t = b(X_t, t)\frac{\partial g}{\partial x}\mathrm{d}W_t^d. \tag{2.30}$$

Integrating from $t = 0$ to T, we have

$$g_T = g_0 + \int_0^T b(X_t, t)\frac{\partial g}{\partial x}\mathrm{d}W_t^d.$$

Taking expectations, and recognising that the expectation of the Itô integral above is zero, we have

$$g_0 = \mathbf{E}^d[g_T].$$

We therefore have, as in (2.26), $g(X_0, 0) = \mathbf{E}^d[h(X_T)]$.

In the presence of a forcing term f, i.e.

$$\frac{\partial V}{\partial t} + a(x, t)\frac{\partial V}{\partial x} + \frac{1}{2}b^2(x, t)\frac{\partial^2 V}{\partial x^2} + f(x, t)V = 0, \tag{2.31}$$

the analysis above gives

$$\mathrm{d}V_t + f(X_t, t)V\mathrm{d}t = b(X, t, t)\frac{\partial V}{\partial x}\mathrm{d}W_t^d. \tag{2.32}$$

This is amenable to the stochastic integrating factor technique. Multiply the LHS and RHS of (2.32) by $\exp(\int_0^t f(X_s, s)\mathrm{d}s)$ and put $\hat{V}_t = \exp(\int_0^t f(X_s, s)\mathrm{d}s)V_t$. By the chain rule, we have

$$\mathrm{d}\hat{V}_t = \exp\left(\int_0^t f(X_s, s)\mathrm{d}s\right)\mathrm{d}V_t + \exp\left(\int_0^t f(X_s, s)\mathrm{d}s\right)f(X_t, t)V\,\mathrm{d}t.$$

We therefore have, from (2.32),

$$\mathrm{d}\hat{V}_t = \exp\left(\int_0^t f(X_s, s)\mathrm{d}s\right)b(X, t, t)\frac{\partial V}{\partial x}\mathrm{d}W_t^d.$$

Taking expectations as before and recognising that the expectation of the Itô integral above vanishes, we have $\hat{V}_0 = \mathbf{E}^d[V_T]$, i.e.

$$V_0 = \mathbf{E}^d\left[\exp\left(\int_0^t f(X_s, s)\mathrm{d}s\right)V_T\right]. \tag{2.33}$$

In the case where $f(X_s, s)$ is nonstochastic, though potentially a deterministic function of time t, we can take it outside the expectation, obtaining the result $V_0 = \exp(\int_0^t f(X_s, s)\mathrm{d}s)\mathbf{E}^d[\hat{V}_T]$.

Comparing (2.31) with (2.17), we put $a(S,t) = (r^d - r^f)S$, $b(S,t) = \sigma S$ and $f(S,t) = -r^d$, where we use S in place of x. The process (2.27) under which we take the expectation is therefore

$$dS_t = (r^d - r^f)S_t\, dt + \sigma S_t\, dW_t^d \tag{2.34}$$

and the result for the present value today is the discounted risk-neutral expectation under the domestic risk-neutral measure

$$V_0 = e^{-r^d T}\mathbf{E}^d\,[V_T]. \tag{2.35}$$

Fuller discussions of the Feynman–Kac approach can be found in Section 6.2.2.1 of Grigoriu (2002), Chapter VIII of Øksendal (1998), Section 5.8 of Bingham and Kiesel (1998) and Section 4.7 of Lipton (2001).

2.7   RISK NEUTRALITY AND THE PRESUMPTION OF DRIFT

In obtaining the Black–Scholes equations for equity and foreign currency derivatives above, we noticed that the real-world drift term μ does not appear, indicating that all rational market participants can be assumed to price derivatives identically no matter what value of μ is assumed for the expected drift. We saw in Section 2.6 above that the present value (in units of domestic currency) can be identified as the discounted expectation under a particular measure, which we refer to as the domestic risk-neutral measure.

In this section, we attempt to give a clearer introduction to the risk-neutral measure, which is often understood as taking a particular choice of drift μ in the price of the risky asset, so that the investor's expectation of the returns of the two assets available to him or her are identical. But what are these two assets? For equity derivatives, they are the equity and the domestic bond. However for FX, we have two bonds, but where the FX spot rate must be used to convert one into the numeraire currency. This gives two choices, and therefore not one but *two* risk-neutral measures. We refer the reader to Section 3.4 of Baxter and Rennie (1996) for further details of the change of measure approach in continuous time finance.

2.7.1   Equity derivatives (without dividends)

The domestic equity investor sees the equity S_t as the risky asset, driven by a Brownian motion W_t, which at time t has the distribution

$$S_t = S_0 \exp\left(\sigma W_t + \left(\mu - \frac{1}{2}\sigma^2\right)t\right). \tag{2.36}$$

Comparing this with the domestic bond $B_t^d = e^{r^d t}$, a truly risk-neutral investor must expect the two assets to have the same expected returns. The ratio of these should therefore be a martingale. We have

$$
\begin{aligned}
Z_t &= S_t/B_t^d \\
&= S_0 \exp\left(\sigma W_t + \left(\mu - \frac{1}{2}\sigma^2\right)t\right)\exp(-r^d t) \\
&= S_0 \exp\left(\sigma W_t - \frac{1}{2}\sigma^2 t\right)\exp((\mu - r^d)t).
\end{aligned}
$$

Now $\exp\left(\sigma W_t - \frac{1}{2}\sigma^2 t\right)$ is an exponential martingale, which means that if $\mu = r^d$ then Z_t is a martingale, as desired.

Therefore, under the domestic risk-neutral measure $\mathbf{P}^d$, we can write

$$S_t = S_0 \exp\left(\sigma W_t^d + \left(r^d - \frac{1}{2}\sigma^2\right)t\right) \tag{2.37}$$

or, equivalently,

$$dS_t = r^d S_t \, dt + \sigma S_t \, dW_t^d.$$

Note that the drift change required is

$$W_t^d = W_t + \frac{\mu - r^d}{\sigma}t, \tag{2.38}$$

which gives a Radon–Nikodym derivative at time T (annotated with an extra superscript to avoid confusion with the other Radon–Nikodym derivatives below) of

$$\frac{d\mathbf{P}^{d:\mathrm{EQ}}}{d\mathbf{P}} = \exp\left(-\gamma^{\mathrm{EQ}} W_T - \frac{1}{2}[\gamma^{\mathrm{EQ}}]^2 T\right), \quad \text{where } \gamma^{\mathrm{EQ}} = \frac{\mu - r^d}{\sigma}. \tag{2.39}$$

2.7.2 FX derivatives – domestic risk-neutral measure

In contrast, the domestic investor sees the foreign bond B_t^f as the risky asset, which, denominated in domestic currency, is valued at $B_t^f S_t$. Construct the ratio of this against the domestic bond:

$$
\begin{aligned}
Z_t &= S_t B_t^f / B_t^d \\
&= S_0 \exp\left(\sigma W_t + \left(\mu - \frac{1}{2}\sigma^2\right)t\right) \exp\left((r^f - r^d)t\right) \\
&= S_0 \exp\left(\sigma W_t - \frac{1}{2}\sigma^2 t\right) \exp\left((\mu + r^f - r^d)t\right).
\end{aligned}
$$

To attain the martingale property we require that

$$\mu = \mu^d \equiv r^d - r^f \tag{2.40}$$

(μ^d is used to avoid confusion below), so under the domestic risk-neutral measure $\mathbf{P}^d$ we write

$$S_t = S_0 \exp\left(\sigma W_t^d + \left(r^d - r^f - \frac{1}{2}\sigma^2\right)t\right),$$

$$dS_t = (r^d - r^f)S_t \, dt + \sigma S_t \, dW_t^d. \tag{2.41}$$

The drift change required is

$$W_t^d = W_t + \frac{\mu - \mu^d}{\sigma}t, \tag{2.42}$$

which gives a Radon–Nikodym derivative at time T of

$$\frac{d\mathbf{P}^d}{d\mathbf{P}} = \exp\left(-\gamma^d W_T - \frac{1}{2}[\gamma^d]^2 T\right), \quad \text{where } \gamma^d = \frac{\mu - \mu^d}{\sigma}. \tag{2.43}$$

2.7.3   FX derivatives – foreign risk-neutral measure

The result of Section 2.7.2 is of no surprise, but it leads naturally into construction of the foreign risk-neutral measure, which is not so widely known.

The foreign investor sees the domestic bond B_t^d as the risky asset, which denominated in foreign currency is valued at B_t^d / S_t or, equivalently, $B_t^d \hat{S}_t$, where $\hat{S}_t = 1/S_t$ denotes the flipped spot rate. By taking the reciprocal we have $\hat{S}_t = \hat{S}_0 \exp\left(-\sigma W_t + (\frac{1}{2}\sigma^2 - \mu)t\right)$ and therefore

$$B_t^d \hat{S}_t = \hat{S}_0 \exp\left(-\sigma W_t + \left(\frac{1}{2}\sigma^2 - \mu + r^d\right)t\right).$$

Construct the ratio of this quantity divided by the foreign bond B_t^f:

$$\begin{aligned}
\hat{Z}_t &= \hat{S}_t B_t^d / B_t^f \\
&= \hat{S}_0 \exp\left(-\sigma W_t + \left(\frac{1}{2}\sigma^2 - \mu + r^d - r^f\right)t\right) \\
&= \hat{S}_0 \exp\left(-\sigma W_t - \frac{1}{2}\sigma^2 t\right) \exp\left((-\mu + r^d - r^f + \sigma^2)t\right).
\end{aligned}$$

This indicates that $\hat{Z}_t$ is a martingale if

$$\mu = \mu^f \equiv r^d - r^f + \sigma^2, \tag{2.44}$$

so under the foreign risk-neutral measure $\mathbf{P}^f$ we write

$$\hat{S}_t = \hat{S}_0 \exp\left(-\sigma W_t^f + \left(\frac{1}{2}\sigma^2 - \mu^f\right)t\right)$$

or, alternatively, we can express the nonflipped spot rate

$$S_t = S_0 \exp\left(\sigma W_t^f + \left(\mu^f - \frac{1}{2}\sigma^2\right)t\right).$$

Therefore, under the foreign risk-neutral measure $\mathbf{P}^f$ we write

$$\begin{aligned}
S_t &= S_0 \exp\left(\sigma W_t^f + \left(r^d - r^f + \frac{1}{2}\sigma^2\right)t\right), \\
dS_t &= (r^d - r^f + \sigma^2)S_t \, dt + \sigma S_t \, dW_t^f.
\end{aligned} \tag{2.45}$$

The drift change required is

$$W_t^f = W_t + \frac{\mu - \mu^f}{\sigma}t, \tag{2.46}$$

which gives a Radon–Nikodym derivative at time T of

$$\frac{d\mathbf{P}^f}{d\mathbf{P}} = \exp\left(-\gamma^f W_T - \frac{1}{2}[\gamma^f]^2 T\right), \quad \text{where } \gamma^f = \frac{\mu - \mu^f}{\sigma}. \tag{2.47}$$

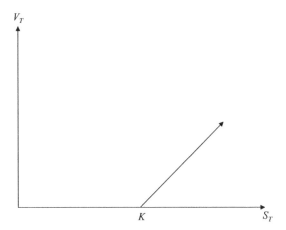

Figure 2.1 Payout function V_T for European call

2.8 VALUATION OF EUROPEAN OPTIONS

Consider a European call option with payout function $V_T = \max(S_T - K, 0) = (S_T - K)^+$ at time T, shown in Figure 2.1. By risk-neutral expectation, we can compute the price of such an option today by

$$
\begin{aligned}
V_0 &= \mathrm{e}^{-r^d T} \mathbf{E}^d \left[(S_T - K)^+ \right] \\
&= \mathrm{e}^{-r^d T} \mathbf{E}^d \left[(S_T - K)\mathbf{1}_{\{S_T \geq K\}} \right] \\
&= \mathrm{e}^{-r^d T} \mathbf{E}^d \left[S_T \mathbf{1}_{\{S_T \geq K\}} - K\mathbf{1}_{\{S_T \geq K\}} \right] \\
&= \mathrm{e}^{-r^d T} \mathbf{E}^d \left[S_T \mathbf{1}_{\{S_T \geq K\}} \right] - K\mathrm{e}^{-r^d T} \mathbf{E}^d \left[\mathbf{1}_{\{S_T \geq K\}} \right] \\
&= \mathrm{e}^{-r^d T} \mathbf{E}^d \left[S_T \mathbf{1}_{\{S_T \geq K\}} \right] - K\mathrm{e}^{-r^d T} \mathbf{P}^d \left[S_T \geq K \right]
\end{aligned}
\tag{2.48}
$$

In FX derivatives, the Black–Scholes price obtained in this way, in the absence of any term structure of interest rates or volatility, is referred to as the *theoretical value* and is usually denoted 'TV' in the pricing systems.

Computation of $\mathbf{P}^d [S_T \geq K]$, i.e. the domestic risk-neutral probability that $S_T \geq K$, is relatively trivial as we know the distribution of S_T. The other component requires a Radon–Nikodym change of measure argument, which in FX has a nice symmetry to it.

From Section 2.7, we have Radon–Nikodym derivatives relating domestic and foreign risk-neutral measures to the real-world measure (assuming μ), but we need to construct the Radon–Nikodym derivative relating one risk-neutral measure to the other. From (2.43) and (2.47) we have

$$
\frac{\mathrm{d}\mathbf{P}^d}{\mathrm{d}\mathbf{P}} = \exp\left(-\gamma^d W_T - \frac{1}{2}[\gamma^d]^2 T \right), \quad \text{where } \gamma^d = \frac{\mu - \mu^d}{\sigma}
\tag{2.49}
$$

and

$$
\frac{\mathrm{d}\mathbf{P}^f}{\mathrm{d}\mathbf{P}} = \exp\left(-\gamma^f W_T - \frac{1}{2}[\gamma^f]^2 T \right), \quad \text{where } \gamma^f = \frac{\mu - \mu^f}{\sigma},
\tag{2.50}
$$

which gives

$$\frac{\mathrm{d}\mathbf{P}^f}{\mathrm{d}\mathbf{P}^d} = \exp\left(-\gamma^{f,d}W_T^d - \frac{1}{2}[\gamma^{f,d}]^2 T\right), \quad \text{where } \gamma^{f,d} = \frac{\mu^d - \mu^f}{\sigma}. \tag{2.51}$$

We basically have

$$W_t^f = W_t^d + \frac{\mu^d - \mu^f}{\sigma}t = W_t^d - \sigma t. \tag{2.52}$$

From (2.40) and (2.44) we have $\mu^f - \mu^d = \sigma^2$ and so $\gamma^{f,d} = (\mu^d - \mu^f)/\sigma = -\sigma$. This gives

$$\frac{\mathrm{d}\mathbf{P}^f}{\mathrm{d}\mathbf{P}^d} = \exp\left(\sigma W_T^d - \frac{1}{2}\sigma^2 T\right) \tag{2.53}$$

or, equivalently,

$$W_t^f = W_t^d + \sigma t. \tag{2.54}$$

We can now use (2.53) to complete (2.48). Consider $\mathbf{E}^d\left[S_T\mathbf{1}_{\{S_T \geq K\}}\right]$. We have

$$\mathbf{E}^d\left[S_T\mathbf{1}_{\{S_T \geq K\}}\right] = \mathbf{E}^d\left[S_0\exp\left(\left(r^d - r^f - \frac{1}{2}\sigma^2\right)T + \sigma W_T^d\right)\mathbf{1}_{\{S_T \geq K\}}\right]$$

$$= S_0 e^{(r^d - r^f)T}\mathbf{E}^d\left[\exp\left(\sigma W_T^d - \frac{1}{2}\sigma^2 T\right)\mathbf{1}_{\{S_T \geq K\}}\right]$$

$$= S_0 e^{(r^d - r^f)T}\mathbf{E}^d\left[\frac{\mathrm{d}\mathbf{P}^f}{\mathrm{d}\mathbf{P}^d}\mathbf{1}_{\{S_T \geq K\}}\right]$$

$$= S_0 e^{(r^d - r^f)T}\mathbf{E}^f\left[\mathbf{1}_{\{S_T \geq K\}}\right]$$

$$= S_0 e^{(r^d - r^f)T}\mathbf{P}^f\left[S_T \geq K\right]. \tag{2.55}$$

We therefore have

$$V_0 = S_0 e^{-r^f T}\mathbf{P}^f\left[S_T \geq K\right] - K e^{-r^d T}\mathbf{P}^d\left[S_T \geq K\right]. \tag{2.56}$$

We now need to calculate the two risk-neutral probabilities (in $\mathbf{P}^d$ and $\mathbf{P}^f$) that $S_T \geq K$. From (2.41) and (2.45) we have

$$S_T = S_0 \exp\left(\sigma W_T^d + \left(r^d - r^f - \frac{1}{2}\sigma^2\right)T\right), \tag{2.57a}$$

$$S_T = S_0 \exp\left(\sigma W_T^f + \left(r^d - r^f + \frac{1}{2}\sigma^2\right)T\right). \tag{2.57b}$$

We unify the notation by introducing the index i which takes values in $\{1, 2\}$ and $X(\cdot)$ defined such that $X(1) \equiv f$ and $X(2) \equiv d$, the reason for which will become apparent below, obtaining

$$S_T = S_0 \exp\left(\sigma W_T^{X(i)} + \left(r^d - r^f + \left[\frac{1}{2} - (i-1)\right]\sigma^2\right)T\right). \tag{2.58}$$

The probabilities to be computed in (2.56) are easily computed for domestic and foreign risk-neutral measures by computing $\mathbf{P}^{X(i)}[S_T \geq K]$ for $i = 1, 2$. We use (2.58) above to write

$$\mathbf{P}^{X(i)}\left[S_0 \exp\left(\sigma W_T^{X(i)} + \left(r^d - r^f + \left[\frac{1}{2} - (i-1)\right]\sigma^2\right)T\right) \geq K\right]$$

$$= \mathbf{P}^{X(i)}\left[\exp\left(\sigma W_T^{X(i)} + \left(r^d - r^f + \left[\frac{1}{2} - (i-1)\right]\sigma^2\right)T\right) \geq \frac{K}{S_0}\right]$$

$$= \mathbf{P}^{X(i)}\left[\sigma W_T^{X(i)} + \left(r^d - r^f + \left[\frac{1}{2} - (i-1)\right]\sigma^2\right)T \geq \ln\left(\frac{K}{S_0}\right)\right]$$

$$= \mathbf{P}^{X(i)}\left[\sigma W_T^{X(i)} \geq \ln\left(\frac{K}{S_0}\right) - \left(r^d - r^f + \left[\frac{1}{2} - (i-1)\right]\sigma^2\right)T\right]$$

$$= \mathbf{P}^{X(i)}\left[-\sigma W_T^{X(i)} \leq \ln\left(\frac{S_0}{K}\right) + \left(r^d - r^f + \left[\frac{1}{2} - (i-1)\right]\sigma^2\right)T\right]$$

$$= \mathbf{P}\left[\sigma\sqrt{T}\xi \leq \ln\left(\frac{S_0}{K}\right) + \left(r^d - r^f + \left[\frac{1}{2} - (i-1)\right]\sigma^2\right)T\right]$$

$$= \mathbf{P}\left[\xi \leq \frac{\ln(S_0/K) + \left(r^d - r^f + \left[\frac{1}{2} - (i-1)\right]\sigma^2\right)T}{\sigma\sqrt{T}}\right],$$

where ξ is a standard $N(0, 1)$ normal distribution, noting that $W_T^{X(i)}, -W_T^{X(i)}, \sqrt{T}\xi$ and $-\sqrt{T}\xi$ all have the same distribution (by symmetry). We can therefore put

$$d_i = \frac{\ln(S_0/K) + \left(r^d - r^f + \left[\frac{1}{2} - (i-1)\right]\sigma^2\right)T}{\sigma\sqrt{T}}, \tag{2.59}$$

obtaining

$$\mathbf{P}^{X(i)}[S_T \geq K] = N(d_i), \tag{2.60}$$

where $N(x) = \int_{-\infty}^{x} n(u)\,du$ is the cumulative distribution function (CDF) and

$$n(u) = (2\pi)^{-1/2} \exp\left(-\frac{1}{2}u^2\right) \tag{2.61}$$

is the probability density function (PDF) for the standard normal distribution $N(0, 1)$.

Substituting (2.60) into (2.56) yields the standard Garman–Kohlhagen formula for a European call

$$V_0^C = S_0 e^{-r^f T} N(d_1) - K e^{-r^d T} N(d_2), \tag{2.62}$$

where $d_{1,2}$ are, in a more familiar form obtained from (2.59),

$$d_{1,2} = \frac{\ln(S_0/K) + \left(r^d - r^f \pm \frac{1}{2}\sigma^2\right)T}{\sigma\sqrt{T}}. \tag{2.63}$$

The same argument applies for the European put option, with payout function $V_T = \max(K - S_T, 0) = (K - S_T)^+$ at time T shown in Figure 2.2, for which we obtain

$$V_0^P = K e^{-r^d T} N(-d_2) - S_0 e^{-r^f T} N(-d_1). \tag{2.64}$$

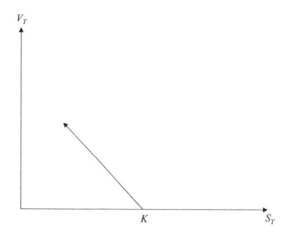

Figure 2.2   Payout function V_T for European put

For clarity, we use a more unified notation – introduce the variable ω which is $+1$ for a call and -1 for a put. We obtain

$$V_0^{C/P} = \omega S_0 e^{-r^f T} N(\omega d_1) - \omega K e^{-r^d T} N(\omega d_2). \tag{2.65}$$

2.8.1   Forward

The same argument applies for a forward contract, with payout function $V_T = S_T - K$ at time T shown in Figure 2.3.

As this contract can have a negative value as well as a forward value, depending on the strike K, it is customary to solve for the value of K that makes the forward costless to enter into. This choice of strike K for which $V_0 = e^{-r^d T} \mathbf{E}^d [S_T - K] = 0$ is denoted $F_{0,T}$, i.e. $F_{0,T} = \mathbf{E}^d [S_T]$.

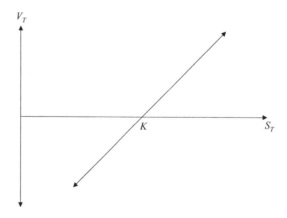

Figure 2.3   Payout function V_T for European forward

By (2.41) we easily obtain

$$F_{0,T} = \mathbf{E}^d [S_T]$$

$$= S_0 \mathbf{E}^d \left[\exp \left(\sigma W_T^d + \left(r^d - r^f - \frac{1}{2}\sigma^2 \right) T \right) \right]$$

$$= S_0 e^{(r^d - r^f)T} \mathbf{E}^d \left[\exp \left(\sigma W_T^d - \frac{1}{2}\sigma^2 T \right) \right]$$

$$= S_0 e^{(r^d - r^f)T}. \tag{2.66}$$

Note that with this we can rewrite (2.65) as

$$V_0 = \omega e^{-r^d T} [F_{0,T} N(\omega d_1) - K N(\omega d_2)] \tag{2.67}$$

and (2.63) can be rewritten as

$$d_{1,2} = \frac{\ln \left(F_{0,T}/K \right) \pm \frac{1}{2}\sigma^2 T}{\sigma \sqrt{T}}. \tag{2.68}$$

Note that $F_{0,T}$ represents the price at $t = 0$ to enter into the forward maturing at time T, and hence the choice of notation $F_{t,T}$ to denote the price at t for a forward contract maturing at T. The result (2.67) is nothing more than the price of European call or put options, priced using the Black (1976) model, where one directly models the driftless forward process $F_{t,T}$.

More generally, we have for times t other than zero

$$F_{t,T} = S_t \frac{D_{t,T}^f}{D_{t,T}^d}, \tag{2.69}$$

where $D_{t,T}^d \ D_{T(t)}^d$ and $D_{t,T}^f \ D_{T(t)}^f$ denote the domestic and foreign discount factors respectively, applicable between times t and T.

2.9   THE LAW OF ONE PRICE

The analysis in Section 2.8 above assumes that the European options are valued from the reference point of the domestic investor. In this section, I want to show that if the other currency is taken as the reference point, then exactly the same price is obtained.

This is quite crucial, otherwise counterparties to an FX options transaction will not be able to agree a Black–Scholes TV price between themselves. Even though most trades do not go through at the TV price due to the well-known shortcomings of the Black–Scholes model (to be discussed in a later chapter), it is important that a consensus for it can be obtained.

Suppose there are two currencies, A and B, and the domestic investor has ccy B as their domestic currency and ccy A as their foreign currency. The foreign investor will therefore have ccy A as *their* domestic currency and ccy B as their foreign currency.

Let us start by assuming that the domestic investor has already priced a long position in a call option with strike K and ccy A notional N_A (and therefore ccy B notional $N_B = K \cdot N_A$) and obtained the result seen earlier in (2.62):

$$V_0 = S_0 e^{-r^A T} N(d_1) - K e^{-r^B T} N(d_2),$$

where d_1 and d_2 are quoted in (2.63).

For the domestic investor who is long the option, this contract represents the right but not the obligation to exchange $N_2 = K \cdot N_A$ units of their domestic currency (ccy B) for $N_1 = N_A$ units of their foreign currency (ccy A).

For the foreign investor, the roles of domestic and foreign currency are interchanged. We shall therefore use 'hatted' symbols to denote the flipped spot rate, i.e. $\hat{S}_t = 1/S_t$ and the flipped strike $\hat{K} = 1/K$.

From the point of view of a foreign investor who is short the option, the same contract represents the *obligation* but not the right to exchange N_A units of their domestic currency (ccy A) for N_B units of their foreign currency (ccy B). So the foreign investor sees a risk notional of $N_1 = N_B$ and a base notional of $N_2 = N_A$.

For the foreign investor, the value at expiry of the short put option is always negative, and can be expressed in ccy A as

$$\hat{V}_T = K \left(\hat{S}_T - \hat{K} \right)^- = K \left(\hat{S}_T - \hat{K} \right) \mathbf{1}_{\{\hat{S}_T \leq \hat{K}\}}.$$

The value today $\hat{V}_0$ *in units of foreign currency* can be computed as

$$
\begin{aligned}
\hat{V}_0 &= e^{-r^f T} \mathbf{E}^f [\hat{V}_T] \\
&= K e^{-r^f T} \mathbf{E}^f \left[\left(\hat{S}_T - \hat{K} \right) \mathbf{1}_{\{\hat{S}_T \leq \hat{K}\}} \right] \\
&= K e^{-r^f T} \mathbf{E}^f \left[\hat{S}_T \mathbf{1}_{\{S_T \geq K\}} \right] - e^{-r^f T} \mathbf{E}^f \left[\mathbf{1}_{\{S_T \geq K\}} \right] \\
&= K \hat{S}_0 e^{(\sigma^2 - \mu^f) T} e^{-r^f T} \mathbf{E}^f \left[\frac{d\mathbf{P}^d}{d\mathbf{P}^f} \mathbf{1}_{\{S_T \geq K\}} \right] - e^{-r^f T} \mathbf{P}^f \left[S_T \geq K \right] \\
&= K \hat{S}_0 e^{-r^d T} \mathbf{P}^d \left[S_T \geq K \right] - e^{-r^f T} \mathbf{P}^f \left[S_T \geq K \right] \\
&= \frac{K}{S_0} e^{-r^d T} N(d_2) - e^{-r^f T} N(d_1).
\end{aligned}
$$

Converting this price into units of domestic currency today at the spot rate S_0 we obtain

$$
\begin{aligned}
\hat{S}_0 \hat{V}_0 &= K e^{-r^d T} N(d_2) - S_0 e^{-r^f T} N(d_1) \\
&= -V_0.
\end{aligned}
\tag{2.70}
$$

The same argument applies for European puts and other contingent claims. We therefore see that domestic and foreign investors, though pricing using different risk-neutral measures, agree on a consistent price when converted into the same currency using today's spot rates.

2.10   THE BLACK–SCHOLES TERM STRUCTURE MODEL

The Black–Scholes model of Section 2.1 is unrealistic, in that it does not allow for any term structure of interest rates (or volatility, for that matter). For that reason the model in (2.1) can be extended to

$$dS_t = \mu_t S_t \, dt + \sigma_t S_t \, dW_t, \tag{2.71}$$

where both μ_t and σ_t are deterministic processes. By risk neutrality, as in Section 2.7, we obtain

$$\mu_t = r_t^d - r_t^f. \tag{2.72}$$

From (2.71), we obtain

$$dS_t / S_t = \mu_t \, dt + \sigma_t \, dW_t. \tag{2.73}$$

As in Section 2.4, we let $X_t = f(S_t)$, defined by $f(x) = \ln(x)$. Following (2.19a) we obtain

$$dX_t = \frac{dS_t}{S_t} - \frac{1}{2} \frac{dS_t^2}{S_t^2}$$

$$= \mu_t \, dt + \sigma_t \, dW_t - \frac{1}{2} \sigma_t^2 \, dt. \tag{2.74}$$

This integrates to give

$$X_T = X_0 + \int_0^T \mu_s \, ds - \frac{1}{2} \int_0^T \sigma_s^2 \, ds + \int_0^T \sigma_s \, dW_s. \tag{2.75}$$

Since μ_t and σ_t are deterministic, though time-varying, the only stochastic component in (2.75) is the final term $\int_0^T \sigma_s \, dW_s$.

As shown in Corollary 13.3 in Bain (2009), this can be integrated through use of the Itô isometry, and has the distribution

$$\int_0^T \sigma_s \, dW_s \sim N(0, \bar{\sigma}_T^2 T),$$

where

$$\bar{\sigma}_T^2 = \frac{1}{T} \int_0^T \sigma_s^2 \, ds$$

defines the effective volatility $\bar{\sigma}_T$ applicable over the time interval $[0, T]$.

We can therefore write (2.75) as

$$X_T = X_0 + \left[\bar{\mu}_T - \frac{1}{2} \bar{\sigma}_T^2 \right] T + \bar{\sigma}_T \sqrt{T} \xi, \tag{2.76}$$

where $\xi \sim N(0, 1)$ and

$$\bar{\mu}_T = \frac{1}{T} \int_0^T \mu_s \, ds.$$

Note the similarity of (2.76) to (2.23). As a result, the methods of Section 2.8 are entirely applicable to a valuation of European options with expiry T, with r^d, r^f and σ in (2.65) replaced by their effective counterparts $\bar{r}_T^d$, $\bar{r}_T^f$ and $\bar{\sigma}_T$, where

$$\bar{r}_T^{d;f} = \frac{1}{T} \int_0^T r_s^{d;f} \, ds$$

are the effective (continuously compounded) domestic and foreign rates respectively over the interval $[0, T]$.

The prices obtained under the Black–Scholes term structure model are often referred to as the term structure price ('TS' price) What this means is that the Black–Scholes term structure price coincides with the Black–Scholes TV price for European options with maturity T, assuming that the interest rate and volatility parameters used in the Black–Scholes model are set to the effective values $\bar{r}_T^{d;f}$ and $\bar{\sigma}_T$ given above. For path-dependent options, however, the prices will probably *not* coincide.

2.11 BREEDEN–LITZENBERGER ANALYSIS

Suppose that we have a continuum of prices available for call options with strike K (all with the same time to expiry T). It was originally shown in Breeden and Litzenberger (1978) that this information is equivalent to an implied distribution. The argument is basically this.

We know that a call price is

$$C(K, T) = e^{-r^d T} \mathbf{E}^d \left[(S_T - K)^+ \right]$$

$$= e^{-r^d T} \int_0^\infty (s - K)^+ f_{S_T}^d(s) \, ds$$

$$= e^{-r^d T} \int_K^\infty (s - K) f_{S_T}^d(s) \, ds, \tag{2.77}$$

where $f_{S_T}^d(s)$ is the probability distribution function for spot S_T under the domestic risk-neutral measure.

Taking the first derivative with respect to K follows by differentiating under the integral sign. The result we use is the following. Let $F(x)$ be defined by the following:

$$F(x) = \int_{a(x)}^{b(x)} f(x, s) \, ds. \tag{2.78}$$

We then have

$$\frac{d}{dx} F(x) = f(x, b(x)) b'(x) - f(x, a(x)) a'(x) + \int_{a(x)}^{b(x)} \frac{\partial}{\partial x} f(x, s) \, ds. \tag{2.79}$$

For the Breeden–Litzenberger result, we need to compute (replacing K with x and forgetting about the discount factor for now)

$$\frac{d}{dx} \int_x^\infty (s - x) f_{S_T}^d(s) \, ds,$$

which is equivalent to $(d/dx) F(x)$ with $F(x)$ as in (2.78) with $a(x) = x$, $b(x) = \infty$ and $f(x, s) = (s - x) f_{S_T}^d(s)$ – noting that $(\partial/\partial x) f(x, s) = -f_{S_T}^d(s)$.

From (2.79), we therefore have

$$\frac{d}{dx} F(x) = -f(x, a(x)) a'(x) + \int_{a(x)}^{b(x)} \frac{\partial}{\partial x} f(x, s) \, ds$$

$$= f(x, x) + \int_x^\infty \frac{\partial}{\partial x} f(x, s) \, ds$$

$$= \int_x^\infty \frac{\partial}{\partial x} f(x, s) \, ds$$

$$= -\int_x^\infty f_{S_T}^d(s) \, ds.$$

A second differentiation under the integral sign gives

$$\frac{d^2}{dx^2} F(x) = -\frac{d}{dx} \int_x^\infty f_{S_T}^d(s) \, ds$$

$$= f_{S_T}^d(s). \tag{2.80}$$

Table 2.1 European digitals

Product code	Name	Payout function V_T
D1C	Foreign call digital	$S_T \mathbf{1}_{\{S_T \geq U\}}$
D1P	Foreign put digital	$S_T \mathbf{1}_{\{S_T \leq L\}}$
D2C	Domestic call digital	$\mathbf{1}_{\{S_T \geq U\}}$
D2P	Domestic put digital	$\mathbf{1}_{\{S_T \leq L\}}$

From (2.77) we have $F(K) = \int_K^\infty (s - K) f_{S_T}^d(s)\,ds = e^{r^d T} C(K, T)$ and therefore, by differentiating twice with respect to K and using (2.80), we have the *Breeden–Litzenberger formula*

$$f_{S_T}^d(K) = e^{r^d T} \frac{\partial^2 C(K, T)}{\partial K^2}. \tag{2.81}$$

2.12 EUROPEAN DIGITALS

Another type of European option differs from calls and puts by having a discontinuous payout profile. Such a product is called a *digital* as it either pays 0 or 1, and is basically a bet – a product familiar to gamblers – which pays out either a certain cash amount or nothing at all depending on whether a particular event (let's denote it ε) has happened or not.

In FX, the cash can either be domestic or foreign, which means at time T the digital can either pay (a) 1 unit of domestic currency or (b) 1 unit of foreign currency, which is worth S_T when expressed in domestic currency. Conditional on the event ε, the payout function at expiry will either be $\mathbf{1}_\varepsilon$ or $S_T \mathbf{1}_\varepsilon$.

There are therefore four types of European digitals, which we list in Table 2.1. It may come as a pleasant surprise to realise that we have actually already valued each of these in Section 2.8, as these terms (with K instead of L or U) occur as components of the payout functions in $V_T = \max(S_T - K, 0)$ or $V_T = \max(K - S_T, 0)$, as a review of (2.56) will show.

Tempting as it to use K to denote the digital barrier level, this can easily lead to confusion as the strike variable K is often used for quote style conversion, as in Section 3.1. Some of these quote styles are meaningless for digitals – e.g. a domestic call digital only has a domestic notional, so domestic/foreign and %foreign quote styles are meaningless. Restricting the barrier level variables to L and U avoids potential quote style errors for European digitals. Using a generalised moneyness notation similar to Section 10.5 in Zhang (1998), we can write this in terms of probabilities of S_T exceeding not the strike K but an arbitrary level X, as $\mathbf{P}^{X(i)}[S_T \geq X] = N(d_i(X))$ with

$$d_{1,2}(S_0, X) = \frac{\ln(S_0/X) + (r^d - r^f \pm \sigma^2)T}{\sigma\sqrt{T}}. \tag{2.82}$$

We therefore have

$$V_0^{\text{D1C}} = S_0 e^{-r^f T} N(d_1(S_0, U)), \tag{2.83a}$$

$$V_0^{\text{D1P}} = S_0 e^{-r^f T} N(-d_1(S_0, L)), \tag{2.83b}$$

$$V_0^{\text{D2C}} = e^{-r^d T} N(d_2(S_0, U)), \tag{2.83c}$$

$$V_0^{\text{D2P}} = e^{-r^d T} N(d_2(S_0, -L)). \tag{2.83d}$$

2.12.1   Static replication for bid/offer digital pricing

Suppose we are asked to price a European domestic call digital, with the up-and-in European barrier U, and we can trade European calls or puts with any strike. We can build a call spread by going long N units of a call option at strike K and short N units of a call option at strike $K + \epsilon$, where $\epsilon = 1/N$. This will underprice the call digital (as the payout profile from this call spread slightly truncates that of the European call digital). Conversely, we can go long N units of a call option at strike $K - \epsilon$ and short N units of a call option at strike K, with the same ϵ, that will systematically overestimate the price. This provides us with a simple yet robust method we can use to estimate the price of digitals, both on the bid and offer side, subject to constraints that limit the amount of the notional of the underlying hedge Europeans that can be traded to no more (or less) than $\pm N$. As $N \rightarrow \infty$, these prices converge to that of the digital without any trading constraints.

2.13   SETTLEMENT ADJUSTMENTS

Recall from Chapter 1 that FX spot transactions generally (not always) settle in two business days and that we have four dates of importance for option contracts: today, spot, expiry and delivery. The delivery date is usually set to the expiry spot, i.e. so that delivery bears the same spot settlement relationship to expiry.

How should the formulae in (2.62) and (2.83) be adjusted to handle this and how should we adapt the numerical methods in Chapter 7? We let the following denote the four times respectively:

$$T_{\text{today}} \quad T_{\text{spot}} \quad \longrightarrow \quad T_{\text{exp}} \quad T_{\text{es}}$$

and we (usually) have the delivery time $T_{\text{del}} = T_{\text{es}}$.

If a European option expires in the money, the payout is known and therefore fixed on the expiry date. Whether it is cash settled (in which case it is expressed in units of the settlement currency at expiry) or whether it involves delivery settlement (in which case N_d and N_f are physically exchanged at T_{es}) is reasonably irrelevant. Either way, cash is transferred on the expiry spot date.

The premium we are asked to compute for such an option is for how much the counterparty would be charged today for such an option, and for which he or she would have to make the funds available on the premium value date – which coincides with the spot date T_{spot}.

Therefore, FX spot volatility is applicable over the period $T_{\text{today}} \leq t \leq T_{\text{exp}}$, but the option value at delivery needs to be discounted back from T_{del} to today (T_{today}) and then forward valued to T_{spot}.

From (2.62) and (2.63), we have

$$V_0^C = S_0 e^{-r^f T} N(d_1) - K e^{-r^d T} N(d_2) \tag{2.84}$$

with

$$d_{1,2} = \frac{\ln(S_0/K) + \left(r^d - r^f \pm \frac{1}{2}\sigma^2\right) T}{\sigma \sqrt{T}}, \tag{2.85}$$

but it is clear from considering the four time points that an exact price should instead be

$$V_0^C = S_0 e^{-r^f (T_{\text{es}} - T_{\text{spot}})} N(d_1) - K e^{-r^d (T_{\text{es}} - T_{\text{spot}})} N(d_2) \tag{2.86}$$

with

$$d_{1,2} = \frac{\ln(S_0/K) + (r^d - r^f)(T_{es} - T_{spot}) \pm \frac{1}{2}\sigma^2(T_{exp} - T_{today})}{\sigma\sqrt{T_{exp} - T_{today}}}. \qquad (2.87)$$

If $T_{es} - T_{spot}$ were equal to $T_{exp} - T_{today}$, then we could just use $T = T_{exp} - T_{today}$ and get the same results. For the purposes of this book we can assume that we use a common practitioners' trick and use rates $\hat{r}^d$ and $\hat{r}^f$ adapted so that

$$r^{d;f}(T_{es} - T_{spot}) = \hat{r}^{d;f}(T_{exp} - T_{today})$$

and then everything can be priced relative to T_{today} and T_{exp}.

Although a fairly unsophisticated but pragmatic approximation, to describe more extensively the various settlement effects (ACT/365, ACT/360, etc.) involving interest rate conventions for the various country markets we may (and do) encounter in FX takes us well beyond the scope of this work. Chances are that anyone who needs to handle these with such precision will be best advised to talk with the section of their bank responsible for yield curve stripping. A thorough description of the details of the various market conventions in bond markets can be found in Stigum and Robinson (1996) and a comprehensive survey of yield curve stripping methods can be found in Hagan and West (2006). In the meantime, where we see rates $r^{d;f}$ and their term structure counterparts $r_t^{d;f}$ below, these should be understood to be rates adjusted so that the same T can be used for Black–Scholes pricing, as described above.

2.14 DELAYED DELIVERY ADJUSTMENTS

Suppose the delivery date does not coincide with the expiry spot and we therefore have $T_{del} > T_{es}$. Then

$$T_{today} \quad T_{spot} \quad \longrightarrow \quad T_{exp} \quad T_{es} \quad \longrightarrow \quad T_{del}.$$

How should we adjust prices to compensate for this?

2.14.1 Delayed delivery adjustments – digitals

It is easiest if we begin by explaining how this works for the case of digitals. Let's assume that these four dates described in Section 2.13 are all known. In the case where the payment of the digital is not deferred, the cash amount is paid out at time T_{es}. Consequently, if the delivery date T_{del} is further along in time than the typical expiry spot date T_{es}, then the only required adjustment is the discount factor (in either domestic or foreign currency) applicable between T_{es} and T_{del}. This is nothing more than a multiplicative correction of either $D^d_{T_{exp}}(T_{del})$ (for domestic cash-or-nothing digitals) or $D^f_{T_{exp}}(T_{del})$ (for foreign cash-or-nothing digitals).

We therefore have, following (2.83),

$$V_0^{DIC;dd} = D^f_{T_{del}}(T_{exp})S_0 e^{-r^f T} N(d_1(S_0, U)), \qquad (2.88a)$$

$$V_0^{DIP;dd} = D^f_{T_{del}}(T_{exp})S_0 e^{-r^f T} N(-d_1(S_0, L)), \qquad (2.88b)$$

$$V_0^{D2C;dd} = D^d_{T_{del}}(T_{exp})e^{-r^d T} N(d_2(S_0, U)), \qquad (2.88c)$$

$$V_0^{D2P;dd} = D^d_{T_{del}}(T_{exp})e^{-r^d T} N(-d_2(S_0, L)). \qquad (2.88d)$$

2.14.2 Delayed delivery adjustments – Europeans

One can see from Section 2.14.1 that the delayed delivery adjustment can sometimes be either the discount factor in domestic currency, or in foreign currency, over the time interval $[T_{exp}, T_{del}]$. Which one do we use for Europeans? Or do we use neither? The answer is that it actually depends on whether the European is cash settled or involves physical settlement. If it's cash settled in domestic currency, we use $D^d_{T_{del}}(T_{exp})$ and if it's cash settled in foreign currency we use $D^f_{T_{del}}(T_{exp})$.

Much more interesting is the case where the option involves physical settlement. It's interesting because it provides a rare example of a scenario in which it can actually be optimal to exercise an option which is *out* of the money. Why would one do this? If the spot at expiry is sufficiently close to the strike that the expected drift in the spot date between expiry spot and the (delayed) delivery date is sufficient to make the expectation of $S_{T_{del}} - K$ positive for a call (or negative for a put), then one should exercise into what is effectively a position in the T_{del} forward FX contract. In other words, a European option with delayed delivery is basically just an option on a forward, and should be priced as such.

Consider, therefore, a European call option with expiry time T on an FX forward with maturity T_{del}. At time T, the value is $V_T = D^d_{T,T_{del}}[F_{T,T_{del}} - K]^+$ and therefore under risk-neutral valuation, this has a PV at $t = 0$ of

$$V^{C;dd}_0 = D^d_{0,T} \mathbf{E}^d \left[D^d_{T,T_{del}}(F_{T,T_{del}} - K)^+ \right]. \tag{2.89}$$

Using (2.69), we can write $F_{T,T_{del}} = S_T D^f_{T,T_{del}}/D^d_{T,T_{del}}$, which allows (2.89) to be expressed in terms of S_T as

$$V^{C;dd}_0 = D^d_{0,T} \mathbf{E}^d \left[D^d_{T,T_{del}} \left(S_T \frac{D^f_{T,T_{del}}}{D^d_{T,T_{del}}} - K \right)^+ \right]. \tag{2.90}$$

Define K' by

$$K' = K \frac{D^d_{T,T_{del}}}{D^f_{T,T_{del}}}$$

and (2.90) reduces to

$$\begin{aligned}
V^{C;dd}_0(K, T) &= D^d_{0,T} \mathbf{E}^d \left[D^d_{T,T_{del}} \left(S_T \frac{D^f_{T,T_{del}}}{D^d_{T,T_{del}}} - K' \frac{D^f_{T,T_{del}}}{D^d_{T,T_{del}}} \right)^+ \right] \\
&= D^d_{0,T} \mathbf{E}^d \left[D^f_{T,T_{del}}(S_T - K')^+ \right]. \\
&= D^f_{T,T_{del}} D^d_{0,T} \mathbf{E}^d \left[(S_T - K')^+ \right] \\
&= D^f_{T,T_{del}} V^C_0(K', T).
\end{aligned}$$

We therefore see that the effect of having a physically settled European option on the forward, not the spot, is to introduce an additional discount factor $D^f_{T,T_{del}}$ and a strike adjustment $K' = K D^d_{T,T_{del}}/D^f_{T,T_{del}}$.

In the case where all five dates are to be considered, the delayed delivery adjustment depends only on the time interval $[T_{es}, T_{del}]$, and is of the form

$$V_0^{C;dd}(K, T_{exp}) = D_{T_{es}, T_{del}}^f \cdot V_0^C(K', T_{exp}),$$

(2.91)

where

$$K' = K \frac{D_{T_{es}, T_{del}}^d}{D_{T_{es}, T_{del}}^f}.$$

The same strike adjustment applies for puts, straddles and any other option expiring at time T_{exp}, with a strike K applicable for physical settlement of currency A against currency B at a delayed delivery date T_{del} beyond the usual expiry spot date T_{es}.

2.15   PRICING USING FOURIER METHODS

The treatment in this section follows that of Zhu (2000), and while it may seem unnecessarily arcane at first when compared to the closed-form Black–Scholes prices in (2.65), this method actually extends to the stochastic volatility models in Chapter 6. What this means is that we can obtain semi-analytic prices for European options under the Black–Scholes model and some stochastic volatility models, requiring only a one-dimensional numerical integration and some functions involving $\mathbb{C}$ – the set of complex numbers.

Note that while this only works for pricing European options, models are often calibrated to European options and a fast semi-analytic algorithm for pricing Europeans is therefore a useful piece of machinery to have in our toolbox.

The present value of a European option with terminal payout function $V_T = V_T(S_T)$ can be obtained under the risk-neutral expectation

$$V_0 = e^{-r^d T} \mathbb{E}^d [V_T(S_T)]$$

(2.92)

or, alternatively, for a European call or put, as a pair of expectations in foreign and domestic risk-neutral measures respectively:

$$V_0 = S_0 e^{-r^f T} \mathbb{E}^f [\mathbf{1}_\epsilon] - K e^{-r^d T} \mathbb{E}^d [\mathbf{1}_\epsilon],$$

(2.93)

where ϵ denotes the event $\{S_T \geq K\}$.

If the probability distribution functions for S_T under the domestic and foreign risk-neutral measures respectively are denoted by $f_{S_T}^{d;f}(s)$, as in Section 2.11, then (2.92) can be written as

$$V_0 = e^{-r^d T} \int_0^\infty V_T(s) f_{S_T}^d(s) \, ds$$

(2.94)

or, equivalently,

$$V_0 = e^{-r^d T} \int_{-\infty}^\infty h(x) f_{X_T}^d(x) \, dx,$$

(2.95)

where $X_T = \ln S_T$, $h(x) = V_T(e^x)$ denotes the terminal value as a function of the logspot, and $f_{X_T}^d(x)$ is the probability distribution function for logspot X_T – once again under the domestic risk-neutral measure.

The integral in (2.95) can be identified as an inner product acting on a function space, and Parseval's theorem (Kammler, 2007) indicates that inner products of this type are preserved under Fourier transforms (up to a factor of 2π). Consequently, we have

$$2\pi \int_{-\infty}^{\infty} h(x) f_{X_T}^{\mathrm{d}}(x)\,\mathrm{d}x = \int_{-\infty}^{\infty} \hat{h}(\phi) \hat{f}_{X_T}^{\mathrm{d}}(\phi)\,\mathrm{d}\phi, \tag{2.96}$$

where

$$\hat{h}(\phi) = \int_{-\infty}^{\infty} e^{i\phi x} h(x)\,\mathrm{d}x \tag{2.97}$$

is the Fourier transform of the payout function (in logspot coordinates) and

$$\hat{f}_{X_T}^{d;f}(\phi) = \int_{-\infty}^{\infty} e^{i\phi x} f_{X_T}^{d;f}(x)\,\mathrm{d}x = \mathbf{E}^{d;f}\left[e^{i\phi X_T}\right] \tag{2.98}$$

is the characteristic function of X_T, in either a domestic or foreign risk-neutral measure. With this, the expectation in (2.92) can be calculated in ϕ-space as

$$\mathbf{E}^d\left[V_T(S_T)\right] = \frac{1}{2\pi}\int_{-\infty}^{\infty} \hat{h}(\phi) \hat{f}_{X_T}^d(\phi)\,\mathrm{d}\phi, \tag{2.99}$$

as can those in (2.93).

The expectations $\mathbf{E}^{d;f}\left[\mathbf{1}_{\{S_T \ge K\}}\right] = \mathbf{E}^{d;f}\left[\mathbf{1}_{\{X_T \ge \ln K\}}\right]$ correspond to the choice of $h(x) = \mathbf{1}_{\{x \ge \ln K\}}$. We can obtain the Fourier transform of this via

$$\hat{h}(\phi) = \int_{-\infty}^{\infty} \mathbf{1}_{\{x \ge \ln K\}} e^{i\phi x}\,\mathrm{d}x - \int_{\ln K}^{\infty} e^{i\phi x}\,\mathrm{d}x = \left.\frac{e^{i\phi x}}{i\phi}\right|_{x=\ln K}^{\infty}$$

This has a complex pole at the origin ($\phi = 0$) and the limit as $x \to \infty$ of $e^{i\phi x}$ isn't formally defined, but we can still use this in practice by choosing a contour of integration that avoids $\phi = 0$ and introduces a suitable dampening factor into $e^{i\phi x}$; if we put $\phi = \phi_r + i\phi_i$, then

$$e^{i\phi x} = e^{i(\phi_r + i\phi_i)x} = e^{i\phi_r x} \cdot e^{-\phi_i x},$$

and clearly both issues are resolved by integrating over $\phi = \phi_r + i\phi_i$ from $\phi_r = -\infty$ to $+\infty$ with a choice of $\phi_i > 0$. As ϕ_i can be very small, so long as it is strictly positive, we omit it in the rest of this discussion to illustrate the main ideas behind the Fourier pricing approach. Obviously a correct numerical implementation should include this ϕ_i offset in the complex plane, which is fairly straightforward.

The Fourier inversion formula (Heston, 1993; Bates, 1996; Bakshi *et al.*, 1997) follows:

$$\mathbf{P}^{d;f}\left[S_T \ge K\right] = \frac{1}{2} + \frac{1}{\pi}\int_0^{\infty} \mathrm{Re}\left[\hat{f}_{X_T}^{d;f}(\phi)\frac{\exp(-i\phi \ln K)}{i\phi}\right]\mathrm{d}\phi. \tag{2.100}$$

We need to compute the characteristic functions $\hat{f}_{X_T}^{d;f}(\phi)$ for the logspot asset process. The approach here will generalise to more complex models later. Assume volatility σ is constant. The spot process follows:

$$\mathrm{d}S_t = (r^d - r^f)S_t\,\mathrm{d}t + \sigma S_t\,\mathrm{d}W_t,$$

with logspot following

$$\mathrm{d}X_t = \left(r^d - r^f - \frac{1}{2}\sigma^2\right)\mathrm{d}t + \sigma\,\mathrm{d}W_t.$$

Integrating this, we have

$$X_t = X_0 + \left(r^d - r^f - \frac{1}{2}\sigma^2 \right) t + \sigma(W_t - W_0),$$

which is normally distributed with mean $X_0 + (r^d - r^f - \frac{1}{2}\sigma^2)t$ and variance $\sigma^2 t$.

An $N(\mu, \sigma^2)$ random variable X with the PDF

$$F_X(x) = \frac{1}{\sqrt{2\pi}\sigma} \exp \left(\frac{-(x-\mu)^2}{2\sigma^2} \right)$$

has the characteristic function (this follows after completing the square)

$$\hat{f}_X(\phi) = \frac{1}{\sqrt{2\pi}\sigma} \int_{-\infty}^{\infty} e^{i\phi x} \exp \left(\frac{-(x-\mu)^2}{2\sigma^2} \right) dx = \exp \left(i\mu\phi - \frac{1}{2}\sigma^2\phi^2 \right).$$

This means that the characteristic functions in domestic and foreign risk-neutral measures describing the asset price process at the terminal time T can be written

$$\hat{f}_{X_T}^{d;f}(\phi) = \exp \left(i \left[\left(r^d - r^f \pm \frac{1}{2}\sigma^2 \right) T + X_0 \right] \phi - \frac{1}{2}\sigma^2 T \phi^2 \right) \qquad (2.101)$$

and we can use (2.101) in (2.100), computing $\mathbf{P}^{d;f}[S_T \geq K]$ numerically.

Obviously, the integral in (2.100) will have to be computed on a truncated domain, between 0 and ϕ_{max}. But what value of ϕ_{max} makes sense?

Note that the integrand in (2.100) can be written as

$$\mathrm{Re} \left[\hat{f}_{X_T}^{d;f}(\phi) \frac{e^{-i\phi \ln K}}{i\phi} \right] = \frac{e^{-\frac{1}{2}\sigma^2 T \phi^2}}{\phi} \times \sin \left(\left[\left(r^d - r^f \pm \frac{1}{2}\sigma^2 \right) T + X_0 - \ln K \right] \phi \right),$$

which decomposes into the product of an envelope of the form $(1/\phi)e^{-\frac{1}{2}\sigma^2 T\phi^2}$ and an oscillatory term. It therefore suffices to examine the behaviour of the envelope to determine a sensible upper limit on the integrand, seeking to establish a value for ϕ_{max} for which we perform a simple trapezoidal integration from 0 to ϕ_{max}. Note that the argument in the exponential must be dimensionless (due to the Taylor series for e^x summing terms involving unity, x, x^2, ...) and so we require $\sigma^2 T \phi_{max}^2$ to be constant. From this, we choose

$$\phi_{max} = \frac{Q}{\sigma\sqrt{T}}.$$

A value for Q is chosen that gives suitably close convergence to the Black–Scholes closed-form formulae. Numerical experiments suggest that a value for Q somewhere between 2 and 5 works well in practice.

2.15.1 European option pricing involving one numerical integral

The approach described above is easy to visualise and has a clear relationship to the Black–Scholes approach. For practical purposes, however, superior convergence can be obtained by formulating the European option pricing problem as a single Fourier integral. This is described in Chapter 2 of Lewis (2000), which introduces the Fourier transform of the value function in equation (2.2), which the reader will immediately relate to (2.97) in this work. This requires us to use (2.92) with $V_T = V_T(S_T) = \max(S_T - K, 0)$ for a European call, instead of (2.93).

We have $h(x) = (e^x - K)^+$, which yields

$$\hat{h}(\phi) = \int_{-\infty}^{\infty} (e^x - K)^+ e^{i\phi x} \, dx$$

$$= \int_{\ln K}^{\infty} (e^x - K) e^{i\phi x} dx$$

$$= \left(\frac{e^{(i\phi+1)x}}{i\phi + 1} - K \frac{e^{i\phi x}}{i\phi} \right) \Bigg|_{x=\ln K}^{\infty} \tag{2.102a}$$

$$= -\frac{K^{i\phi+1}}{\phi^2 - i\phi} \tag{2.102b}$$

where in order to reduce (2.102a) to (2.102b), ϕ should be chosen so that $\phi = \phi_r + i\phi_i$ with $\phi_i > 1$, so that both $e^{(i\phi+1)x}$ and $e^{i\phi x}$ decay suitably to zero for large values of x. However, as pointed out by Lewis (2000) in the discussion entitled 'Call Option Solution II' (page 41), the numerical integration can in practice be performed along a contour with $\phi_i = \frac{1}{2}$.

2.16 LEPTOKURTOSIS – MORE THAN FAT TAILS

To conclude this chapter, which has been quite dense in mathematical notation, we go to the other extreme and present a handful of figures that will hopefully give the reader more of an intuitive introduction to leptokurtic distributions. Later, in Chapters 5 and 6, we shall be examining various models that attempt to explain the volatility smile, appealing to the notion of a leptokurtic distribution. It is natural, then, to ask what features leptokurtic distributions typically have. Furthermore, how might these features impact upon the prices for derivatives? It's no bad idea to know what these distributions actually look like.

Recall from (2.61) the probability density function $f_Z(z) = n(z)$ of the standard normal distribution, with mean 0, variance 1 and skewness and kurtosis of zero. We can compare this with a family of leptokurtic distributions, e.g. the Pearson type VII family of distributions, parameterised with kurtosis γ_2. For these distributions, we have probability density functions

$$f(x; \gamma_2) = \frac{\Gamma(m)}{a\sqrt{\pi}\Gamma(m - \frac{1}{2})} \left(1 + \left(\frac{x}{a} \right)^2 \right)^{-m}$$

with $a = \sqrt{2 + 6/\gamma_2}$ and $m = \frac{5}{2} + 3/\gamma_2$, using the Gamma function $\Gamma : \mathbb{C} \to \mathbb{C}$ (we only need it on $\mathbb{R}^+$) defined by $\Gamma(x) = \int_0^\infty s^{x-1} e^{-s} ds$, which can be more easily evaluated as $\Gamma(n) = (n-1)!$ when n is an integral.

Examining these densities $f(x; \gamma_2)$ visually in Figure 2.4 for values of kurtosis γ_2 in $\{\frac{1}{4}, \frac{1}{2}, 1, 3, 1000\}$, and comparing against the reference case of the normal distribution $N(0, 1)$, one has to look really closely to see the excess probability mass in the tails. However, it is obvious from Figure 2.4(a) that as kurtosis increases, the height of the central peak of the density function increases also. The overwhelming visual signature is in the central body of the distribution. Since the area under the density function has to integrate to unity by definition, the excess probability mass in the tails has to come from somewhere, hence the loss of probability mass in the shoulder, which has to be balanced by extra probability mass accumulation near the mean of the distribution, all in order to match the first two moments to those for $N(0, 1)$.

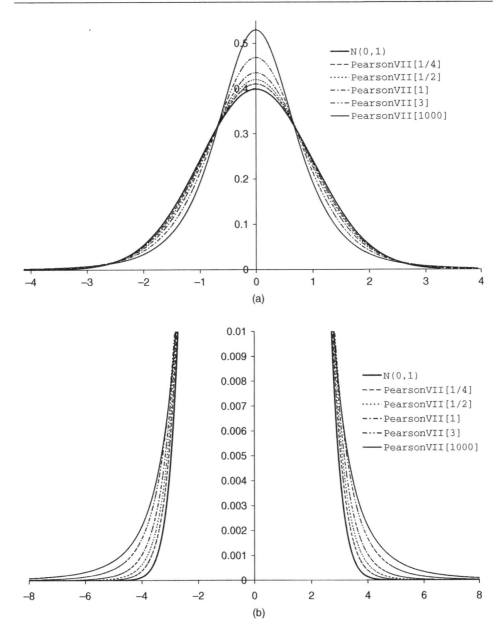

Figure 2.4 Sample leptokurtic density functions: (a) leptokurtic density functions – large-scale view; (b) leptokurtic density functions – tail region

Basically, a leptokurtic density function resembles an animal[5] with a sharply pointed head, narrow shoulders and fat tails. The fat tails, while difficult to see in Figure 2.4, are considerably

---

[5] Aardvark, beaver, peacock, pheasant, platypus or unicorn, my friends helpfully suggest, but I prefer Rebecca's suggestion of rat – rat with two tails, ideally.

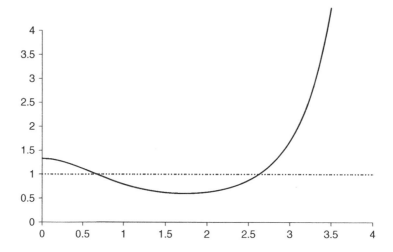

Figure 2.5 Leptokurtic likelihood ratio: `Pearson VII(1000)` relative to $N(0, 1)$

more apparent if we consider the *relative* differences between the most leptokurtic `Pearson VII` distribution with $\gamma_2 = 1000$ and the reference normal distribution $N(0, 1)$, expressed as a likelihood ratio, illustrated in Figure 2.5. For this particular fat-tailed distribution relative to a normal distribution, a zero standard deviation move is 33 % more likely than the reference normal distribution, but a ± 2 standard deviation move is only two thirds as likely to occur. Out beyond ± 3 standard deviations, however, the likelihoods are at least doubled, and considerably greater still in relative terms for rare events. Indeed, I calculate a ± 5 standard deviation move to be five hundred times more likely with the `Pearson VII(1000)` distribution than under $N(0, 1)$.

Financially, this means that if we use a leptokurtic distribution to model daily logreturns for an asset, then two scenarios are more likely under this assumption than with a lognormal distribution: extreme market moves and episodes of little asset price movement. This is quite consistent with historical observations for most if not all tradeable assets, and particularly so for FX, which can often be rangebound for extended periods of time before the next period of heightened market volatility.

3

Deltas and Market Conventions

While the Black–Scholes model introduced in Chapter 2 is the industry benchmark and an important market reference, it has several deficiencies when it comes to describing realistic FX markets. The assumption of constant interest rates in foreign and domestic currencies is inadequate, as is the assumption of a single volatility σ sufficient to price options of different maturities and strikes correctly. We have already shown how Black–Scholes term structure models can remedy some of these deficiencies, but the inability of a Black–Scholes model equipped solely with a single volatility to price options of various strikes cannot be remedied by the imposition of a term structure.

However, Black–Scholes prices provide a natural *starting point* for a fuller and more accurate description of the volatility surfaces encountered in the FX markets, which can be used in developing more advanced models, such as the ones discussed in this work.

Given a Black–Scholes price for an option, one can calculate the change in that price for infinitesimal changes in the underlying spot rate (or forward rate for that matter). This gives us the notion of the option delta, which is normally thought of as the instantaneous sensitivity of the price to infinitesimal changes in the price of the underlying asset. In most asset classes other than FX, the delta is perfectly straightforward. We shall see that this is not true in FX – the explanation is simple, even though it gets little mention in the existing literature: if there are several different types of quote styles for price, then there *must* be several types of delta. Not only that, but the sensitivities can be quoted with respect to changes in the spot or the forward.

The crucial point to stress here is that the market conventions for FX markets, as introduced in this chapter, are specified predominantly in terms of the price and volatility attributes of options with various delta characteristics. If we are going to develop any more advanced model than Black–Scholes, we must be able to calibrate it to the market. We therefore need to understand the intricacies of the various types of FX delta and how they are used in the description of market volatility surfaces; otherwise our work is of little practical use.

This chapter therefore provides a thorough description of all the different types of delta encountered. This is especially important in FX, as the entire concept of the FX volatility smile is based on parameterisation with respect to delta. We introduce and describe the various market conventions used in practice, and while we encourage readers to check with any traders they can ask, we have attempted to provide a reliable set of rules for typical market conventions.

We then describe, for a single expiry time T, the conditions that a volatility smile must satisfy in order to be consistent with the market description of the volatilities, and we introduce two numerical methods that can be used in practice to build smiles that are consistent with the market, illustrating both by example.

3.1 QUOTE STYLE CONVERSIONS

In currency markets, as opposed to equity markets, options can be quoted in one of four relative quote styles – domestic per foreign (d/f), percentage foreign $(\%f)$, percentage domestic $(\%d)$

and foreign per domestic (f/d). This is because, unlike equities, investors can have one of two numeraires:[1] currency 1 [ccy1] or currency 2 [ccy2] – since currencies are legal tender and have economic purchasing power in their respective home countries, whereas equities do not have this property anywhere – and because there are two notionals. A risk-neutral investor in the domestic currency can therefore obtain a domestic per domestic price or a domestic per foreign price. Similarly, a risk-neutral investor in the foreign currency can obtain a foreign per domestic price or a foreign per foreign price.

Consider now the standard Black–Scholes formula for a European call/put option, as derived in Chapter 2:

$$V_{d;\text{pips}} \equiv V_{d/f} = \omega S_0 e^{-r^f T} N(\omega d_1) - \omega K e^{-r^d T} N(\omega d_2)$$
$$= \omega e^{-r^d T} [F N(\omega d_1) - K N(\omega d_2)]. \tag{3.1}$$

Whether a call or put, it is nevertheless an option to effect an exchange of K units of domestic currency for 1 unit of foreign currency, valued in domestic currency – so it is the domestic/foreign price, and is therefore denoted as $V_{d/f}$ above. It is also sometimes called the ccy2/ccy1 price or the domestic pips (or, more rarely, points) price. Dimensionally, the terms 'pips' and 'points' are synonymous with domestic per foreign – 'pips' is more common in the spot market, whereas 'points' is more common in the forward market.

If one wants to express this as a ccy1/ccy1 price, the conversion is easy: one merely takes the ccy2/ccy1 price above and converts the ccy2 value into ccy1 terms using today's spot rate S_0:

$$V_{\%f} = \frac{\omega}{S_0} e^{-r^d T} [F N(\omega d_1) - K N(\omega d_2)] = \frac{V_{d/f}}{S_0}.$$

For the %ccy2 price, we start with the ccy2/ccy1 price, this being the price in ccy2 of an option with a unit notional in the foreign currency. Equivalently, since the strike is predetermined, it is *also* the price in ccy2 of an option with a notional of K in the domestic currency. So the ccy2/ccy1 price, divided by K, is the %ccy2 price, i.e. the % domestic price:

$$V_{\%d} = \frac{\omega}{K} e^{-r^d T} [F N(\omega d_1) - K N(\omega d_2)] = \frac{V_{d/f}}{K}.$$

The ccy1/ccy2 price is obtained from the %ccy2 price by converting the ccy2 value of this option into ccy1. Since 1 unit of ccy2 is worth $1/S_0$ units of ccy1, the price is

$$V_{f;\text{pips}} \equiv V_{f/d} = \frac{1}{S_0} V_{\%d} = \frac{V_{d/f}}{S_0 K}.$$

The ccy1/ccy2 price is also sometimes called the foreign/domestic price or the foreign pips price.

Finally, the four prices above are relative to notionals of K in the domestic currency. and 1 in the foreign currency. We can also obtain two absolute prices V_d (domestic) and V_f (foreign) given actual notionals N_d and N_f in domestic and foreign currencies respectively,

---

[1] **Important footnote.** Note that the true numeraires are really the money market accounts, in either currency. In accordance with typical short dated FX market practice, we assume that discount factors are deterministic and can be removed from the expectations. Consequently, we refer to ccy A and ccy B numeraires, where we should really call them *quasi*-numeraires. We return to this point later in Chapter 11. Don't forget.

where $N_d = K \cdot N_f$. The possible quote styles (four relative and two absolute) are summarised below:

$$V_{d;pips} \equiv V_{d/f} = \omega e^{-r^d T}[FN(\omega d_1) - KN(\omega d_2)]$$

$$V_{\%f} = \frac{V_{d/f}}{S_0}$$

$$V_{\%d} = \frac{V_{d/f}}{K},$$

$$V_{f;pips} \equiv V_{f/d} = \frac{V_{d/f}}{S_0 K}$$

$$V_d = N_f \cdot V_{d/f}$$

$$V_f = \frac{1}{S_0} N_f \cdot V_{d/f}.$$

It is very important to note, and I particularly want to stress this to the reader, that this technique of constructing all these different quote styles *only* works where there are two notionals, in foreign and domestic currencies, and there is a fixed relationship between them, which is known from the start. This is true for European and American style vanilla options, even in the presence of barriers and accrual features (more on these exotic features later), but is most definitely *not* true for digital options. Suppose one has a cash-or-nothing digital which pays one USD if the EURUSD FX rate fixes at time T above a particular level (sometimes called 'strike', which I believe leads to the confusion). The digital clearly has a USD notional ($= \$1$) so we can obtain %USD and EUR/USD prices. However, there is no EUR notional at all so the other two quote styles are meaningless.

3.2 THE LAW OF MANY DELTAS

We saw in Section 2.9 – 'The Law of One Price' – that investors must agree on the Black–Scholes price of an FX option, no matter which they regard as their domestic and their foreign currencies, so long as they agree on market parameters such as spot, volatility and interest rates. Unfortunately, just as there are several ways to quote the prices of currency options, there are several ways to quote the deltas.

This is not surprising, as the delta is meant to be the instantaneous derivative of price with respect to changes in the asset price. Therefore, if there are several quote styles for the price, then there will almost certainly be several ways to construct a delta.

For clarity, we use expression (2.65) for the Black–Scholes price of a European:

$$V_{d;pips} = \omega S_0 e^{-r^f T} N(\omega d_1) - \omega K e^{-r^d T} N(\omega d_2),$$

with moneyness terms from (2.68):

$$d_{1,2} = \frac{\ln(F_{0,T}/K) \pm \frac{1}{2}\sigma^2 T}{\sigma\sqrt{T}}.$$

In order to derive the deltas, not forgetting that as well as the S_0 term in (2.65), both d_1 and d_2 are functions of S_0 also, we use the following propositions (the proofs of which are all just simple algebra and are left as an exercise for the reader):

Proposition 3.2.1

$$\frac{\partial d_1}{\partial S_0} = \frac{\partial d_2}{\partial S_0} = \frac{1}{\sigma S_0 \sqrt{T}}.$$

Proposition 3.2.2

$$\frac{\partial N(\omega d_k)}{\partial S_0} = \frac{\omega}{\sigma S_0 \sqrt{T}} n(\omega d_k) \quad \text{for } k \in \{1, 2\}.$$

Proposition 3.2.3 *Note that while we are only concerned with $\omega = \pm 1$, for which $\omega^2 = 1$, the result holds in general:*

$$n(\omega d_1) = n(\omega d_2) \exp(\omega^2 [r^f - r^d] T)(K/S_0)^{\omega^2}.$$

With this, we start by taking the derivative of $V_{d;\,\text{pips}}$ with respect to S_0, which gives the first of our deltas.

3.2.1   Pips spot delta

The pips spot delta is the ratio of the change in present value (PV) of the option to the change in spot – both expressed in ccy2/ccy1 terms:

$$\Delta_{S;\,\text{pips}} = \lim_{\Delta S_0 \to 0} \frac{\Delta V_{d;\,\text{pips}}}{\Delta S_0} = \frac{\partial V_{d;\,\text{pips}}}{\partial S_0},$$

where $\Delta V_x \equiv V_x(S_0 + \Delta S_0) - V_x(S_0)$ for any quote style x:

$$
\begin{aligned}
\Delta_{S;\,\text{pips}} &\equiv \frac{\partial V_{d;\,\text{pips}}}{\partial S_0} \\
&= \omega e^{-r^f T} N(\omega d_1) + \omega S_0 e^{-r^f T} \frac{\partial N(\omega d_1)}{\partial S_0} - \omega K e^{-r^d T} \frac{\partial N(\omega d_2)}{\partial S_0} \\
&= \omega e^{-r^f T} N(\omega d_1) + \frac{\omega^2}{\sigma S_0 \sqrt{T}} \left(S_0 e^{-r^f T} n(\omega d_1) - K e^{-r^d T} n(\omega d_2) \right) \\
&= \omega e^{-r^f T} N(\omega d_1) \quad \text{from Proposition 3.2.3 with } |\omega| = 1.
\end{aligned}
\tag{3.2}
$$

Up to a factor of $e^{-r^f T}$, as required in FX, this is just the standard Black–Scholes delta. It is sometimes referred to as the points spot delta, e.g. in FENICS.

If we think of a delta hedge, it is just the number of units of foreign currency we need to hold in order to hedge an option with a notional of 1 unit of foreign currency and an equivalent notional of K units of domestic currency. So the spot delta is expressed as a percentage of foreign currency.

3.2.2 Percentage spot delta (premium adjusted)

The percentage spot delta, in contrast, is the ratio of the change in PV of the option – *in %
foreign terms* – to the change in spot – *in % foreign terms*:

$$\Delta_{S;\%} = \lim_{\Delta S_0 \to 0} \frac{\Delta V_{\%f}}{\Delta S_0/S_0} = \frac{\partial(V_{d;\text{pips}}/S_0)}{\partial(\ln S_0)}$$

$$= S_0 \frac{\partial(V_{d;\text{pips}}/S_0)}{\partial(S_0)} = S_0 \frac{(\partial V_{d;\text{pips}}/\partial S_0)S_0 - V_{d;\text{pips}}}{S_0^2} = \frac{\partial V_{d;\text{pips}}}{\partial S_0} - \frac{V_{d;\text{pips}}}{S_0}.$$

We therefore obtain the result that the percentage spot delta is the *premium-adjusted* spot pips
delta

$$\Delta_{S;\%} = \Delta_{S;\text{pips}} - V_{\%f}. \tag{3.3}$$

3.2.3 Pips forward delta

The pips forward delta is the ratio of the change in future value (FV) – note this is the future
and not present value! – of the option to the change in the relevant forward, both quoted in
ccy2/ccy1 terms:

$$\Delta_{F;\text{pips}} = \frac{\partial \mathbf{E}^d[V_T]}{\partial F_{0,T}} = e^{r^d T} \lim_{\Delta F_{0,T} \to 0} \frac{\Delta V_{d;\text{pips}}}{\Delta F_{0,T}}$$

$$= \frac{e^{r^d T}}{\partial F_{0,T}/\partial S} \frac{\partial V_{d;\text{pips}}}{\partial S_0} = e^{r^f T} \Delta_{S;\text{pips}}$$

$$= \omega N(\omega d_1). \tag{3.4}$$

Note that this is *not* the same as the forward delta introduced as equation (1.59) in Wystup
(2006), which is the ratio of the change in PV of the option to the change in the relevant
forward, both quoted in ccy2/ccy1 terms. It *is*, however, the same as the forward delta in
Wystup (2008).

3.2.4 Percentage forward delta (premium adjusted)

The percentage forward delta is the ratio of the change in FV of the option – *in % foreign
terms* – to the change in the relevant forward – *in % foreign terms*:

$$\Delta_{F;\%} = e^{r^d T} \lim_{\Delta F_{0,T} \to 0} \frac{\Delta V_{\%f}}{\Delta F_{0,T}/F_{0,T}} = \frac{\partial(V_{d;\text{pips}}/S_0)}{\partial(\ln F_{0,T})}$$

$$= e^{r^f T}\left[\Delta_{S;\text{pips}} - V_{\%f}\right]$$

$$= \omega \frac{K}{F_{0,T}} N(\omega d_2). \tag{3.5}$$

3.2.5 Simple delta

The last 'delta' we introduce isn't actually a delta in the usual sense of a sensitivity of any
price to changes in spot or the forward. Being defined as an intermediate type of moneyness
between $\omega N(\omega d_1)$ and $\omega N(\omega d_2)$, it is a simplified measure of moneyness, somewhere in

principle between the two forward deltas $\Delta_{F;\text{pips}}$ and $\Delta_{F;\%}$ (suitably scaled), and is used for ease of computation instead of other deltas when we construct parametric functions of delta:

$$\Delta_{\text{simple}} = \omega N(\omega d), \quad \text{where } d = \frac{\ln\left(F_{0,T}/K\right)}{\sigma\sqrt{T}}. \tag{3.6}$$

Note that d is the arithmetic average of d_1 and d_2 in (2.68).

3.2.6 Equivalence between pips and percentage deltas

An interesting note is that the spot percentage delta for an investor with ccy2 numeraire is related to the spot pips delta for an investor with ccy1 numeraire by a constant (negative) multiple.

Proof: Suppose we are working with currency 2 as the numeraire. We therefore have a spot pips delta $\Delta_{S;\text{pips}} = \partial V_{d;\text{pips}}/\partial S_0$. For an investor who has a numeraire of currency 1, *their* pips delta will be

$$
\begin{aligned}
\hat{\Delta}_{S;\text{pips}} &= \frac{\partial V_{f;\text{pips}}}{\partial \hat{S}_0} = \frac{\partial S_0}{\partial (S_0)^{-1}} \frac{\partial V_{f;\text{pips}}}{\partial S_0} \\[2mm]
&= \frac{\partial S_0}{\partial (S_0)^{-1}} \frac{\partial (V_{d;\text{pips}} S_0^{-1} K^{-1})}{\partial S_0} \\[2mm]
&= \frac{-S_0^2}{K} \left[S_0 \frac{\partial V_{d;\text{pips}}}{\partial S_0} - V_{d;\text{pips}} \right] \\[2mm]
&= \frac{-S_0}{K} \left[\frac{\partial V_{d;\text{pips}}}{\partial S_0} - \frac{V_{d;\text{pips}}}{S_0} \right] \\[2mm]
&= \frac{-S_0}{K} \left[\Delta_{S;\text{pips}} - V_{\%f} \right] \\[2mm]
&= \frac{-S_0}{K} \Delta_{S;\%}.
\end{aligned}
$$

This leads after a little algebra to the important results

$$
\begin{aligned}
\Delta_{S;\%} &= K/S_0 \cdot \omega e^{-r^d T} N(\omega d_2), \\
\Delta_{F;\%} &= K/F_{0,T} \cdot \omega N(\omega d_2),
\end{aligned}
$$

which we leave as an exercise to the reader, though a worked example of the latter can be found in pages 12–14 of Wystup (2008). The point well worth making is that due to the *duality* between the two currencies, there is a clear relationship between the two styles of delta (pips and percentage), due naturally to the change of measure between domestic and foreign risk-neutral measures.

3.2.7 Premium adjustment

It is worthwhile at this stage to think about why premium adjustment is required. Consider the case of a EURUSD call option or, to be more thorough, a EUR call/USD put. If the two counterparties to such a trade are euro based and US dollar based respectively, then we already know from Section 2.9 that they will agree on the price. However, the price will be expressed and actually exchanged in one of two currencies: EUR or USD. Since market convention in this case is for the premium to be in USD, the premium is itself riskless from the dollar investor's frame of reference and adds no further complexity to their risk calculations. However, the premium itself constitutes an extra source of currency risk from the euro investor's point of view, and as a result the euro based investor will premium adjust the delta.

This actually means that a euro based investor can either obtain premium adjusted deltas for FX call options on the spot rate for EURUSD, or he/she can construct pips deltas (without premium adjustment) for FX put options on the flipped spot rate USDEUR – a rate that is nothing more than the FX spot price of 1 USD, a risky asset for a euro denominated investor, as expressed in units of EUR (being his/her numeraire currency).

3.2.8 Summary

$$\Delta_{S;\text{pips}} = \omega e^{-r^f T} N(\omega d_1),$$

$$\Delta_{S;\%} = \omega e^{-r^d T} \frac{K}{S_0} N(\omega d_2),$$

$$\Delta_{F;\text{pips}} = \omega N(\omega d_1),$$

$$\Delta_{F;\%} = \omega \frac{K}{F_{0,T}} N(\omega d_2),$$

$$\Delta_{\text{simple}} = \omega N(\omega d).$$

3.3 FX DELTA CONVENTIONS

FX volatility smiles are characterised by providing volatilities, not as a function of strike, but as a function of delta (with the sole exception of the few cases in which the at-the-money is taken to be at-the-money-forward). The choice of delta as the parameter describing the volatility smile is sensible, as otherwise a strike that might correspond to a considerably out-of-the-money option for small T would be very close to at-the-money for large T. Parameterising the smile by delta allows better coverage of the volatility smile for many maturities given a known selection of deltas.

However, we saw above that in FX there is no such thing as *the* delta. As well as pips and percentage deltas, corresponding to risk exposures in ccy1 and ccy2 respectively, there are spot and forward delta versions of both. Which are to be used?

3.3.1 To premium adjust or not?

The choice of whether to apply the premium adjustment, i.e. whether to use pips or percentage delta, completely depends on which currency pair we are dealing with, and is determined by the choice of the premium currency (this is one of the FX market conventions) (see Table 3.1). Basically if the premium currency is ccy2 then no premium adjustment is applied and one uses the pips delta, whereas if the premium currency is ccy1 then the premium adjustment *is* applied and one uses the percentage delta. For example, with currency pair EURUSD, since the premium currency is USD (ccy2), the pips delta is used, whereas for currency pair USDJPY, since the premium currency is USD (ccy1), the percentage delta is used.

Typically the premium currency is taken to be the more commonly traded currency of the two – with the exception of JPY, which is rarely the premium currency. Therefore, for virtually

Table 3.1 Delta conventions for common currency pairs

Currency pair	ccy1	ccy2	Premium ccy	Δ convention
EURUSD	EUR	USD	USD	Pips
USDJPY	USD	JPY	USD	%
EURJPY	EUR	JPY	EUR	%
USDCHF	USD	CHF	USD	%
EURCHF	EUR	CHF	EUR	%
GBPUSD	GBP	USD	USD	Pips
EURGBP	EUR	GBP	EUR	%
AUDUSD	AUD	USD	USD	Pips
AUDJPY	AUD	JPY	AUD	%
USDCAD	USD	CAD	USD	%
USDBRL	USD	BRL	USD	%
USDMXN	USD	MXN	USD	%

all currency pairs involving the US dollar, the premium currency will be USD. For currency pairs including the euro and not including the US dollar, it will be EUR. For currency pairs involving the Japanese yen, it often *won't* be JPY unless the currency being quoted against the yen is an emerging market currency other than CZK, PLN, TRY or MXN (all of which dominate JPY in premium terms).

A basic hierarchy of which currencies dominate in premium currency terms can be written:

$$USD>EUR>GBP>AUD>NZD>CAD>CHF>\{NOK,SEK,DKK\}>\{CZK,PLN,TRY,MXN\}>JPY>....$$

However, in general, it is best to check. Table 3.2 shows the choice of premium currency for various currency pairs (only valid pairs of ccy1 and ccy2 are shown, e.g. USDJPY but not JPYUSD).

3.3.2 Spot delta or forward delta?

Since the credit crunch of 2008 and the associated low levels of liquidity in short-term interest rate products, it became unfeasible for banks to agree on spot deltas (which include discount factors) and, as a result, market practice at the time this book went to press has largely shifted

Table 3.2 Premium currency for major currency pairs

ccy1	USD	EUR	GBP	AUD	NZD	CAD	CHF	JPY
					ccy2			
USD						USD	USD	USD
EUR	USD		EUR	EUR	EUR	EUR	EUR	EUR
GBP	USD			GBP	GBP	GBP	GBP	GBP
AUD	USD				AUD	AUD	AUD	AUD
NZD	USD					NZD	NZD	NZD
CAD							CAD	CAD
CHF								CHF
JPY								

to using forward deltas exclusively in the construction of the FX smile, which do not include any discounting.

This has not always been the case, however. Historically, the answer used to depend on the time to expiry T, depending on whether the currency pair contained at least one emerging market currency. In that case, market practice used to be using forward deltas exclusively in our description of the market, due to the typically high interest rates in what is generally ccy2. However, if the currency pair contained only currencies from the more developed OECD economies, a comprehensive list of which used to be {USD, EUR, JPY, GBP, AUD, NZD, CAD, CHF, NOK, SEK, DKK}, and notably *not* including ISK, TRY, MXN, CZK, KRW, HUF, PLN, ZAR or SGD, then spot deltas were used out to and including 1Y, and forward deltas for all longer dated tenors. It was believed – not unreasonably – that short dated options could be hedged in the spot market, whereas longer dated options were hedged with forwards.

The events of 2008 show how market conditions can cause market conventions to evolve, and therefore it is always advisable to check current market practice, particularly in or after extreme market conditions.

3.3.3 Notation

Once the currency pair and the expiry time T are known, we know from Sections 3.3.1 and 3.3.2 which delta is meant. Let Δ_Q be defined by choosing whichever of $\{\Delta_{S;\text{pips}}, \Delta_{S;\%}, \Delta_{F;\text{pips}}, \Delta_{F;\%}\}$ is to be used.

For ease of notation, let $V(\omega, K, T, \sigma)$ denote the Black–Scholes domestic/foreign price for a call/put option ($\omega = \pm 1$ respectively) with strike K and time to expiry T, i.e. $V(\omega, K, T, \sigma) = V_{d;\text{pips}}$, and let $\Delta_Q(\omega, K, T, \sigma)$ denote the Δ_Q delta for a call/put ($\omega = \pm 1$ respectively), both using volatility σ.

We are now in a position to interpret typical FX market volatility smiles and to relate the market quotes to European options with strikes chosen to satisfy certain requirements on the deltas and prices, now that we know which delta is to be used.

3.4 MARKET VOLATILITY SURFACES

Because Black–Scholes is inadequate to price options of all strikes and maturities consistently with the market, it is necessary to construct a volatility smile $\sigma_X(K)$ that ascribes a volatility to each strike K. However, there is a notable absence of material in the literature that discusses the way in which the deviation of markets from Black–Scholes behaviour is expressed, in terms of market parameters. Malz (1997) provides a good description, but what he refers to as the 'strangle' is the 'smile strangle', which does not correspond to the typical strangles observed and traded in the markets (known as 'market strangles'). Furthermore, he does not clarify which deltas are to be used, nor what the at-the-money strike is required to be. We provide a more complete and thorough discussion in the rest of this chapter.

Malz correctly points out that the 25-delta call and the 25-delta put are commonly traded, and indeed these are important benchmark strikes for FX volatility surfaces. He suggests on page 23 that a 75-delta call can be used instead of a 25-delta put. However, the reader will now be aware that this only holds true for one *particular* choice of delta – the forward pips delta – in which case the 50-delta call strike is equivalent to the (forward pips) delta-neutral straddle.

Table 3.3 Sample market volatility surface for EURUSD

	EURUSD (spot reference 1.3465)				
Tenor	ATM vol	25-d-MS	10-d-MS	25-d-RR	10-d-RR
1M	21.000 %	0.650 %	2.433 %	−0.200 %	−1.258 %
2M	21.000 %	0.750 %	2.830 %	−0.250 %	−1.297 %
3M	20.750 %	0.850 %	3.228 %	−0.300 %	−1.332 %
6M	19.400 %	0.900 %	3.485 %	−0.500 %	−1.408 %
1Y	18.250 %	0.950 %	3.806 %	−0.600 %	−1.359 %
2Y	17.677 %	0.850 %	3.208 %	−0.562 %	−1.208 %

We therefore have prescribed volatilities for the 25-delta put, at-the-money and 25-delta call, which we denote by σ_{25-d-P}, σ_{ATM} and σ_{25-d-C} respectively. Prescribing volatilities at three strikes gives what is known as a three-point smile.

Somewhat less liquid but also available are 10-delta put and 10-delta call vols, denoted by σ_{10-d-P} and σ_{10-d-C}. These combined with the three above give a five-point smile.

3.4.1 Sample market volatility surfaces

The market snapshot below was collected on 15 December 2008 (see Tables 3.3 and 3.4). We shall use this market data in providing examples of the construction of the volatility surface in this chapter. The typical market volatility surfaces below describe measurements of three aspects of the volatility surface: at-the-money (ATM), market strangle (MS) and risk reversal (RR). All of these provide separate and somewhat nonoverlapping constraints on the volatility smile required. Our intent in the remainder of this chapter is to describe what these market parameters require in terms of describing a volatility surface.

3.5 AT-THE-MONEY

The at-the-money option is meant to correspond, as the name suggests, to an option that is midway between being in the money and out of the money. There are basically two possibilities that are used in practice. The ATM strike can be either set to be the forward or it can be set to be the delta neutral straddle (using whichever delta is specified by Section 3.3.1 and 3.3.2). Let us describe what these two cases correspond to.

Table 3.4 Sample market volatility surface for USDJPY

	EURJPY (spot reference 90.72)				
Tenor	ATM vol	25-d-MS	10-d-MS	25-d-RR	10-d-RR
1M	21.500 %	0.350 %	3.704 %	−8.350 %	−15.855 %
2M	20.500 %	0.325 %	4.047 %	−8.650 %	−16.467 %
3M	19.850 %	0.300 %	4.396 %	−8.950 %	−17.114 %
6M	18.000 %	0.225 %	4.932 %	−9.250 %	−17.882 %
1Y	15.950 %	0.175 %	5.726 %	−9.550 %	−18.855 %
2Y	14.009 %	0.100 %	5.709 %	−9.500 %	−18.217 %

3.5.1 At-the-money – ATMF

This is the easy one. For a particular maturity T, the strike K_{ATM} is set to the forward $F_{0,T}$ as defined in Section 2.6.1:

$$K_{\text{ATM}} = K_{\text{ATMF}} \equiv F_{0,T}. \tag{3.7}$$

This convention is only used for currency pairs including a Latin American emerging market currency, e.g. MXN, BRL, etc.

3.5.2 At-the-money – DNS

A more natural way to define the at-the-money strike is the strike K_{ATM} for which it is possible to buy a straddle that corresponds to a pure long vega (as introduced in Chapter 2) position with no net delta. This is known as the delta-neutral straddle and has the advantage that such a trade can be effected without any spot or forward trade being needed. It is the purest way to buy volatility at a fairly central level of strike and has presumably become the industry standard choice of strike for the at-the-money for this reason.

The delta-neutral straddle strike is defined by $K_{\text{ATM}} = K_{\text{DNS}}$, where K_{DNS} is chosen such that

$$\Delta_\varrho(+1, K_{\text{DNS}}, T, \sigma_{\text{ATM}}) + \Delta_\varrho(-1, K_{\text{DNS}}, T, \sigma_{\text{ATM}}) = 0. \tag{3.8}$$

Note that while spot deltas have a discount factor and forward deltas do not, this is irrelevant for (3.8) since the discount factor (if it appears) is just a constant factor. Consequently, the only two possibilities that need to be considered are using $\Delta_{F;\text{pips}}$ and $\Delta_{F;\%}$ – which one to choose is explained in Section 3.3.1.

We can actually solve for K analytically in both cases.

At-the-money – DNS – pips delta

We attempt to solve

$$\Delta_{F;\text{pips}}(+1, K, T, \sigma_{\text{ATM}}) + \Delta_{F;\text{pips}}(-1, K, T, \sigma_{\text{ATM}}) = 0,$$

the solution of which we denote by $K_{\text{DNS;pips}}$. By (3.4), $\Delta_{F;\text{pips}} = \omega N(\omega d_1)$ and so we require that $N(d_1) = N(-d_1)$. Using (2.68), we have $d_1 = [\ln\left(F_{0,T}/K\right) + \frac{1}{2}\sigma^2 T]/\sigma\sqrt{T}$ and therefore require

$$N\left(\frac{\ln F_{0,T} - \ln K + \frac{1}{2}\sigma^2 T}{\sigma\sqrt{T}}\right) = N\left(\frac{\ln K - \ln F_{0,T} - \frac{1}{2}\sigma^2 T}{\sigma\sqrt{T}}\right),$$

which, as $N(\cdot)$ is monotonically increasing, means we need K such that

$$\frac{\ln F_{0,T} - \ln K + \frac{1}{2}\sigma^2 T}{\sigma\sqrt{T}} = \frac{\ln K - \ln F_{0,T} - \frac{1}{2}\sigma^2 T}{\sigma\sqrt{T}}.$$

Forgetting the denominator and grouping numerator terms, we need $2\ln K = 2\ln F_{0,T} + \sigma^2 T$, which has the exact solution

$$K_{\text{DNS;pips}} = F_{0,T}\exp\left(\frac{1}{2}\sigma^2 T\right).$$

At-the-money – DNS – percentage delta

This time, one attempts to solve for that value of K (call it $K_{\text{DNS};\%}$) for which

$$\Delta_{F;\%}(+1, K, T, \sigma_{\text{ATM}}) + \Delta_{F;\%}(-1, K, T, \sigma_{\text{ATM}}) = 0.$$

By (3.5), $\Delta_{F;\%} = \omega(K/F_{0,T})N(\omega d_2)$ and so, after cancelling out $K/F_{0,T}$ we require that $N(d_2) = N(-d_2)$. The algebra is almost exactly the same as above, and it easily follows that the required delta-neutral strike is

$$K_{\text{DNS};\%} = F_{0,T} \exp\left(-\frac{1}{2}\sigma^2 T\right).$$

ATMF is actually delta-neutral with respect to simple delta

We see above that either $N(d_1) = N(-d_1)$ or $N(d_2) = N(-d_2)$ give the delta-neutral strikes corresponding to pips and percentage deltas respectively. Suppose we try instead to solve for the strike $K_{\text{DNS};\text{simple}}$ that makes the straddle zero delta, with respect to simple delta (3.6). For this, we require $N(d) = N(-d)$ and the solution is just $\ln F_{0,T} - \ln K = \ln K - \ln F_{0,T}$, i.e. $K_{\text{DNS};\text{simple}} = K_{\text{ATMF}} = F_{0,T}$.

3.5.3 At-the-money strikes – summary

$$K_{\text{ATMF}} = F_{0,T},$$

$$K_{\text{DNS};\text{pips}} = F_{0,T} \exp\left(\frac{1}{2}\sigma^2 T\right),$$

$$K_{\text{DNS};\%} = F_{0,T} \exp\left(-\frac{1}{2}\sigma^2 T\right).$$

Rule of thumb. If the ATM strike is above (below) the forward, the market convention must be that deltas for that currency pair are quoted as pips (percentage) deltas.

3.5.4 Example – EURUSD 1Y

We see from Table 3.3 that the 1Y EURUSD ATM volatility is 18.25 %. Interest rates out to 1Y are $r^f = 3.46\%$ (EUR) and $r^d = 2.94\%$ (USD), with discount factors of $D_T^f(0) = 0.966\,001$ and $D_T^d(0) = 0.971\,049$ respectively.
We calculate

$$F_{0,T} = S_0 D_T^f(0)/D_T^d(0) = 1.3465 \times 0.966\,001/0.971\,049 = 1.3395.$$

We now apply Section 3.5.2, with $\exp\left(\frac{1}{2}\sigma^2 T\right) = \exp(\frac{1}{2} \times 0.1825^2) = 1.016\,793$, and then $K_{\text{DNS};\text{pips}} = 1.3395 \times 1.016\,793 = 1.3620$ (to the nearest pip).

Figure 3.1 shows the pips price of a 1Y straddle with $K = 1.3620$ as a function of spot S_0, from which we can see that the spot pips delta is indeed zero at the current level of spot $S_0 = 1.3465$.

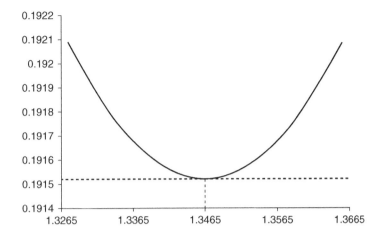

Figure 3.1 $V_{d;\,\text{pips}}$ value profile for delta-neutral straddle ($T = 1.0,\ \ K = 1.3620$)

3.5.5   Example – USDJPY 1Y

From Table 3.4 the 1Y USDJPY ATM volatility is 15.95 %. Interest rates out to 1Y are $r^f = 2.94\,\%$ (USD) and $r^d = 1.71\,\%$ (JPY), with discount factors of $D_T^f(0) = 0.971\,049$ and $D_T^d(0) = 0.983\,050$ respectively. Spot $S_0 = 90.72$.

From Table 3.1, we use the percentage (or premium adjusted) delta to compute the ATM strike. We have $F_{0,T} = S_0 D_T^f(0)/D_T^d(0) = 90.72 \times 0.971\,049/0.983\,050 = 89.6125$.

Applying Section 3.5.2, with $\exp\left(-\tfrac{1}{2}\sigma^2 T\right) = \exp(-\tfrac{1}{2} \times 0.1595^2) = 0.987\,36$, then $K_{\text{DNS};\%} = 89.6125 \times 0.987\,36 = 88.4798$ (to the nearest pip).

3.6   MARKET STRANGLE

Suppose that we neglect the effect of volatility skew and presume that volatility, while nonconstant across various strikes, is basically symmetric. The concept of the market strangle is that we buy an out-of-the-money put and an out-of-the-money call with strikes placed a similar distance away from the at-the-money strike in moneyness terms. For the sake of clarity, we shall suppose we are talking about the 25-delta market strangle, though the market strangle for any delta can be dealt with similarly.

The idea here is that, without needing to know the actual volatility smile, we can nevertheless estimate the volatility that is needed to price a market strangle instrument consistently with the market, by taking the at-the-money volatility and adding a strangle premium $\sigma_{25-d-\text{MS}}$ to it. The premium thus added, in volatility terms, is called the market strangle.

The important point to make is that the strikes for the calls and puts are both calculated subject to the Black–Scholes model with a single constant volatility of $\sigma_{\text{ATM}} + \sigma_{25-d-\text{MS}}$; these strikes are known as the market strangle strikes $K_{25-d-P-\text{MS}}$ and $K_{25-d-C-\text{MS}}$. With that, we obtain strikes for calls and puts that have deltas of $+0.25$ and -0.25 respectively, as shown in Figures 3.2 and 3.3.

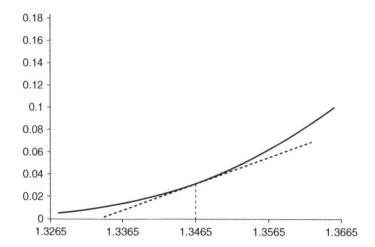

Figure 3.2 $V_{d;\text{pips}}$ value profile for 25-delta market strangle (call component) $(T = 1.0, \ K = 1.5449)$

This requires solution of

$$\Delta_\varrho(-1, K_{25-d-P-MS}, T, \sigma_{ATM} + \sigma_{25-d-MS}) = -0.25,$$
$$\Delta_\varrho(+1, K_{25-d-C-MS}, T, \sigma_{ATM} + \sigma_{25-d-MS}) = +0.25. \qquad (3.9)$$

The crucial part of this, and we shall return to this point later, is that even if the volatility smile is not symmetric, and therefore neither the call with strike $K_{25-d-C-MS}$ nor the put with strike $K_{25-d-P-MS}$ should actually be priced with volatility $\sigma_{ATM} + \sigma_{25-d-MS}$, the *aggregate* price obtained for the market strangle (long a call with strike $K_{25-d-C-MS}$ and long a put with strike $K_{25-d-P-MS}$) under the actual market volatility smile should be identical to the

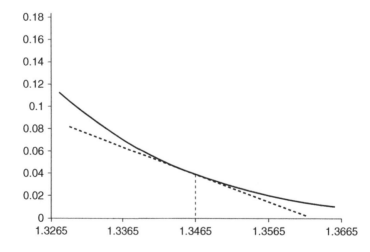

Figure 3.3 $V_{d;\text{pips}}$ value profile for 25-delta market strangle (put component) $(T = 1.0, K = 1.2050)$

same aggregate price for the same market strangle instrument, under the assumption of Black–Scholes volatility of $\sigma_{ATM} + \sigma_{25-d-MS}$.

In other words, the market strangle $\sigma_{25-d-MS}$ provides the *adjustment* to σ_{ATM} which, if substituted into a Black–Scholes model and used to calculate 25-delta call and put strikes and then to price a straddle with those strikes, gives the *same* aggregate price as we would obtain if we priced the two components with those strikes using a full volatility smile (though the two price components may well differ, the sum must agree).

We put

$$V_{25-d-MS} = V(-1, K_{25-d-P-MS}, T, \sigma_{ATM} + \sigma_{25-d-MS})$$
$$+ V(+1, K_{25-d-C-MS}, T, \sigma_{ATM} + \sigma_{25-d-MS}). \qquad (3.10)$$

3.6.1 Example – EURUSD 1Y

We see from Table 3.3 that the 1Y EURUSD ATM volatility is 18.25 % and the 25-delta market strangle is 0.950 %. These sum to 19.20 % and since the market convention for EURUSD for 1Y and a shorter expiry is pips spot delta, the market strangle strikes are obtained by solving

$$\Delta_{S;pips}(+1, K_{25-d-C-MS}, 1.0, 19.20\%) = 0.25,$$
$$\Delta_{S;pips}(-1, K_{25-d-P-MS}, 1.0, 19.20\%) = -0.25. \qquad (3.11)$$

We obtain strikes of $K_{25-d-C-MS} = 1.5449$ and $K_{25-d-P-MS} = 1.2050$.

3.7 SMILE STRANGLE AND RISK REVERSAL

The at-the-money volatility and market strangle volatility provide two degrees of freedom, which allow a volatility smile to be described but without a skew. To introduce a market parameter corresponding to skew, we use the risk reversal as described in Malz (1997). In order to do this, however, we need to suppose that a volatility smile of the form $\sigma_X(K)$ exists, because each European option with different strike K is priced using the smile volatility $\sigma_X(K)$, unlike the at-the-money or market strangle for which we can use a single volatility (which we know in advance). Let us describe the conditions we have on this smile from Sections 3.5 and 3.6:

$$\sigma_X(K_{ATM}) = \sigma_{ATM}, \qquad (3.12)$$
$$V_{25-d-MS} = V(-1, K_{25-d-P-MS}, T, \sigma_X(K_{25-d-P-MS}))$$
$$+ V(+1, K_{25-d-C-MS}, T, \sigma_X(K_{25-d-C-MS})). \qquad (3.13)$$

The task is now to find 25-delta smile strikes K_{25-d-C} and K_{25-d-P} for which the Black–Scholes delta is ± 0.25 subject to using smile volatilities $\sigma_X(K_{25-d-C})$ and $\sigma_X(K_{25-d-P})$ respectively. We therefore need to solve

$$\Delta_\varrho(-1, K_{25-d-P}, T, \sigma_X(K_{25-d-P})) = -0.25,$$
$$\Delta_\varrho(+1, K_{25-d-C}, T, \sigma_X(K_{25-d-C})) = +0.25. \qquad (3.14)$$

Once these strikes have been determined, we set $\sigma_{25-d-P} = \sigma_X(K_{25-d-P})$ and $\sigma_{25-d-C} = \sigma_X(K_{25-d-C})$. The 25-delta risk reversal is calculated from the difference. However, the market generally imposes a sign convention that indicates whether the risk reversal is defined as $\sigma_{25-d-C} - \sigma_{25-d-P}$ or $\sigma_{25-d-P} - \sigma_{25-d-C}$. We use $\phi_{RR} \in \{-1, +1\}$ to denote which is meant, depending on whether positive risk reversals favour (i.e. attribute higher implied volatilities to) calls on ccy1 or calls on ccy2, and put

$$\sigma_{25-d-RR} = \phi_{RR} \cdot [\sigma_{25-d-C} - \sigma_{25-d-P}]. \tag{3.15}$$

Equations (3.12), (3.13) and (3.15) provide us with conditions necessary for $\sigma_X(K)$ to be consistent with the market, as parameterised by σ_{ATM}, $\sigma_{25-d-MS}$ and $\sigma_{25-d-RR}$. If other deltas on the smile are quoted, most commonly 10-delta, then conditions (3.13) and (3.15) are applied in the exact same way except using $\sigma_{10-d-MS}$ and $\sigma_{10-d-RR}$.

It is important to note that the smile strikes K_{25-d-C} and K_{25-d-P} are in general *not* the same as the market strangle strikes $K_{25-d-C-MS}$ and $K_{25-d-P-MS}$. The 25-delta smile strangle is given by the average volatility of the 25-delta call and 25-delta put, expressed as a premium over the at-the-money volatility:

$$\sigma_{25-d-SS} = \frac{1}{2}[\sigma_{25-d-C} + \sigma_{25-d-P}] - \sigma_{ATM}. \tag{3.16}$$

Note that if $\sigma_{25-d-RR} = 0$ then by (3.15) we have $\sigma_{25-d-C} = \sigma_{25-d-P}$ and therefore $\sigma_{25-d-SS} = \sigma_{25-d-C} - \sigma_{ATM} = \sigma_{25-d-P} - \sigma_{ATM}$. Consequently, $\sigma_{25-d-MS} = \sigma_{25-d-SS}$ in the case where $\sigma_{25-d-RR} = 0$, but in general this is not so. The discrepancy is most notable for currency pairs where the risk reversals are large in absolute value, e.g. USDJPY.

We therefore have several strikes – even without including the 10-delta smile, we have $\{K_{25-d-P}, K_{25-d-P-MS}, K_{ATM}, K_{25-d-C}, K_{25-d-C-MS}\}$. There is unfortunately no unique prescription for $\sigma_X(K)$ and we therefore need to calibrate a smile $\sigma_X(K)$ that satisfies

$$\sigma_X(K_{ATM}) = \sigma_{ATM}, \tag{3.17}$$

$$V_{25-d-MS} = V(-1, K_{25-d-P-MS}, T, \sigma_X(K_{25-d-P-MS}))$$
$$+ V(+1, K_{25-d-C-MS}, T, \sigma_X(K_{25-d-C-MS})), \tag{3.18}$$

$$\sigma_{25-d-RR} = \phi_{RR} \cdot [\sigma_X(K_{25-d-C}) - \sigma_X(K_{25-d-P})], \tag{3.19}$$

where the strikes are determined as detailed above. When these three equations are satisfied, we have

$$\sigma_{25-d-SS} = \frac{1}{2}[\sigma_X(K_{25-d-C}) + \sigma_X(K_{25-d-P})] - \sigma_X(K_{ATM}). \tag{3.20}$$

The tricky part is that (3.14) is an *implicit* equation for K_{25-d-P} and K_{25-d-C} respectively – there is an entire family of solutions with Δ_ρ of ± 0.25 depending on the balance between K and σ. Consequently, the calibration procedure needs to take into account the fact that as we change our parametric form $\sigma_X(K)$ for the smile, we will have shifted the smile strikes K_{25-d-P} and K_{25-d-C} (not K_{ATM}, $K_{25-d-P-MS}$ and $K_{25-d-C-MS}$, however, which are fully determined and independent of what choice of smile interpolation is used). We see two examples of this in practice in Sections 3.9 and 3.10 below.

The following is an algorithm that can be used to fit a smile, and thereby obtain smile strangles from market strangles.

3.7.1 Smile strangle from market strangle – algorithm

1. Decide on a parametric form $\sigma_X(K)$ for volatility, e.g. (3.21) or (3.23).
2. Determine K_{ATM} by using either (3.7) or (3.8) with σ_{ATM}, depending on market convention.

3. Use (3.9), together with σ_{ATM} and $\sigma_{25-d-MS}$, to determine $K_{25-d-P-MS}$ and $K_{25-d-C-MS}$.
4. Use (3.10) to determine $V_{target} = V_{25-d-MS}$.
5. Choose an initial guess for $\sigma_{25-d-SS}$, such as $\sigma_{25-d-SS} = \sigma_{25-d-MS}$.
6. Using σ_{ATM}, $\sigma_{25-d-SS}$ and $\sigma_{25-d-RR}$, find parameters for $\sigma_X(K)$ using a least squares optimiser that satisfies (3.17), (3.19) and (3.20), with smile strikes K_{25-d-C} and K_{25-d-P} given by $\sigma_X(K)$, i.e. satisfying (3.14).
7. Price up the market strangle with strikes $K_{25-d-P-MS}$ and $K_{25-d-C-MS}$ using the $\sigma_X(K)$ parameters obtained in step 6, i.e. $V_{trial} = V_{25-d-MS}$ using (3.18).
8. If $V_{trial} \approx V_{target}$ then $\sigma_X(K)$ satisfies the smile conditions and the algorithm is complete. Otherwise, revise the guess for $\sigma_{25-d-SS}$ (downwards if $V_{trial} > V_{target}$ and upwards if $V_{trial} < V_{target}$) and repeat steps 5 through to 7.

In practice, the inner optimisation in step 6, together with the outer optimisation in steps 5 to 8, are performed with an optimiser such as Levenberg–Marquardt (Press *et al.*, 2002).

3.8 VISUALISATION OF STRANGLES

The discussion above of the difference between market strangle and smile strangle is somewhat technical, and a diagrammatic representation may be useful. In Figure 3.4 we show a smile volatility $\sigma_X(K)$, basically parabolic in shape even though constructed using the SABR methodology described in Section 3.10, which we have constructed to fit the 1Y EURUSD market as described above. The 25-delta put (25-d-P) and call (25-d-C) strikes are shown with respect to the volatilities on the smile, as is the at-the-money (ATM). Note that this is not the at-the-money-forward; it is whatever is prescribed in Section 3.5.

In Figure 3.4, the horizontal dotted lines indicate the volatilities at these three strikes. The graph depicts the risk reversal (RR) as the difference between the 25-delta call and the 25-delta put volatilities (the small + and − signs denote which sign convention is intended). The oblique dotted line segment connecting the 25-delta call and 25-delta put points on the graph is bisected, so that the midpoint of that line segment has a volatility equal to the average of σ_{25-d-P} and σ_{25-d-C}. The vertical distance of that midpoint above the ATM level is therefore the smile strangle (SS), as indicated on the graph.

The market strangle is more difficult to explain visually. Figure 3.5 shows the market strangle (MS) as a spread to the at-the-money volatility. As well as the long horizontal dotted

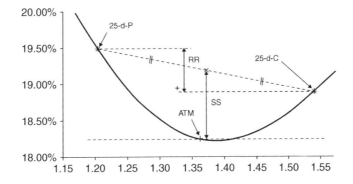

Figure 3.4 Schematic illustration of the smile strangle

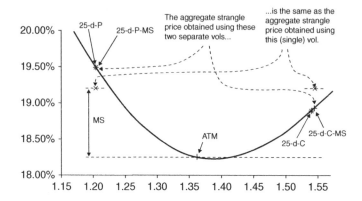

Figure 3.5   Schematic illustration of the market strangle

line showing the ATM volatility level, two shorter horizontal dotted lines at the same vertical level indicate the market strangle vol. *This* volatility, not the ATM volatility nor the smile volatility, is used to calculate strikes that are 25-delta strikes for the put and the call, indicated by X-shaped tickmarks on the graph at the market strangle volatility level (the level indicated by the two shorter horizontal dotted lines).

Now the crucial point about the market strangle is that, if one prices the put and the call with those two strikes, using the market strangle volatility, the aggregate price obtained is the *same* as if one prices the put and call, with the exact same strikes, on the smile $\sigma_X(K)$, using the volatilities indicated at the 25-d-P-MS and 25-d-C-MS tickmarks on the smile.

The discrepancy between the strikes corresponding to smile strangles and market strangles is relatively small in the example of 1Y EURUSD shown in Figure 3.5. This is by no means always the case. Figure 3.6 shows that in the case where the risk reversal is large, as is typically the case for USDJPY, the strikes can be markedly different. The discrepancy between smile strangle and market strangle strikes increases for large absolute values of risk reversal.

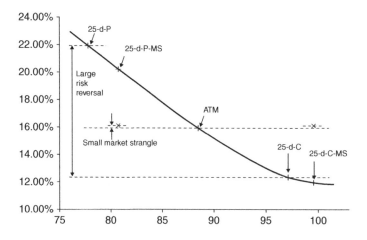

Figure 3.6   Highly skewed smile (1Y USDJPY)

3.9   SMILE INTERPOLATION – POLYNOMIAL IN DELTA

The first technique we present here involves construction of a polynomial

$$\sigma_X(K) = \exp(f(\ln(F_{0,T}/K))) \qquad (3.21a)$$

with

$$f(x) = c_0 + c_1\delta(x) + c_2[\delta(x)]^2, \qquad (3.21b)$$

where, letting $\sigma_0 = \exp(c_0)$, we have

$$\delta(x) = N(x/(\delta_0\sqrt{T})). \qquad (3.22)$$

Note that $\delta(x)$ in (3.22) is similar to Δ_{simple} in (3.6), as we use $x = \ln(F_{0,T}/K)$, but considering only δ_0. We are therefore constructing a parametric fit to $\sigma_X(K)$ using interpolation in simple delta.

Parameters c_0, c_1 and c_2 are numerically chosen in order to minimise a suitably chosen error function that takes into account the degree to which $\sigma_X(K)$ fails to satisfy conditions (3.17), (3.18) and (3.19). A solver such as Powell or Levenberg–Marquardt is used, as described in Press et al. (2002).

Note that a quadratic such as used in (3.21b) can be tuned between parabolic shapes of the form x^2 and a V-shaped profile of the form $|x|$ by changing from a quadratic term c_2x^2 to a damped quadratic term $c_2x^2/(1+l|x|)$. As $|x| \to \infty$, $c_2x^2/(1+l|x|) \to c_2x^2/l|x| = c_2/l^{-1}|x|$. The linearity parameter l determines how quickly we approach linear behaviour as $x \to \infty$.

3.9.1   Example – EURUSD 1Y – polynomial in delta

Applying the procedure above, given the market data in Table 3.5, we obtain $c_0 = -1.701\,005$, $c_1 = 0.050\,131$ and $c_2 = 0.800\,801$, for which we back out the smile strikes and volatilities below. Note that $\sigma_{25-d-C} - \sigma_{25-d-P} = -0.60\,\%$, in agreement with the market. The ATM vol is similarly correct.

We now verify that the market strangle is priced correctly. Comparing prices in Table 3.6 by summing the first two bold elements in the column headed $\sigma = 19.20\,\%$ and the corresponding bold elements in the two rightmost columns, we see that the aggregate price of 0.078 637 for the market strangle obtained using put and call volatilities of 18.92 % and 19.48 % respectively is in very close agreement with the price of 0.078 630 obtained using the single market strangle volatility of 19.20 %, indicating that this particular smile interpolation $\sigma_X(K)$ recovers the market strangle as well as the at-the-money volatility and the risk reversal.

Table 3.5   1Y EURUSD smile with polynomial delta parameterisation

K_{25-d-P}	1.2034	19.50 %
$K_{25-d-P-MS}$	1.2050	19.48 %
K_{ATM}	1.3620	18.25 %
K_{25-d-C}	1.5410	18.90 %
$K_{25-d-C-MS}$	1.5449	18.92 %

Table 3.6   1Y EURUSD Black–Scholes prices under delta polynomial

		EURUSD (spot reference 1.3465)			
		$V_{d;\,pips}$ under several BS volatility scenarios			
	K	$\sigma = 18.25\%$	$\sigma = 19.20\%$	$\sigma = 18.92\%$	$\sigma = 19.48\%$
25-d-P	1.2034	0.038 664	0.042 613	0.041 462	0.043 771
25-d-P-MS	1.2050	0.039 155	**0.043 123**	0.041 966	**0.044 285**
ATM	1.3620	0.191 520	0.201 379	0.198 520	0.204 240
25-d-C	1.5410	0.032 299	0.036 277	0.035 112	0.037 452
25-d-C-MS	1.5449	0.031 565	**0.035 507**	**0.034 352**	0.036 672
			0.078 630	**0.078 637**	

3.10   SMILE INTERPOLATION – SABR

One criticism of the volatility smile obtained by a quadratic polynomial in simple delta in Section 3.9 is that it fails to have enough volatility in the 'wings', i.e. for call and put strikes deeply in-the-money. The approach can of course be extended to polynomials of higher order, and the 10-delta market strangle and risk reversal similarly fit with the extra parameters, but the danger of using a quartic in d is one of overfitting.

An alternative scheme is proposed in Hagan *et al.* (2002), in which the authors derive useful closed-form approximations for implied volatilities for European options under a particular type of stochastic volatility model. A fuller discussion of the model itself is in Chapter 6 below, and we merely present the expressions for implied volatility here.

Subject to the choice of a β parameter, which scales between stochastic normal ($\beta = 0$) and stochastic lognormal ($\beta = 1$) and which is constrained to lie in the interval [0,1], the SABR model has three parameters:

α – initial volatility
ν – volatility of volatility
ρ – correlation between spot and volatility

These are the three parameters we shall use as decision variables in optimising for a choice of $\sigma_X(K)$ to fit the volatility smile, analogous to c_0, c_1 and c_2 in Section 3.9.

The implied volatility for a European option with strike K and expiry T can be obtained, as in (2.17) of Hagan *et al.* (2002). Note that we follow the authors' advice and neglect all the higher order terms marked with '...' in the original paper, and merely state

$$\sigma_X(K) =$$
$$\frac{\alpha}{(F_{0,T}K)^{(1-\beta)/2}\left\{1 + [(1-\beta)^2/24]\log^2(F_{0,T}/K) + [(1-\beta)^4/1920]\log^4(F_{0,T}/K)\right\}}$$
$$\cdot\left(\frac{z}{\chi(z)}\right) \cdot \left\{1 + \left[\frac{(1-\beta)^2}{24}\frac{\alpha^2}{(F_{0,T}K)^{1-\beta}} + \frac{1}{4}\frac{\rho\beta\nu\alpha}{(F_{0,T}K)^{(1-\beta)/2}} + \frac{2-3\rho^2}{24}\nu^2\right]T\right\}, \quad (3.23a)$$

where

$$z = \frac{\nu}{\alpha}(F_{0,T}K)^{(1-\beta)/2}\log(F_{0,T}/K) \qquad (3.23b)$$

Table 3.7 1Y EURUSD smile with SABR parameterisation

K_{25-d-P}	1.2034	19.49 %
$K_{25-d-P-MS}$	1.2050	19.47 %
K_{ATM}	1.3620	18.25 %
K_{25-d-C}	1.5410	18.89 %
$K_{25-d-C-MS}$	1.5449	18.93 %

and

$$\chi(z) = \log\left\{ \frac{\sqrt{1 - 2\rho z + z^2} + z - \rho}{1 - \rho} \right\}. \tag{3.23c}$$

Though (3.23a) looks very complicated, numerical implementation of this is no more difficult in principle than (3.21a). The parameter β is specified in advance (we find $\beta = 1$ sufficient for our needs, and the algebra is certainly simpler), and since K and $F_{0,T}$ are known also, the only parameters that admit any variation are α, ν and ρ – exactly the decision variables mentioned above. As in Section 3.9, parameters α, ν and ρ are numerically chosen using a solver such as Powell or Levenberg–Marquardt in order to minimise a suitably chosen error function.

3.10.1 Example – EURUSD 1Y – SABR

Using the technique described above, with the choice of $\beta = 1$, we obtain $\alpha = 0.174\,310\,60$, $\nu = 0.816\,940\,72$ and $\rho = -0.112\,683\,06$, from which the smile strikes and volatilities can be computed, as tabulated in Table 3.7. Note that $\sigma_{25-d-C} - \sigma_{25-d-P} = -0.60\,\%$, in agreement with Table 3.3, even though the 25-d-C and 25-d-P vols differ slightly from Section 3.9.1.

Comparing prices in Table 3.8, the price of 0.078 633 for the market strangle obtained using put and call volatilities of 18.93 % and 19.47 % respectively agrees to six decimal places with the price obtained using the single market strangle volatility of 19.20 % (summing elements as in Table 3.6).

We therefore see that the smile parameterisation $\sigma_X(K)$ quoted in (3.23a) can be calibrated to capture all the required market volatility characteristics of the 1Y EURUSD smile.

Table 3.8 1Y EURUSD Black–Scholes prices under SABR

		EURUSD (spot reference 1.3465)			
		$V_{d;pips}$ under several BS volatility scenarios			
	K	$\sigma = 18.25\%$	$\sigma = 19.20\%$	$\sigma = 18.93\%$	$\sigma = 19.47\%$
25-d-P	1.2034	0.038 670	0.042 619	0.041 472	0.043 765
25-d-P-MS	1.2050	0.039 156	**0.043 124**	0.041 971	**0.044 275**
ATM	1.3620	0.191 520	0.201 379	0.198 530	0.204 211
25-d-C	1.5410	0.032 308	0.036 286	0.035 125	0.037 449
25-d-C-MS	1.5449	0.031 567	**0.035 509**	**0.034 358**	0.036 662
			0.078 633	**0.078 633**	

3.11 CONCLUDING REMARKS

In this chapter, we have made the connection between the different quote styles encountered in FX and the different deltas that can be constructed. There is no concept of 'the' delta in FX. Since the FX volatility surface is specified in terms of volatilities corresponding to different available deltas, market participants need a clear understanding of which deltas are available, and this is where the connection between deltas and market conventions arises. We have described the market conventions extensively, and given examples of how these can be used in practice to construct volatility smiles that are consistent with the market.

Having introduced the concept of a market volatility smile, the next issue to discuss is how these smiles, which correspond to separate marginal distributions for S_T for different expiries T, are coupled together into a volatility surface, which one can interpolate to estimate smiles between tenors and price options with maturities in between the liquid tenor points. We discuss the problem of volatility surface construction in the next chapter.

4

Volatility Surface Construction

FX markets are particularly liquid at benchmark tenors, such as 1M, 2M, 3M, 6M, 1Y, 2Y and possibly longer dated options. Figures 4.1 and 4.2 show typical market volatility surfaces for EURUSD and USDJPY, obtained by kind permission of Bloomberg Finance L.P.

Note that the screenshots provide some information regarding the market conventions used for these currency pairs; for example, premium is included in the delta for USDJPY but not for EURUSD (as we know from Chapter 3). Vol surface representations as provided by various systems may differ, as seen above by use of spot delta out beyond 1Y and the use of the smile strangle not the market strangle (in contrast, this can be toggled on and off in Murex). It is always best to check directly what the smile benchmarks correspond to; the objective of this text is to describe what the various possible modes are.

As well as the liquid benchmark tenors, we need to be able to price options with arbitrary times to expiry, i.e. broken dated options. Even if we confine our trading to instruments with the benchmark tenors above, a 6M option bought today will be a 5M option in a month's time.

How should we use our knowledge of implied volatilities at benchmark tenors to estimate the volatility to be used in the Black–Scholes equation, to price an option in between tenors? Suppose the implied volatilities $\sigma_{\mathrm{imp}}(\cdot, t)$ are known for expiry times t_1 and t_2 ($t_1 < t_2$) and we wish to estimate the implied volatility

$$\sigma_{\mathrm{imp}}(K, t^*)$$

to be used to price an option with strike K and time to expiry t^*, where $t_1 < t^* < t_2$.

At first, one may be tempted to use a technique such as bilinear or bicubic interpolation of the implied volatility. This is inadvisable for FX and is not used in practice. Firstly, it is meaningless to regard options at different maturities with the same numerical level of strike as related when it comes to interpolating smiles. We already know that FX smiles are parameterised in terms of the volatility for options at various deltas, roughly corresponding to various levels of moneyness. Secondly, even naive linear interpolation with regard to time can lead to unrealistic forward volatility dynamics, as I shall show below.

If we relax the assumption that the volatility depends on the strike, thereby flattening the smile, we have $\sigma_1 = \sigma_{\mathrm{imp}}(\cdot, t_1)$ and $\sigma_2 = \sigma_{\mathrm{imp}}(\cdot, t_2)$. The effective variance to time t_2 is $\sigma_2^2 t_2$ and the effective variance to t_1 is $\sigma_1^2 t_1$. We require $\sigma_2^2 t_2 \geq \sigma_1^2 t_1$; otherwise we have a negative forward variance error, which our code should test for and throw an exception if found.

By additivity of variance, we can write

$$\sigma_2^2 t_2 = \sigma_1^2 t_1 + \sigma_{12}^2 (t_2 - t_1), \tag{4.1}$$

where σ_{12} is the forward volatility applicable between times t_1 and t_2 (Taleb, 1997, pages 154–157). We trivially solve to get

$$\sigma_{12} = \sqrt{\frac{\sigma_2^2 t_2 - \sigma_1^2 t_1}{t_2 - t_1}}. \tag{4.2}$$

GRAB   CurncyOVDV
Click vol price for details

| 91) Actions | 92) Charts | 93) Settings | 94) Refresh | | | FX Volatility Surface |

EURUSD   02/19/10   Bloomberg BGN   Default   ● RR/BF   ● Bid/Ask
              Calendar Weekdays   ○ Put/Call   ○ Mid/Spread

	ATM		25D RR	25D BF	10D RR	10D BF
Exp	Bid	Ask	Mid	Mid	Mid	Mid
1D	7.556	8.778	-0.636	0.084	-1.251	0.299
1W	11.550	12.350	-1.432	0.270	-2.540	0.840
2W	11.650	12.300	-1.510	0.257	-2.750	0.808
3W	11.490	12.030	-1.558	0.265	-2.857	0.823
1M	11.540	12.040	-1.660	0.260	-3.042	0.795
2M	11.605	12.005	-1.667	0.315	-3.075	0.990
3M	11.795	12.195	-1.677	0.365	-3.103	1.165
6M	12.340	12.690	-1.680	0.445	-3.132	1.460
1Y	12.590	12.915	-1.683	0.520	-3.158	1.743
18M	12.420	12.750	-1.577	0.525	-3.000	1.735
2Y	12.315	12.665	-1.520	0.495	-2.872	1.665
3Y	11.915	12.310	-1.407	0.457	-2.683	1.572
5Y	11.075	11.520	-1.183	0.417	-2.217	1.363
7Y	10.144	10.626	-1.205	0.353	-2.382	1.157

96)Hide Quick Pricer   ATM DNS | Spot & excl Prem | RR=EUR Call-Put | BF=(C+P)/2-ATMD   Interpolated

98)Launch OVML   Bid   Ask   Mid   Deposit

Maturity 1M   Delta 49.989 C   Vol   11.540   12.040   Fwd   1.3498 EUR   0.286%
Expiry 03/19/10   Strike   1.3506 USD Price   1.248%   1.303%   Spot   1.3499 USD   0.229%

Australia 61 2 9777 8600 Brazil 5511 3048 4500 Europe 44 20 7330 7500 Germany 49 69 9204 1210 Hong Kong 852 2977 6000
Japan 81 3 3201 8900   Singapore 65 6212 1000   U.S. 1 212 318 2000   Copyright 2010 Bloomberg Finance L.P.
                                               G700-810-3 19-Feb-10 15:34:28

Figure 4.1 Volatility surface for EURUSD. © 2010 Bloomberg Finance L.P. All rights reserved. Used with permission

GRAB   CurncyOVDV
Click vol price for details

| 91) Actions | 92) Charts | 93) Settings | 94) Refresh | | | FX Volatility Surface |

USDJPY   02/19/10   Bloomberg BGN   Default   ● RR/BF   ● Bid/Ask
              Calendar Weekdays   ○ Put/Call   ○ Mid/Spread

	ATM		25D RR	25D BF	10D RR	10D BF
Exp	Bid	Ask	Mid	Mid	Mid	Mid
1D	6.871	8.780	0.014	0.077	0.031	0.278
1W	10.830	12.080	0.060	0.245	0.010	0.840
2W	11.205	12.005	-0.285	0.265	-0.523	0.843
3W	11.390	12.000	-0.475	0.293	-0.865	0.913
1M	11.435	11.910	-0.585	0.287	-1.100	0.907
2M	11.720	12.120	-0.985	0.305	-1.843	1.060
3M	12.085	12.500	-1.292	0.328	-2.452	1.207
6M	13.045	13.375	-1.813	0.345	-3.503	1.415
1Y	13.710	14.020	-2.383	0.390	-4.678	1.680
18M	14.045	14.425	-2.687	0.370	-5.245	1.712
2Y	14.245	14.645	-2.910	0.305	-5.705	1.685
3Y	14.430	14.930	-3.475	0.290	-6.783	1.745
5Y	14.995	15.695	-4.550	0.240	-8.937	1.905
7Y	16.800	17.538	-5.425	0.413	-11.062	3.090

96)Hide Quick Pricer   ATM DNS | Spot & incl Prem | RR=USD Call-Put | BF=(C+P)/2-ATMD   Interpolated

98)Launch OVML   Bid   Ask   Mid   Deposit

Maturity 1M   Delta 49.966 C   Vol   11.435   11.910   Fwd   91.87 USD   0.229%
Expiry 03/18/10   Strike   91.82 USD Price   1.266%   1.317%   Spot   91.88 JPY   0.052%

Australia 61 2 9777 8600 Brazil 5511 3048 4500 Europe 44 20 7330 7500 Germany 49 69 9204 1210 Hong Kong 852 2977 6000
Japan 81 3 3201 8900   Singapore 65 6212 1000   U.S. 1 212 318 2000   Copyright 2010 Bloomberg Finance L.P.
                                               G700-810-3 19-Feb-10 15:35:11

Figure 4.2 Volatility surface for USDJPY. © 2010 Bloomberg Finance L.P. All rights reserved. Used with permission

At this stage it is useful to clarify the notation. Let $\sigma_{\text{imp}}(t)$ denote the implied volatility for options expiring at time t and $\sigma_{\text{fwd}}(t_1, t_2)$ denote the forward volatility applicable between t_1 and t_2. In the limit as $t_2 - t_1 \to 0$, we have the instantaneous forward volatility at time t_1, which we denote by $\sigma_{\text{fwd}}(t_1)$. In the notation above, we have

$$[\sigma_{\text{imp}}(t_2)]^2 t_2 = [\sigma_{\text{imp}}(t_1)]^2 t_1 + \int_{t_1}^{t_2} \sigma_{\text{fwd}}^2(s)\, ds.$$

In the absence of any further a priori information about exactly when the forward volatility feeds through into the asset price process between t_1 and t_2, we attempt to avoid introducing any additional bias or expectations about where the forward volatility arises by supposing flat forward volatility between t_1 and t_2, i.e.

$$\sigma_{\text{fwd}}(t) = \sigma_{12} \,\forall\, t \in (t_1, t_2),$$

where σ_{12} is as given in (4.2). In this case, the implied volatility $\sigma_{\text{imp}}(t^*)$ to time t^*, where $t^* \in (t_1, t_2)$, is

$$[\sigma_{\text{imp}}(t^*)]^2 t^* = \sigma_1^2 t_1 + \sigma_{12}^2(t^* - t_1). \tag{4.3}$$

This scheme is known as *flat forward volatility interpolation*, and we detail it for an entire volatility term structure in Section 4.1 below.

Following the cautionary note above, suppose a term structure of volatility at two time points (1Y and 2Y) is provided, with $\sigma_{\text{imp}}(1.0) = 20\,\%$ and $\sigma_{\text{imp}}(2.0) = 15\,\%$. The forward volatility σ_{12} between these two points is $7.07\,\%$ – small, but certainly possible. Now, if we use naive linear interpolation of $\sigma_{\text{imp}}(t)$ then we obviously have $\sigma_{\text{imp}}(1.5) = 17.5\,\%$, which looks sensible at first, until one works out that this implies a negative forward variance between $t_1 = 1.5$ and $t_2 = 2.0$, with $\sigma_{12}^2(t_2 - t_1) = -0.000\,94$ over the $[1.5, 2.0]$ time interval. This is why linear interpolation of implied volatility is never used.

Linear interpolation of variance is similarly inadmissible. In the example above, linearly interpolating between the 1Y variance of $0.04 = (20\,\%)^2$ and the 2Y variance of $0.0225 = (15\,\%)^2$ gives a 1.5Y variance of $0.031\,25$, and therefore a volatility of $17.68\,\%$. This also gives negative forward variance between $t_1 = 1.5$ and $t_2 = 2.0$.

In Figure 4.3, we clearly see that linear interpolation in either volatility or variance violates the upper bound on the implied volatility between the two tenor points (1Y and 2Y) – where the bounds are shown using solid lines – so something else is needed. A much better idea is to use linear interpolation in *integrated* variance, i.e. in $f(t) = \int_0^t [\sigma_{\text{fwd}}(s)]^2\, ds$, which is equivalent to the flat forward volatility interpolation, shown and described below, and clearly in accordance with the natural upper and lower bounds on volatility within the period of interest.

4.1   VOLATILITY BACKBONE – FLAT FORWARD INTERPOLATION

Suppose that time points $t_0 = 0, t_1, \ldots, t_N$ are given, and the implied volatilities for each of these time points (excluding the $t = t_0$ point) are $\sigma_1, \ldots, \sigma_N$. Following the recipe above, we have the flat forward volatility interpolator

$$\sigma_{\text{imp}}^{\text{flat fwd}}(t) = \begin{cases} \sigma_1, & t < t_1, \\ \sqrt{\left[\sigma_i^2 t_i + \sigma_{i,i+1}^2(t - t_i)\right]/t}, & t_i \le t < t_{i+1} \text{ for } i < N, \\ \sigma_N, & t \ge t_N, \end{cases} \tag{4.4a}$$

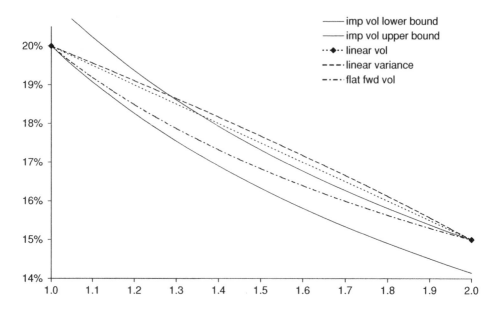

Figure 4.3   Upper and lower bounds for interpolated volatility term structure

where

$$\sigma_{i,i+1}^2 = \frac{\sigma_{i+1}^2 t_{i+1} - \sigma_i^2 t_i}{t_{i+1} - t_i}. \tag{4.4b}$$

This can certainly be used to interpolate volatility for time points in between known tenors.

Theorem: The scheme above is equivalent to linear interpolation in total variance $f(t) = \int_0^t \sigma_s^2 \, ds$.

Proof: Suppose without loss of generality that $t_1 < t < t_2$, where $\sigma_{\mathrm{imp}}(t_1) = \sigma_1$ and $\sigma_{\mathrm{imp}}(t_2) = \sigma_2$. Linear interpolation in total variance locates $\sigma_{\mathrm{imp}}(t)$ at a point such that $[\sigma_{\mathrm{imp}}(t)]^2 t$ lies directly on the line segment connecting $\sigma_1^2 t_1$ with $\sigma_2^2 t_2$, i.e.

$$[\sigma_{\mathrm{imp}}(t)]^2 t = \frac{t_2 - t}{t_2 - t_1}\sigma_1^2 t_1 + \frac{t - t_1}{t_2 - t_1}\sigma_2^2 t_2. \tag{4.5}$$

Now from (4.4a) describing interpolation assuming flat forward volatility, we obtain

$$\sigma_{\mathrm{imp}}^{\mathrm{flat\ fwd}}(t) = \sqrt{\left[\sigma_1^2 t_1 + \sigma_{12}^2(t - t_1)\right]/t},$$

i.e.

$$[\sigma_{\mathrm{imp}}^{\mathrm{flat\ fwd}}(t)]^2 t = \sigma_1^2 t_1 + \sigma_{12}^2(t - t_1).$$

Using (4.4b) to write $\sigma_{12}^2 = (\sigma_2^2 t_2 - \sigma_1^2 t_1)/(t_2 - t_1)$, we have

$$[\sigma_{\text{imp}}^{\text{flat fwd}}(t)]^2 t = \sigma_1^2 t_1 + (\sigma_2^2 t_2 - \sigma_1^2 t_1)\frac{t - t_1}{t_2 - t_1}$$

$$= \frac{1}{t_2 - t_1}\left[\sigma_2^2 t_2(t - t_1) + \sigma_1^2 t_1(t_2 - t)\right]. \tag{4.6}$$

Comparing (4.6) with (4.5), the result is proven.

4.2 VOLATILITY SURFACE TEMPORAL INTERPOLATION

In Section 4.1 earlier, we see how one can estimate the implied volatility for times t^* in between benchmark tenors t_1 and t_2 in the absence of a volatility smile. This might work reasonably well, if all we want to do is price an at-the-money option, and we know the ATM volatilities for times t_1 and t_2. However, one of the major themes we want to develop in this book is how to price options consistently with volatility surfaces – *including* smiles.

How, then, should we build a smile at time t^*, if we know the volatility surface at times t_1 and t_2?

4.2.1 Volatility smile extrapolation

Daglish *et al.* (2007) give a partial answer, in Section 5.3, quoting the 'square root of time rule'. This allows a volatility smile at *one* specific maturity to be used, in conjunction with a fully specified term structure of at-the-money volatilities, to be used to construct an entire volatility surface. The approach is basically to suppose that the volatility smile at the maturity T for which a smile is known can be used to fit a function $\Phi(\cdot)$ – not to be confused with the cumulative distribution function for the normal distribution, which we denote by $N(\cdot)$ – that satisfies

$$\sigma_{\text{imp}}(K, T) = \Phi\left(\frac{\ln(K/F_T)}{\sqrt{T}}\right) \cdot \sigma_{\text{imp}}(F_T, T). \tag{4.7}$$

Note that when $K = F_T$, we have $\Phi(0)$ in the RHS of (4.7) and therefore require $\Phi(0) = 1$. Note also the similarity of the argument in $\Phi(\cdot)$ to the simple delta d given in (3.6). In fact, with (3.6) in mind, we argue instead for recasting this 'square root' relationship as

$$\sigma_{\text{imp}}(K, T) = \Phi\left(\frac{\ln(K/F_T)}{\sigma_{\text{ATMF}}(T) \cdot \sqrt{T}}\right) \cdot \sigma_{\text{ATMF}}(T), \tag{4.8}$$

where $\sigma_{\text{ATMF}}(T) = \sigma_{\text{imp}}(F_T, T)$. With this, we have

$$\sigma_{\text{imp}}(K, T) = \Phi(d) \cdot \sigma_{\text{ATMF}}(T)$$

with $d = \ln(F_T/K)/[\sigma_{\text{ATMF}}(T)\sqrt{T}]$. For other times t^*, we apply the same functional form $\Phi(d)$, obtaining

$$\sigma_{\text{imp}}(K, t^*) = \Phi(d) \cdot \sigma_{\text{ATMF}}(t^*)$$

with $d = \ln(F_{t^*}/K)/[\sigma_{\text{ATMF}}(t^*)\sqrt{t^*}]$.

This technique involves assuming that the volatility surface can be effectively factorised into two separable components: an at-the-money term structure component (for which we can use flat forward interpolation as described in Section 4.1) and a function $\Phi(\cdot)$ of moneyness.

As illustrated above, we use purely the ATMF representation of the ATM point (i.e. not delta-neutral) and we use moneyness in terms of simple delta, not pips nor percentage delta. However, the choice is somewhat arbitrary, as all we're basically trying to do is to preserve the same overall shape of the volatility smile but 'smeared out' further for longer maturities. One could certainly use flat forward volatility interpolation for the at-the-money volatilities as described by delta-neutral strikes, together with smiles parameterised by various types of delta. It does, however, make less sense to use spot deltas due to the presence of the discount factor, and so the sensible choices are basically functions of simple delta, forward pips delta or forward percentage delta.

4.2.2   Volatility smile interpolation

Of course, we generally have a fully specified volatility smile at times t_1 and t_2, and the method above cannot be guaranteed to fit the smile at t_1 *and* at t_2. A single functional form $\Phi(\cdot)$ places too many constraints on the smile. There are a number of different methods that can be used.

To begin with, we sketch the considerations that need to be borne in mind, together with some practical issues that are worth consideration.

ATM volatility interpolation

Suppose the at-the-money vols are given at t_1 and t_2, both subject to the same ATM convention (be it delta-neutral or ATMF). We can use the method of Section 4.1 to obtain an interpolated volatility for $\sigma_{\mathrm{imp}}(t^*)$. The only complicating factor is if the ATM conventions for t_1 and t_2 are not the same, e.g. if we have volatility smiles for EURUSD with 10Y and 12Y expiries and want to estimate the 11Y ATM vol. In that case, we need to choose one ATM convention to work with and then obtain $\sigma_{\mathrm{imp}}(K_{\mathrm{ATM};t_1}, t_1)$ and $\sigma_{\mathrm{imp}}(K_{\mathrm{ATM};t_2}, t_2)$ for the 2 ATM strikes $K_{\mathrm{ATM};t_1}$ and $K_{\mathrm{ATM};t_2}$, obtained using the *same* ATM convention for both t_1 and t_2. We then use flat forward interpolation.

Volatility smile interpolation in the wings

Suppose we have parametric shapes for $\Phi(\cdot)$ at times t_1 and t_2, such as polynomial in delta (with parameters c_0, c_1 and c_2) or SABR (with parameters α, ν and ρ), such as presented in Sections 3.9 or 3.10. We will therefore, in general, have two sets of smile parameters – one for t_1 and one for t_2. One possibility is to interpolate in parameter space – e.g. a piecewise linear function connecting $c_i|_{t=t_1}$ at $t = t_1$ to $c_i|_{t=t_2}$ at $t = t_2$ for $i \in \{0, 1, 2\}$ – and similarly for SABR. However, this probably will not satisfy the flat forward volatility condition for the at-the-money strikes.

Another quite reasonable possibility is to use flat forward volatility interpolation, not just for the at-the-money strike but independently for *all* the benchmark strikes, i.e. the 25-d-P and 25-d-C strikes (and also the 10-d-P and 10-d-C strikes if a five point smile is used). The advantage of this scheme is that it is guaranteed to distribute the forward volatility uniformly over the forward time interval (t_1, t_2) for in-the-money puts and calls of comparable moneyness, as well as for the at-the-money strikes. The disadvantage is that a separate smile calibration is required for each interim time t^*, and as well as introducing extra computational effort, this can also introduce numerical calibration noise in the smile parameters – undesirable in itself, and especially problematic for backing out local volatility using the method to appear in Chapter 5.

Nevertheless, this is a fairly safe way to proceed, and has been successfully used by many practitioners, so it is worth presenting.

4.2.3 Flat forward vol interpolation in smile strikes

Suppose we have volatility smiles, consisting of an ATM vol, market strangle vol(s) and risk reversal(s) at times t_1 and t_2. A recipe for obtaining a smile at an interim time t^* (where $t_1 < t^* < t_2$) is:

Step 1. Use a method from Chapter 3, together with the relevant market conventions for the currency pair and the expiry time, to fit parametric smiles $\sigma_{X;t_1}(K)$ and $\sigma_{X;t_2}(K)$ from the market smiles at t_1 and t_2 respectively.

Step 2. Choose a *consistent* set of smile conventions for marking an ATM strike and 25-delta strikes at times t_1 and t_2. We already note that spot deltas are an inferior choice due to the presence of the embedded discount factor.

　　The easiest choice is ATMF for the ATM and simple delta for the strikes; a more pragmatic choice is to choose whether pips or percentage delta should be used, and then to have delta-neutrality as the choice for the ATM strike and 25-delta call and put strikes given with respect to forward pips delta or forward percentage delta. Similarly for 10-delta or any other strikes in the wings, though we only describe it using 25-delta for simplicity.

　　Once this is done, we obtain at times t_1 and t_2 new strikes $\hat{K}_{\text{ATM}}(t_{1;2})$, $\hat{K}_{25\text{-d-P}}(t_{1;2})$ and $\hat{K}_{25\text{-d-C}}(t_{1;2})$, where the hatted symbols denote that these are with respect to artificial smile conventions, held constant for all maturities.

Step 3. At t_1 and t_2, use the volatility smiles $\sigma_{X;t_{1;2}}(K)$ to look up the implied vols at strikes $\hat{K}_{\text{ATM}}(t_{1;2})$, $\hat{K}_{25\text{-d-P}}(t_{1;2})$ and $\hat{K}_{25\text{-d-C}}(t_{1;2})$, which we denote by $\hat{\sigma}_{\text{ATM}}(t_{1;2})$, $\hat{\sigma}_{25\text{-d-P}}(t_{1;2})$ and $\hat{\sigma}_{25\text{-d-C}}(t_{1;2})$ respectively. We end up with an incompletely populated matrix, where we wish to interpolate the blank entries by applying flat forward volatility interpolation to each column in turn (see Table 4.1).

Step 4. Use flat forward interpolation (4.6) on $\hat{\sigma}_{25\text{-d-P}}(t)$, $\hat{\sigma}_{\text{ATM}}(t)$ and $\hat{\sigma}_{25\text{-d-C}}(t)$, each of which is now known at temporal endpoints t_1 and t_2. For each of $X \in \{$ 25-d-P, ATM, 25-d-C $\}$,

$$\hat{\sigma}_X^2(t^*)t^* = \frac{1}{t_2 - t_1}\left[\hat{\sigma}_X^2(t_2)t_2(t^* - t_1) + \hat{\sigma}_X^2(t_1)t_1(t_2 - t^*)\right],$$

i.e.

$$\hat{\sigma}_X(t^*) = \sqrt{\frac{t_2(t^* - t_1)}{t^*(t_2 - t_1)}\hat{\sigma}_X^2(t_2) + \frac{t_1(t_2 - t^*)}{t^*(t_2 - t_1)}\hat{\sigma}_X^2(t_1)}. \tag{4.9}$$

Step 5. Use $\hat{\sigma}_{25\text{-d-P}}(t^*)$, $\hat{\sigma}_{\text{ATM}}(t^*)$ and $\hat{\sigma}_{25\text{-d-C}}(t^*)$ to calibrate an entire smile $\sigma_X(K)$, using the approach from Chapter 3.

Table 4.1 Flat forward volatility interpolation by smile strike

	$\hat{\sigma}_{25\text{-d-P}}(t)$	$\hat{\sigma}_{\text{ATM}}(t)$	$\hat{\sigma}_{25\text{-d-C}}(t)$
t_1	$\hat{\sigma}_{25\text{-d-P}}(t_1)$	$\hat{\sigma}_{\text{ATM}}(t_1)$	$\hat{\sigma}_{25\text{-d-C}}(t_1)$
t^*			
t_2	$\hat{\sigma}_{25\text{-d-P}}(t_2)$	$\hat{\sigma}_{\text{ATM}}(t_2)$	$\hat{\sigma}_{25\text{-d-C}}(t_2)$

Table 4.2 EURUSD market strangle and risk reversal at 1Y and 2Y

Tenor	ATM vol	25-d-MS	25-d-RR
1Y	18.250 %	0.950 %	−0.600 %
2Y	17.677 %	0.850 %	−0.562 %

Table 4.3 EURUSD smile at 1Y and 2Y

Tenor		$\sigma_{25-d-P}(t)$	$\sigma_{ATM}(t)$	$\sigma_{25-d-C}(t)$
1Y	K	1.2034	1.3620	1.5410
	σ	19.494 %	18.250 %	18.894 %
2Y	K	1.1538	1.3748	1.6393
	σ	18.801 %	17.677 %	18.239 %

4.2.4 Example – EURUSD 18M from 1Y and 2Y tenors – SABR

From Table 3.3, we have the volatilities given in Table 4.2 (in this example, we just show how this works with regard to a three point smile). The extension to a five point smile works the same way, merely requiring a more complex functional form $\sigma_X(K)$. From these volatilities and (4.9) we get the 1Y and 2Y smiles given in Table 4.3, with respect to the market conventions at those tenors.

Note that the 1Y and 2Y options above do *not* share the same market conventions – for 1Y, deltas are defined as spot pips deltas, but for 2Y they are forward pips deltas. Having fit $\sigma_X(K)$ to the 1Y tenor, we can use the *same* smile equation $\sigma_X(K)$ and find strikes $\hat{K}_{25-d-P}$ and $\hat{K}_{25-d-C}$, which have forward pips deltas of ± 0.25, computed using a Black–Scholes volatility of $\sigma_X(\hat{K}_{25-d-P})$ and $\sigma_X(\hat{K}_{25-d-C})$ respectively.

This doesn't affect the ATM strike by the way (we would only need to adjust this if the market convention is ATMF for one or both of the tenors). In this example, only the wing strikes need to be adjusted (see Table 4.4).

Note that the 1Y smile is more pronounced when marked using forward deltas. Failing to take this into account introduces a mismatch of slightly under 0.1 of a vol – large enough to be relevant for calibration and pricing, but small enough that it may not be noticed at first.

We now use flat forward interpolation in all three smile strikes, noting that for this particular example with $t_1 = 1$, $t_2 = 2$ and $t^* = 1.5$, (4.9) reduces to $\hat{\sigma}_X(t^*) = [\frac{1}{3}\hat{\sigma}_X^2(t_1) + \frac{2}{3}\hat{\sigma}_X^2(t_2)]^{1/2}$ – not exactly just a simple linear interpolation in volatility or variance. Using this, we obtain Table 4.5.

Finally, we use the three strikes {1.1733, 1.3689, 1.5974} and corresponding smile volatilities {19.068 %, 17.870 %, 18.485 %} from above to obtain a fitted smile $\sigma_X(K)$ for any strike K at time t^*.

4.3 VOLATILITY SURFACE TEMPORAL INTERPOLATION – HOLIDAYS AND WEEKENDS

FX markets are famous for being truly 24-hour markets, with a daily turnover of $3.21 trillion in April 2007[1] – about ten times the daily turnover of global equity markets. Most books

---

[1] Source: Bank of International Settlements Triennial Survey 2007.

Table 4.4 EURUSD smile at 1Y and 2Y with consistent market conventions

Tenor		$\hat{\sigma}_{25-d-P}(t)$	$\hat{\sigma}_{ATM}(t)$	$\hat{\sigma}_{25-d-C}(t)$
1Y	K	1.1964	1.3620	1.5501
	$\hat{\sigma}$	19.590 %	18.250 %	18.967 %
2Y	K	1.1538	1.3748	1.6393
	$\hat{\sigma}$	18.801 %	17.677 %	18.239 %

Table 4.5 Interpolated 18M EURUSD smile

Tenor		$\hat{\sigma}_{25-d-P}(t)$	$\hat{\sigma}_{ATM}(t)$	$\hat{\sigma}_{25-d-C}(t)$
1Y	K	1.1964	1.3620	1.5501
	$\hat{\sigma}$	19.590 %	18.250 %	18.967 %
18M	K	1.1733	1.3689	1.5974
	$\hat{\sigma}$	19.068 %	17.870 %	18.485 %
2Y	K	1.1538	1.3748	1.6393
	$\hat{\sigma}$	18.801 %	17.677 %	18.239 %

mention this in Chapter 1 to motivate the reader, but as you've read this far, it's fair to presume we don't need to worry about motivation.

Admittedly, the largest component of this is the FX swap market, and spot transactions only make up $1 trillion of that daily volume. This is still a lot. Even considered by itself, the FX spot market is an enormous continuously traded market, which experiences volatility over the entire 24-hour period as trading books are passed from centre to centre: from Asia to Europe to North America, trading volumes being highest in Europe and lowest in North America on average (Tsuyuguchi and Wooldridge, 2008) and then over to Asia to start all over again the next trading day.

Until close of business in NYC on Friday, that is. At that point (assuming Friday isn't an NY holiday), the liquid market stops. The markets close at 5 pm New York time[2] and reopen Monday morning in New Zealand at about 8:15 pm UTC on Sunday evening, followed by Asia and Australia.

As a result, if you have a currency pair with a reasonably flat term structure of volatility of about 12 %, such as EURUSD as observed on Friday 19 February 2010, and you look at the term structure of volatility specifically on a Friday, you are likely to see something like that shown in Table 4.6.

Note that the overnight volatility is much lower than the other marks. Is the market really saying that there is likely to be less market uncertainty over the weekend? No. What the market is saying is that there is one business day of volatility, but this is effective over three calendar days. Hence the overnight volatility σ_{ON}, when integrated over three business days, gives us a total integrated variance of $(\sigma_{ON})^2 \times 3/365$. One would expect this to be about a fifth of the one week integrated variance of $(\sigma_{1W})^2 \times 7/365$, if forward volatility was equally distributed

---

[2] 10 pm UTC (or 9 pm UTC when daylight savings is in effect in NYC).

Table 4.6 Typical term structure of volatility on a Friday

T	σ
ON	8.15 %
1W	11.95 %
2W	11.97 %
3W	11.75 %
1M	11.80 %
$\vdots$	$\vdots$

over each and every *trading* day. And indeed it is:

$$\frac{(\sigma_{ON})^2 \times 3/365}{(\sigma_{1W})^2 \times 7/365} = \frac{3 \times (8.15\,\%)^2}{7 \times (11.95\,\%)^2} = \frac{0.019\,926\,75}{0.100\,015\,75} \approx \frac{1}{5}.$$

French (1984) proposed a separate concept of volatility time, thereby decoupling the time t used for discounting in the Black–Scholes equation from the time t used for integrating the Brownian motion W_t. In his analysis there are 365 calendar days per year that need to be considered for discounting, but only 252 (or so) business days that actually contribute to any possible volatility in the asset price process (the asset price cannot experience any volatility if the market is closed).

An easy way to set up a usable short dated volatility model is to use a mask function that kills the forward volatility on weekends and holidays, and assumes forward volatility is constant for all trading days between specified tenors. To be consistent with the market implied volatility, we need to construct a sequence of daily forward volatilities $\sigma_{fwd}(t_i)$ in such a manner that the integrated variance over each interval $[0, T_i]$ matches $[\sigma_{imp}(T_i)]^2 T_i$. The condition we need, for each N such that t_N is a benchmark volatility date, is that

$$\sum_{i=1}^{N} [\omega(t_i)\sigma_{fwd}(t_i)]^2 (t_i - t_{i-1}) = [\sigma_{imp}(t_N)]^2 \cdot t_N,$$

where $\omega(t)$ is zero if t is a weekend or a holiday, and unity otherwise. This enables us to bootstrap a suitable form for $\sigma_{fwd}(t_i)$.

We can rewrite this as

$$\int_{t_1}^{t_2} \omega(t)[\sigma_{fwd}(t_1; t_2)]^2 \, dt = [\sigma_{imp}(t_2)]^2 \cdot t_2 - [\sigma_{imp}(t_2)]^2 \cdot t_1. \tag{4.10}$$

where we use a piecewise constant effective forward volatility $\sigma_{fwd}(t_1; t_2)$ applicable over $[t_1, t_2]$, but multiplied by a mask function $w(t)$, which removes any variance contribution from nontrading days. In the EURUSD example here, we obtain Table 4.7.

Note that the forward volatilities on nonbusiness days are identically zero, as required. Further, with the exception of the trading days between the 2W and 3W tenor points, the daily forward volatilities on business days over the entire month are nearly constant – remarkably so, in fact. One almost wonders if the 3W implied volatility, being a tenor less frequently updated by traders, is out of date.

Note that while this scheme is described above with reference to ATM vols, it can equally be used to interpolate 25-delta calls and puts (or 10-deltas or whatever) to equivalent effect.

Table 4.7 Sample shortdated EURUSD
day weights

		σ_{fwd}	σ_{imp}
	Sa	0.00 %	0.00 %
	Su	0.00 %	0.00 %
ON	Mo	14.12 %	**8.15 %**
	Tu	14.15 %	9.99 %
	We	14.15 %	10.95 %
	Th	14.15 %	11.55 %
1W	Fr	14.15 %	**11.95 %**
	Sa	0.00 %	11.18 %
	Su	0.00 %	10.54 %
	Mo	14.18 %	10.96 %
	Tu	14.18 %	11.29 %
	We	14.18 %	11.56 %
	Th	14.18 %	11.78 %
2W	Fr	14.18 %	**11.97 %**
	Sa	0.00 %	11.56 %
	Su	0.00 %	11.20 %
	Mo	13.37 %	11.34 %
	Tu	13.37 %	11.46 %
	We	13.37 %	11.57 %
	Th	13.37 %	11.66 %
3W	Fr	13.37 %	**11.75 %**
	Sa	0.00 %	11.48 %
	Su	0.00 %	11.23 %
	Mo	14.15 %	11.36 %
	Tu	14.15 %	11.49 %
	We	14.15 %	11.60 %
	Th	14.15 %	11.71 %
1M	Fr	14.15 %	**11.80 %**
	$\vdots$	$\vdots$	$\vdots$

One can therefore use this in place of step 4 in Section 4.2.3 for smile interpolation as well as at-the-money volatility interpolation.

4.4   VOLATILITY SURFACE TEMPORAL INTERPOLATION – INTRADAY EFFECTS

In Section 4.3, a simple digital {0, 1} mask function was used to extinguish any forward volatility completely on Saturdays and Sundays. Suppose we want to be even more precise in correctly apportioning forward volatility over the course of a typical trading week, perhaps for pricing very short dated options including considerations of New York and Tokyo cuts (cf. Section 1.6).

Since we're excluding weekends (and holidays) from contributing forward volatility, it makes little economic sense to assume that the forward volatility over the $46\frac{1}{4}$ hours from 10 pm UTC Friday evening to 8:15 pm UTC Sunday evening is comparable to that over the remaining $121\frac{3}{4}$ hours. If we want to be even more precise, we could use a weighted interpolation in integrated variance, where the weights are estimated by typical trading volumes

Table 4.8 Sample intraday
EURUSD weights

Day/time (London)	Intraday
⋮	⋮
Sun 21:59:59	0.000
Sun 22:00:00	0.210
Mon 07:29:59	0.210
Mon 07:30:00	1.830
Mon 08:59:59	1.830
Mon 09:00:00	1.390
Mon 12:29:59	1.390
Mon 12:30:00	2.621
Mon 16:59:59	2.621
Mon 17:00:00	0.520
Mon 21:59:59	0.520
Mon 22:00:00	0.210
⋮	⋮
Fri 21:59:59	0.520
Fri 22:00:00	0.000
⋮	⋮

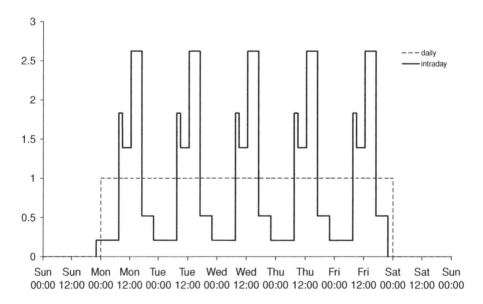

Figure 4.4 Intraday forward volatility mask for EURUSD

in that particular hour. I believe this was used to some effect in J.P. Morgan in the late 1990s. It does, however, mean there are 168 hours to keep track of (though obviously one would look for repeated structure). Sundkvist and Vikström (2000) presented the same idea in their continuous time using discrete approximations (CTDA) model, which proposed estimating intraday volatility over time intervals that are 30 minutes in length.

More recently, Cai *et al.* (2006) provide a very nice pair of graphs in Figure 1 of their paper showing typical high-frequency trading volumes for EURUSD and USDJPY in the electronic broking services (EBS) market. Having done so, they identify five structural periods in the course of a typical trading day in FX: (i) Asia only, (ii) Asia/Europe, (iii) Europe only, (iv) Europe/North America and (v) North America only.[3] Figure 4 in their paper shows average trading volumes for EURUSD and USDJPY, averaged over each of these five periods, and we could do much worse than use this to provide sensible intraday weights to apportion forward volatility. I have estimated these weights for EURUSD visually and tabulated them in Table 4.8 (the following 4 days exactly repeat the Sun 22:00:00–Mon 21:59:59 period). Figure 4.4 then graphs over an entire trading week the mask function $\omega(t)$ constructed from these weights, compared to the simplistic but adequate $\{0, 1\}$ mask function used in Section 4.3 above. We see that the new mask function provides some extra fine grain structure should we need this kind of precision.

The algorithm for bootstrapping a short dated forward volatility structure then proceeds in basically the same way as in Section 4.3 – we take the integral representation (4.10) and perform a piecewise integration over the relevant time slice, where $\omega(t)$ is as described above. This allows us to solve for a suitable constant $\sigma_{\text{fwd}}(t_1; t_2)$, which, when multiplied by the mask function $\omega(t)$ and used to obtain the total forward variance over $[t_1, t_2]$, matches the forward variance between t_1 and t_2 using implied volatilities $\sigma_{\text{imp}}(t_1)$ and $\sigma_{\text{imp}}(t_2)$.

I expect high-frequency volatility analysis to become increasingly popular over the lifetime of this book, as more market participants move to electronic trading of FX options. The interested reader is referred to Andersen *et al.* (2003), as well as more recent papers citing the references given herein.

---

[3] The North America/Asia handover is excluded from their analysis because, in their words, 'it is very short (half an hour or so) and trading is very light'.

5

Local Volatility and Implied Volatility

5.1 INTRODUCTION

It is well known that a single Black–Scholes model of the form

$$dS_t = \mu S_t \, dt + \sigma S_t \, dW_t \tag{5.1}$$

is inadequate to describe the prices of traded options accurately, for two reasons. Firstly, no term structure can be generated by a simple Black–Scholes model, though this can be easily added by imposing a term structure upon the drift and volatility terms

$$dS_t = \mu_t S_t \, dt + \sigma_t S_t \, dW_t, \tag{5.2}$$

where μ_t and σ_t are deterministic. Note that the volatility term σ_t is an instantaneous volatility, and the implied volatility $\sigma_{imp}(T)$ for an option with time to maturity T will be a root-mean-square quantity of the form

$$\sigma_{imp}(T) = \sqrt{\frac{1}{T} \int_0^T \sigma_t^2 \, dt} \tag{5.3}$$

by additivity of variance.

Secondly, even with term structure taken into account, a different instantaneous volatility will in general be required for options with different strike K.

Dupire (1993) attempted to answer the question – is it possible to construct a state-dependent instantaneous volatility $\sigma_{loc}(S, t)$ that, when fed into a one-dimensional diffusion of the form

$$dS_t = \mu_t S_t \, dt + \sigma_{loc}(S_t, t) S_t \, dW_t, \tag{5.4}$$

recovers the entire implied volatility surface $\sigma_{imp}(K, T)$? He found an answer in the affirmative together with a simple method for construction of $\sigma_{loc}(S, t)$.

The approach works by expressing the marginal probability distribution φ_T in terms of the second partial derivative of European call prices $C(K, T)$ with respect to strike K (the Breeden–Litzenberger result) and realising that the marginal probability distributions can be thought of as timeslices of forward transition probabilities. Since the forward Fokker–Planck equation describes the time evolution of forward transition probabilities, we can isolate the volatility coefficient that recovers the prices of tradeable call options for all strikes and all times.

The relationship of local volatility to an implied volatility surface is very much like the relationship of instantaneous volatility to the term structure of implied volatility that we saw in Chapter 4.

Suppose a term structure of implied volatility is given, without any volatility smile or skew, as in Table 5.1. This has a 1Y into 2Y forward volatility of 20.62 % and, consequently, the instantaneous volatilities we would use in either a forward time-stepping Monte Carlo or a backward time-stepping PDE/tree pricing algorithm are as given in Table 5.2.

Table 5.1   A trivial upward sloping
two-period term structure of implied
volatility

	σ_{imp}
1Y	5 %
2Y	15 %

Note that this is only a function of time and not of the asset level S_t. If we had a denser set of time points $\{1M, 2M, 3M, 6M, 9M, 1Y, 2Y\}$ then we can do exactly the same thing, as shown in Table 5.3.

Once again, $\sigma_{fwd}(t)$ is independent of the asset price level S_t. If, on the other hand, we have a volatility surface that has no smile or skew out to the 1Y tenor, but has a smile in the 2Y tenor, of the form given in Table 5.4, then the instantaneous volatilities we would use in either a forward time-stepping Monte Carlo or a backward time-stepping PDE/tree pricing algorithm are something like Table 5.5, where the local volatilities are tabulated for values of logspot $X_t = \ln S_t$ ranging from -0.20 to $+0.20$, and for values of time t from $t = 0$ to $t = 2$. We see this in Figure 5.1.

The point is that the local volatility is effectively a state-dependent generalisation of instantaneous volatility, which is capable of recovering the entire term structure of the volatility surface instead of just the term structure of the at-the-money implied volatilities.

The crucial question is how do we get from the implied volatilities, which we see quoted in the market, to a consistent local volatility?

The answer is that the Fokker–Planck equation, together with the Dupire construction of local volatility, allows us to obtain exactly this equivalence, both analytically in the case of simple local volatility models and numerically in the case of higher dimensional models such as LSV and longdated FX models. Even though this chapter is quite theoretical, it is of direct relevance to practitioners seeking to fit models containing local volatility terms to a market surface specified by implied volatilities. Most FX options pricing libraries will have some code that implements these techniques, and as such this is important to discuss in a practitioner's guide.

5.2   THE FOKKER–PLANCK EQUATION

Clear derivations of the Fokker–Planck equation (also known as the forward Kolmogorov equation) are surprisingly difficult to locate in the literature. We present a step-by-step version of the rather elegant derivation given in Grigoriu (2002) for the one-dimensional case, followed by a derivation of the multidimensional Fokker–Planck equation.

Table 5.2   Forward volatility
consistent with upward sloping
implied volatility

	$\sigma_{fwd}(t)$
$t \leq 1$	5 %
$1 < t \leq 2$	20.62 %

Table 5.3 Implied and forward volatilities for a typical ATM volatility structure

	$\sigma_{imp}(t)$	$\sigma_{fwd}(t)$
1M	12.0 %	12.000 %
2M	11.0 %	9.899 %
3M	10.0 %	7.616 %
6M	9.8 %	9.596 %
9M	9.7 %	9.497 %
1Y	9.6 %	9.294 %
2Y	10.0 %	10.385 %

5.2.1 Derivation of the one-dimensional Fokker–Planck equation

Suppose a one-dimensional stochastic differential equation is given as

$$dX_t = a(X_t, t)\, dt + b(X_t, t)\, dW_t,\tag{5.5}$$

where $a(X_t, t)$ is the drift term and $b(X_t, t)$ is the diffusion term. Suppose $g(x)$ is an arbitrary function of x such that $\lim_{x\to\pm\infty} g(x) = 0$. Let $G_t = g(X_t)$. Then, since g is purely a function of x, we use the Itô formula to obtain $dG_t = (\partial g/\partial x)\, dX_t + \frac{1}{2}(\partial^2 g/\partial x^2)\, dX_t^2$, yielding

$$dG_t = \left(a(x, t)\frac{\partial g}{\partial x} + \frac{1}{2}b^2(x, t)\frac{\partial^2 g}{\partial x^2}\right) dt + b(x, t)\frac{\partial g}{\partial x}\, dW_t.\tag{5.6}$$

Consider the quantity $(d/dt)\mathbf{E}[G_t]$. Since W_t is driftless, we have

$$\frac{d}{dt}\mathbf{E}[G_t] = \mathbf{E}\left[a(x, t)\frac{\partial g}{\partial x} + \frac{1}{2}b^2(x, t)\frac{\partial^2 g}{\partial x^2}\right].\tag{5.7}$$

We can express the RHS of (5.7) as an integral over the forward transition probability density $p(x, t; x_0, t_0)$, where we often suppress the initial state (x_0, t_0) and use the notation $p(x, t) \equiv p(x, t; x_0, t_0)$ for brevity:

$$\mathbf{E}\left[a(x, t)\frac{\partial g}{\partial x} + \frac{1}{2}b^2(x, t)\frac{\partial^2 g}{\partial x^2}\right] = \int_x p(x, t)\left[a(x, t)\frac{\partial g}{\partial x} + \frac{1}{2}b^2(x, t)\frac{\partial^2 g}{\partial x^2}\right] dx.\tag{5.8}$$

After we break this into two integrals and integrate by parts (once for the first and twice for the second integral), making use of the asymptotic limits for $g(x)$ required above, we obtain

$$\mathbf{E}\left[a(x, t)\frac{\partial g}{\partial x} + \frac{1}{2}b^2(x, t)\frac{\partial^2 g}{\partial x^2}\right] = -\int_x \frac{\partial[a(x, t)p(x, t)]}{\partial x}g(x)\, dx$$

$$+ \frac{1}{2}\int_x \frac{\partial^2[b(x, t)p(x, t)]}{\partial x^2}g(x)\, dx.\tag{5.9}$$

Table 5.4 Example of implied volatility surface with convexity only beyond 1Y

	σ_{ATM}	$\sigma_{25-d-MS}$	$\sigma_{25-d-RR}$
1Y	10.00 %	0.00 %	0.00 %
2Y	10.00 %	0.50 %	0.00 %

Table 5.5 Example of local volatility surface with convexity only beyond 1Y

					$\ln S_t$				
t	−0.20	−0.15	−0.10	−0.05	0.00	0.05	0.10	0.15	0.20
0	10.00 %	10.00 %	10.00 %	10.00 %	10.00 %	10.00 %	10.00 %	10.00 %	10.00 %
0.2	10.00 %	10.00 %	10.00 %	10.00 %	10.00 %	10.00 %	10.00 %	10.00 %	10.00 %
0.4	10.00 %	10.00 %	10.00 %	10.00 %	10.00 %	10.00 %	10.00 %	10.00 %	10.00 %
0.6	10.00 %	10.00 %	10.00 %	10.00 %	10.00 %	10.00 %	10.00 %	10.00 %	10.00 %
0.8	10.00 %	10.00 %	10.00 %	10.00 %	10.00 %	10.00 %	10.00 %	10.00 %	10.00 %
1	17.03 %	14.43 %	12.22 %	10.65 %	9.42 %	10.43 %	11.85 %	13.95 %	16.48 %
1.2	16.93 %	14.14 %	11.87 %	10.30 %	9.66 %	10.05 %	11.41 %	13.52 %	16.18 %
1.4	16.40 %	13.75 %	11.58 %	10.07 %	9.44 %	9.79 %	11.05 %	13.03 %	15.53 %
1.6	15.87 %	13.39 %	11.34 %	9.90 %	9.29 %	9.59 %	10.76 %	12.60 %	14.91 %
1.8	15.41 %	13.08 %	11.14 %	9.77 %	9.17 %	9.44 %	10.53 %	12.24 %	14.38 %
2	13.11 %	11.66 %	10.41 %	9.49 %	9.08 %	9.25 %	9.96 %	11.04 %	12.36 %

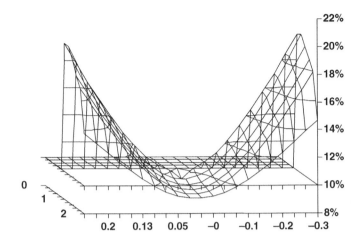

Figure 5.1   Sample local volatility

What now of the LHS of (5.7)? We can obtain $\mathbf{E}[G_t]$ by integrating with respect to the forward transition probability density $p(x, t)$:

$$\mathbf{E}[G_t] = \int_x p(x, t) g(x) \, dx. \tag{5.10}$$

Differentiating (5.10) with respect to t, we get

$$\frac{d}{dt}\mathbf{E}[G_t] = \int_x \frac{\partial p(x, t)}{\partial t} g(x) \, dx. \tag{5.11}$$

Substituting (5.9) and (5.11) into (5.7), we have

$$\int_x \frac{\partial p(x, t)}{\partial t} g(x) \, dx = \int_x \left[-\frac{\partial [a(x, t) p(x, t)]}{\partial x} + \frac{1}{2} \frac{\partial^2 [b^2(x, t) p(x, t)]}{\partial x^2} \right] g(x) \, dx.$$

Since the function $g(x)$ is arbitrary, we have the celebrated *Fokker–Planck equation* (FPE):

$$\frac{\partial p(x, t)}{\partial t} = -\frac{\partial [a(x, t) p(x, t)]}{\partial x} + \frac{1}{2} \frac{\partial^2 [b^2(x, t) p(x, t)]}{\partial x^2}. \tag{5.12}$$

Note that the source solution at time t_0 is generally taken to be a Dirac delta function, assuming that the value of the stochastic process is known at time t_0 to be x_0 almost surely, i.e.

$$p(x, t_0) \equiv p(x, t_0; x_0, t_0) = \delta_{x_0}(x). \tag{5.13}$$

Fokker–Planck equation for Black–Scholes model

The Black–Scholes model is given by (2.19b) with $\mu = \mu^d$ as in (2.40), i.e. $dX_t = (\mu^d - \frac{1}{2}\sigma^2) \, dt + \sigma \, dW_t$, from which after immediate comparison with (5.5) we can read off the convection term $a(x, t) = \mu^d - \frac{1}{2}\sigma^2$ and diffusion term $b = \sigma$. Substituting these terms into (5.12), we get

$$\frac{\partial p(x, t)}{\partial t} = \frac{1}{2}\sigma^2 \frac{\partial^2 [p(x, t)]}{\partial x^2} + \left(\frac{1}{2}\sigma^2 - \mu^d \right) \frac{\partial [p(x, t)]}{\partial x}.$$

5.2.2   The multidimensional Fokker–Planck equation

This is described in Section 4.7 of Risken (1989); we shall sketch how the derivation in this work extends to the multidimensional case. Suppose

$$d\mathbf{X}_t = \mathbf{a}(\mathbf{X}_t, t)\,dt + \mathbf{B}(\mathbf{X}_t, t)\,d\mathbf{W}_t \tag{5.14}$$

is an m-dimensional stochastic process, where the drift vector is given by $\mathbf{a}(\mathbf{X}_t, t) = \left[a_1(\mathbf{X}_t, t)\ldots a_m(\mathbf{X}_t, t)\right]^\top$ and the volatility matrix is

$$\mathbf{B}(\mathbf{X}_t, t) = \begin{bmatrix} B_{11}(\mathbf{X}_t, t) & \cdots & B_{1n}(\mathbf{X}_t, t) \\ \vdots & \ddots & \vdots \\ B_{m1}(\mathbf{X}_t, t) & \cdots & B_{mn}(\mathbf{X}_t, t) \end{bmatrix}.$$

$\mathbf{X}_t = \left[X_t^{(1)} \ldots X_t^{(m)}\right]^\top$ is an m-dimensional stochastic process driven by an n-dimensional Brownian motion $\mathbf{W}_t = \left[W_t^{(1)} \ldots W_t^{(n)}\right]^\top$, where (importantly!) $\langle W_t^{(i)}, W_t^{(j)}\rangle = \rho_{ij}\,dt$. We shall need the multidimensional Itô formula for $G_t = g(\mathbf{X}_t)$, where $g : \mathbb{R}^m \to \mathbb{R}$ is an arbitrary function of the process $\mathbf{X}_t$ and *not* of time t, subject once again to an asymptotic condition such as $g(\mathbf{x}) \to 0$ as $||\mathbf{x}|| \to \infty$ for a suitable choice of norm. We have

$$dG_t = \sum_{i=1}^{m} \frac{\partial g}{\partial x_i}\,dX_t^{(i)} + \frac{1}{2}\sum_{i,j=1}^{m} \frac{\partial^2 g}{\partial x_i x_j}\langle dW_t^{(i)}, dW_t^{(j)}\rangle. \tag{5.15}$$

Use

$$dX_t^{(i)} = a_i(\mathbf{X}_t, t) + \sum_{k=1}^{n} B_{ik}(\mathbf{X}_t, t)\,dW_t^{(k)}, \quad \forall i \in \{1, \ldots, m\}$$

to obtain

$$\langle dX_t^{(i)}, dX_t^{(j)}\rangle = \sum_{k,l=1}^{n} B_{ik}(\mathbf{X}_t, t)B_{jl}(\mathbf{X}_t, t)\langle dW_t^{(k)}, dW_t^{(l)}\rangle$$

$$= \sum_{k=1}^{n} B_{ik}(\mathbf{X}_t, t)B_{jk}(\mathbf{X}_t, t)\,dt.$$

From this we get

$$dG_t = \left[\sum_{i=1}^{m} \frac{\partial g}{\partial x_i}a_i(\mathbf{x}, t) + \frac{1}{2}\sum_{i,j=1}^{m} \frac{\partial^2 g}{\partial x_i x_j}\sum_{k=1}^{n} B_{ik}(\mathbf{x}, t)B_{jk}(\mathbf{x}, t)\right]dt$$

$$+ \sum_{i=1}^{m} \frac{\partial g}{\partial x_i}\sum_{k=1}^{n} B_{ik}(\mathbf{x}, t)\,dW_t^{(k)}. \tag{5.16}$$

Once again, since $\mathbf{W}_t$ is driftless in each of its components, we have

$$\frac{d}{dt}\mathbf{E}[G_t] = \mathbf{E}\left[\sum_{i=1}^{m} \frac{\partial g}{\partial x_i}a_i(\mathbf{x}, t) + \frac{1}{2}\sum_{i,j=1}^{m} \frac{\partial^2 g}{\partial x_i x_j}\sum_{k=1}^{n} B_{ik}(\mathbf{x}, t)B_{jk}(\mathbf{x}, t)\right].$$

We express the expectation as an integral over a multivariate forward transition density $p(\mathbf{x}, t; \mathbf{x}_0, t_0)$, which we shorten to $p(\mathbf{x}, t)$ for brevity, allowing the additional arguments $\mathbf{x}_0, t_0$ to be implicit in the notation:

$$\frac{d\mathbf{E}[G_t]}{dt} = \int_{\mathbb{R}^m} p(\mathbf{x}, t) \left[\sum_{i=1}^m \frac{\partial g}{\partial x_i} a_i(\mathbf{x}, t) + \frac{1}{2} \sum_{i,j=1}^m \frac{\partial^2 g}{\partial x_i x_j} \sum_{k=1}^n B_{ik}(\mathbf{x}, t) B_{jk}(\mathbf{x}, t) \right] dV,$$

where the infinitesimal volume element $dV = \prod_{i=1}^m dx_i$.

Each of the partial derivatives of $g(\mathbf{x})$ with respect to x_i must similarly be reduced using integration by parts. We obtain

$$\frac{d}{dt} \mathbf{E}[G_t] = \int_{\mathbb{R}^m} \left[-\sum_{i=1}^m \frac{\partial [a_i(\mathbf{x}, t) p(\mathbf{x}, t)]}{\partial x_i} \right.$$

$$\left. + \frac{1}{2} \sum_{i,j=1}^m \frac{\partial^2 [\sum_{k=1}^n B_{ik}(\mathbf{x}, t) B_{jk}(\mathbf{x}, t) p(\mathbf{x}, t)]}{\partial x_i \partial x_j} \right] g(\mathbf{x}) \, dV. \qquad (5.17)$$

However, as in (5.11), we have

$$\frac{d}{dt} \mathbf{E}[G_t] = \int_{\mathbb{R}^m} \frac{\partial p(\mathbf{x}, t)}{\partial t} g(\mathbf{x}) \, dV, \qquad (5.18)$$

which, when combined with (5.17), gives

$$\int_{\mathbb{R}^m} \left[\frac{\partial p(\mathbf{x}, t)}{\partial t} + \sum_{i=1}^m \frac{\partial [a_i(\mathbf{x}, t) p(\mathbf{x}, t)]}{\partial x_i} \right.$$

$$\left. - \frac{1}{2} \sum_{i,j=1}^m \frac{\partial^2 [\sum_{k=1}^n B_{ik}(\mathbf{x}, t) B_{jk}(\mathbf{x}, t) p(\mathbf{x}, t)]}{\partial x_i \partial x_j} \right] g(\mathbf{x}) \, dV = 0.$$

Since $g(\mathbf{x})$ is arbitrary, this yields the *multidimensional Fokker–Planck equation*:

$$\frac{\partial p(\mathbf{x}, t)}{\partial t} + \sum_{i=1}^m \frac{\partial [a_i(\mathbf{x}, t) p(\mathbf{x}, t)]}{\partial x_i} - \frac{1}{2} \sum_{i,j=1}^m \frac{\partial^2 [\sum_{k=1}^n B_{ik}(\mathbf{x}, t) B_{jk}(\mathbf{x}, t) p(\mathbf{x}, t)]}{\partial x_i \partial x_j} = 0. \quad (5.19)$$

5.3   DUPIRE'S CONSTRUCTION OF LOCAL VOLATILITY

Dupire (1993) posed the question: 'Knowing all the densities conditional on an initial fixed (x_0, t_0), is there a unique diffusion process which generates these densities?' Specifically, the diffusion process sought by Dupire is a one-dimensional *state-dependent* diffusion, of the form

$$dS_t = \mu_t S_t \, dt + \sigma_{\mathrm{loc}}(S_t, t) S_t \, dt. \qquad (5.20)$$

From the Breeden–Litzenberger analysis in Section 2.11, we know the (marginal) densities for all times t, the collection of which must satisfy the one-dimensional Fokker–Planck equation derived above. Can a suitable diffusion be found?

In fact, the subset of the same question regarding existence was asked earlier (and answered) in Gyöngy (1986), though not in the context of financial mathematics. Note that this approach has been extended to the 'Markovian projection' approach of Piterbarg (2006a) and Antonov and Misirpashaev (2006). Uniqueness of such a diffusion, however, only follows when a suitable condition on the drift, such as risk neutrality, is prescribed.

5.3.1 Dupire's local volatility – the $r^d = r^f = 0$ case

To begin with, for illustrative purposes, we follow Dupire (1993, 1994) and assume that domestic and foreign interest rates are identically zero. In this case, the marginal distributions in (2.81) reduce to

$$\varphi_T(K) \equiv f_{S_T}^d(K) = \frac{\partial^2 C(K, T)}{\partial K^2}, \tag{5.21}$$

and the drift and diffusion terms $a(S_t, t)$ and $b(S_t, t)$ in (5.5) reduce to 0 and $\sigma_{\mathrm{loc}}(S_t, t)S_t$ respectively. In the absence of a convection term, the one-dimensional Fokker–Planck equation simplifies to

$$\frac{\partial p(x, t)}{\partial t} - \frac{1}{2} \frac{\partial^2 [b^2(x, t)p(x, t)]}{\partial x^2} = 0 \tag{5.22}$$

or, in (K, T) coordinates,

$$\frac{\partial p(K, T)}{\partial T} - \frac{1}{2} \frac{\partial^2 [b^2(K, T)p(K, T)]}{\partial K^2} = 0. \tag{5.23}$$

Recognising that $p(K, T) = \varphi_T(K) = \partial^2 C/\partial K^2$, (5.23) reduces to

$$\frac{1}{2} \frac{\partial^2 [b^2(K, T)\varphi_T(K)]}{\partial K^2} = \frac{\partial}{\partial T} \left[\frac{\partial^2 C}{\partial K^2} \right]$$

$$= \frac{\partial^2}{\partial K^2} \left[\frac{\partial C}{\partial T} \right]. \tag{5.24}$$

Integrating twice with respect to K gives

$$\frac{1}{2} b_{\alpha, \beta}^2(K, T)\varphi_T(K) = \frac{\partial C}{\partial T} + \alpha(T)K + \beta(T).$$

However, both $\alpha(T)$ and $\beta(T)$ must vanish, due to the asymptotic behaviour of European call option prices, and we are left with

$$\frac{1}{2} b^2(K, T)\varphi_T(K) = \frac{\partial C}{\partial T}. \tag{5.25}$$

Since $\varphi_T(K) = \partial^2 C/\partial K^2$, the diffusion term $b(K, T)$ can be written out directly:

$$b(K, T) = \sqrt{\frac{2\partial C/\partial T}{\partial^2 C/\partial K^2}}. \tag{5.26}$$

Since $b(S_t, t) = \sigma_{\mathrm{loc}}(S_t, t)S_t$, or equivalently $b(K, T) = \sigma_{\mathrm{loc}}(K, T)K$, this gives

$$\sigma_{\mathrm{loc}}(K, T) = \sqrt{\frac{2\partial C/\partial T}{K^2 \partial^2 C/\partial K^2}}. \tag{5.27}$$

5.3.2 Dupire's local volatility – with nonzero but constant interest rates

This analysis is somewhat complicated when a term structure of domestic and foreign interest rates r_t^d and r_t^f is required. A simplified treatment assumes that domestic and foreign interest rates r^d and r^f are provided but assumed to be constant, in which case we have

$$\sigma_{\text{loc}}(K, T) = \sqrt{2 \frac{\partial C/\partial T + (r^d - r^f)K\partial C/\partial K + r^f C}{K^2 \partial^2 C/\partial K^2}}, \qquad (5.28)$$

a result derived in Appendix A of Derman and Kani (1998) and quoted in Jex *et al.* (1999) and Ren *et al.* (2007).[1] For the case of equities without dividends, i.e. when $r^f = 0$, (5.28) reduces to equation (2.4) in Lee (2004).

We show that (5.28) satisfies the Fokker–Planck equation. By risk neutrality, the diffusion for S_t is constrained to be of the form

$$\begin{aligned} dS_t &= a(S_t, t)dt + b(S_t, t)dW_t \\ &= (r^d - r^f)S_t\, dt + \sigma_{\text{loc}}(S_t, t)S_t\, dW_t \end{aligned} \qquad (5.29)$$

where, written in terms of (K, T) coordinates,

$$a(K, T) = (r^d - r^f)K, \qquad (5.30)$$

$$b(K, T) = \sigma_{\text{loc}}(K, T)K. \qquad (5.31)$$

The one-dimensional Fokker–Planck equation (5.12), also expressed in (K, T) coordinates, reads

$$\frac{\partial p(K, T)}{\partial T} + \frac{\partial[a(K, T)p(K, T)]}{\partial K} - \frac{1}{2}\frac{\partial^2[b^2(K, T)p(K, T)]}{\partial K^2} = 0, \qquad (5.32)$$

which we need to show is satisfied by $p(K, T) = \varphi_T(K) = e^{r^d T}\partial^2 C/\partial K^2$ and terms (5.30) and (5.31) above, where $\sigma_{\text{loc}}(K, T)$ comes from (5.28) and consequently

$$b(K, T) = \sigma_{\text{loc}}^2(K, T)K^2 = 2\frac{\partial C/\partial T + (r^d - r^f)K\partial C/\partial K + r^f C}{\partial^2 C/\partial K^2}.$$

Firstly,

$$\frac{\partial p(K, T)}{\partial T} = \frac{\partial}{\partial T}\left[e^{r^d T}\frac{\partial^2 C}{\partial K^2}\right] = e^{r^d T}\frac{\partial^3 C}{\partial T \partial K^2} + r^d e^{r^d T}\frac{\partial^2 C}{\partial K^2}.$$

As for partial derivatives with respect to strike K, the $e^{r^d T}$ term in $p(K, T)$ falls out, so the LHS of (5.32) becomes

$$e^{r^d T}\frac{\partial^3 C}{\partial T \partial K^2} + r^d e^{r^d T}\frac{\partial^2 C}{\partial K^2} + e^{r^d T}\frac{\partial[a(K, T)\partial^2 C/\partial K^2]}{\partial K} - e^{r^d T}\frac{1}{2}\frac{\partial^2[b^2(K, T)\partial^2 C/\partial K^2]}{\partial K^2}$$

and it suffices to show that the following term vanishes:

$$\frac{\partial^3 C}{\partial T \partial K^2} + r^d\frac{\partial^2 C}{\partial K^2} + \frac{\partial}{\partial K}\left[a(K, T)\frac{\partial^2 C}{\partial K^2}\right] - \frac{\partial^2}{\partial K^2}\left[\frac{1}{2}b^2(K, T)\frac{\partial^2 C}{\partial K^2}\right]. \qquad (5.33)$$

---

[1] Note a typo in the third equation on page 139; the term $(r - q)C_K$ in the numerator should read $(r - q)KC_K$.

From above, we have

$$a(K, T) = (r^d - r^f)K \quad \text{and} \quad b(K, T) = \frac{\partial C/\partial T + (r^d - r^f)K\partial C/\partial K + r^f C}{\partial^2 C/\partial K^2}.$$

Substituting these into (5.33) gives

$$\frac{\partial^3 C}{\partial T \partial K^2} + r^d \frac{\partial^2 C}{\partial K^2} + (r^d - r^f)\frac{\partial}{\partial K}\left[K\frac{\partial^2 C}{\partial K^2}\right] - \frac{\partial^2}{\partial K^2}\left[\frac{\partial C}{\partial T} + (r^d - r^f)K\frac{\partial C}{\partial K} + r^f C\right]$$

$$= \frac{\partial^3 C}{\partial T \partial K^2} + r^d \frac{\partial^2 C}{\partial K^2} + (r^d - r^f)\left[\frac{\partial^2 C}{\partial K^2} + K\frac{\partial^3 C}{\partial K^3}\right] - \frac{\partial^3 C}{\partial T \partial K^2}$$

$$- (r^d - r^f)\frac{\partial^2}{\partial K^2}\left[K\frac{\partial C}{\partial K}\right] - r^f \frac{\partial^2 C}{\partial K^2}$$

$$= (r^d - r^f)\left[2\frac{\partial^2 C}{\partial K^2} + K\frac{\partial^3 C}{\partial K^3} - \frac{\partial^2}{\partial K^2}\left(K\frac{\partial C}{\partial K}\right)\right]. \tag{5.34}$$

We now use

$$\frac{\partial^2}{\partial K^2}\left[K\frac{\partial C}{\partial K}\right] = K\frac{\partial^3 C}{\partial K^3} + 2\frac{\partial^2 C}{\partial K^2},$$

which, when substituted into (5.34), yields

$$(r^d - r^f)\left[2\frac{\partial^2 C}{\partial K^2} + K\frac{\partial^3 C}{\partial K^3} - \left\{K\frac{\partial^3 C}{\partial K^3} + 2\frac{\partial^2 C}{\partial K^2}\right\}\right],$$

which identically vanishes. This shows that (5.28) satisfies the Fokker–Planck equation, as required.

5.4   IMPLIED VOLATILITY AND RELATIONSHIP TO LOCAL VOLATILITY

The analysis above shows that we can construct an instantaneous state-dependent diffusion term $\sigma_{loc}(S, t)$ that recovers the shape of the implied volatility surface $\sigma_{imp}(K, T)$ since equation (5.28) constructs a local volatility surface with the observed call option $C(K, T)$ (and partial derivatives thereof), all of which can be obtained directly from an implied volatility surface $\sigma_{imp}(K, T)$. Note that the parameters of the two volatility functions are different – (S, t) in one, (K, T) in the other. This is because the local volatility is an instantaneous measure of the volatility expected for the FX spot process at time t, conditional on $S_t = K$, whereas the implied volatility is the value that, if used in the Black–Scholes formula, recovers the market price for an option with strike K at time T. Implied volatility basically tells us how much volatility an option (with strike K and time to maturity T) prices in for the underlying asset price process, averaged over the interval $[0, T]$, whereas local volatility lets us narrow down exactly where the volatility feeds into the asset price process, as a function of time and asset price level.

These are very different representations of volatility and it is important not to get the two confused.

5.5   LOCAL VOLATILITY AS CONDITIONAL EXPECTATION

Gatheral (2006) provides a clear and succinct discussion on pages 13–14 of the relationship between local volatility and instantaneous volatility, which we show here. The result is presented assuming that domestic and foreign interest rates vanish, for notational simplicity, but holds in the general case.

We have seen in Section 5.3 that local volatility can be obtained from implied volatility, and clearly the implied volatility for an option with expiry T depends on the instantaneous volatility over the entire time interval $[0, T]$. We present the argument in the case where the domestic and foreign interest rates vanish, for simplicity.

Suppose that we have a geometric Brownian motion for the asset price S_t driven by a variance[2] process v_t:

$$dS_t = \sqrt{v_t} S_t \, dW_t. \tag{5.35}$$

Consider the value of a European option with strike K, i.e. $C(S_T, K) = \mathbf{E}^d[(S_T - K)^+]$. Differentiating with respect to K gives

$$\frac{\partial C}{\partial K} = -\mathbf{E}^d[H(S_T - K)], \tag{5.36a}$$

$$\frac{\partial^2 C}{\partial K^2} = \mathbf{E}^d[\delta(S_T - K)], \tag{5.36b}$$

with $H(\cdot)$ and $\delta(\cdot)$ being the Heaviside step function and the Dirac delta function respectively.

Considering the function $f(S_t) = (S_t - K)\mathbf{1}_{\{S_t \geq K\}}$ and using Itô's lemma, we have

$$d(S_t - K)^+ = df(S_t)$$

$$= f'(S_t)dS_t + \frac{1}{2}f''(S_t)dS_t^2$$

$$= H(S_t - K)dS_t + \frac{1}{2}\delta(S_t - K)v_t S_t^2 \, dt. \tag{5.37}$$

The stochastic differential of C can be expressed as

$$dC = d\mathbf{E}^d[(S_T - K)^+]$$

$$= \mathbf{E}^d\left[H(S_t - K)dS_t + \frac{1}{2}\delta(S_t - K)v_t S_t^2 \, dt\right]$$

$$= \frac{1}{2}\mathbf{E}^d\left[\delta(S_t - K)v_t S_t^2\right] dt$$

$$= \frac{1}{2}\mathbf{E}^d[v_t|S_t = K]\,\mathbf{E}^d\left[\delta(S_t - K)\right] K^2 \, dt$$

$$= \frac{1}{2}\mathbf{E}^d[v_t|S_t = K]\frac{\partial^2 C}{\partial K^2}K^2 \, dt. \tag{5.38}$$

We can therefore use T in place of t and write

$$\frac{\partial C}{\partial T} = \frac{1}{2}\mathbf{E}^d[v_T|S_T = K]K^2\frac{\partial^2 C}{\partial K^2}.$$

---

[2] To avoid ambiguity, I use lower case v_t for variance and upper case V_t for value.

Referring back to (5.27), we have

$$\sigma_{\text{loc}}^2(K, T) = \frac{2\partial C/\partial T}{K^2 \partial^2 C/\partial K^2} = \mathbf{E}^d\left[v_T \mid S_T = K\right].$$

(5.39)

This result shows us that the local variance $\sigma_{\text{loc}}^2(K, T)$ (i.e. the square of the local volatility) has a natural interpretation as the domestic risk-neutral expectation of the instantaneous variance v_T at time T conditional on the asset price S_T being equal to K.

5.6   LOCAL VOLATILITY FOR FX MARKETS

The analysis above shows us how local volatility can be computed from market prices for European call options, and specifically their derivatives with respect to strike and time to expiry, as presented in (5.27) and (5.28). However, from Chapters 2 and 3, we already know that the market quotes prices for European options in terms of their implied volatilities, and these are generally expressed with respect to delta, not strike. So what we really need is an expression for local volatility, computed not in terms of C but in terms of $\sigma_{\text{imp}}(K, T)$.

Such an expression is available as (22.7) in Wilmott (1998) or (16) in Andersen and Brotherton-Ratcliffe (1998); we quote it here:

$$\sigma_{\text{loc}}^2(K, T) = \frac{\sigma_{\text{imp}}^2 + 2T\sigma_{\text{imp}}\partial\sigma_{\text{imp}}/\partial T + 2(\bar{r}_T^d - \bar{r}_T^f)KT\sigma_{\text{imp}}\partial\sigma_{\text{imp}}/\partial K}{\left(1 + Kd_1 T\partial\sigma_{\text{imp}}/\partial K\right)^2 + K^2 T\sigma_{\text{imp}}\left(\partial^2\sigma_{\text{imp}}/\partial K^2 - d_1 T\left(\partial\sigma_{\text{imp}}/\partial K\right)^2\right)},$$

(5.40)

where, in contrast to the simpler Black–Scholes expression in (2.59),

$$d_1 = \frac{\ln\left(\frac{S_0}{K}\right) + \left(\bar{r}_T^d - \bar{r}_T^f + \frac{1}{2}\sigma_{\text{imp}}^2(K, T)\right)T}{\sigma_{\text{imp}}(K, T)\sqrt{T}}.$$

For equity derivatives, this is perfect. However, in FX, implied volatilities are parameterised in terms of delta – effectively a measure of moneyness – as opposed to absolute levels of strike. Suppose we define a reparameterised implied volatility $\hat{\sigma}_{\text{imp}}$ by $\hat{\sigma}_{\text{imp}}(x, T) = \sigma_{\text{imp}}(F_T e^x, T)$, where log-moneyness x^* is defined by

$$x^* = \ln\left(\frac{K}{S_0 \exp(\int_0^T r_s^d - r_s^f \, ds)}\right) = \ln\left(\frac{K}{F_T}\right).$$

One should be careful not to confuse logmoneyness x^* with logspot X_t. Comparing logmoneyness to simple delta

$$\Delta_{\text{simple}} = \omega N(\omega d), \quad \text{where } d = \frac{\ln(F_T/K)}{\sigma\sqrt{T}},$$

and we see immediately the relationship

$$d = \frac{-x^*}{\sigma\sqrt{T}}.$$

With this parameterisation of implied volatility $\hat{\sigma}_{\text{imp}}(x^*, T) = \sigma_{\text{imp}}(F_T e^{x^*}, T)$, we have

$$\sigma_{\text{loc}}^2(x^*, T) = \frac{2T\hat{\sigma}_{\text{imp}}\partial\hat{\sigma}_{\text{imp}}/\partial T + \hat{\sigma}_{\text{imp}}^2}{\left[1 - (x^*/\hat{\sigma}_{\text{imp}})(\partial\hat{\sigma}_{\text{imp}}/\partial x^*)\right]^2 + T\hat{\sigma}_{\text{imp}}\partial^2\hat{\sigma}_{\text{imp}}/\partial x^{*2} - \frac{1}{4}T^2\hat{\sigma}_{\text{imp}}^2\left(\partial\hat{\sigma}_{\text{imp}}/\partial x^*\right)^2},$$
(5.41)

a result stated in Lee (2004).

Given a continuum of implied volatilities $\hat{\sigma}_{\text{imp}}(x^*, T)$ for all conceivable values of log-moneyness x^* and for all expiry times T up to some sensible upper limit T_{max}, we could then use (5.41) to construct the local volatility function. Of course, the implied volatilities we see in the market are far from a continuum, as we know from Chapters 3 and 4, where we described how a continuous implied volatility surface can be constructed from the relatively few discrete points describing the market quotes. However, implied volatility only gives us a single number σ_{imp}, which we can use to price European options accurately, and while we can get a Black–Scholes price for path-dependent options using a single implied volatility, the price achieved will ignore the effect of the term structure of volatility and the entire volatility smile surface. Further, what number should be taken from the implied volatility surface for a path-dependent option? For a barrier option such as we discuss in Chapter 8, with strike K and up-and-out barrier U, do we use $\sigma_{\text{imp}}(K, T)$ or $\sigma_{\text{imp}}(U, T)$? Or should we use $\sigma_{\text{imp}}(U, t^*)$ for some interim t^* between 0 and T, on the basis that the barrier is more likely to be touched somewhere during the lifetime of the option? None of these choices seems particularly appropriate.

Local volatility, in contrast, is quite unambiguous about how the diffusion varies for possible future scenarios for the asset level at future times. This chapter tells us how to go from an implied volatility surface to a local volatility σ_{loc}, which is *consistent* with the implied volatilities and capable of pricing path-dependent options.

Finally, it should be noted that the local volatility $\sigma_{\text{loc}}(x^*, T)$ obtained in (5.41) is particularly prone to numerical noise as a result of the partial derivatives $\partial\hat{\sigma}_{\text{imp}}/\partial T$, $\partial\hat{\sigma}_{\text{imp}}/\partial x^*$ and $\partial^2\hat{\sigma}_{\text{imp}}/\partial x^{*2}$. This is not so much of a problem for obtaining prices using a pure local volatility model, but it will be particularly troublesome for calibrating the mixed local-stochastic volatility model seen in Chapter 6. What does this mean in practice? Choosing a parameterisation for the implied volatility surface for which we have, and use, analytic expressions for the partial derivatives in (5.41) will give a much more regular local volatility surface – without this, a very large number of timesteps will probably be needed for convergence.

5.7 DIFFUSION AND PDE FOR LOCAL VOLATILITY

We know that the diffusion for spot is given by

$$dS_t = (r_t^d - r_t^f)S_t \, dt + \sigma_{\text{loc}}(S_t, t)S_t \, dW_t.$$
(5.42)

This can be easily written in terms of logspot X_t:

$$dX_t = \left(r_t^d - r_t^f - \frac{1}{2}\sigma_{\text{loc}}^2(S_t, t)\right) dt + \sigma_{\text{loc}}(S_t, t) \, dW_t,$$
(5.43)

as can the equivalent parabolic PDE (with local volatility):

$$\frac{\partial V}{\partial t} + \frac{1}{2}\sigma_{\text{loc}}^2(S, t)S^2\frac{\partial^2 V}{\partial S^2} + (r^d - r^f)S\frac{\partial V}{\partial S} - r^d V = 0,$$
(5.44)

which becomes

$$\frac{\partial V}{\partial t} + \frac{1}{2}\hat{\sigma}_{\mathrm{loc}}^2(x,t)\frac{\partial^2 V}{\partial x^2} + \left(r^d - r^f - \frac{1}{2}\hat{\sigma}_{\mathrm{loc}}^2(x,t)\right)\frac{\partial V}{\partial x} - r^d V = 0, \qquad (5.45)$$

where $\hat{\sigma}_{\mathrm{loc}}(x,t) = \sigma_{\mathrm{loc}}(e^x, t)$ denotes the local volatility as parameterised by logspot. Note the similarity of these PDEs to (2.17) and (2.24).

The coefficients in these equations can be directly used in the numerical methods presented in Chapter 7 below.

5.8   THE CEV MODEL

The analysis above shows how a full local volatility surface $\sigma_{\mathrm{loc}}(S_t, t)$ can be fitted to an implied volatility surface for traded options. A simplified local volatility surface can be obtained by supposing a parametric form for the local volatility surface. The CEV model (Cox and Ross, 1976; Cox, 1996) can be written

$$dS_t = \mu S_t\, dt + \sigma S_t^\beta\, dW_t, \qquad (5.46)$$

which clearly reduces to (2.1) when $\beta = 1$. We rewrite this as

$$dS_t = \mu S_t\, dt + \sigma S_t^{\beta-1} S_t\, dW_t$$
$$= \mu S_t\, dt + \sigma_{\mathrm{loc}}(S_t, t) S_t\, dW_t$$

with $\sigma_{\mathrm{loc}}(S_t, t) = \sigma S_t^{\beta-1}$. Transforming this from a stochastic differential equation in spot S_t to one in logspot $X_t = \ln S_t$, we obtain

$$dX_t = \left(\mu - \frac{1}{2}\sigma^2 e^{2(\beta-1)X_t}\right) dt + \sigma e^{(\beta-1)X_t}\, dW_t. \qquad (5.47)$$

Similarly to (2.24), we obtain the pricing PDE, expressed in logspot coordinates, as

$$\frac{\partial V}{\partial t} + \frac{1}{2}\sigma^2 e^{2(\beta-1)X}\frac{\partial^2 V}{\partial X^2} + \left(r^d - r^f - \frac{1}{2}\sigma^2 e^{2(\beta-1)X}\right)\frac{\partial V}{\partial X} - r^d V = 0. \qquad (5.48)$$

Useful further references regarding the CEV model are Schroder (1989), Lo *et al.* (2000), Davydov and Linetsky (2001) and Lu and Hsu (2005).

Note that the SABR model presented in Chapter 6 reduces to the CEV model when the volatility of volatility ('vovol') α is set to zero. In fact, the singular perturbation expansion for SABR in Hagan *et al.* (2002) was presented earlier for the CEV model in Appendix A of Hagan and Woodward (1999), and it is instructive to present their analysis here, both for its intrinsic applicability and also to introduce the approach before presenting the fuller SABR model in Chapter 6. Perturbation theory is an important numerical method in applied mathematics and finance, and we have the opportunity to see an example of this in practice in this section.

Suppose the forward $F_{t;T}$ is modelled directly, which we denote F_t for brevity, suppressing the expiry time T. Presuming a CEV process, we have

$$dF_t = \sigma F_t^\beta\, dW_t. \qquad (5.49)$$

The parameters $A(f)$ and $\alpha(t)$ in the Hagan and Woodward (1999) paper, where they use $dF_t = \alpha(t)A(F_t)dW_t$, are of a simple form indeed with the CEV model – merely $A(f) = f^\beta$ and $\alpha(t) = \sigma$.

Writing the value at time t of a call option (with strike K) as $V(f, t)$, we have

$$V(f, t) = e^{-r^d T} E^d \left[(F_T - K)^+ | F_t = f \right]$$

or, equivalently, as in Hagan and Woodward (1999), we can strip out the discount factor and write

$$V(f, t) = e^{-r^d T} Q(f, t)$$

with

$$Q(f, t) = E^d \left[(F_T - K)^+ | F_t = f \right]$$

subject to the obvious terminal condition $Q(f, T) = (f - K)^+$.

This quantity $Q(f, t)$ is described by the convectionless partial differential equation

$$\frac{\partial Q}{\partial t} + \frac{1}{2} \sigma^2 f^{2\beta} \frac{\partial^2 Q}{\partial f^2} = 0. \tag{5.50}$$

5.8.1 Asymptotic expansion

Let the quantities ϵ, τ and x be given by

$$\epsilon = K^\beta, \tag{5.51a}$$

$$\tau = \sigma^2 [T - t], \tag{5.51b}$$

$$x = \frac{1}{\epsilon} (f - K), \tag{5.51c}$$

and rewrite (5.50) in terms of $\tilde{Q}(x, \tau) = \frac{1}{\epsilon} Q(f, t)$, using $\partial Q / \partial t = -\epsilon \sigma^2 \partial \tilde{Q} / \partial \tau$ and $\partial Q / \partial f^2 = (1/\epsilon)(\partial^2 \tilde{Q} / \partial x^2)$, thereby obtaining

$$\frac{\partial \tilde{Q}}{\partial \tau} - \frac{1}{2} \left(\frac{f}{K} \right)^{2\beta} \frac{\partial^2 \tilde{Q}}{\partial x^2} = 0$$

Since $f = K + \epsilon x$ from (5.51c), we have

$$\frac{\partial \tilde{Q}}{\partial \tau} - \frac{1}{2} \left(\frac{K + \epsilon x}{K} \right)^{2\beta} \frac{\partial^2 \tilde{Q}}{\partial x^2} = 0, \tag{5.52}$$

which is just (A.7a) in Hagan and Woodward (1999), i.e.

$$\frac{\partial \tilde{Q}}{\partial \tau} - \frac{1}{2} \frac{A^2(K + \epsilon x)}{A^2(K)} \frac{\partial^2 \tilde{Q}}{\partial x^2} = 0$$

when $A(f) = f^\beta$. The same initial condition $\tilde{Q}(x, 0) = \max\{x, 0\}$ applies at $\tau = 0$.

Using the $A(f)$ notation of Hagan and Woodward (1999) and following their approach, we write

$$A(f) = A(K + \epsilon x) = A(K) \left\{ 1 + \epsilon v_1 x + \frac{1}{2} \epsilon v_2 x^2 + \cdots \right\}$$

with $v_1 = A'(K)/A(K) = \beta/K$ and $v_2 = A''(K)/A(K) = \beta(\beta - 1)/K^2$. We have

$$\frac{A(f)}{A(K)} = 1 + \epsilon v_1 x + \frac{1}{2} \epsilon v_2 x^2 + \cdots,$$

which we can square and, collecting terms in ϵ up to second order, write

$$\frac{A^2(f)}{A^2(K)} = \left[1 + \epsilon v_1 x + \frac{1}{2}\epsilon v_2 x^2 + \cdots\right]\left[1 + \epsilon v_1 x + \frac{1}{2}\epsilon v_2 x^2 + \cdots\right]$$

$$= 1 + 2\epsilon v_1 x + \epsilon^2[v_1^2 + v_2]x^2 + O(\epsilon^3).$$

Following this, transform (5.52) to

$$\frac{\partial \tilde{Q}}{\partial \tau} - \frac{1}{2}\frac{\partial^2 \tilde{Q}}{\partial x^2} = \epsilon v_1 x \frac{\partial^2 \tilde{Q}}{\partial x^2} + \frac{1}{2}\epsilon^2(v_1 + v_1^2)x^2\frac{\partial^2 \tilde{Q}}{\partial x^2}. \tag{5.53}$$

We write

$$\tilde{Q}(x, \tau) = \tilde{Q}^{(0)}(x, \tau) + \epsilon \tilde{Q}^{(1)}(x, \tau) + \epsilon^2 \tilde{Q}^{(2)}(x, \tau) + \cdots. \tag{5.54}$$

Substituting (5.54) into (5.53), one obtains

$$\tilde{Q}_\tau^{(0)} + \epsilon \tilde{Q}_\tau^{(1)} + \epsilon^2 \tilde{Q}_\tau^{(2)} - \frac{1}{2}\left[\tilde{Q}_{xx}^{(0)} + \epsilon \tilde{Q}_{xx}^{(1)} + \epsilon^2 \tilde{Q}_{xx}^{(2)}\right].$$

$$= \left[\epsilon v_1 x + \frac{1}{2}\epsilon^2(v_1^2 + v_2)x^2\right]\left[\tilde{Q}_{xx}^{(0)} + \epsilon \tilde{Q}_{xx}^{(1)} + \epsilon^2 \tilde{Q}_{xx}^{(2)}\right]. \tag{5.55}$$

Collecting terms in zeroth, first and second order in ϵ respectively, one obtains

$$\tilde{Q}_\tau^{(0)} - \frac{1}{2}\tilde{Q}_{xx}^{(0)} = 0, \tag{5.56a}$$

$$\tilde{Q}_\tau^{(1)} - \frac{1}{2}\tilde{Q}_{xx}^{(1)} = v_1 x \tilde{Q}_{xx}^{(0)}, \tag{5.56b}$$

$$\tilde{Q}_\tau^{(2)} - \frac{1}{2}\tilde{Q}_{xx}^{(2)} = v_1 x \tilde{Q}_{xx}^{(1)} + \frac{1}{2}(v_1^2 + v_2)x^2\tilde{Q}_{xx}^{(1)}, \tag{5.56c}$$

which must obey the initial conditions $\tilde{Q}^{(0)}(x, 0) = \max\{x, 0\}$ and $\tilde{Q}^{(1)}(x, 0) = \tilde{Q}^{(2)}(x, 0) = 0$ at $\tau = 0$.

Equation (5.56a) is nothing more than the heat equation and, interestingly, given the initial condition above on $\tilde{Q}^{(0)}$, corresponds to the price of a call option with strike of 0 (remarkably!) given a driftless Bachelier model, such as described briefly in (2.1). This has solution

$$\tilde{Q}^{(0)}(x, \tau) = G(x, \tau) = xN(x/\sqrt{\tau}) + \sqrt{\frac{\tau}{2\pi}}\exp(-x^2/2\tau). \tag{5.57}$$

The other terms in the expansion (5.54) can be picked out similarly. The various partial derivatives of $G(x, \tau)$ with respect to x and τ (including higher order derivatives) are given in Hagan and Woodward (1999). To take one for example, $G_{xx} = e^{-x^2/2\tau}/\sqrt{2\pi\tau}$, which can be directly plugged into (5.56b) to give

$$\tilde{Q}_\tau^{(1)} - \frac{1}{2}\tilde{Q}_{xx}^{(1)} = v_1 x e^{-x^2/2\tau}/\sqrt{2\pi\tau}.$$

One obtains, subject to the initial condition,

$$\tilde{Q}^{(1)} = v_1 \tau x G_\tau.$$

For (5.56c), more algebra gives

$$\tilde{Q}^{(2)} = \frac{1}{2}v_1^2\tau^2 x^2 G_{\tau\tau} + \frac{1}{12}v_1^2(x^2 - \tau)\tau G_\tau + \frac{1}{6}v_2(2x^2 + \tau)\tau G_\tau.$$

Using terms $\tilde{Q}^{(0)}$, $\tilde{Q}^{(1)}$ and $\tilde{Q}^{(2)}$ as obtained above, we write (5.54) as (dropping terms above $O(\epsilon^2)$ in the expansion)

$$\tilde{Q}(x, \tau) = G(x, \tau) + \epsilon v_1 \tau x G_\tau + \frac{1}{2}\epsilon^2 v_1^2 \tau^2 x^2 G_{\tau\tau}$$

$$+ \frac{1}{12}\epsilon^2 \left((4v_2 + v_1^2)x^2 + (2v_2 - v_1^2)\tau\right)\tau G_\tau. \tag{5.58}$$

This looks suspiciously like an expansion in τ, and can in fact be written as $\tilde{Q}(x, \tau) = G(x, \tilde{\tau})$ with

$$\tilde{\tau} = \tau\left[1 + \epsilon v_1 x + \frac{\epsilon^2}{12}\left((4v_2 + v_1^2)x^2 + (2v_2 - v_1^2)\tau\right)\right].$$

Scaling back from $\tilde{Q}(x, \tau)$ to $V(x, t)$, we get

$$V(f, t) = e^{-r^d T} G(f - K, \tau^*) \tag{5.59}$$

with

$$\tau^* = A^2(K)\tau\left[1 + v_1(f - K) + \frac{4v_2 + v_1^2}{12}(f - K)^2 + \frac{2v_2 - v_1^2}{12}A^2(K)\tau\right].$$

Translating this price $V(f, t)$ into the equivalent implied volatility yields the desired expression $\sigma_{\text{imp}}(K, T)$. We take $f_{\text{av}} = \frac{1}{2}(F + k)$ and write $\gamma_1 = A'(f_{\text{av}})/A(f_{\text{av}})$, $\gamma_2 = A''(f_{\text{av}})/A(f_{\text{av}})$, for which we still have (5.59), but with τ^* required to obey

$$\sqrt{\tau^*} = A(f_{\text{av}})\sqrt{\tau}\left[1 + \frac{\gamma_2 - 2\gamma_1^2}{24}(f - K)^2 + \frac{2\gamma_2 - \gamma_1^2}{24}A^2(f_{\text{av}})\right].$$

Using the same analysis, as suggested in the Hagan and Woodward paper, but with a constant volatility σ_B, i.e. $dF_t = \sigma_B F_t dW_t$, gives $V(f, t) = e^{-r^d T} G(f - K, \tau_B)$, but with

$$\sqrt{\tau_B} = \sigma_B f_{\text{av}}\sqrt{T}\left[1 + \frac{(f - K)^2}{12 f_{\text{av}}^2} + \frac{\sigma_B^2 T}{24}\right].$$

Equating τ^* and τ_B and solving for σ_B, we have

$$\sigma_B = a\frac{A(f_{\text{av}})}{f_{\text{av}}}\left[1 + \left(\gamma_2 - 2\gamma_1^2 + \frac{2}{f_{\text{av}}}\right)\frac{(f - K)^2}{24} + \left(2\gamma_2 - \gamma_1^2 + \frac{1}{f_{\text{av}}^2}\right)\frac{a^2 A^2(f_{\text{av}})T}{24}\right] \tag{5.60}$$

with $a = \frac{1}{T}\int_0^T \alpha^2(u)du$.

For the CEV model (5.46), since $\alpha(t) = \sigma$ and $A(f) = f^\beta$, we can simplify this somewhat, obtaining

$$\sigma_B = \frac{\sigma}{f_{\text{av}}^{1-\beta}}\left[1 + \frac{1}{24}(1 - \beta)(2 + \beta)\left(\frac{F_0 - K}{f_{\text{av}}}\right)^2 + \frac{1}{24}(1 - \beta)^2\frac{\sigma^2 T}{f_{\text{av}}^{2-2\beta}}\right]. \tag{5.61}$$

A discussion of the asymptotic volatility skews generated by the CEV model in the extreme wings (i.e. for extreme strike) can be found in Benaim *et al.* (2008).

6

Stochastic Volatility

6.1 INTRODUCTION

A local volatility model such as introduced in the previous chapter has the advantage of being able to fit the market for European vanillas, with little extra computational cost compared with similar numerical techniques for a term-structure Black–Scholes model (both being one-dimensional models). On the other hand, a purely local volatility model will underestimate the forward smile and skew in the market, and as such is a poor candidate for a model designed to match market prices for exotic options. Further, a historical time-series analysis of any FX currency pair immediately shows that the realised historical volatility is far from constant. For these reasons, various stochastic volatility models have been proposed in the literature, many of which have gained some acceptance in the practitioner community.

In this chapter, I will attempt to describe some of these models and, perhaps most crucially from the industry perspective, introduce some of the numerical techniques that can be used for their calibration and for pricing (some of the discussion will necessarily have to wrap over into the next chapter). A model that is difficult to calibrate is of limited use indeed in practical applications.

To begin, we consider a much simpler candidate model than a full continuous time stochastic volatility model, but which shares surprisingly many features – an uncertain volatility model.

6.2 UNCERTAIN VOLATILITY

We already have prices for European options $V_0^C(K, T)$ under the Black–Scholes model, under the assumption that volatility is a constant value σ. Let's denote this price by $V_0^C(K, T; \sigma)$.

Now what if we don't actually know σ, but can suppose it to be described by a statistical distribution. The simplest nontrivial random distribution we could imagine is a two-state case, basically a binomial model for volatility: at time $t = 0$, volatility goes into one of two states, σ_+ or σ_-, and remains constant thereafter over the entire lifetime of the option. We assign equal probabilities to these two events and have

$$
\sigma = \begin{cases} \sigma_+, & p = 1/2, \\ \\ \sigma_-, & p = 1/2. \end{cases} \tag{6.1}
$$

We clearly have the expected volatility $\bar{\sigma} = \frac{1}{2}[\sigma_+ + \sigma_-]$ and can construct prices of European options under this simple model, obtaining

$$
V_0^{C;UV}(K, T) = \frac{1}{2} V_0^C(K, T; \sigma_+) + \frac{1}{2} V_0^C(K, T; \sigma_-).
$$

What sort of prices do we see and what does this tell us about the implied volatilities generated? We know that an ATMF European option has PV approximately equal to $0.04\sigma\sqrt{T}$ and, being linear in volatility, the price of the ATMF European option is nothing more than

$$V_0^{\text{C;UV}}(K_{\text{ATMF}}, T) = \frac{1}{2} V_0^{\text{C}}(K_{\text{ATMF}}, T; \sigma_+) + \frac{1}{2} V_0^{\text{C}}(K_{\text{ATMF}}, T; \sigma_-)$$

$$\approx \frac{1}{2} \left[0.04\sigma_+ \sqrt{T} + 0.04\sigma_- \sqrt{T} \right]$$

$$= 0.04\bar{\sigma} \sqrt{T},$$

from which we immediately see that the implied ATM volatility is nothing more than $\bar{\sigma}$.

This holds because the price of ATM European options is very close to being purely linear in volatility. Out-of-the-money options, however, are *convex* in volatility, and so we have

$$V_0^{\text{C;UV}}(K_{\text{OTM}}, T) = \frac{1}{2} V_0^{\text{C}}(K_{\text{OTM}}, T; \sigma_+) + \frac{1}{2} V_0^{\text{C}}(K_{\text{OTM}}, T; \sigma_-)$$

$$> V_0^{\text{C}}(K_{\text{OTM}}, T; \bar{\sigma}).$$

From this, we can make the important observation that OTM options have implied volatilities *greater* than $\bar{\sigma}$ in an uncertain volatility model and, therefore, even a simple toy model as this is capable of generating volatility smiles.

Stochastic volatility is really all about generating an ensemble of possible future scenarios for volatility over the time interval $[0, T]$. The uncertain volatility model above is as simple a way of doing that as it gets.

Note that an uncertain *variance* model, of the form

$$v = \sigma^2 = \begin{cases} v_+ = \sigma_+^2, & p = 1/2, \\ v_- = \sigma_-^2, & p = 1/2, \end{cases}$$

with expected variance $\bar{v} = \frac{1}{2}[v_+ + v_-]$, will generate an implied ATM volatility somewhat *less* then $\sqrt{\bar{v}}$, due to convexity – one can see this by considering

$$V_0^{\text{C;UV}}(K_{\text{ATMF}}, T) = \frac{1}{2} V_0^{\text{C}}(K_{\text{ATMF}}, T; \sqrt{v_+}) + \frac{1}{2} V_0^{\text{C}}(K_{\text{ATMF}}, T; \sqrt{v_-})$$

$$\approx \frac{1}{2} \left[0.04\sqrt{v_+}\sqrt{T} + 0.04\sqrt{v_-}\sqrt{T} \right]$$

$$< 0.04\sqrt{\bar{v}}\sqrt{T} \quad \text{due to the concavity of } f(x) = \sqrt{x}.$$

The same behaviour is evident for the Heston model, a stochastic variance model, for which the same effect in the ATM implied volatilities is apparent. What is happening here is that if a nontrivial stochastic process is driftless in variance, it cannot be simultaneously driftless in volatility, due to the concavity of $f(x) = \sqrt{x}$, as shown in Figure 6.1.

6.3 STOCHASTIC VOLATILITY MODELS

There is an extra level of complexity attached to moving into stochastic volatility models, however. All the models presented so far to describe the evolution of the spot FX rate, such as (2.1) for Black–Scholes, (2.71) for Black–Scholes with term structure and (5.29) for local volatility, are one-factor models. As such, they can written in general terms as $dS_t = a(S_t, t)dt + b(S_t, t)dW_t$ or perhaps $dX_t^{(1)} = \mu(X_t^{(1)}, t)dt + \sigma(X_t^{(1)}, t)dW_t^{(1)}$, where $X_t^{(1)} = \ln S_t$ and $W_t^{(1)}$ is a one-dimensional Brownian motion.

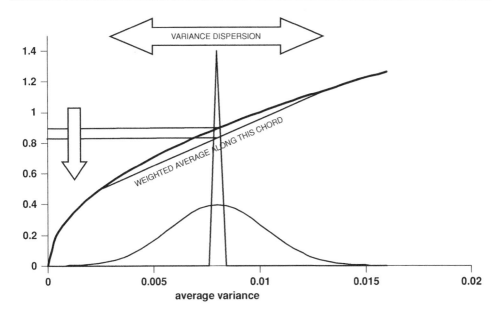

Figure 6.1 Increasing dispersion of a driftless variance process reduces σ_{ATM}

In contrast, a second factor is needed to describe the additional variance or volatility process in stochastic volatility models. Suppose we let $\mathbf{X}_t = \left(X_t^{(1)}, X_t^{(2)} \right)$ denote the state vector consisting of logspot $X_t^{(1)}$ and a state variable $X_t^{(2)}$ that drives the volatility of $X_t^{(1)}$. We can then write, in general,

$$d\mathbf{X}_t = \boldsymbol{\mu}(\mathbf{X}_t, t)dt + \boldsymbol{\Sigma}(\mathbf{X}_t, t)d\mathbf{W}_t, \tag{6.2}$$

where

$$\boldsymbol{\mu}(\mathbf{X}_t, t) = \begin{bmatrix} \mu^{(1)}(X_t^{(1)}, X_t^{(2)}, t) \\ \mu^{(2)}(X_t^{(1)}, X_t^{(2)}, t) \end{bmatrix}, \tag{6.3a}$$

$$\boldsymbol{\Sigma}(\mathbf{X}_t, t) = \begin{bmatrix} \sigma^{(11)}(X_t^{(1)}, X_t^{(2)}, t) & \sigma^{(12)}(X_t^{(1)}, X_t^{(2)}, t) \\ \sigma^{(21)}(X_t^{(1)}, X_t^{(2)}, t) & \sigma^{(22)}(X_t^{(1)}, X_t^{(2)}, t) \end{bmatrix}, \tag{6.3b}$$

$$\mathbf{W}_t = \left(W_t^{(1)}, W_t^{(2)} \right). \tag{6.3c}$$

The vector notation is clearly a much more compact representation. For example, a selection of the entries for some stochastic volatility models listed in Table 2.2 in Zhu (2000) reads in our notation as given in Table 6.1, where we understand that the logspot process follows $dX_t^{(1)} = (r^d - r^f - \frac{1}{2}\sigma_t^2)dt + \sigma_t \, dW_t^{(1)}$ and that the two diffusions $W_t^{(1)}$ and $W_t^{(2)}$ may be correlated, with $\langle dW_t^{(1)}, dW_t^{(2)} \rangle = \rho \, dt$.

The imposition of correlation between $W_t^{(1)}$ and $W_t^{(2)}$ adds to the descriptive power of these models, but also complicates somewhat the analysis, as we see in Section 6.5 below.

Let's introduce some commonly encountered stochastic volatility models, which we shall consider later in this chapter.

Table 6.1   Common stochastic volatility models in the literature

$dX_t^{(2)} = \kappa X_t^{(2)}\,dt + \alpha X_t^{(2)}\,dW_t^{(2)}$	$\sigma_t = X_t^{(2)}$	Johnson and Shanno (1987)
$dX_t^{(2)} = \kappa(\theta - X_t^{(2)})dt + \alpha\,dW_t^{(2)}$	$\sigma_t = \exp(X_t^{(2)})$	Scott (1987)
$dX_t^{(2)} = \kappa(\theta - X_t^{(2)})dt + \alpha\,dW_t^{(2)}$	$\sigma_t = X_t^{(2)}$	Stein and Stein (1991), Schöbel and Zhu (1999)
$dX_t^{(2)} = \kappa(\theta - X_t^{(2)})dt + \alpha\sqrt{X_t^{(2)}}\,dW_t^{(2)}$	$\sigma_t = \sqrt{X_t^{(2)}}$	Heston (1993)

6.3.1   The Heston model

Heston (1993) proposed a stochastic variance model as an extension to the Black–Scholes model, in the form

$$dS_t = \mu_t S_t\,dt + \sqrt{v_t}\,S_t\,dW_t^{(1)}, \tag{6.4a}$$

$$dv_t = \kappa(m - v_t)dt + \alpha\sqrt{v_t}\,dW_t^{(2)}, \tag{6.4b}$$

with $< dW_t^{(1)},\,dW_t^{(2)}> = \rho\,dt$. Transforming (6.4a) into logspot, we obtain

$$dX_t = \left(\mu_t - \frac{1}{2}v_t\right)dt + \sqrt{v_t}\,dW_t^{(1)}. \tag{6.4c}$$

This model is characterised by several constant parameters, given in Table 6.2.

Note that some of these parameters can be made time-dependent; see Elices (2008), Halai (2008) and Benhamou et al. (2009). For now we stick to the original Heston model.

The volatility process in (6.4b) is the same as the short rate process $dr_t = a[b - r_t]\,dt + \sigma_r\sqrt{r_t}\,dW_t^r$ in the CIR process (Cox et al., 1985), a process originally mentioned in the literature by Feller (1951). One supposed advantage of process (6.4b) is that, if $v_0 > 0$ and the so-called Feller condition is satisfied, then the variance v_t remains strictly positive with probability one for all times t.

The Feller condition

Lemma. $v_0 > 0 \cap \beta \equiv 2\kappa m/\alpha^2 \geq 1 \Rightarrow v_t > 0\,\forall t > 0.$

Unfortunately in FX, the Feller condition is almost never satisfied for the smiles typically encountered in practice, due to the convexities encountered in practice, as shown by the values for β in Table 6.3 (market data as of 16 September 2008). It is exactly this reason that practitioners in FX especially are concerned with violation of the Feller condition and correct treatment of variance absorption at the $v = 0$ boundary.

Table 6.2   Parameters of the Heston model

Initial variance	v_0
Spot/variance correlation	ρ
Vovariance	α
Mean reversion rate	κ
Mean reversion level	m

Table 6.3   Violation of Heston Feller condition in typical FX markets

ccypair	tenor	ATM	25-d-MS	25-d-RR	v_0	ρ	α	κ	m	β
EURUSD	3M	12.70%	0.28%	−0.55%	0.02	−0.13	0.49	6.02	0.02	0.9050
EURUSD	6M	11.87%	0.38%	−0.55%	0.02	−0.13	0.41	3.02	0.02	0.5879
EURUSD	1Y	11.50%	0.40%	−0.55%	0.02	−0.13	0.31	1.50	0.02	0.4918
EURUSD	2Y	11.45%	0.40%	−0.55%	0.02	−0.14	0.20	0.75	0.02	0.5640
EURUSD	3Y	11.30%	0.40%	−0.55%	0.02	−0.15	0.16	0.50	0.02	0.5549
EURUSD	4Y	11.13%	0.40%	−0.56%	0.01	−0.16	0.14	0.38	0.01	0.5442
EURUSD	5Y	10.75%	0.38%	−0.55%	0.01	−0.17	0.12	0.30	0.01	0.5625
USDJPY	3M	15.10%	0.18%	−4.65%	0.03	−0.60	0.89	6.02	0.03	0.4252
USDJPY	6M	13.00%	0.18%	−4.95%	0.02	−0.64	0.72	3.02	0.02	0.2717
USDJPY	1Y	11.80%	0.18%	−5.25%	0.02	−0.67	0.62	1.50	0.02	0.1692
USDJPY	2Y	10.60%	0.10%	−5.40%	0.02	−0.70	0.46	0.75	0.02	0.1382
USDJPY	3Y	10.25%	0.05%	−5.45%	0.02	−0.71	0.41	0.50	0.02	0.1151
USDJPY	4Y	10.10%	0.03%	−5.55%	0.02	−0.71	0.40	0.38	0.02	0.0956
USDJPY	5Y	10.10%	0.00%	−5.60%	0.02	−0.71	0.39	0.30	0.02	0.0845
GBPUSD	3M	11.95%	0.30%	−1.05%	0.02	−0.23	0.51	6.02	0.02	0.7432
GBPUSD	6M	11.40%	0.33%	−0.98%	0.02	−0.22	0.38	3.02	0.02	0.6253
GBPUSD	1Y	11.10%	0.35%	−0.95%	0.01	−0.22	0.29	1.50	0.01	0.5207
GBPUSD	2Y	10.95%	0.38%	−0.93%	0.01	−0.22	0.20	0.75	0.01	0.5599
GBPUSD	3Y	10.83%	0.38%	−0.85%	0.01	−0.21	0.16	0.50	0.01	0.5558
GBPUSD	4Y	10.70%	0.38%	−0.77%	0.01	−0.21	0.14	0.38	0.01	0.5519
GBPUSD	5Y	10.60%	0.33%	−0.70%	0.01	−0.20	0.11	0.30	0.01	0.6422
EURGBP	3M	8.90%	0.23%	0.80%	0.01	0.23	0.37	6.02	0.01	0.7925
EURGBP	6M	8.90%	0.28%	0.85%	0.01	0.22	0.29	3.02	0.01	0.6323
EURGBP	1Y	8.90%	0.29%	0.85%	0.01	0.23	0.21	1.50	0.01	0.6008
EURGBP	2Y	8.90%	0.28%	1.10%	0.01	0.31	0.13	0.75	0.01	0.7931
EURGBP	3Y	9.00%	0.23%	0.85%	0.01	0.27	0.09	0.50	0.01	1.0792
EURGBP	4Y	9.10%	0.20%	0.75%	0.01	0.26	0.07	0.38	0.01	1.3758
EURGBP	5Y	9.20%	0.18%	0.55%	0.01	0.20	0.06	0.30	0.01	1.5344
AUDUSD	3M	18.50%	0.38%	−2.70%	0.04	−0.39	0.76	6.02	0.04	0.8121
AUDUSD	6M	16.50%	0.40%	−2.75%	0.03	−0.42	0.56	3.02	0.03	0.6182
AUDUSD	1Y	14.75%	0.43%	−2.80%	0.03	−0.45	0.43	1.50	0.03	0.4465
AUDUSD	2Y	14.15%	0.40%	−2.70%	0.03	−0.46	0.26	0.75	0.03	0.5604
AUDUSD	3Y	13.65%	0.40%	−2.40%	0.02	−0.43	0.20	0.50	0.02	0.5622
AUDUSD	4Y	13.38%	0.40%	−2.19%	0.02	−0.42	0.17	0.38	0.02	0.5670
AUDUSD	5Y	13.25%	0.40%	−2.00%	0.02	−0.40	0.15	0.30	0.02	0.5756
USDBRL	3M	16.00%	0.60%	3.50%	0.03	0.43	0.90	6.02	0.03	0.4497
USDBRL	6M	14.00%	0.63%	3.50%	0.02	0.46	0.63	3.02	0.02	0.3686
USDBRL	1Y	14.30%	0.65%	3.50%	0.02	0.45	0.44	1.50	0.02	0.3848
USDBRL	2Y	15.20%	0.70%	3.50%	0.03	0.44	0.31	0.75	0.03	0.4196
USDBRL	3Y	16.20%	0.75%	3.50%	0.03	0.42	0.26	0.50	0.03	0.4516
USDBRL	4Y	17.66%	0.77%	3.55%	0.03	0.42	0.22	0.38	0.03	0.5204
USDBRL	5Y	18.80%	0.78%	3.50%	0.04	0.41	0.20	0.30	0.04	0.6084
AUDJPY	3M	21.40%	0.22%	−5.00%	0.05	−0.50	1.13	6.02	0.05	0.5123
AUDJPY	6M	19.50%	0.20%	−5.80%	0.05	−0.55	0.96	3.02	0.05	0.3223
AUDJPY	1Y	18.00%	0.20%	−6.50%	0.05	−0.58	0.97	1.50	0.05	0.1609
AUDJPY	2Y	18.10%	0.25%	−6.80%	0.05	−0.55	0.78	0.75	0.05	0.1337
AUDJPY	3Y	18.20%	0.33%	−7.20%	0.07	−0.54	0.93	0.50	0.07	0.0800
AUDJPY	4Y	18.30%	0.33%	−7.75%	0.09	−0.55	1.26	0.38	0.09	0.0450
AUDJPY	5Y	18.35%	0.33%	−8.30%	0.18	−0.58	2.44	0.30	0.18	0.0183
USDTRY	3M	17.30%	0.60%	5.00%	0.04	0.60	0.89	6.02	0.04	0.5376
USDTRY	6M	17.40%	0.65%	5.25%	0.04	0.63	0.61	3.02	0.04	0.5714

(continued)

Table 6.3   (continued)

ccypair	tenor	ATM	25-d-MS	25-d-RR	v_0	ρ	α	κ	m	β
USDTRY	1Y	17.75%	0.70%	5.50%	0.04	0.70	0.39	1.50	0.04	0.7143
USDTRY	2Y	19.15%	0.80%	5.15%	0.04	0.76	0.23	0.75	0.04	1.1821
USDTRY	3Y	20.60%	1.00%	5.10%	0.05	0.78	0.17	0.50	0.05	1.4996
USDTRY	4Y	22.10%	1.10%	5.40%	0.05	0.77	0.14	0.38	0.05	1.8480
USDTRY	5Y	23.60%	1.00%	5.70%	0.06	0.78	0.15	0.30	0.06	1.6305
EURCHF	3M	6.65%	0.23%	−1.85%	0.01	−0.50	0.45	6.02	0.01	0.3299
EURCHF	6M	6.10%	0.26%	−1.80%	0.01	−0.49	0.36	3.02	0.01	0.2436
EURCHF	1Y	5.80%	0.29%	−1.80%	0.00	−0.48	0.29	1.50	0.00	0.1745
EURCHF	2Y	5.30%	0.25%	−1.65%	0.00	−0.48	0.17	0.75	0.00	0.2085
EURCHF	3Y	5.10%	0.22%	−1.50%	0.00	−0.47	0.13	0.50	0.00	0.2233
EURCHF	4Y	4.80%	0.21%	−1.53%	0.00	−0.49	0.11	0.37	0.00	0.1999
EURCHF	5Y	4.50%	0.15%	−1.55%	0.00	−0.54	0.09	0.30	0.00	0.2178

A modern proof of the Feller condition is surprisingly hard to track down in the literature. The original source is in Feller (1951). A proof, in the context of the mathematically equivalent CIR model (actually for the more general shifted CIR process), is in Section 5 of Gorovoi and Linetsky (2004). To accompany this, I recommend the very readable introduction to scale measure and speed measure density and their use in the Feller classification of boundaries in Section 6.5 of Durrett (1996). Section 4.4 of Lipton (2002) also discusses scale and speed measure, and in particular Example 4.5 describes the Feller classification of boundary conditions for the Bessel process. See also Section 9.2 of Lewis (2000). Note that various authors' definitions differ slightly, often by a factor of 2.

The Feller condition – method A

The most straightforward approach, as used in Wang (2007), is to appeal to Bessel processes. Consider the n-dimensional Bessel process

$$dX_t = \frac{n-1}{2X_t}\,dt + dW_t.$$

It can be shown that if $n \geq 2$, then X_t will never reach the origin for strictly positive times t. A proof for integral n can be found in Proposition 3.22 of Karatzas and Shreve (1991). For the more general case of real-valued n, Lipton (2002) uses speed and scale measure to show that this is true for a Bessel process $dX_t = (1 - 2v)/(2X_t)\,dt + dW_t$ if and only if $v \leq 0$, which corresponds to $n \geq 2$.

The question is whether v_t can be related to a Bessel process X_t. Wang (2007) recognises that it is sufficient to show that the adjusted process (in a neighbourhood of $v_t = 0$)

$$dv_t^* = \kappa m\,dt + \alpha\sqrt{v_t^*}\,dW_t \tag{6.5}$$

is locally equivalent to the square of a Bessel process of dimension ≥ 2. The adjusted process just replaces the mean reverting term with a constant drift term of the same magnitude at the $v_t = 0$ boundary. The approach taken there is to put $v_t^* = \frac{1}{4}\alpha^2 X_t^2$, with X_t a Bessel process of dimension n, and see what the required dimension is (which will tell us whether 0 is attainable or not). Applying Itô's lemma to $f(x) = \frac{1}{2}\alpha^2 x^2$ gives

$$dv_t^* = \frac{1}{2}\alpha^2 X_t \, dW_t + \frac{1}{4}\alpha^2 n \, dt. \tag{6.6}$$

With $v_t^* = \frac{1}{4}\alpha^2 X_t^2$, we have $X_t = (2/\alpha)\sqrt{v_t^*}$ and (6.6) then becomes

$$dv_t^* = \alpha\sqrt{v_t^*} \, dW_t + \frac{1}{4}\alpha^2 n \, dt. \tag{6.7}$$

Comparing (6.7) to (6.5), we see that the diffusion terms are identical, and if n is chosen so that $\frac{1}{4}\alpha^2 n = \kappa m$, then the drift terms match also. This gives

$$n = \frac{4\kappa m}{\alpha^2}.$$

The condition $n \geq 2$ for strict nonattainability of $X_t = 0$ is therefore equivalent to showing that $2\kappa m/\alpha^2 \geq 1$ implies that $v_t^* = 0$ is unreachable. This demonstrates that $v_t = 0$ is similarly unattainable when the Feller condition is satisfied.

A similar discussion, not invoking the adjusted process v_t^*, can be found in Section 5.3 of Rajabpour (2009) in the context of the CIR process. With this, the variance process v_t can be written

$$v_t = e^{-\kappa t} X_{t^*}^2,$$

where $t^* = (\alpha^2/4\kappa)(e^{-\kappa t} - 1)$ and X_t is a Bessel process of dimension $n = 4\kappa m/\alpha^2$. The condition $n \geq 2$ for nonattainability of the origin is nothing more than the same $2\kappa m/\alpha^2 \geq 1$ condition, as above.

The Feller condition – method B

Approaching the important proof of the Feller condition from a lower level, and approaching the concepts of scale and speed measure head on, we present Gorovoi and Linetsky's proof here. Suppose a diffusion X_t is given, with

$$dX_t = \mu(X_t)dt + \sigma(X_t)dW_t$$

with drift and diffusion terms $\mu(\cdot)$ and $\sigma(\cdot)$ respectively, where $\mu, \mu', \sigma, \sigma'$ and σ'' are required to be continuous over $(0, \infty)$ and σ required to be strictly positive in $(0, \infty)$. Following (2.3) and (2.4) in Gorovoi and Linetsky (2004), define the scale and speed densities by

$$\mathfrak{s}(x) = \exp\left\{-\int^x \frac{2\mu(y)}{\sigma^2(y)} dy\right\}, \tag{6.8a}$$

$$\mathfrak{m}(x) = \frac{2}{\sigma^2(x)\mathfrak{s}(x)}, \tag{6.8b}$$

with the associated scale function

$$S(x) = \int_{x_0}^x \mathfrak{s}(y) \, dy. \tag{6.8c}$$

For the Heston variance process (6.4b), quoting equations (5.2) in Gorovoi and Linetsky (2004) with $l = 0$, we have scale and speed densities

$$\mathfrak{s}(x) = x^{-\beta} \exp(2\kappa x / \alpha^2) \qquad \text{and} \qquad \mathfrak{m}(x) = \frac{2}{\alpha^2} x^{\beta-1} \exp(-2\kappa x / \alpha^2),$$

where $\beta = 2\kappa m / \alpha^2$.

Finiteness of $\int_0^\epsilon \mathfrak{m}(x) dx$ within an ϵ-neighbourhood of zero when $\beta > 0$ follows from $\mathfrak{m}(x) \leq (2/\alpha^2) x^{\beta-1}$, since $\int x^{\beta-1} dx = x^\beta / \beta + c$ for $\beta \neq 0$ and $\int x^{\beta-1} dx = \ln x + c$ for $\beta = 0$. For a CIR or equivalent Heston process, we would expect $\beta > 0$ since all quantities κ, m and α can realistically be expected to be positive.

In order to show (assuming $v_0 > 0$) that $v_t > 0 \, \forall t > 0$ if $\beta \geq 1$, we examine the behaviour of two real-valued integrals

$$I = \int_0^\epsilon \mathfrak{s}(x) dx, \tag{6.9a}$$

$$J = \int_0^\epsilon S(x) \mathfrak{m}(x) dx, \tag{6.9b}$$

both computed over an ϵ-neighbourhood of $x = 0$. Following Gorovoi and Linetsky (2004), if we can demonstrate that $I = \infty$, then $x = 0$ must be either an unattainable entrance boundary or an attainable natural boundary – these being two of the possible four Feller boundary classifications, as described on page 231 of Durrett (1996). The terminology is somewhat cryptic at first but makes sense – an entrance boundary means that you can't exit via that boundary having started elsewhere in the state space. An attainable boundary, on the other hand, can be reached.

The $J < \infty$ case corresponds to the case where v_t is unattainable, which the Feller condition describes, while the $J = \infty$ case corresponds to the attainable case where the Feller condition is violated.

Note that the integral I here differs from that in Durrett, but since we know that $\int_0^\epsilon \mathfrak{m}(x) dx$ is finite over the ϵ-neighbourhood of zero, it suffices to show that the integral I defined herein is infinite.

Let's examine these two integrals in turn.

Consider $I = \int_0^\epsilon \mathfrak{s}(x) dx = \int_0^\epsilon x^{-\beta} \exp(2\kappa x / \alpha^2) dx$. Similarly to our discussion of $\int_0^\epsilon \mathfrak{m}(x) dx$ above, for x in $[0, \epsilon]$, $x^{-\beta} \leq \mathfrak{s}(x) \leq C x^{-\beta}$ for a suitably chosen constant $C = \exp(2\kappa \epsilon / \alpha^2)$. From elementary calculus we have $\int x^{-\beta} dx = x^{1-\beta} / (1 - \beta) + c$ for $\beta \neq 1$, and for $\beta = 1$, $\int x^{-\beta} dx = \ln x + c$. From this we see that $\int_0^\epsilon x^{-\beta} dx$ is infinite for $\beta \geq 1$, and therefore $\int_0^\epsilon \mathfrak{s}(x) dx = \infty$ if $\beta \geq 1$ also.

It remains only to show that $J = \int_0^\epsilon S(x) \mathfrak{m}(x) dx < \infty$ for $\beta \geq 1$. Put

$$J = \frac{2}{\alpha^2} \int_0^\epsilon x^{\beta-1} \exp(-2\kappa x / \alpha^2) \int_{x_0}^x y^{-\beta} \exp(2\kappa y / \alpha^2) dy \, dx.$$

We have $J \leq C \int_0^\epsilon x^{\beta-1} \int_{x_0}^x y^{-\beta} dy \, dx$ for a suitably chosen finite constant C. Clearly,

$$\int_{x_0}^x y^{-\beta} dy = \left[\frac{y^{1-\beta}}{1 - \beta} \right]_{x_0}^x = \frac{1}{1 - \beta} \left[x^{1-\beta} - x_0^{1-\beta} \right] \qquad \text{for } \beta > 1$$

and therefore we have

$$J \leq \frac{C}{1-\beta} \int_0^\epsilon x^{\beta-1} \left[x^{1-\beta} - x_0^{1-\beta} \right] dx = \frac{C}{1-\beta} \int_0^\epsilon \left(1 - x^{\beta-1} x_0^{1-\beta} \right) dx.$$

This integral is finite for $\beta > 1$.

In the $\beta = 1$ case, the special function $\mathrm{Ei}(x) = \int_{-\infty}^x (e^u/u)\, du$ is required. We have $J = (2/\alpha^2) \int_0^\epsilon \exp(-2\kappa x/\alpha^2) \int_{x_0}^x (1/y) \exp(2\kappa y/\alpha^2)\, dy\, dx$, and for brevity we assume that $2\kappa/\alpha^2 = 1$ (the proof of finiteness of J follows similarly for other values of κ and α subject to extra algebraic manipulations). We have

$$J = \frac{2}{\alpha^2} \int_0^\epsilon e^{-x} \int_{x_0}^x \frac{1}{y} e^y\, dy\, dx$$

$$= \frac{2}{\alpha^2} \int_0^\epsilon e^{-x} [\mathrm{Ei}(x) - \mathrm{Ei}(x_0)]\, dx,$$

which can be shown, potentially with the aid of symbolic algebra computational packages, to be finite.

Enter the expression 'Integrate[Ei[x] * Exp[−x], x,0,1' into Mathematica or www.wolframalpha.com to satisfy yourself that this is so.

Having demonstrated finiteness of J for $\beta \geq 1$, the proof is complete.

The Feller condition states that if initial variance v_0 is nonzero (which of course it will be for any realistic market with any measure of uncertainty), then if the ratio $2m\kappa/\alpha^2$ is greater than or equal to unity, the instantaneous variance v_t will always be nonzero with probability one. Conversely, if the Feller condition is *not* satisfied, then positive times exist for which there is a finite probability of variance v_t going to zero.

Note that for the Feller condition to be satisfied, both the mean reversion parameters m and κ must be nonzero, and simultaneously the vovariance α cannot be too large relative to the mean reversion parameters. The correlation ρ isn't part of the Feller condition, but in order to introduce a volatility skew, the vovariance needs to be large enough to allow the correlated part of $W_t^{(2)}$ to feed through into a volatility skew for X_t. Therefore, calibrating a Heston model to either a volatility skew or a volatility smile will require a positive vovariance α, and typical FX market conditions will require this parameter to be large enough that the Feller condition is often violated in practice.

A simple experiment shows this. Take a Heston model with an initial variance of 0.01 (corresponding to an initial volatility of 10 %) and increase the vovol α while simultanously decreasing the mean reversion parameters so that the Feller condition is satisfied. Price up a strip of European options, all with the same time to expiry T but different strikes, using Fourier inversion. Back out the implied vols and construct a graph of the volatility as a function of strike. Try as you may, you can only get so much convexity out of a Feller condition compliant Heston model.

It is therefore crucial that any numerical schemes we develop are able to deal with the violation of the Feller condition and the absorption of variance at the $v = 0$ boundary. This is discussed in the context of backward PDE schemes in Duffy (2006) and Heston's original paper, in the context of forward Fokker–Planck PDE schemes in Lucic (2008) and in Gatheral (2006) for Monte Carlo methods, where a reflecting boundary is required in the case where the Feller condition fails to be satisfied.

Note that we can transform process (6.4b) for variance v_t into a process for volatility $\sigma_t = \sqrt{v_t}$, as suggested by Zhu (2008), using Itô's lemma. While these exercises in stochastic calculus are easy, they show just how often practical applications of the Itô calculus arise in this business.

Put $f(x) = \sqrt{x}$, for which $f'(x) = \frac{1}{2}x^{-1/2}$ and $f''(x) = -\frac{1}{4}x^{-3/2}$. We then have $\sigma_t = \sqrt{v_t} = f(v_t)$, and can write

$$
\begin{aligned}
d\sigma_t = df(v_t) &= f'(v_t)dv_t + \frac{1}{2}f''(v_t)\,dv_t^2 \\
&= \frac{1}{2}v_t^{-1/2}\,dv_t - \frac{1}{8}v_t^{-3/2}\alpha^2 v_t\,dW_t^2 \\
&= \frac{1}{2}v_t^{-1/2}\left[\kappa(m-v_t)dt + \alpha v_t^{1/2}\,dW_t\right] - \frac{1}{8}v_t^{-3/2}\alpha^2 v_t\,dt \\
&= \frac{1}{2}\alpha\,dW_t + \left(\frac{\kappa m}{2\sigma_t} - \frac{\alpha^2}{8\sigma_t}\right)dt - \frac{1}{2}\kappa\sigma_t\,dt \\
&= \hat{\alpha}\,dW_t + \hat{\kappa}(\hat{m} - \sigma_t)dt
\end{aligned}
$$

with $\hat{\alpha} = \alpha$, $\hat{\kappa} = \kappa$ and $\hat{m} = (m - \alpha^2/4\kappa)/\sigma_t$.

As Zhu (2008) points out, this means that the Heston model for variance is equivalent to an Ornstein–Uhlenbeck process for volatility, but where the mean reversion level is nonstationary and state-dependent (depending on the level of σ_t). In order that the mean reversion level $\hat{m}$ for volatility be positive, we require $m - \alpha^2/4\kappa > 0$, i.e. $\beta = 2\kappa m/\alpha^2 > \frac{1}{2}$. Note that the Feller condition on the underlying Heston process is that $2\kappa m/\alpha^2 \geq 1$, so satisfaction of the Feller condition is sufficient but not necessary for positivity of the mean reversion level for σ_t.

For Monte Carlo simulation, as discussed in Chapter 7, it is possible to simulate numerically either the volatility σ_t as suggested by Zhu (2008) or the variance v_t, possibly using techniques such as recommended by Andersen (2007).

6.3.2   The Stein and Stein model

Stein and Stein (1991) proposed an Ornstein–Uhlenbeck model for mean reverting stochastic volatility, which Schöbel and Zhu (1999) extended to allow correlation between the driving Brownian motions. The model, expressed for FX applications, is

$$dS_t = (r^d - r^f)S_t\,dt + \sigma_t S_t\,dW_t^{(1)}, \tag{6.10a}$$

$$d\sigma_t = \kappa(m - \sigma_t)dt + \alpha\,dW_t^{(2)}, \tag{6.10b}$$

where $<dW_t^{(1)}, dW_t^{(2)}> = \rho\,dt$. This model is characterised by several constant parameters, given in Table 6.4.

Table 6.4   Parameters of the Stein and Stein model

Initial volatility	σ_0
Spot/volatility correlation	ρ
Vovol	α
Mean reversion rate	κ
Mean reversion level	m

Stein and Stein (1991) pointed out an interesting and somewhat undesirable feature of their model, that it allows volatilities to become negative – the same holds true, naturally, in the $\rho \neq 0$ case of Schöbel and Zhu (1999). What this means in practice is that (6.10a) can be written as

$$dS_t = (r^d - r^f)S_t\, dt + |\sigma_t| S_t\, dW_t^{(1)},$$

where $|\sigma_t|$ is driven by a Brownian motion that is positively correlated with $W_t^{(1)}$ for $\sigma_t > 0$ and negatively correlated with $W_t^{(1)}$ for $\sigma_t < 0$. So one has a reflecting volatility barrier at $\sigma_t = 0$, which can be given some economic justification, but with a flipping of correlation upon reflection that is harder to argue for. In the original paper by Stein and Stein (1991), as the correlation ρ was presumed zero, this reflecting barrier is just a straightforward reflection at $\sigma_t = 0$ without the unusual sign-change of correlation.

6.3.3 Longstaff's double square root model

This model was presented as a candidate stochastic volatility model in Zhu (2000), having been originally introduced by Longstaff (1989) for yield curve modelling. We have a process for variance, much like Heston, but where the drift term incorporates mean reversion in volatility and not variance:

$$dS_t = \mu_t S_t\, dt + \sqrt{v_t}\, S_t\, dW_t^{(1)}, \qquad (6.11a)$$

$$dv_t = \kappa(m - \sqrt{v_t})dt + \alpha\sqrt{v_t}\, dW_t^{(2)}, \qquad (6.11b)$$

with $< dW_t^{(1)}, dW_t^{(2)} > = \rho\, dt$. Transforming (6.11a) into logspot, we obtain

$$dX_t = \left(\mu_t - \frac{1}{2}v_t\right) dt + \sqrt{v_t}\, dW_t^{(1)} \qquad (6.11c)$$

The attentive reader will be able to see that this has exactly the same issue with variance absorption at the $v = 0$ boundary as the Heston model, the Feller condition being basically identical, for the same reasons as described in 'The Feller condition – method A' of Section 6.3.1. The required characteristic functions for European option pricing given this double square root model are derived in Zhu (2000), to which we refer the interested reader.

6.3.4 Scott's exponential Ornstein–Uhlenbeck model

Both the Heston and Stein and Stein models have a tendency to experience difficulties at very small levels of volatility or variance, as described above. This was recognised in Section II of Scott (1987); presumably motivated by this, the author presented a mean reverting model for $\ln \sigma_t$. In the context of FX option pricing, we have

$$dS_t = (r^d - r^f)S_t\, dt + \sigma_t S_t\, dW_t^{(1)} \qquad (6.12a)$$

$$d\ln \sigma_t = \kappa(m - \ln \sigma_t)\, dt + \alpha\, dW_t^{(2)} \qquad (6.12b)$$

where $< dW_t^{(1)}, dW_t^{(2)} > = \rho\, dt$. Equation (6.12b) can be straightforwardly transformed into a process for volatility σ_t by yet another application of the Itô calculus. Put $X_t = \ln \sigma_t$, i.e. $\sigma_t = f(X_t)$ with $f(x) = e^x$. Obviously $f''(x) = f'(x) = f(x) = e^x$ and (6.12b) is just

$$dX_t = \kappa(m - X_t)\, dt + \alpha\, dW_t^{(2)}.$$

Therefore,

$$
\begin{aligned}
d\sigma_t = df(X_t) &= f'(X_t)dX_t + \frac{1}{2}f''(X_t)dX_t \\
&= e^{X_t}\,dX_t + \frac{1}{2}e^{X_t}\,dX_t^2 \\
&= \sigma_t\left[\kappa(m - X_t)\,dt + \alpha\,dW_t^{(2)}\right] + \frac{1}{2}\sigma_t\alpha^2\,dt \\
&= \sigma_t\left[\kappa(m - \ln\sigma_t) + \frac{1}{2}\alpha^2\right]dt + \alpha\sigma_t\,dW_t^{(2)}.
\end{aligned}
$$

6.3.5 The SABR model

Hagan *et al.* (2002) presented a particular type of stochastic volatility model that has found widespread acceptance among market practitioners. The model they propose is one for stochastic evolution of the forward process $\hat{F}_t \equiv F_{t,T}$, as defined in (2.69):

$$
d\hat{F}_t = \sigma_t \hat{F}_t^{\beta}\,dW_t^{(1)}, \tag{6.13a}
$$

$$
d\sigma_t = \alpha\sigma_t\,dW_t^{(2)}, \tag{6.13b}
$$

where $<dW_t^{(1)}, dW_t^{(2)}> = \rho\,dt$. Note that the parameter β can be used to tune the model between normal ($\beta = 0$) and lognormal ($\beta = 1$) forward dynamics. For FX, the choice of $\beta = 1$ is common, and not unreasonably so.

Through an application of perturbation theory, similar to that described earlier in Section 5.8, they obtain

$$
\begin{aligned}
\sigma_X(K) = &\frac{\alpha}{(F_T K)^{(1-\beta)/2}\left\{1 + [(1-\beta)^2/24]\log^2(F_T/K) + [(1-\beta)^4/1920]\log^4(F_T/K)\right\}}\left(\frac{z}{\chi(z)}\right) \\
&\times\left\{1 + \left[\frac{(1-\beta)^2}{24}\frac{\alpha^2}{(F_T K)^{1-\beta}} + \frac{1}{4}\frac{\rho\beta\nu\alpha}{(F_T K)^{(1-\beta)/2}} + \frac{2-3\rho^2}{24}\nu^2\right]T\right\},
\end{aligned} \tag{6.14a}
$$

where

$$
z = \frac{\nu}{\alpha}(F_{0,T} K)^{(1-\beta)/2}\log(F_{0,T}/K) \tag{6.14b}
$$

and

$$
\chi(z) = \log\left\{\frac{\sqrt{1 - 2\rho z + z^2} + z - \rho}{1 - \rho}\right\}. \tag{6.14c}
$$

We merely quote the result here. Note, however, that (6.13) describes a full two-factor local-stochastic volatility[1] model of a particular type, and one can therefore price Europeans (and path-dependent exotics, potentially) using such a model directly, not employing the effective implied volatility $\sigma_X(K)$ from above, but instead using numerical methods such as described in Chapter 7. Indeed, doing so is an excellent way to test the validity of the SABR approximation.

---

[1] A pure stochastic volatility model in the $\beta = 1$ case.

6.4   UNCORRELATED STOCHASTIC VOLATILITY

The uncertain volatility and uncertain variance models in Section 6.2 admit no possibility of correlation between the volatility or variance and the asset price S_T at time T. Not co-incidentally, this means that these models can generate a simple volatility smile, but *cannot* generate a skew. While some authors claim that skews are endemic in other asset classes but that volatility smiles in FX tend to be symmetric, this is far from always the case (USD-JPY, EURJPY and AUDJPY in particular are always highly skewed, due to the market's perception that the Bank of Japan is likely to intervene in the markets to stop the yen appreciating to too high a level – i.e. if the spot rate for USDJPY declines substantially in pips terms). It is possible that for some currency pairs with relatively symmetric smiles, one could use a stochastic volatility model uncorrelated with spot and use a local volatility contribution (see Section 6.8 below) to pick up the small residual skew. This has the advantage that the calibration to Europeans would be effortless for even the most complex of stochastic volatility models, but the massive disadvantage that it would fail for skewed currency pairs.

In fact, exactly the same behaviour occurs even if we extend the model to allow either volatility or variance to be a time-varying stochastic process[2] so long as the Brownian motion driving the volatility or variance process is completely uncorrelated with that driving the tradeable asset.

This is discussed in Hull and White (1987), where the price of options under a particular class of stochastic volatility/variance models is related to the integral of Black–Scholes prices convolved with the probability distribution for effective variance (over the time interval of interest). This result holds equivalently for FX options or, equivalently, for equity derivatives paying a constant dividend yield.

Suppose the spot price process is modelled by

$$dS_t = \mu S_t \, dt + \sqrt{v_t} \, S_t \, dW_t^{(1)}, \tag{6.15a}$$

$$dv_t = \alpha(v_t, t)v_t \, dt + \xi(v_t, t)v_t \, dW_t^{(2)}, \tag{6.15b}$$

where $dW_t^{(1)}$ and $dW_t^{(2)}$ are uncorrelated. The drift and volatility of v_t can be basically arbitrary, subject to technical conditions such as boundedness, so long as they do not depend on the asset level S_t. So we're basically just saying that there *is* a stochastic process that describes instantaneous variance, though we don't need to know exactly what specific process it is for now.

If we construct the mean variance $\bar{v}$ over $[0, T]$ by

$$\bar{v} = \frac{1}{T} \int_0^T v_t \, dt, \tag{6.16}$$

then the distribution of S_T at time T conditional on variance $\bar{v}$ is lognormal, and the quantity $\log S_T / \log S_0$ is normally distributed with mean $\mu T - \frac{1}{2}\bar{v}T$ and variance $\bar{v}T$.

---

[2] As opposed to a multistate (possibly binomial) random distribution determined at the start of the option's lifetime and held constant until expiry.

As the Black–Scholes model lets us price options by taking the expectation of contingent claims assuming lognormal dynamics for S_t, we can split the expectation in the following manner:

$$V_0 = e^{-r^d T} \mathbf{E}^d \left[V_T(S_T) \Big| S_0, \{\sigma_t^2\}_{t=0}^T \right] \tag{6.17a}$$

$$= e^{-r^d T} \mathbf{E}^d \left[\int_0^\infty V_T(s) f_{S_T | S_0, \{\sigma_t^2\}_{t=0}^T}(s) \, ds \Big| \{\sigma_t^2\}_{t=0}^T \right], \tag{6.17b}$$

where the expectation in (6.17a) is over possible joint realisations of S_T and $\{\sigma_t^2\}_{t=0}^T$, while that in (6.17b) is merely over possible realisations of the variance process, as we have explicitly introduced the conditional probability distribution function $f_{S_T | S_0, \{\sigma_t^2\}_{t=0}^T}(s)$ into the expectation via an integral.

In fact, as the two Brownian motions in (6.15) are uncorrelated, it suffices to condition over just the mean $\bar{v}$ of the instantaneous variance over $[0, T]$, because variance is additive when integrated in (6.15a). This means we can write

$$V_0 = e^{-r^d T} \mathbf{E}^d \left[\int_0^\infty V_T(s) f_{S_T | S_0, \bar{v}}(s) \, ds \Big| \bar{v} \right]$$

$$= e^{-r^d T} \int_0^\infty \int_0^\infty V_T(s) \, f_{S_T | S_0, \sigma^2 = v}(s) \, ds \, f_{\bar{v}}(v) \, dv$$

$$= \int_0^\infty V_0^{BS} \big|_{\sigma^2 = v} \cdot f_{\bar{v}}(v) \, dv. \tag{6.18}$$

Equation (6.18) tells us that, in the absence of correlation between Brownian motions driving spot and variance, we can obtain stochastic volatility prices for options expiring at time T by integrating the convolution of the Black–Scholes prices conditioned on variance, with the probability density function for mean variance over $[0, T]$.

Using this technique, one can generate Black–Scholes prices for a variety of possible scenarios for mean variance over $[0, T]$ and take the expectation of these prices, given the distribution of the mean variance. In the case where the distribution of the mean variance collapses to two discrete states, each with equal probability, this is equivalent to the method of Section 6.2.

Just as in Section 6.2, this approach is incapable of generating skews. For that, we need to allow the Brownian motions $dW_t^{(1)}$ and $dW_t^{(2)}$ to be correlated.

6.5 STOCHASTIC VOLATILITY CORRELATED WITH SPOT

We generalise (6.15) to

$$dS_t = \mu S_t \, dt + \sqrt{v_t} \, S_t \, dW_t^{(1)}, \tag{6.19a}$$

$$dv_t = \alpha(v_t, t) v_t \, dt + \xi(v_t, t) v_t \, dW_t^{(2)}, \tag{6.19b}$$

with $\langle dW_t^{(1)}, dW_t^{(2)} \rangle = \rho \, dt$, in order to introduce the correlation ρ between spot and stochastic variance. Equivalently, stochastic volatility, as a process σ_t for volatility can be straightforwardly transformed into an equivalent process for variance v_t by simple application of Itô's lemma to $f(x) = x^2$.

Unfortunately, obtaining a closed-form solution for the probability density function $f_{S_T}(s)$ for the spot price S_T at time T, or $f_{X_T}(x)$ for logspot X_T, is not possible in the general case where $\rho \neq 0$. However, the Fourier methods of Section 2.15 are applicable, and we present them here.

The key point is that while we cannot compute the probability density function $f_{X_T}(x)$ in the case of correlated stochastic volatility, we *can* compute the characteristic function. Going back to the definition (2.98), we have $\hat{f}_{X_T}^{d;f}(\phi) = \mathbf{E}^{d;f}\left[e^{i\phi X_T}\right] = \int_{-\infty}^{\infty} e^{i\phi x} f_{X_T}^{d;f}(x)\,dx$.

Following Section 2.2.2 of Zhu (2000), we attempt to compute

$$\hat{f}_{X_T}^{d}(\phi) = \mathbf{E}^{d}\left[e^{i\phi X_T}\right],\tag{6.20a}$$

$$\hat{f}_{X_T}^{f}(\phi) = e^{(r^f - r^d)T}\mathbf{E}^{d}\left[\frac{S_T}{S_0}e^{i\phi X_T}\right] = e^{(r^f - r^d)T}e^{-X_0}\mathbf{E}^{d}\left[e^{(i\phi+1)X_T}\right],\tag{6.20b}$$

both of which require computation of $\mathbf{E}^{d}\left[e^{(i\phi+j)X_T}\right]$, for $j \in \{0, 1\}$.

Consider by way of example the Heston model (6.4):

$$dS_t = \mu S_t\,dt + \sqrt{v_t}\,S_t\,dW_t^{(1)},\tag{6.21}$$

$$dv_t = \kappa(m - v_t)dt + \alpha\sqrt{v_t}\,dW_t^{(2)},\tag{6.22}$$

with $< dW_t^{(1)},\ dW_t^{(2)} > = \rho\,dt$. The logspot process follows (6.4c):

$$dX_t = \left(\mu - \frac{1}{2}v_t\right)dt + \sqrt{v_t}\,dW_t^{(1)}$$

and can be directly integrated to give

$$X_T = X_0 + \mu T - \frac{1}{2}\int_0^T v_t\,dt + \int_0^T \sqrt{v_t}\,dW_t^{(1)}.\tag{6.23}$$

Substituting (6.23) into $\mathbf{E}^{d}\left[e^{(i\phi+j)X_T}\right]$, we obtain

$$\mathbf{E}^{d}\left[e^{(i\phi+j)X_T}\right] = e^{(i\phi+j)(X_0+\mu T)}\mathbf{E}^{d}\left[\exp\left(-\frac{1}{2}\int_0^T v_t\,dt + \int_0^T \sqrt{v_t}\,dW_t^{(1)}\right)\right].$$

We obtain

$$\hat{f}_{X_T}^{d;f}(\phi) = e^{i\phi(X_0+\mu T)}\mathbf{E}^{d}\left[\exp\left\{(i\phi+j)\left(-\frac{1}{2}\int_0^T v_t\,dt + \int_0^T \sqrt{v_t}\,dW_t^{(1)}\right)\right\}\right],\tag{6.24}$$

where $j = 0$ corresponds to $\hat{f}_{X_T}^{d}(\phi)$ and $j = 1$ corresponds to $\hat{f}_{X_T}^{f}(\phi)$. We can apply Cholesky decomposition, writing

$$dW_t^{(1)} = \rho\,dW_t^{(2)} + \bar{\rho}\,dW_t^{(\sim 2)}$$

with $\bar{\rho} = \sqrt{1-\rho^2}$ and where $W_t^{(2)}$ and $W_t^{(\sim 2)}$ are independent Brownian motions. This reduces the expectation in (6.24) to

$$\mathbf{E}^{d}\left[\exp\left\{(i\phi+j)\left(-\frac{1}{2}\int_0^T v_t\,dt + \rho\int_0^T \sqrt{v_t}\,dW_t^{(2)} + \bar{\rho}\int_0^T \sqrt{v_t}\,dW_t^{(\sim 2)}\right)\right\}\right].\tag{6.25}$$

This can be simplified by use of the Girsanov change of measure techniques. We have

$$
\frac{\hat{f}_{X_T}^{d;f}(\phi)}{e^{i\phi(X_0+\mu T)}} = \mathbf{E}^d\left[e^{(i\phi+j)\left(-\frac{1}{2}\int_0^T v_t\,dt + \rho\int_0^T \sqrt{v_t}\,dW_t^{(2)} + \bar{\rho}\int_0^T \sqrt{v_t}\,dW_t^{(\sim 2)}\right)}\right]
$$

$$
= \mathbf{E}^d\left[e^{\int_0^T (i\phi+j)\bar{\rho}\sqrt{v_t}\,dW_t^{(\sim 2)}}\,e^{(i\phi+j)\left(-\frac{1}{2}\int_0^T v_t\,dt + \rho\int_0^T \sqrt{v_t}\,dW_t^{(2)}\right)}\right].
$$

If we could identify the term $e^{\int_0^T (i\phi+j)\bar{\rho}\sqrt{v_t}\,dW_t^{(\sim 2)}}$ as a Radon–Nikodym derivative, then we could transform this using the standard change of measure machinery. In fact this is not too hard. A Radon–Nikodym derivative is of the form

$$
\frac{d\mathbf{P}^{d*}}{d\mathbf{P}^d} = \exp\left(\int_0^T \lambda_t\,dW_t^{(\sim 2)} - \frac{1}{2}\int_0^T \lambda_t^2\,dt\right), \tag{6.26}
$$

so we put $\lambda_t = (i\phi+j)\bar{\rho}\sqrt{v_t}$. With this, we have

$$
\frac{\hat{f}_{X_T}^{d;f}(\phi)}{e^{i\phi(X_0+\mu T)}} = \mathbf{E}^d\left[e^{\int_0^T \lambda_t\,dW_t^{(\sim 2)} - \frac{1}{2}\int_0^T \lambda_t^2\,dt}\,e^{\frac{1}{2}\int_0^T \lambda_t^2\,dt}\,e^{(i\phi+j)\left(-\frac{1}{2}\int_0^T v_t\,dt + \rho\int_0^T \sqrt{v_t}\,dW_t^{(2)}\right)}\right]
$$

$$
= \mathbf{E}^d\left[\frac{d\mathbf{P}^{d*}}{d\mathbf{P}^d}\,e^{\frac{1}{2}\int_0^T \lambda_t^2\,dt}\,e^{(i\phi+j)\left(-\frac{1}{2}\int_0^T v_t\,dt + \rho\int_0^T \sqrt{v_t}\,dW_t^{(2)}\right)}\right]
$$

$$
= \mathbf{E}^{d*}\left[e^{\frac{1}{2}\int_0^T \lambda_t^2\,dt}\,e^{(i\phi+j)\left(-\frac{1}{2}\int_0^T v_t\,dt + \rho\int_0^T \sqrt{v_t}\,dW_t^{(2)}\right)}\right]
$$

$$
= \mathbf{E}^d\left[e^{[\frac{1}{2}(i\phi+j)^2\bar{\rho}^2 - \frac{1}{2}(i\phi+j)]\int_0^T v_t\,dt}\,e^{\rho(i\phi+j)\int_0^T \sqrt{v_t}\,dW_t^{(2)}}\right].
$$

Integrating the Heston process gives

$$
v_T = v_0 + \kappa m T - \kappa\int_0^T v_t\,dt + \alpha\int_0^T \sqrt{v_t}\,dW_t^{(2)},
$$

from which we have

$$
\int_0^T \sqrt{v_t}\,dW_t^{(2)} = \frac{v_T - v_0 - \kappa m T}{\alpha} + \frac{\kappa}{\alpha}\int_0^T v_t\,dt.
$$

Using this, we have

$$
\frac{\hat{f}_{X_T}^{d;f}(\phi)}{e^{i\phi(X_0+\mu T)}} = \mathbf{E}^{d*}\left[e^{[\frac{1}{2}(i\phi+j)^2\bar{\rho}^2 - \frac{1}{2}(i\phi+j)+\rho\kappa/\alpha]\int_0^T v_t\,dt}\,e^{\rho(i\phi+j)(v_T - v_0 - \kappa m T)\alpha}\right].
$$

By suitably defining terms $s_1^{(j)}$ and $s_2^{(j)}$ we have

$$
\hat{f}_{X_T}^{d;f}(\phi) = e^{i\phi(X_0+\mu T)}\exp\left(-(v_0 + \kappa m T)s_2^{(j)}\right)\mathbf{E}^d\left[\exp\left(-s_1^{(j)}\int_0^T v_t\,dt + s_2^{(j)}v_T\right)\right], \tag{6.27}
$$

following the notation of Zhu (2000), in which

$$
s_1^{(j)} = -(i\phi+j)\left(-\frac{1}{2} + \frac{\rho\kappa}{\alpha} + \frac{1}{2}(i\phi+j)(1-\rho^2)\right), \tag{6.28a}
$$

$$
s_2^{(j)} = (i\phi+j)\rho/\alpha. \tag{6.28b}
$$

The expectation in (6.27) is calculated in Zhu (2000), where the author obtains

$$\hat{f}_{X_T}^{d;f}(\phi) = \exp\left(i\phi[X_0 + \mu T] - (v_0 + \kappa m T)s_2^{(j)}\right)\exp\left(A^{(j)}v_0 + C^{(j)}\right),\qquad(6.29)$$

where

$$\gamma_1^{(j)} = \sqrt{\kappa^2 + 2\alpha^2 s_1^{(j)}},\qquad(6.30a)$$

$$\gamma_2^{(j)} = 2\gamma_1^{(j)}e^{-\gamma_1^{(j)}T} + \left(\kappa + \gamma_1^{(j)} - \alpha^2 s_2^{(j)}\right)\left(1 - e^{-\gamma_1^{(j)}T}\right),\qquad(6.30b)$$

$$A^{(j)} = \left[\gamma_1^{(j)}s_2^{(j)}\left(1 + e^{-\gamma_1^{(j)}T}\right) - \left(1 - e^{-\gamma_1^{(j)}T}\right)\left(2s_1^{(j)} + \kappa s_2^{(j)}\right)\right]\bigg/\gamma_2^{(j)},\qquad(6.30c)$$

$$C^{(j)} = \frac{2\kappa m}{\alpha^2}\ln\left[2\gamma_1^{(j)}\exp\left(\frac{1}{2}(\kappa - \gamma_1^{(j)})T\right)\bigg/\gamma_2^{(j)}\right].\qquad(6.30d)$$

Analysis of the characteristic function approach for other stochastic models, such as the Schöbel and Zhu (1999) adaptation of Stein and Stein (1991) to allow nonzero correlation between spot and volatility, and a double square root process for stochastic volatility, can be found in Zhu (2000). As Zhu (2000) states, only a subset of possible stochastic volatility models permits such closed-form semi-analytic option pricing formulae (for European style options) in the case of nonzero correlation between the driving factor $X_t^{(2)}$ for stochastic volatility and logspot $X_t^{(1)}$ – this subset includes models such as the Stein and Stein (1991)/Schöbel and Zhu (1999) and Heston (1993) models. This is probably one good reason why these particular models are popular with practitioners.

Whether the actual stochastic volatility model chosen admits solution using the characteristic function technique or not, all stochastic volatility models with the same attributes such as vovol/vovariance (where 'vovariance' is a commonly used abbreviation for volatility of variance) and spot/vol correlation typically are capable of generating much the same types of volatility surfaces, as discussed in the asymptotic analysis appearing in Chapter 7 of Gatheral (2006). There is therefore no real advantage in using a more complex SV model than necessary, unless there are technical advantages in doing so. Consequently, we use the Heston model as our main example in this discussion of stochastic volatility, in spite of its shortcomings. Extensions to other stochastic volatility models are possible, though not always straightforward.

The method described in this section can be used to price European options given a Heston model with a particular choice of level/skew/boost parameter $\{v_0, \rho, \alpha\}$, requiring only a fast one-dimensional numerical integration. It is fast enough that this pricing method can be embedded within a stochastic volatility calibration routine that varies these decision variables $\{v_0, \rho, \alpha\}$ until a suitably close fit to the implied volatility smile is found, using a suitably chosen objective function. More will be given on this in Chapter 7.

6.6   THE FOKKER–PLANCK PDE APPROACH

While for some candidate stochastic volatility models we have a semi-closed form solution for European option prices obtained using characteristic functions and Fourier integration, there is another approach we can use. It relies upon numerical solution of the forward Fokker–Planck equation, from which we can obtain a marginal probability density function at time T for either spot S_T or logspot X_T. We can solve this on a two-dimensional PDE and use it to compute the value of the European option today, using numerican integration and the domestic discount factor applicable between $t = 0$ and T.

The critical reader will ask: Why go to this trouble, if we can directly obtain European option prices using Fourier techniques? The answer is that the forward Fokker–Planck approach can be adapted to a forward induction approach, used to infer the required local volatility contribution for a mixed local-stochastic volatility model. In order to do so, we will want to be sure that the marginal probability densities coming out from numerical solution of the two-dimensional Fokker–Planck PDE are accurate.

By implementing a numerical solution of the Fokker–Planck equation first, and cross-checking it against the European prices obtained using Fourier methods, one can check that this component is reliable, before building a full LSV calibration engine around it.

We limit ourselves to the common example of the Heston model in this section, though the approach can be applied to any two-dimensional stochastic volatility model by adapting the drift and volatility terms appropriately.

Let $p(X_t, v_t, t)$ denote the transition probability of having logspot X_t and instantaneous variance v_t at time t, conditional on logspot X_0 and variance v_0 at time $t = 0$. Drăgulescu and Yakovenko (2002) quote the forward Fokker–Planck equation for the Heston model in the absence of interest rates:

$$\frac{\partial p}{\partial t} = \kappa \frac{\partial[(v-m)p]}{\partial v} + \frac{1}{2}\frac{\partial[vp]}{\partial X} + \rho\alpha\frac{\partial^2[vp]}{\partial X \partial v} + \frac{1}{2}\frac{\partial^2[vp]}{\partial X^2} + \frac{\alpha^2}{2}\frac{\partial^2[vp]}{\partial v^2}. \tag{6.31}$$

For completeness and rigour, we derive here the above equation using the FPE from Section 5.2.2. Let $\mathbf{X}_t = \left(X_t^{(1)}, X_t^{(2)}\right)$ with $X_t^{(1)} = X_t$, i.e. logspot, and $X_t^{(2)} = v_t$, i.e. instantaneous variance. The drift vector and volatility matrix terms from (6.3) for the case of the Heston model, all being trivariate functions of $(X_t^{(1)}, X_t^{(2)}, t)$, are given (for consistency with Section 5.2.2, we put $a_i = \mu^{(i)}$ and $B_{ij} = \sigma^{(ij)}$) by

$$a_1 = \mu^d - \frac{1}{2}X^{(2)}, \qquad a_2 = -\kappa(X^{(2)} - m), \tag{6.32a}$$

$$B_{11} = \sqrt{X^{(2)}}, \qquad B_{12} = 0, \qquad B_{21} = \rho\alpha\sqrt{X^{(2)}}, \qquad B_{22} = \bar{\rho}\alpha\sqrt{X^{(2)}}. \tag{6.32b}$$

The two-dimensional Fokker–Planck equation (5.19) can be written

$$\frac{\partial p}{\partial t} = -\frac{\partial[a_1 p]}{\partial x_1} - \frac{\partial[a_2 p]}{\partial x_2} + \frac{1}{2}\frac{\partial^2[(B_{11}^2 + B_{12}^2)p]}{\partial x_1^2}$$

$$+ \frac{1}{2}\frac{\partial^2[(B_{11}B_{21} + B_{12}B_{22})p]}{\partial x_1 \partial x_2} + \frac{1}{2}\frac{\partial^2[(B_{21}^2 + B_{22}^2)p]}{\partial x_2^2}. \tag{6.33}$$

Substituting terms (6.32) into (6.33), we get

$$\frac{\partial p}{\partial t} = \left(\frac{1}{2}v - \mu^d\right)\frac{\partial p}{\partial X} + \kappa\frac{\partial[(v-m)p]}{\partial v} + \frac{1}{2}v\frac{\partial^2 p}{\partial X^2} + \rho\alpha\frac{\partial^2[vp]}{\partial X \partial v} + \frac{1}{2}\alpha^2\frac{\partial^2[vp]}{\partial v^2},$$

which reduces to (6.31) in the special case where $\mu^d = 0$. We can simplify this further, obtaining

$$
\frac{\partial p}{\partial t} = \frac{1}{2}v\frac{\partial^2 p}{\partial X^2} + \rho\alpha v\frac{\partial^2 p}{\partial X \partial v} + \frac{1}{2}\alpha^2 v\frac{\partial^2 p}{\partial v^2}
$$

$$
+ \left(\frac{1}{2}v - \mu^d + \rho\alpha\right)\frac{\partial p}{\partial X} + \left(\kappa[v-m] + \alpha^2\right)\frac{\partial p}{\partial v} + \kappa p. \tag{6.34}
$$

The equation above is a forward partial differential equation describing the time evolution of transition probabilities, not the backward evolution of value such as the Black–Scholes equation. In order to price path-dependent securities, we need the Heston PDE.

6.7   THE FEYNMAN–KAC PDE APPROACH

In Section 2.6, we noted that the discounted risk-neutral expectation of the value of a contingent claim could be computed as the solution of a backward partial differential equation. The same applies in higher dimensions, where we have a combination of tradeable stochastic factors such as the FX spot rate S_t and untradeable stochastic factors such as the instantaneous variance v_t.

In the same manner as the Black–Scholes equation, we can derive a pricing PDE for the value of a contingent claim, but with two stochastic factors, corresponding to the FX spot rate S and the instantaneous variance v. We can write the drift and volatility terms for a stochastic variance process in a generic fashion. Suppose the dynamical equations are

$$
dS_t = (r^d - r^f)S_t\, dt + \sqrt{v_t}\, S_t\, dW_t^{(1)}, \tag{6.35a}
$$

$$
dv_t = a(v_t)dt + b(v_t)dW_t^{(2)}, \tag{6.35b}
$$

where $\langle dW_t^{(1)}, dW_t^{(2)}\rangle = \rho\, dt$.

The argument mirrors that of Section 2.3.2, but where the riskless portfolio Π_t needs to be instantaneously delta hedged *and* vega hedged, using an open FX position to hedge the delta (collecting interest at the foreign interest rate r^f) and a traded option, denoted V^H, which we presume is available in the traded markets to hedge the vega.

Similarly to (2.12), we now have

$$
\Pi_t = V_t - \Delta_t S_t B_t^f - \mathcal{V}_t V_t^H(S_t, v_t), \tag{6.36}
$$

where the value V_t^H of the vega hedge instrument crucially depends on the spot rate S_t, time t *and* the untradeable variance v_t. For brevity, we shall omit the arguments and just use V_t^H in the algebra to follow.

Similarly to Section 2.3.2, put

$$
d\Pi_t = dV_t - \Delta_t\, d(S_t B_t^f) - \mathcal{V}_t dV_t^H(S_t, v_t).
$$

It will be useful to put $V_t^* = V_t - \mathcal{V}_t V_t^H$ for much of this section.[3] With this, we have

$$
d\Pi_t = dV_t^* - \Delta_t\, d(S_t B_t^f)
$$

---

[3] My apologies for all the V's. Recall that upper case V denotes value, lower case v denotes variance and the cursive $\mathcal{V}$ is used to denote vega.

and, as in Section 2.3.2, we obtain

$$d\Pi_t = dV_t^* - \Delta_t B_t^f \left[r^d S_t \, dt + \sqrt{v_t} \, S_t \, dW_t^{(1)} \right]. \tag{6.37}$$

Applying Itô's lemma to dV_t^*, we obtain

$$dV_t^* = \frac{\partial V^*}{\partial t} dt + \frac{\partial V^*}{\partial S} \left[(r^d - r^f) S_t \, dt + \sqrt{v_t} \, S_t \, dW_t^{(1)} \right] + \frac{\partial V^*}{\partial v} \left[a(v_t) dt + b(v_t) dW_t^{(2)} \right]$$

$$+ \frac{1}{2} \frac{\partial^2 V^*}{\partial S^2} dS_t^2 + \frac{1}{2} \frac{\partial^2 V^*}{\partial v^2} dv_t^2 + \frac{\partial^2 V^*}{\partial S \partial v} dS_t \, dv_t. \tag{6.38}$$

From (6.35) we have

$$dS_t^2 = v_t S_t^2 \, dt, \qquad dv_t^2 = b^2(v_t) dt, \qquad dS_t \, dv_t = \rho \sqrt{v_t} \, S_t b(v_t) dt, \tag{6.39}$$

which we use to write (6.38) as

$$dV_t^* = \left[\frac{\partial V^*}{\partial t} + \frac{1}{2} v_t S_t^2 \frac{\partial^2 V^*}{\partial S^2} + \frac{1}{2} b^2(v_t) \frac{\partial^2 V^*}{\partial v^2} + \rho \sqrt{v_t} \, S_t b(v_t) \frac{\partial^2 V^*}{\partial S \partial v} \right] dt$$

$$+ \frac{\partial V^*}{\partial S} dS_t + \frac{\partial V^*}{\partial v} dv_t. \tag{6.40}$$

From (6.37), we have

$$d\Pi_t = \left[\frac{\partial V^*}{\partial t} + \frac{1}{2} v_t S_t^2 \frac{\partial^2 V^*}{\partial S^2} + \frac{1}{2} b^2(v_t) \frac{\partial^2 V^*}{\partial v^2} + \rho \sqrt{v_t} \, S_t b(v_t) \frac{\partial^2 V^*}{\partial S \partial v} \right] dt$$

$$+ \frac{\partial V^*}{\partial S} dS_t + \frac{\partial V^*}{\partial v} dv_t - \Delta_t B_t^f \left[r^d S_t \, dt + \sqrt{v_t} \, S_t \, dW_t^{(1)} \right]. \tag{6.41}$$

Substituting in dS_t and dv_t from (6.35), this becomes

$$d\Pi_t = \left[\frac{\partial V^*}{\partial t} + \frac{1}{2} v_t S_t^2 \frac{\partial^2 V^*}{\partial S^2} + \frac{1}{2} b^2(v_t) \frac{\partial^2 V^*}{\partial v^2} + \rho \sqrt{v_t} \, S_t b(v_t) \frac{\partial^2 V^*}{\partial S \partial v} \right] dt$$

$$+ \left[(r^d - r^f) S_t \, dt + \sqrt{v_t} \, S_t \, dW_t^{(1)} \right] \frac{\partial V^*}{\partial S} + \left[a(v_t) dt + b(v_t) dW_t^{(2)} \right] \frac{\partial V^*}{\partial v}$$

$$- \Delta_t B_t^f \left[r^d S_t \, dt + \sqrt{v_t} \, S_t \, dW_t^{(1)} \right], \tag{6.42}$$

i.e.

$$d\Pi_t = \left[\frac{\partial V^*}{\partial t} + \frac{1}{2} v_t S_t^2 \frac{\partial^2 V^*}{\partial S^2} + \frac{1}{2} b^2(v_t) \frac{\partial^2 V^*}{\partial v^2} + \rho \sqrt{v_t} \, S_t b(v_t) \frac{\partial^2 V^*}{\partial S \partial v} \right.$$

$$\left. + (r^d - r^f) S_t \frac{\partial V^*}{\partial S} + a(v_t) \frac{\partial V^*}{\partial v} - \Delta_t B_t^f r^d S_t \right] dt$$

$$+ \left[\sqrt{v_t} \, S_t \frac{\partial V^*}{\partial S} - \Delta_t B_t^f \sqrt{v_t} \, S_t \right] dW_t^{(1)} + b(v_t) \frac{\partial V^*}{\partial v} dW_t^{(2)}. \tag{6.43}$$

As in Section 2.3.2, we find hedge parameters Δ_t and $\mathcal{V}_t$ which render the portfolio Π_t riskless, i.e. which make the coefficients of the $dW_t^{(1)}$ and $dW_t^{(2)}$ terms above vanish.

We require

$$\frac{\partial V^*}{\partial v} = \frac{\partial [V - \mathcal{V}_t V^H]}{\partial v} = 0,$$

from which we obtain

$$\mathcal{V}_t = \frac{\partial V}{\partial v} \Big/ \frac{\partial V^H}{\partial v}. \tag{6.44}$$

Similarly, setting $\sqrt{v_t}\, S_t(\partial V^*/\partial S) - \Delta_t B_t^f \sqrt{v_t}\, S_t$ to zero by choosing Δ_t appropriately is achieved by requiring

$$\Delta_t = \frac{1}{B_t^f}\frac{\partial V^*}{\partial S}.$$

Given such values of Δ_t and $\mathcal{V}_t$, which give an instantaneously risk-free portfolio Π_t, (6.43) reduces to

$$d\Pi_t = \left[\frac{\partial V^*}{\partial t} + \frac{1}{2}v_t S_t^2\frac{\partial^2 V^*}{\partial S^2} + \frac{1}{2}b^2(v_t)\frac{\partial^2 V^*}{\partial v^2} + \rho\sqrt{v_t}\, S_t b(v_t)\frac{\partial^2 V^*}{\partial S\,\partial v}\right.$$
$$\left. + (r^d - r^f)S_t\frac{\partial V^*}{\partial S} + a(v_t)\frac{\partial V^*}{\partial v} - \Delta_t B_t^f r^d S_t\right] dt. \tag{6.45}$$

Since riskless, this must appreciate at the (domestic) risk-free rate, i.e. $d\Pi_t = r^d \Pi_t\, dt = r^d[V_t^* - \Delta_t S_t B_t^f]\, dt$, and therefore we have

$$\frac{\partial V^*}{\partial t} + \frac{1}{2}v S_t^2\frac{\partial^2 V^*}{\partial S^2} + \frac{1}{2}b^2(v)\frac{\partial^2 V^*}{\partial v^2} + \rho\sqrt{v}\, Sb(v)\frac{\partial^2 V^*}{\partial S\,\partial v} + (r^d - r^f)S\frac{\partial V^*}{\partial S}$$
$$+ a(v)\frac{\partial V^*}{\partial v} - \Delta_t B_t^f r^d S = r^d\left[V^* - \Delta_t S B_t^f\right]. \tag{6.46}$$

Note that the $r^d \Delta_t S B_t^f$ terms drop out of both sides, leaving

$$\frac{\partial V^*}{\partial t} + \frac{1}{2}v S^2\frac{\partial^2 V^*}{\partial S^2} + \frac{1}{2}b^2(v)\frac{\partial^2 V^*}{\partial v^2} + \rho\sqrt{v}\, Sb(v)\frac{\partial^2 V^*}{\partial S\,\partial v}$$
$$+ (r^d - r^f)S\frac{\partial V^*}{\partial S} + a(v)\frac{\partial V^*}{\partial v} = r^d V^*, \tag{6.47}$$

which we can express in shorthand form as $\mathcal{L}V^* = 0$ using a differential operator $\mathcal{L}$ defined by

$$\mathcal{L} = \frac{\partial}{\partial t} + \frac{1}{2}v S^2\frac{\partial^2}{\partial S^2} + \frac{1}{2}b^2(v)\frac{\partial^2}{\partial v^2} + \rho\sqrt{v}\, Sb(v)\frac{\partial^2}{\partial S\,\partial v} + (r^d - r^f)S\frac{\partial}{\partial S} + a(v)\frac{\partial}{\partial v} - r^d\mathbf{1}.$$

We're almost done. All that is needed now is to use (6.44) to write $\mathcal{L}V^* = 0$ as $\mathcal{L}V = \mathcal{V}_t\mathcal{L}V^H$, and since $\mathcal{V}_t = (\partial V/\partial v)/(\partial V^H/\partial v)$ by (6.44), this is nothing more than

$$\mathcal{L}V = \frac{\partial V/\partial v}{\partial V^H/\partial v}\mathcal{L}V^H,$$

i.e.

$$\frac{\mathcal{L}V}{\partial V/\partial v} = \frac{\mathcal{L}V^H}{\partial V^H/\partial v}. \tag{6.48}$$

Just as in the technique of separation of variables, this means that both the left-hand side and the right-hand side of (6.48) must be equal, and the value they both equate to can be denoted by a function $\lambda(S, v, t)$, which can be thought of as the market price of volatility risk. This gives

$$\frac{\mathcal{L}V}{\partial V/\partial v} = \lambda(S, v, t),$$

which means we can write the partial differential equation $\mathcal{L}V = \lambda(S, v, t)\partial V/\partial v$, expressed purely in terms of $V(S, v, t)$ and its partial derivatives, obtaining the two-dimensional pricing PDE for a derivative security under a general stochastic variance model with drift $a(\cdot)$ and volatility of variance $b(\cdot)$:

$$\frac{\partial V}{\partial t} + \frac{1}{2}vS^2\frac{\partial^2 V}{\partial S^2} + \frac{1}{2}b^2(v)\frac{\partial^2 V}{\partial v^2} + \rho\sqrt{v}\,Sb(v)\frac{\partial^2 V}{\partial S\,\partial v}$$
$$+ (r^d - r^f)S_t\frac{\partial V}{\partial S} + [a(v) - \lambda(S, v, t)]\frac{\partial V}{\partial v} - r^d V = 0. \tag{6.49}$$

6.7.1 Heston model – example

Given (6.4b) for variance, we have $a(v) = \kappa(m - v)$ and $b(v) = \alpha\sqrt{v}$. Substituting these into (6.49), we have

$$\frac{\partial V}{\partial t} + \frac{1}{2}vS^2\frac{\partial^2 V}{\partial S^2} + \frac{1}{2}\alpha^2 v\frac{\partial^2 V}{\partial v^2} + \alpha\rho v S\frac{\partial^2 V}{\partial S\,\partial v}$$
$$+ (r^d - r^f)S\frac{\partial V}{\partial S} + [\kappa(m - v) - \lambda(S, v, t)]\frac{\partial V}{\partial v} - r^d V = 0. \tag{6.50}$$

Equation (6.50) is easily seen to be identical to equation (6) in Heston (1993) in the case where $r^f = 0$, as required.

Treatment of the boundary conditions for (6.50) is subtle – it is standard to assume that at the $v = 0$ boundary, one merely sets $v = 0$, obtaining

$$\frac{\partial V}{\partial t}\Big|_{v=0} + (r^d - r^f)S\frac{\partial V}{\partial S}\Big|_{v=0} + [\kappa m - \lambda(S, 0, t)]\frac{\partial V}{\partial v}\Big|_{v=0} - r^d V\big|_{v=0} = 0. \tag{6.51}$$

If discretised on a compact configuration space, e.g. $[S_{\min}, S_{\max}] \times [0, V_{\max}]$, such as is required for finite difference methods, then it is usual to require second derivatives normal to the boundary to vanish *on* the boundary.

6.7.2   Heston model – logspot coordinates

As in the Black–Scholes example, the diffusion and convection terms are less inhomogeneous if we use $x = \ln S$ rather than S as one of the independent variables for the PDE. With this, we have

$$\frac{\partial V}{\partial t} + \frac{1}{2}v\frac{\partial^2 V}{\partial x^2} + \frac{1}{2}\alpha^2 v\frac{\partial^2 V}{\partial v^2} + \alpha\rho v\frac{\partial^2 V}{\partial x\partial v}$$

$$+ \left(r^d - r^f - \frac{1}{2}v\right)\frac{\partial V}{\partial x} + \left[\kappa(m-v) - \lambda(x,v,t)\right]\frac{\partial V}{\partial v} - r^d V = 0. \tag{6.52}$$

6.8   LOCAL STOCHASTIC VOLATILITY (LSV) MODELS

In practice, stochastic volatility models are rarely used by themselves. The primary reason for this is that a purely stochastic volatility model generates the same smile irrespective of the initial level of spot, and therefore is a 'sticky-delta' model – the smile stays anchored at points corresponding to the specified deltas. In contrast, a local volatility model parameterised by a local volatility function $\sigma_{loc}(S_t, t)$ clearly depends on the spot level S_t (and its initial level S_0), and is therefore 'sticky-strike'. Neither of these describe what actually happens in FX markets; the reality is somewhere between the two. As a result, it is commonplace to take a model that allows some of the smile to come from stochastic volatility and some to come from a local volatility contribution.

Early work in this area is introduced by Jex et al. (1999), in which a Heston-type model is used together with a multiplicative state-dependent local volatility correction $A(S_t, t)$:

$$dS_t = \left(r_t^d - r_t^f\right)S_t\, dt + \sqrt{v_t}A(S_t, t)S_t\, dW_t^{(1)}, \tag{6.53a}$$

$$dv_t = \kappa(m - v_t)dt + \alpha\sqrt{v_t}\, dW_t^{(2)}, \tag{6.53b}$$

where $<dW_t^{(1)}, dW_t^{(2)}> = \rho\, dt$.

An even more general form of local-stochastic volatility model including jumps (the JLSV model?) was introduced by Lipton and McGhee (2002), with

$$\frac{dS_t}{S_t} = \left(r_t^d - r_t^f\right)dt + \sqrt{v_t}\, A(S_t, t)dW_t^{(1)} + (e^J - 1)dN_t, \tag{6.54a}$$

$$dv_t = \kappa(m - v_t)dt + \alpha\sqrt{v_t}\, dW_t^{(2)}, \tag{6.54b}$$

where $<dW_t^{(1)}, dW_t^{(2)}> = \rho\, dt$, N_t is a Poisson process with Poisson intensity λ and J corresponds to the statistical distribution of jumps. Note that while the original paper uses $\sigma_L(t, S_t)$ for the multiplicative local volatility correction, I use $A(S_t, t)$, for notational consistency. The reader will recognise the jump-diffusion element of this model as similar to that of the Merton (1976) model. While jumps are often invoked as a mechanism to increase the smile in the short end over that of a pure stochastic or local-stochastic volatility model, this comes with the cost of (a) requiring the jump parameters to be included in the calibration and (b) requiring the numerical solution of a partial integro-differential equation (PIDE) rather than a PDE. Both of these considerations add greatly to the complexity of the model and we shall therefore not concern ourselves further with jump diffusions in this text. For those who wish to explore the topic further, a discussion of jump diffusion models can be found in Section 2.4 of Zhu (2000), where characteristic functions for asset price processes including jump diffusion elements are covered, and in Cont and Tankov (2004), notably including Chapter 12 on the challenging topic of partial integro-differential equations.

Numerical methods for PIDEs, a complicated topic at best, are covered in Duffy (2006). They differ from the standard convection–diffusion approach by requiring nonlocal terms to be included in the backward induction for option pricing, corresponding to integration over all possible post-jump scenarios, and the Fokker–Planck equation for forward transition probabilities will similarly contain nonlocal transition probability terms corresponding to jumps.

We therefore consider only local-stochastic volatility models here, which have become something of an industry standard for FX option pricing over the first decade of this century. LSV modelling features have been incorporated into front office systems such as Murex's 'Tremor' model, which is basically an LSV model coupling a Heston-type stochastic variance process with a parametric form $f(\cdot)$ for local volatility.

More up-to-date references on LSV models is Ren *et al.* (2007) and Henry-Labordère (2009), which demonstrates the ongoing interest in such models. Clearly, while a lot of the implementation details of these models is proprietary, there are keynote references such as the above in the public domain, which means the topic is definitely open for presentation in a book such as this.

6.8.1   Calibration of local volatility in LSV models

We shall use the earlier result (5.39) that the local volatility $\sigma_{\mathrm{loc}}(K, T)$ is the square root of the expectation of the future instantaneous variance at time T, conditional on spot $S_T = K$.

We directly read off the instantaneous volatility term $\sqrt{v_t}A(S_t, t)$ driving the spot process under an LSV model from (6.53a); instantaneous variance is just this quantity squared, so

$$\sigma_{\mathrm{loc}}^2(K, T) = \mathbb{E}^d\left[v_T A^2(S_T, T)|S_T = K\right]. \tag{6.55}$$

The local variance contribution $A^2(S_T, T)$ conditioned on $S_T = K$ is nothing more than $A^2(K, T)$ and can be taken outside the expectation, giving $\sigma_{loc}^2(K, T) = A^2(K, T)\mathbb{E}^d[v_T|S_T = K]$, i.e.

$$A(K, T) = \sqrt{\frac{\sigma_{\mathrm{loc}}^2(K, T)}{\mathbb{E}^d[v_T|S_T = K]}}. \tag{6.56}$$

We compute the denominator in (6.56) by

$$\mathbb{E}^d[v_T|S_T = K] = \frac{\mathbb{E}^d[v_T\delta_{\{S_T - K\}}]}{\mathbb{E}^d[\delta_{\{S_T - K\}}]}. \tag{6.57}$$

or, equivalently, when expressed in logspot terms and with logstrike $k = \ln K$,

$$\mathbb{E}^d[v_T|X_T = k] = \frac{\mathbb{E}^d[v_T\delta_{\{X_T - k\}}]}{\mathbb{E}^d[\delta_{\{X_T - k\}}]}. \tag{6.58}$$

It is worth noting that (6.56), together with the numerical recipe (6.58) for computing it, hold irrespective of the particular form of stochastic variance model assumed. We'll illustrate this with the particular LSV model of the form (6.53) built using Heston as the stochastic variance component; the analysis of local-stochastic models involving other volatility/variance processes is left as an exercise for the reader.

Let's suppose that we have managed to obtain (perhaps by solving the forward Fokker–Planck equation numerically, which we discuss in Section 6.8.2 below) an expression for the forward transition probabilities $p(X, v, T)$ for the joint probability distribution for logspot X and stochastic variance v at time T, conditional on initial values $\{X_0, v_0\}$ at time $t = 0$. We can then compute (6.58) by taking two integrals along the v axis of the joint probability density function:

$$\mathbb{E}^d[\delta_{\{X_T - k\}}] = \int_v p(k, v, T)\, dv, \tag{6.59a}$$

$$\mathbb{E}^d[v_T \delta_{\{X_T - k\}}] = \int_v v \cdot p(k, v, T)\, dv. \tag{6.59b}$$

So we need to use numerical methods for constructing values of the joint probability density function $p(k, v, T)$ – i.e. numerical solution of the Fokker–Planck equation, from which we can recover the local volatility contribution $A(k, T)$ (in logstrike coordinates) using

$$A(k, T) = \sigma_{\text{loc}}^2(\exp(k), T) \sqrt{\frac{I_0(k, T)}{I_1(k, T)}}, \tag{6.60a}$$

where

$$I_n(k, T) = \int_v v^n \cdot p(k, v, T)\, dv, \quad \text{for } n \in \{0, 1\}. \tag{6.60b}$$

6.8.2 Fokker–Planck equation for the LSV model

We therefore need an expression for the Fokker–Planck equation for the LSV model, similar to that derived in Section 6.6, but using stochastic dynamics (6.53). Transforming (6.53a) into a process for logspot X_t using Itô's lemma, we have

$$dX_t = \left[r^d - r^f - \frac{1}{2} v_t A^2(X_t, t) \right] dt + \sqrt{v_t}\, A(S_t, t)\, dW_T^{(1)}, \tag{6.61}$$

where with mild abuse of notation we now let $A(X_t, t)$ denote the multiplicative local volatility correction term as a function of logspot and time.

As before, let $\mathbf{X}_t = \left(X_t^{(1)}, X_t^{(2)} \right)$ with $X_t^{(1)} = X_t$, i.e. logspot, and $X_t^{(2)} = v_t$, i.e. stochastic variance, so that

$$dX_t^{(1)} = \left[r^d - r^f - \frac{1}{2} X_t^{(2)} A^2(X_t^{(1)}, t) \right] dt + \sqrt{X_t^{(2)} t}\, A(X_t^{(1)}, t)\, dW_T^{(1)}, \tag{6.62}$$

$$dX_t^{(2)} = \kappa(m - X_t^{(2)})dt + \rho\alpha\sqrt{X_t^{(2)}}\, dW_t^{(1)} + \bar{\rho}\alpha\sqrt{X_t^{(2)}}\, dW_t^{(1\perp)}. \tag{6.63}$$

Drift vector and diffusion matrix terms are

$$a_1 = \mu^d - \frac{1}{2} X^{(2)} A^2\left(X^{(1)}, t \right), \quad a_2 = -\kappa(X^{(2)} - m), \tag{6.64a}$$

$$B_{11} = \sqrt{X^{(2)}} A(X^{(1)}, t), \quad B_{12} = 0, \quad B_{21} = \rho\alpha\sqrt{X^{(2)}}, \quad B_{22} = \bar{\rho}\alpha\sqrt{X^{(2)}}. \tag{6.64b}$$

The approach is similar to Section 6.6 but with terms a_1 and B_{11} now including the multiplicative local volatility correction $A(X_t^{(1)}, t)$. Substituting (6.64) into (6.33), we obtain

$$
\frac{\partial p}{\partial t} = \frac{1}{2}\frac{\partial^2[vA^2(X,t)p]}{\partial X^2} + \rho\alpha\frac{\partial^2[vA(X,t)p]}{\partial X \partial v} + \frac{1}{2}\alpha^2\frac{\partial^2[vp]}{\partial v^2}
$$
$$
+ \frac{\partial}{\partial X}\left[\left(\frac{1}{2}vA^2(X,t) - \mu^d\right)p\right] + \kappa\frac{\partial[(v-m)p]}{\partial v}. \tag{6.65}
$$

A little algebra allows us to reduce this to

$$
\frac{\partial p}{\partial t} = \frac{1}{2}\frac{\partial^2[vA^2(X,t)p]}{\partial X^2} + \rho\alpha\frac{\partial^2[vA(X,t)p]}{\partial X \partial v} + \frac{1}{2}\alpha^2\frac{\partial^2[vp]}{\partial v^2}
$$
$$
+ \frac{\partial}{\partial X}\left[\left(\frac{1}{2}vA^2(X,t) - \mu^d\right)p\right] + \kappa\frac{\partial[(v-m)p]}{\partial v},
$$

which after a few algebraic manipulations reduces to

$$
\frac{\partial p}{\partial t} = \frac{A^2v}{2}\frac{\partial^2 p}{\partial X^2} + \rho\alpha Av\frac{\partial^2 p}{\partial X \partial v} + \frac{\alpha^2 v}{2}\frac{\partial^2 p}{\partial v^2} + \left(\frac{1}{2}A^2v + 2AA'v + \rho\alpha A - \mu^d\right)\frac{\partial p}{\partial X}
$$
$$
+ \left(\kappa[v-m] + \alpha^2 + \rho\alpha A'v\right)\frac{\partial p}{\partial v} + \left[AA'v + \rho\alpha A' + AA''v + [A']^2v + \kappa\right]p, \tag{6.66}
$$

where $A = A(X,t)$, $A' = \partial A(X,t)/\partial X$ and $A'' = \partial^2 A(X,t)/\partial X^2$.

Note that in the case where $A(X,t) = 1$ $\forall\{X,t\}$, (6.66) reduces to (6.34), just as one would expect.

6.8.3   Forward induction for local volatility calibration on LSV

The approach therefore taken is something like bootstrapping the yield curve, but attempting to infer a surface $A(X,t)$ rather than a curve. Suppose a sequence of N timepoints $\{0, t_1, t_2, \ldots, t_N\}$ is given, with $t_N = T_{\text{CAL}}$. The approach is to solve (6.66) numerically, marching forward timestep by timestep, and after each iteration in the solution of (6.66) refine the function $A(X,t)$ by use of (6.60):

Step 1. Start at time $t = 0$ with an initial local volatility correction $A(X,0) = 1$ for all X, and initial condition

$$
p(X, v, 0) = \delta_{\{X-X_0\}} \cdot \delta_{\{v-v_0\}},
$$

illustrated in Figure 6.2.

Step 2. Construct a forward timestepping scheme for (6.66) using a finite scheme for the PDE such as either explicit[4] finite differencing (EFD) or ADI timestepping (both discussed in Chapter 7). Spatial derivatives A' and A'' of the local volatility contribution function can be estimated at time t by setting a function $f(X) = A(X,t)$ equal to a cubic spline and extracting first- and second-order derivatives by symbolic differentiation of $f(X)$,

---

[4] EFD is likely to be prohibitively slow, but being simpler it could be wise to start with this to build experience before tackling the ADI implementation.

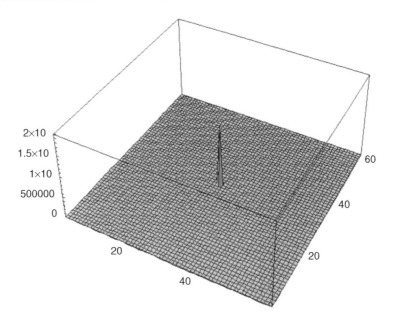

Figure 6.2 Initial probability distribution for the forward Fokker–Planck equation

for which we know the coefficients. Alternatively, one can attempt to fit a parametric function $\hat{f}(X) = A(X, t)$ and obtain the derivatives of $\hat{f}(X)$ once again by symbolic differentiation.

Note that for $t > 0$, $p(X, v, 0)$ can be visually depicted as shown in Figure 6.3.

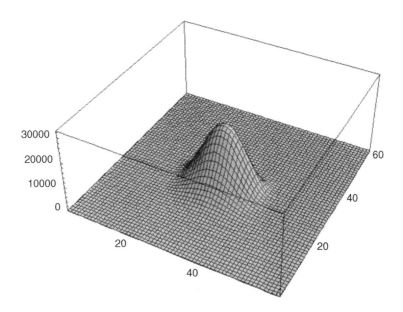

Figure 6.3 Interim probability distribution from the forward Fokker–Planck equation

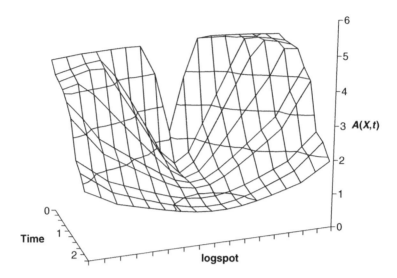

Figure 6.4 Bootstrapped local volatility contribution $A(X, t)$ for EURUSD as of September 2008

Step 3. Refine $A(X, t)$ by use of (6.60), by calculating the two integrals I_0 and I_1 in (6.60b) at each required level of X, taking numerical integrals in the variance dimension. Then update the diffusion, convection and force terms in (6.66).

We hope to end up with something resembling Figure 6.4 or 6.5. These graphs were generated using mixing weights of 0.65 for both convexity and skew, albeit in quite extreme markets during the so-called credit crunch. Note that the axes are with respect to logspot as measured from the logforward, and therefore do not show any drift.

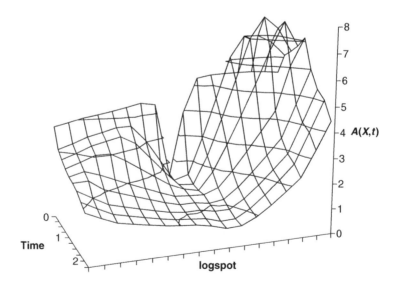

Figure 6.5 Bootstrapped local volatility contribution $A(X, t)$ for USDJPY as of September 2008

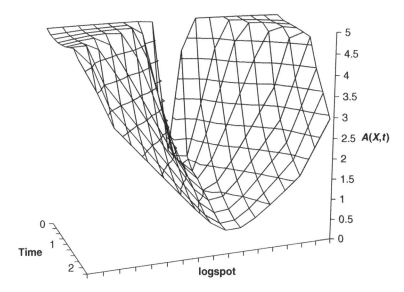

Figure 6.6 Bootstrapped local volatility contribution $A(X, t)$ for USDJPY as of September 2008 with $\rho \approx 0$

Perhaps counterintuitively, the skew for USDJPY looks to be flipped. This is because the risk reversals were so high in these markets that the spot/variance correlation of ρ was sufficiently distant from zero, at $\rho = -0.64$, that the local volatility parameter $A(X, t)$ ends up having to fight SABR and actually has to augment it for high strikes. If the mixing weight for skew was set to zero, so that ρ ends up at or near zero, we see a more intuitive solution (see Figure 6.6). Basically, we start with a Dirac delta function for $p(X, v, 0)$ and $A(X, 0) = 1$. We use $A(X, 0)$ in (6.66), solve forward to t_1 to obtain $p(X, v, t_1)$, from which we can infer $A(X, t_1)$. Having obtained $A(X, t_1)$, we then use *that* to infer $p(X, v, t_2)$, from which $A(X, t_2)$ can be computed, and so on, thereby inferring $A(X, t_{i+1})$ and $p(X, v, t_{i+1})$ from $A(X, t_i)$ and $p(X, v, t_i)$.

Technically, the scheme is correct as described for the explicit finite difference scheme, as we know $A(X, t_i)$ and $p(X, v, t_i)$ and can infer $p(X, v, t_{i+1})$. For an ADI scheme, however, we are actually attempting to use $A(X, t_{i+1})$ and $p(X, v, t_i)$ to infer $p(X, v, t_{i+1})$, and we don't actually know $A(X, t_{i+1})$ yet. We therefore have to estimate it – the naive approach is to just use $A(X, t_i)$. A better approach would be to use $A(X^*, t_i)$, where the moneyness of logspot X^* at t_i is equal to the moneyness of X at t_{i+1} – in other words, we just expect the local volatility contribution going forward from one timepoint to the next to be roughly constant with respect to moneyness, not with respect to logspot.

Numerical issues likely to be faced by this scheme are:

1. The initial condition for the Fokker–Planck equation is highly singular, and we therefore benefit greatly from having an aggressively nonuniform mesh to pack more meshpoints in around (X_0, v_0) in the spatial dimension, and $t = 0$ in the time dimension. After a small amount of time has elapsed, the source distribution of probability diffuses out somewhat, and fewer meshpoints are needed due to the presence of less convexity.
2. FX volatility surfaces with skew will require a nontrivial ρ, which can be problematic for finite difference schemes. We present schemes in Chapter 7 to meet this need.

3. It is advantagous to minimise the convection term in (6.66) by modelling the logforward
   $\ln F_{t,T}$ as opposed to logspot X_T. This has the effect of removing the μ^d term and then
   constructs a multiplicative local volatility function in terms of logforward $\ln F_{t,T}$ and time
   t. Translation from one to the other is basically trivial and just requires an offset to be
   applied.
4. If the Feller condition is violated, then probability mass will tend to pile up against the
   $v = 0$ boundary. For this reason, we find that a nonuniform mesh in variance which has a
   concentration of points in a boundary layer adjoining $v = 0$ helps considerably.
5. The calibration works best for shorter dated maturities for currency pairs with relatively
   symmetric smiles. For longer dated calibrations to skewed currency pairs, such as 3Y
   USDJPY and EURJPY, we find that the numerics are much more challenging. In contrast,
   EURCHF is much easier to work with.

We benefit from having nonuniform mesh points in (X_t, v_t) aggressively concentrated
around (X_0, v_0) to handle the Dirac delta function and LSV forward induction, together with
a boundary layer of increased density around v_0 to handle mass absorption due to violation of
the Feller condition. I show the sort of mesh I have in mind schematically in Figure 6.7(a) and
give a realistic example of such a mesh built using 50 space steps in either direction in Figure
6.7(b). Time grids for forward induction are similarly concentrated around $t = 0$ and allowed
to take larger timesteps as the probability distribution diffuses outwards from (X_0, v_0).

6.8.4 Calibrating stochastic and local volatilities

We now have the machinery required to build and calibrate an entire LSV model. A two-stage
calibration procedure is required.

1. *Stochastic volatility.* Mark down the implied volatility convexity by a multiplicative factor
   less than unity η, often called 'mixing weight' in the industry,[5] and calibrate the purely
   stochastic volatility model to this market. In FX, reducing the convexity requires us to mark
   down strangles and risk reversals by η, straightforwardly multiplying market strangles
   and risk reversals by the multiplicative factor η and then calibrating a purely stochastic
   volatility model to that volatility surface with reduced convexity. The calibration to implied
   volatilities requires the Fourier transform techniques of Section 6.5 together with a nonlinear
   least squares minimisation for calibration, as will be discussed in Section 7.2.
2. *Local volatility.* Having described a portion of the implied volatility smile using stochastic
   volatility, we attempt to pick up the residual smile by construction of the multiplicative
   local volatility correction $A(X_t, t)$, as detailed in Section 6.8.3.

The first of these calibrations is considerably faster than the second, as we benefit from
the semi-analytic expressions for the prices of European options under a stochastic volatility
model. For the second stage, we require numerical solution of the forward Fokker–Planck
equation using a two-dimensional PDE engine.

---

[5] Typical values for η are in the vicinity of 0.60 or 0.65, though typically a little higher for LSV models to price increasingly
short dated options, i.e. with three months or less to maturity. The mixing weight η can be inferred by examining the price of double
no-touches and seeing what value for η is consistent with the market, or estimated from historical analysis of moves in risk reversals
as a function of daily changes in spot.

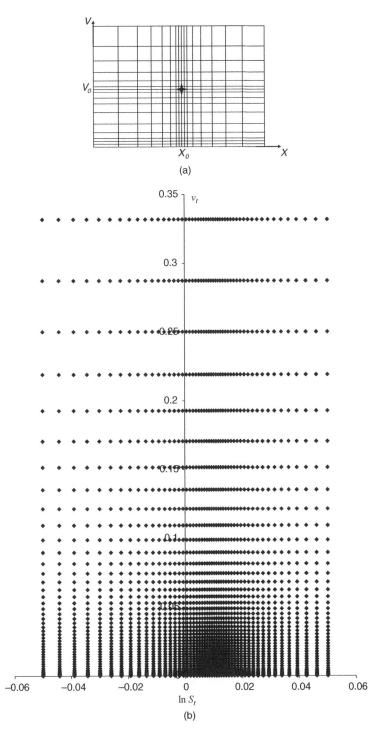

Figure 6.7 Mesh for two-dimensional Fokker–Planck equation: (a) schematic mesh; (b) realistic mesh (50×50)

Table 6.5 Violation of Heston Feller condition even after 65% mixing weight

ccypair	tenor	ATM	25-d-MS	25-d-RR	v_0	ρ	α	κ	m	β
EURUSD	3M	12.70%	0.28%	−0.55%	0.02	−0.10	0.38	6.02	0.02	1.4299
EURUSD	6M	11.87%	0.38%	−0.55%	0.02	−0.10	0.31	3.02	0.02	0.9538
EURUSD	1Y	11.50%	0.40%	−0.55%	0.01	−0.11	0.24	1.50	0.01	0.8026
EURUSD	2Y	11.45%	0.40%	−0.55%	0.01	−0.11	0.15	0.75	0.01	0.9116
EURUSD	3Y	11.30%	0.40%	−0.55%	0.01	−0.12	0.13	0.50	0.01	0.8992
EURUSD	4Y	11.13%	0.40%	−0.56%	0.01	−0.13	0.11	0.38	0.01	0.8828
EURUSD	5Y	10.75%	0.38%	−0.55%	0.01	−0.13	0.09	0.30	0.01	0.9111
USDJPY	3M	15.10%	0.18%	−4.65%	0.03	−0.51	0.62	6.02	0.03	0.7960
USDJPY	6M	13.00%	0.18%	−4.95%	0.02	−0.54	0.47	3.02	0.02	0.5417
USDJPY	1Y	11.80%	0.18%	−5.25%	0.02	−0.56	0.38	1.50	0.02	0.3632
USDJPY	2Y	10.60%	0.10%	−5.40%	0.01	−0.59	0.27	0.75	0.01	0.3117
USDJPY	3Y	10.25%	0.05%	−5.45%	0.01	−0.59	0.23	0.50	0.01	0.2717
USDJPY	4Y	10.10%	0.03%	−5.55%	0.01	−0.59	0.21	0.38	0.01	0.2354
USDJPY	5Y	10.10%	0.00%	−5.60%	0.01	−0.58	0.20	0.30	0.01	0.2122
GBPUSD	3M	11.95%	0.30%	−1.05%	0.02	−0.18	0.40	6.02	0.02	1.1878
GBPUSD	6M	11.40%	0.33%	−0.98%	0.01	−0.18	0.29	3.02	0.01	1.0221
GBPUSD	1Y	11.10%	0.35%	−0.95%	0.01	−0.18	0.22	1.50	0.01	0.8544
GBPUSD	2Y	10.95%	0.38%	−0.93%	0.01	−0.17	0.15	0.75	0.01	0.9131
GBPUSD	3Y	10.83%	0.38%	−0.85%	0.01	−0.17	0.12	0.50	0.01	0.9068
GBPUSD	4Y	10.70%	0.38%	−0.77%	0.01	−0.16	0.10	0.38	0.01	0.8991
GBPUSD	5Y	10.60%	0.33%	−0.70%	0.01	−0.16	0.08	0.30	0.01	1.0373
EURGBP	3M	8.90%	0.23%	0.80%	0.01	0.18	0.28	6.02	0.01	1.2635
EURGBP	6M	8.90%	0.28%	0.85%	0.01	0.18	0.22	3.02	0.01	1.0347
EURGBP	1Y	8.90%	0.29%	0.85%	0.01	0.18	0.16	1.50	0.01	0.9786
EURGBP	2Y	8.90%	0.28%	1.10%	0.01	0.25	0.10	0.75	0.01	1.2938
EURGBP	3Y	9.00%	0.23%	0.85%	0.01	0.22	0.07	0.50	0.01	1.7306
EURGBP	4Y	9.10%	0.20%	0.75%	0.01	0.21	0.05	0.38	0.01	2.1939
EURGBP	5Y	9.20%	0.18%	0.55%	0.01	0.16	0.05	0.30	0.01	2.4116
AUDUSD	3M	18.50%	0.38%	−2.70%	0.04	−0.32	0.58	6.02	0.04	1.3341
AUDUSD	6M	16.50%	0.40%	−2.75%	0.03	−0.34	0.42	3.02	0.03	1.0573
AUDUSD	1Y	14.75%	0.43%	−2.80%	0.03	−0.36	0.31	1.50	0.03	0.7820
AUDUSD	2Y	14.15%	0.40%	−2.70%	0.02	−0.37	0.19	0.75	0.02	0.9649
AUDUSD	3Y	13.65%	0.40%	−2.40%	0.02	−0.35	0.15	0.50	0.02	0.9590
AUDUSD	4Y	13.38%	0.40%	−2.19%	0.02	−0.34	0.13	0.38	0.02	0.9600
AUDUSD	5Y	13.25%	0.40%	−2.00%	0.02	−0.32	0.11	0.30	0.02	0.9695
USDBRL	3M	16.00%	0.60%	3.50%	0.03	0.35	0.66	6.02	0.03	0.7814
USDBRL	6M	14.00%	0.63%	3.50%	0.02	0.37	0.45	3.02	0.02	0.6488
USDBRL	1Y	14.30%	0.65%	3.50%	0.02	0.37	0.32	1.50	0.02	0.6723
USDBRL	2Y	15.20%	0.70%	3.50%	0.03	0.36	0.23	0.75	0.03	0.7221
USDBRL	3Y	16.20%	0.75%	3.50%	0.03	0.34	0.19	0.50	0.03	0.7678
USDBRL	4Y	17.66%	0.77%	3.55%	0.03	0.34	0.17	0.38	0.03	0.8893
USDBRL	5Y	18.80%	0.78%	3.50%	0.04	0.33	0.15	0.30	0.04	0.9964
AUDJPY	3M	21.40%	0.22%	−5.00%	0.05	−0.42	0.81	6.02	0.05	0.9273
AUDJPY	6M	19.50%	0.20%	−5.80%	0.04	−0.46	0.67	3.02	0.04	0.6010
AUDJPY	1Y	18.00%	0.20%	−6.50%	0.04	−0.47	0.60	1.50	0.04	0.3419
AUDJPY	2Y	18.10%	0.25%	−6.80%	0.04	−0.44	0.47	0.75	0.04	0.2909
AUDJPY	3Y	18.20%	0.33%	−7.20%	0.05	−0.42	0.49	0.50	0.05	0.2009
AUDJPY	4Y	18.30%	0.33%	−7.75%	0.05	−0.42	0.54	0.38	0.05	0.1404
AUDJPY	5Y	18.35%	0.33%	−8.30%	0.06	−0.43	0.62	0.30	0.06	0.0969
USDTRY	3M	17.30%	0.60%	5.00%	0.03	0.51	0.63	6.02	0.03	0.9946
USDTRY	6M	17.40%	0.65%	5.25%	0.03	0.54	0.44	3.02	0.03	1.0557

(continued)

Table 6.5 (continued)

ccypair	tenor	ATM	25-d-MS	25-d-RR	v_0	ρ	α	κ	m	β
USDTRY	1Y	17.75%	0.70%	5.50%	0.03	0.62	0.27	1.50	0.03	1.3583
USDTRY	2Y	19.15%	0.80%	5.15%	0.04	0.70	0.16	0.75	0.04	2.3604
USDTRY	3Y	20.60%	1.00%	5.10%	0.04	0.74	0.12	0.50	0.04	3.0614
USDTRY	4Y	22.10%	1.10%	5.40%	0.05	0.75	0.10	0.38	0.05	4.0019
USDTRY	5Y	23.60%	1.00%	5.70%	0.06	0.74	0.07	0.30	0.06	6.7681
EURCHF	3M	6.65%	0.23%	−1.85%	0.01	−0.41	0.32	6.02	0.01	0.6026
EURCHF	6M	6.10%	0.26%	−1.80%	0.00	−0.40	0.24	3.02	0.00	0.4575
EURCHF	1Y	5.80%	0.29%	−1.80%	0.00	−0.39	0.19	1.50	0.00	0.3397
EURCHF	2Y	5.30%	0.25%	−1.65%	0.00	−0.39	0.11	0.75	0.00	0.3959
EURCHF	3Y	5.10%	0.22%	−1.50%	0.00	−0.38	0.09	0.50	0.00	0.4200
EURCHF	4Y	4.80%	0.21%	−1.53%	0.00	−0.40	0.07	0.37	0.00	0.3839
EURCHF	5Y	4.50%	0.15%	−1.55%	0.00	−0.44	0.06	0.30	0.00	0.4224

Note that the marking down of the convexity parameters reduces the vovariance in the calibrated Heston model, but not to the extent that the Feller condition is satisfied in the case of typical mixing weights. Table 6.5 shows the effect of a 65 % mixing weight, in comparison to the Heston calibration to the unmodified FX market in Table 6.3 – one sees that the Feller condition is still violated.

6.8.5 The pricing PDE for LSV models

As in Section 6.7, suppose that instead of (6.35) we have a local volatility correction $A(S_t, t)$ included, i.e.

$$dS_t = (r^d - r^f)S_t\, dt + \sqrt{v_t}A(S_t, t)S_t\, dW_t^{(1)}, \qquad (6.67a)$$

$$dv_t = a(v_t)dt + b(v_t)dW_t^{(2)}, \qquad (6.67b)$$

where $\langle dW_t^{(1)}, dW_t^{(2)}\rangle = \rho\, dt$. Following the earlier argument, we now have

$$dS_t^2 = v_t A^2(S_t, t)S_t^2\, dt, \qquad dv_t^2 = b^2(v_t)dt, \qquad dS_t\, dv_t = \rho\sqrt{v_t}A(S_t, t)S_t b(v_t)dt.$$

The same analysis as Section 6.7, but with these Itô terms, leads to

$$\frac{\partial V}{\partial t} + \frac{1}{2}v A^2(S, t)S^2\frac{\partial^2 V}{\partial S^2} + \frac{1}{2}b^2(v)\frac{\partial^2 V}{\partial v^2} + \rho\sqrt{v}A(S, t)Sb(v)\frac{\partial^2 V}{\partial S\, \partial v}$$
$$+ (r^d - r^f)S_t\frac{\partial V}{\partial S} + \left[a(v) - \lambda(S, v, t)\right]\frac{\partial V}{\partial v} - r^d V = 0, \qquad (6.68)$$

which for the case of a pure Heston stochastic volatility model is

$$\frac{\partial V}{\partial t} + \frac{1}{2}v A^2(S, t)S^2\frac{\partial^2 V}{\partial S^2} + \frac{1}{2}\alpha^2 v\frac{\partial^2 V}{\partial v^2} + \alpha\rho v A(S, t)S\frac{\partial^2 V}{\partial S\, \partial v}$$
$$+ (r^d - r^f)S\frac{\partial V}{\partial S} + \left[\kappa(m - v) - \lambda(S, v, t)\right]\frac{\partial V}{\partial v} - r^d V = 0. \qquad (6.69)$$

Transforming to logspot coordinates is trivial and one obtains

$$
\frac{\partial V}{\partial t} + \frac{1}{2} v A^2(x,t) \frac{\partial^2 V}{\partial x^2} + \frac{1}{2} \alpha^2 v \frac{\partial^2 V}{\partial v^2} + \alpha \rho v A(x,t) \frac{\partial^2 V}{\partial x \partial v}
$$

$$
+ \left(r^d - r^f - \frac{1}{2} v A^2(x,t) \right) \frac{\partial V}{\partial x} + \left[\kappa(m-v) - \lambda(x,v,t) \right] \frac{\partial V}{\partial v} - r^d V = 0, \quad (6.70)
$$

where, with some abuse of notation, $A(x,t) = A(\exp(x), t)$ refers to the local volatility contribution parameterised either in logspot or spot coordinates.

Solving (6.70) numerically is less trivial. We shall need Chapter 7 to discuss the numerical solution of PDEs such as this.

7

Numerical Methods for Pricing
and Calibration

The models presented in this book have the advantage that they have the flexibility to provide prices for exotic options that are more consistent with the market. The downside is that the extra complexity means that closed-form solutions do not exist, in all but a few simple examples, and therefore we are forced to resort to numerical methods for pricing options with these models. This is an extensive subject, and in this chapter we can only scratch the surface. Further references are given for those who wish to follow up in more detail, but this is a practical subject and the best way to learn is to implement these techniques in code.

This chapter covers numerical techniques used for both calibration and pricing. Though it may seem counterintuitive we shall (a) start with simple numerical optimisation schemes that we find useful for calibration, then (b) consider pricing using techniques such as Monte Carlo and numerical methods for partial differential equations and, finally, (c) return to calibration, but this time considering the sometimes difficult issue of the calibration of the LSV model using numerical methods for the forward Fokker–Planck equation.

7.1 ONE-DIMENSIONAL ROOT FINDING – IMPLIED VOLATILITY CALCULATION

The simplest numerical method to begin with is an implied volatility calculator – a routine for a Black–Scholes model with known domestic and foreign interest rates r^d and r^f and initial spot S_0. The requirement is that it should take in the strike K and time to expiry T for a European call (or put), together with an observed market price $V_{mkt}^{C/P}$ of that instrument, and return the volatility σ_{imp} for which $V_0^{C/P} = V_{mkt}^{C/P}$, where $V_0^{C/P}$ is computed using (2.65).

The implied volatility calculator described can be thought of as a very simple calibration engine: it takes in a market price $V_{mkt}^{C/P}$ and returns a calibrated Black–Scholes model with volatility σ_{imp}. Since the other parameters S_0, r^d, r^f, K and T are known, and it is only σ that is to be determined in (2.65), we set $V_0^{C/P}$ as a function of σ holding all other parameters constant, i.e.

$$V_0^{C/P}(\sigma) = \omega S_0 e^{-r^f T} N(\omega d_1) - \omega K e^{-r^d T} N(\omega d_2).$$

An easy way to implement this is to set up a price error function

$$F(\sigma) = V_0^{C/P}(\sigma) - V_{mkt}^{C/P}, \tag{7.1}$$

recognising that σ_{imp} is nothing more than that particular value of volatility σ for which $F(\sigma) = 0$. Since $F(\cdot)$ is a monotonically increasing function, we can find the root numerically. The simplest scheme to use is probably the bisection method, which requires initial values x_0 and x_1 (I assume without loss of generality that $x_0 < x_1$) that bracket the root, i.e. for which $F(x_0) \cdot F(x_1) < 0$. Setting $x_2 = \frac{1}{2}(x_0 + x_1)$, we can then work out which of the smaller intervals (x_0, x_2) or (x_2, x_1) brackets the root, and continue the bisection method with *that* interval, until we reach a final interval that is suitably compact. Another quite straightforward scheme is the secant method, which requires initial values x_0 and x_1 and then calculates subsequent approximations x_i using

$$x_{i+1} = x_i + \frac{x_i - x_{i-1}}{F(x_i) - F(x_{i-1})} F(x_i),$$

which can be iterated until a value x_n is found for which $|F(x_n)| < \epsilon$ for a suitable tolerance ϵ. These two schemes, both described in Chapter 10 of Hildebrand (1974), are basically just possible starting points and hardly the most efficient choice of root-finding algorithm – we merely relate these by way of introduction.

A better choice of one-dimensional root finder is Brent's method which combines attributes from the bisection method, secant method and inverse quadratic interpolation. The Brent method is described in Section 9.3 of Press *et al.* (2002), where an implementation (named zbrent) can be found. One needs to start with values a and b (we can assume the ordering $a < b$) for which

$$F(a) < 0 \qquad \text{and} \qquad F(b) > 0. \tag{7.2}$$

The easiest way to achieve this is to start with financially sensible initial guesses for a and b (perhaps 10 % for FX), and then use a bracketing scheme such as zbrak in Press *et al.* (2002) to reduce a and/or increase b until the condition (7.2) is met. We then use the Brent scheme to find σ for which $|F(\sigma)| < \epsilon$ for a suitably small ϵ. This forms our numerical method for finding σ_{imp}. Extending it to handle straddles is equally straightforward.

7.2 NONLINEAR LEAST SQUARES MINIMISATION

What we have effectively done in Section 7.1 is calibrated a Black–Scholes model to a market – a simple market comprising only one European option, with strike K and time to expiry T. Given a market price $V_{\text{mkt}}^{\text{C/P}}$, we obtained the model parameter σ_{imp} chosen suitably to reprice the European option.

The same approach, in more dimensions, can be used to calibrate a model such as the Heston model. As well as the market parameters common to both Black–Scholes and Heston, i.e. r^d, r^f and S_0, the Heston model has five model parameters: initial variance v_0, correlation ρ, vovariance α, mean reversion rate κ and mean reversion level m. We already know from Chapter 6 that the first three correspond to level, skew and convexity of the volatility surface respectively, whereas increasing the mean reversion rate leads to a flattening of the butterflies.

For this reason, a simple calibration routine for a pure Heston model, attempting to calibrate out to time T_{CAL}, will do reasonably well to employ a heuristic choice of mean reversion parameters to attempt to flatten the butterflies out in the vicinity of T_{CAL}. A somewhat heuristic choice that seems to work well in practice is

$$\kappa = 2.75/T_{\text{CAL}}, \tag{7.3a}$$

$$m = \sigma_{\text{ATM}}(T_{\text{CAL}}). \tag{7.3b}$$

Suppose initial Heston parameter values are given by the mean reversion parameters specified a priori in (7.3), together with three decision variables v_0, ρ and α.

We then need a nonlinear least squares minimisation scheme that attempts to minimise a suitably chosen error function by changing v_0, ρ and α, subject to obvious model constraints

$v_0 > 0, \alpha > 0$ and $\rho \in (-1, 1)$. Suppose that market implied volatilities $\sigma_{\text{imp}}(K_i)$ are available for three benchmark strikes, e.g. $K_1 = K_{25\text{-d-P}}$, $K_2 = K_{\text{ATM}}$ and $K_3 = K_{25\text{-d-C}}$.

Given a choice of Heston model parameters, we use the characteristic function technique to obtain semi-analytic prices $V_0^{C/P}(K_i, T_{\text{CAL}}; v_0, \rho, \alpha)$ for the three strikes K_i (realistically, we'd probably price a put for K_1, a straddle for K_{ATM} and a call for K_3) and then use the method of Section 7.1 to obtain model implied volatilities, denoted $\sigma_{\text{Heston}}(K_i; v_0, \rho, \alpha)$, for those three strikes given the Heston parameters V_0, ρ and α.

A suitable error function is then given by

$$F(v_0, \rho, \alpha) = \sum_{i=1}^{3} \left| \sigma_{\text{Heston}}(K_i; v_0, \rho, \alpha) - \sigma_{\text{imp}}(K_i) \right|^2 \tag{7.4}$$

and we can use a nonlinear least squares minimisation scheme such as Powell or Levenberg–Marquardt (Press *et al.*, 2002; Nocedal and Wright, 2006) to locate a set of parameters $\{v_0, \rho, \alpha\}$ that minimises the objective error function $F(v_0, \rho, \alpha)$

The only issue now is ensuring that the constraints are adhered to. An easy way to do this is, instead of using constrained decision variables v_0, ρ, α, to use unconstrained decision variables x_1, x_2, x_3, subject to a mapping that maps $\mathbb{R}$ into $(0, \infty)$, $(-1, 1)$ and $(0, \infty)$ respectively. Such a choice is given by

$$v_0 = \exp(x_1), \tag{7.5a}$$

$$\rho = \tanh(x_2), \tag{7.5b}$$

$$\alpha = \exp(x_3), \tag{7.5c}$$

with inverse

$$x_1 = \ln(v_0), \tag{7.6a}$$

$$x_2 = \tanh^{-1}(\rho) = \log\left(\sqrt{\frac{1+\rho}{1-\rho}} \right), \tag{7.6b}$$

$$x_3 = \ln(\alpha). \tag{7.6c}$$

We can therefore use an unconstrained nonlinear least squares minimisation algorithm on

$$F(x_1, x_2, x_3) = \sum_{i=1}^{3} \left| \sigma_{\text{Heston}}(K_i; e^{x_1}, \tanh(x_2), e^{x_3}) - \sigma_{\text{imp}}(K_i) \right|^2$$

and transform the final values of the decision variables x_1, x_2, x_3 back into financial coordinates using (7.5). Starting values for x_1, x_2, x_3 can be easily chosen by applying transformation (7.6) to typical market parameters; e.g. $V_0 = 0.01$, $\rho = 0$ and $\alpha = 0.05$ seems as good a choice as any.

7.3   MONTE CARLO SIMULATION

Perhaps the simplest numerical method for pricing to start with is Monte Carlo simulation. In contrast to various other business areas, Monte Carlo methods probably get used least in FX compared to other asset classes. The reason for this is simple: foreign currency option pricing models are often quite low dimensional[1] and can therefore be handled with PDEs, and FX options often have a continuous knock-out feature that is a perfect candidate for pricing using PDEs with associated Dirichlet conditions.

Nevertheless, it is always a good idea to have a Monte Carlo engine available for pricing. It can be successfully employed to cross-check against other algorithms, and it is massively easier to build a generic pricer (one asset or multiasset) using a generic payoff description language[2] and Monte Carlo simulation than it is to do the same with PDE schemes or, even more challengingly, both.[3]

We know the initial value of the state variables, which in a two-factor stochastic or stochastic/local volatility model may correspond to (a) logspot X_t and (b) volatility σ_t or variance v_t. In a one-factor world, such as Black–Scholes or a pure local volatility model, we only have logspot X_t as the state variable requiring simulation, and in Chapter 11 we introduce a three-factor model that requires (a) logspot X_t, (b) the domestic short rate r_t^d and (c) the foreign short rate r_t^f as state variables. Even more generally, Chapter 10 discusses multidimensional models for derivative products that derive their value from a number of tradeable currency pairs, in which case the dimensionality is the number of risky assets relative to a numeraire currency.

Whatever the components, and whatever the dimensionality – which we denote here by N – we let $\mathbf{X}_t = \left[X_t^{(1)} \cdots X_t^{(N)} \right]$ denote the state vector. Some of these factors may correspond to tradeable assets, while others will correspond to untradeable factors such as stochastic volatility or domestic and foreign instantaneous short rates. We suppose that there are N_{TF} tradeable factors, corresponding to logspot for each of those FX rates, and $N - N_{\mathrm{TF}}$ untradeable factors. Suppose we write the diffusion for $\mathbf{X}_t$ in vector form

$$d\mathbf{X}_t = \boldsymbol{\mu}(t, \mathbf{X}_t)dt + \boldsymbol{\Sigma}(t, \mathbf{X}_t)d\mathbf{W}_t, \tag{7.7}$$

where $\boldsymbol{\mu}(t, \mathbf{X}_t)$ and $\boldsymbol{\Sigma}(t, \mathbf{X}_t)$ denote the drift and diffusion terms respectively, and $\mathbf{W}_t$ denotes a standardised N-dimensional Brownian motion. If we consider a small time increment Δt, then the Euler scheme (Section 4.2.1 in Jäckel, 2002) can be written as

$$\begin{aligned}
\mathbf{X}_{t+\Delta t} &= \mathbf{X}_t + \int_t^{t+\Delta t} d\mathbf{X}_s \\
&= \mathbf{X}_t + \int_t^{t+\Delta t} \boldsymbol{\mu}(s, \mathbf{X}_s)ds + \int_t^{t+\Delta t} \boldsymbol{\Sigma}(s, \mathbf{X}_s)d\mathbf{W}_s \\
&\approx \mathbf{X}_t + \boldsymbol{\mu}(t, \mathbf{X}_t)\Delta t + \boldsymbol{\Sigma}(t, \mathbf{X}_t)[\mathbf{W}_{t+\Delta t} - \mathbf{W}_t].
\end{aligned}$$

If an increasing sequence of time points $\{t_0, t_1, \ldots, t_M\}$ is prescribed, with $t_0 = 0$ and $t_M = T$, then we have

$$\mathbf{X}_{t_{i+1}} = \mathbf{X}_{t_i} + \boldsymbol{\mu}(t_i, \mathbf{X}_{t_i})[t_{i+1} - t_i] + \boldsymbol{\Sigma}(t_i, \mathbf{X}_{t_i})[\mathbf{W}_{t_{i+1}} - \mathbf{W}_{t_i}]. \tag{7.8}$$

---

[1] Stochastic volatility and LSV require only two dimensions; long-dated FX/IR models even with local volatility still only require three dimensions.

[2] Where the payout is specified at run time, not at compile time, by a textual representation of the product's value, e.g. 'MAX(S[EURUSD]-K,0)'. Useful resources for those wanting to build their own syntactical language for evaluating payoffs at expiry are Boost.Spirit and the Kaleidoscope page at http://llvm.org/docs/tutorial/.

[3] I am interested to hear from people who have made progress towards an elegant solution to this challenging problem of inferring the correct boundary conditions and auxiliary states for PDE algorithms directly from a payout description language. The ideal would be a mechanism that could price Europeans (easy), barrier options (hard) and the strongly path-dependent options of Chapter 9 (harder) using either Monte Carlo simulation or PDE schemes, given the exact same payout description syntax. Many practitioners including myself would be very interested to see this.

Note that we can write

$$\mathbf{W}_{t_{i+1}} - \mathbf{W}_{t_i} = \mathbf{Z}_i \sqrt{t_{i+1} - t_i},$$ (7.9)

where, for each i, $\mathbf{Z}_i = [Z_i^{(1)} \cdots Z_i^{(N)}]^\perp$ is an N-dimensional random vector, comprised of N independent and identically distributed $N(0, 1)$ random variables. Because of the independent increments property of Brownian motion, we require that the random vectors $\mathbf{Z}_i$ and $\mathbf{Z}_j$ are independent for $i \neq j$ (correlations within the model are absorbed in the volatility matrix $\boldsymbol{\Sigma}$).

The numbers generated to comprise $\mathbf{Z}_i$ are more correctly referred to as pseudo-random numbers; a thorough discussion of the various pseudo-random number generators available is beyond the scope of this text. A commonly used choice for generation of uniformly distributed pseudo-random numbers U_i drawn from $U[0, 1]$ is the Mersenne twister (Matsumoto and Nishimura, 1998), good implementations of which can be easily located. Mapping these into normally distributed random numbers Z_i (Jäckel, 2002; Glassermann, 2004) can be achieved by a rejection scheme such as the Box–Muller method or by using an implementation of the inverse normal distribution function $F_Z^{-1}(u)$. Since the cumulative distribution function $F_Z(z)$ maps the real line into $[0, 1]$, its inverse $F_Z^{-1}(u)$ maps $[0, 1]$ into $\mathbb{R}$, and therefore can be used to generate normally distributed pseudo-random numbers from samples drawn from $U[0, 1]$. This approach is generally preferred by practitioners over rejection methods.

Equation (7.8) for the Euler scheme can be written

$$\mathbf{X}_{t_{i+1}} = \mathbf{X}_{t_i} + \boldsymbol{\mu}(t_i, \mathbf{X}_{t_i})[t_{i+1} - t_i] + \boldsymbol{\Sigma}(t_i, \mathbf{X}_{t_i}) \begin{bmatrix} Z_i^{(1)} \\ \vdots \\ Z_i^{(N)} \end{bmatrix} \sqrt{t_{i+1} - t_i}.$$ (7.10)

Having obtained a trajectory for $\mathbf{X}_{t_i}$, we can obtain the price of a European option (with expiry $t_M = T$) given that simulation by mapping the N_{TF} tradeable stochastic factors to $S_{t_i}^{(i)} = \exp(X_{t_i}^{(i)})$, which we can denote by an N_{TF} vector $\mathbf{S}_{t_i} = (S_T^{(1)}, S_T^{(2)}, \ldots, S_T^{(N_{\mathrm{TF}})})$ and computing

$$V_T = V_T(\mathbf{S}_T) = V_T\big(S_T^{(1)}, \ldots, S_T^{(N_{\mathrm{TF}})}\big).$$ (7.11a)

Obtaining the value at expiry for a path-dependent option conditional on a discretely monitored path and not having any Bermudan or callable feature (which requires estimation of early exercisability; we return to this later) is equally straightforward:

$$V_T = V_T\big(\mathbf{S}_{t_0}, \mathbf{S}_{t_1}, \ldots, \mathbf{S}_{t_{N_{\mathrm{TF}}}}\big).$$ (7.11b)

Either way, letting $V_T(i)$ denote the value attained in the appropriate payout expression in (7.11) for the ith simulation, we have the Monte Carlo estimate for the price of the European option by averaging across all simulations:

$$V_0^{\mathrm{MC}} = \mathrm{e}^{-r^d T} \frac{1}{N_{\mathrm{sims}}} \sum_{i=1}^{N_{\mathrm{sims}}} V_T(i).$$ (7.12)

In its simplest form, the Monte Carlo method is nothing more than (7.12).

Higher order schemes such as the Milstein scheme introduce higher order terms in the Itô expansion of (7.7), terms that include partial derivatives of components of $\boldsymbol{\Sigma}(t, \mathbf{X}_t)$ with respect to components $X_t^{(i)}$ of the state vector $\mathbf{X}_t$. For simpler models where the diffusion term

$\Sigma(t, \mathbf{X}_t)$ is homogeneous with respect to the state variables, there is nothing to be gained by including the Milstein correction.

An example of a one-dimensional model with an *inhomogeneous* diffusion term is the local volatility model, seen in Chapter 5, for which we have

$$dX_t = \left(r_t^d - r_t^f - \frac{1}{2}\sigma_{\mathrm{loc}}^2(X_t, t)\right)dt + \sigma_{\mathrm{loc}}(X_t, t)dW_t,$$

for which the vector representation (7.7) can be written in scalar form – we have $\mu(t, \mathbf{X}_t) = \mu(t, X_t^{(1)})$ and $\Sigma(t, \mathbf{X}_t) = \sigma(t, X_t^{(1)})$, with $\mu(t, X_t) = r^d - r^f - \frac{1}{2}\sigma_{\mathrm{loc}}^2(X_t, t)$ and $\sigma(t, X_t) = \sigma_{\mathrm{loc}}(X_t, t)$. The Milstein scheme (Kloeden and Platen, 1992) is introduced in the one-dimensional case in Section 3.2 of Seydel (2004) and Chapter 3 of McLeish (2005), where the following result is obtained:

$$X_{t_{i+1}} = X_{t_i} + \mu(t_i, X_{t_i})\Delta t + \sigma_{\mathrm{loc}}(X_{t_i}, t_i)Z_i\sqrt{\Delta t}$$
$$+ \frac{1}{2}\sigma_{\mathrm{loc}}(X_{t_i}, t_i)\frac{\partial\sigma_{\mathrm{loc}}(X_{t_i}, t_i)}{\partial X_{t_i}}\left[\left(Z_i\sqrt{\Delta t}\right)^2 - \Delta t\right], \qquad (7.13)$$

with $\Delta t = t_{i+1} - t_i$.

For multidimensional models with $N > 1$, computation of the Milstein correction is more involved, and we leave this for the interested reader to pursue further. Notes on the Milstein scheme for the Heston model, for example, can be found in Schmitz (2010) and in pages 22–23 of Gatheral (2006).

7.3.1 Handling large timesteps with local volatility

One advantage of Milstein over Euler timestepping is improved convergence when Δt is noninfinitesimal. In that case, we can take larger timesteps and get by with a smaller number of timesteps N_{times}. Even if we resort to the simpler Euler discretisation, we would like to get by with as few timesteps as possible.

However, we already know that local volatility is an *instantaneous* diffusion term which, in the continuous limit, reprices Europeans with the implied volatility observed in the markets. The question therefore is: what effective local volatility should be used over a macroscopic time slice for Monte Carlo simulation? Additionally, one should ask: what effective drift should be used?

Symbolically, the first question is: if we are using Euler timestepping, for which

$$X_{t_{i+1}} \approx X_{t_i} + \mu(t_i, X_{t_i})\Delta t + \sigma_{\mathrm{loc}}(t_i, X_{t_i})Z_i\sqrt{\Delta t}$$

in the limit of small Δt, what values of $\hat{\mu}_{\mathrm{loc}}(t_i, X_{t_i}; \Delta t)$ and $\hat{\sigma}_{\mathrm{loc}}(t_i, X_{t_i}; \Delta t)$ should we use when Δt is noninfinitesimal, such that

$$X_{t_{i+1}} = X_{t_i} + \hat{\mu}_{\mathrm{loc}}(t_i, X_{t_i}; \Delta t)\Delta t + \hat{\sigma}_{\mathrm{loc}}(t_i, X_{t_i}; \Delta t)Z_i\sqrt{\Delta t}? \qquad (7.14)$$

Effective drift, in the absence of any state dependent term, is given straightforwardly by

$$\hat{\mu}_{\mathrm{loc}}(t_i, X_{t_i}; \Delta t) = \int_{t_i}^{t_i+\Delta t} \mu_t\, dt,$$

and can be trivially computed from discount factors at times t_i and $t_i + \Delta t$.

For effective volatility, a useful approach is hinted at in Chapter 3 of Gatheral (2006), which presents a very nice path integral interpretation of Black–Scholes implied variance.

Equation (3.8) in his book is tantamount to saying that the forward implied variance applicable between X_{t_i} and $X_{t_{i+1}}$ is the path integral of local variance $\hat{\sigma}_{loc}^2(t, x)$, integrated over the transition probabilities for a Brownian bridge connecting (t_i, X_{t_i}) to $(t_{i+1}, X_{t_{i+1}})$. We can hardly expect to know the endpoint $(t_{i+1}, X_{t_{i+1}})$ before we calculate $\hat{\sigma}_{loc}(t_i, X_{t_i})$, which is itself used in (7.14) for timestepping forward to compute $X_{t_{i+1}}$. What we can do, however, is take a zeroth-order estimate of $E[X_{t_{i+1}}|\mathcal{F}_{t_i}] = X_{t_i} + \mu(t_i, X_{t_i})\Delta t$. A simple pathwise integral of local variance over paths connecting (t_i, X_{t_i}) to $X_{t_i} + \mu(t_i, X_{t_i})\Delta t$, taking into account only the two endpoints, is just

$$\hat{\sigma}_{loc}^2(t_i, X_{t_i}; \Delta t) = \frac{1}{2}\sigma_{loc}^2(t_i, X_{t_i}) + \frac{1}{2}\sigma_{loc}^2(t_{i+1}, E[X_{t_{i+1}}|\mathcal{F}_{t_i}]). \tag{7.15}$$

Note that this approximation will still underestimate forward convexity – a better idea may be a moment matching approximation that picks two equally probable future realisations $(t_{i+1}, X_{t_{i+1}}^-)$ and $(t_{i+1}, X_{t_{i+1}}^+)$ with $X_{t_{i+1}}^- + X_{t_{i+1}}^+ = E[X_{t_{i+1}}|\mathcal{F}_{t_i}]$ and with the difference between $X_{t_{i+1}}^-$ and $X_{t_{i+1}}^+$ chosen to match $Var[X_{t_{i+1}}|\mathcal{F}_{t_i}]$ (for this, I imagine we have to use (7.15) to estimate the variance). With that, one could obtain a higher order estimate for effective local variance $\hat{\sigma}_{loc}^2(t_i, X_{t_i}; \Delta t)$ obtained from

$$\hat{\sigma}_{loc}^2(t_i, X_{t_i}; \Delta t) = \frac{1}{2}\sigma_{loc}^2(t_i, X_{t_i}) + \frac{1}{4}\sigma_{loc}^2(t_{i+1}, X_{t_{i+1}}^-) + \frac{1}{4}\sigma_{loc}^2(t_{i+1}, X_{t_{i+1}}^+).$$

Methods for finding effective local volatilities applicable over larger time slices are somewhat neglected in the literature, and more rigorous analysis on this point would be welcomed by many. While inexact, the simplicity of (7.15) has much to commend it in practice.

7.3.2   Monte Carlo convergence goes as $1/\sqrt{N}$

One issue with the Monte Carlo method is its relatively slow convergence, which turns out to be really quite slow – of order $1/\sqrt{N}$. We can easily prove this using sampling theory, as discussed in Chapter 7 of DeGroot (1986) and many other statistical texts.

Suppose we have N simulations $\{V_1, \ldots, V_N\}$ of a price, where the V_i represent independent and identically distributed random variables, each with expectation $E[V_i] = \mu$ (population mean) and $Var[V_i] = \sigma_V^2$ (population variance). In our example, μ is the 'true' price of the option, which we're trying to estimate using N simulations, and σ_V^2 comes from measurement error.

We don't know μ (nor σ_V^2) but we can certainly estimate μ using a suitably chosen statistic. A statistic is nothing more than just a function of several random variables that are to be experimentally observed.

The sample mean $\bar{V} = (1/N)\sum_{i=1}^{N} V_i$ is an unbiased estimator of μ, since the first moment $E[\bar{V}] = (1/N)\sum_{i=1}^{N} E[V_i] = (1/N)\sum_{i=1}^{N} \mu = \mu$. Once these random variables $\{V_1, \ldots, V_N\}$ are actually observed, the sample mean $\bar{V}$ is just the arithmetic average of these observations.

More interestingly, we can compute the second central moment of $\bar{V}$, i.e. its variance. We obtain $Var[\bar{V}] = Var[(1/N)\sum_{i=1}^{N} V_i] = (1/N^2)Var[\sum_{i=1}^{N} V_i] = (1/N)Var[V_i] = (1/N)\sigma_V^2$. We don't know the population variance σ_V^2, but we can estimate it using the sample variance, another statistic:

$$s_{\bar{V}}^2 = \frac{\sum_{i=1}^{N} V_i^2 - N\bar{V}^2}{N - 1}. \tag{7.16}$$

The $N - 1$ term (Bessel's correction) in the denominator ensures that $s_{\bar{V}}^2$ is an unbiased estimator of $\sigma_{\bar{V}}^2$.

We therefore have $(1/N)s_{\bar{V}}^2$ as our estimate of $\mathbf{Var}[\bar{V}]$, and the *standard error* of $\bar{V}$ is just the square root of this quantity:

$$SE_{\bar{V}} = \frac{1}{\sqrt{N}}s_{\bar{V}} = \frac{1}{\sqrt{N}}\sqrt{\frac{\sum_{i=1}^{N} V_i^2 - N\bar{V}^2}{N - 1}}. \qquad (7.17)$$

We can use the standard error to construct a confidence interval for our estimate of μ, so, for example, we expect that about 68.3% of the time μ will lie within the interval $\bar{V} \pm SE_{\bar{V}}$ (within one standard error) and 95% of the time μ will be within $\bar{V} \pm 1.96SE_{\bar{V}}$. As we increase the number of simulations N, we expect $SE_{\bar{V}}$ to decrease as $1/\sqrt{N}$, and can therefore be increasingly confident with our estimate $\bar{V}$ for the price of the option.

Consequently, it makes sense then for a practical Monte Carlo implementation to return both the sample mean $\bar{V}$ *and* the standard error $SE_{\bar{V}}$, as the only extra bookkeeping involved is keeping track of $\sum_{i=1}^{N} V_i^2$ as well as $\sum_{i=1}^{N} V_i$.

Figure 7.1 shows exactly this $1/\sqrt{N}$ convergence for the simple case of an ATMS 1Y call option with $S_0 = K = 1$, domestic and foreign interest rates set to zero and $\sigma = 10\%$ in a Black–Scholes model, using a one-dimensional Monte Carlo algorithm with a simple Mersenne twister pseudo-random number generator, implemented in C++ by the author.

In practice, this means if we want to reduce the confidence intervals around a point estimate for the PV of an option by a factor of 2, i.e. to halve the error bounds around the price estimate, then we need to use four times the many simulations. The error bounds in Figure 7.1 for the 120 000 simulation case are indeed about half as wide as the 30 000 simulation case

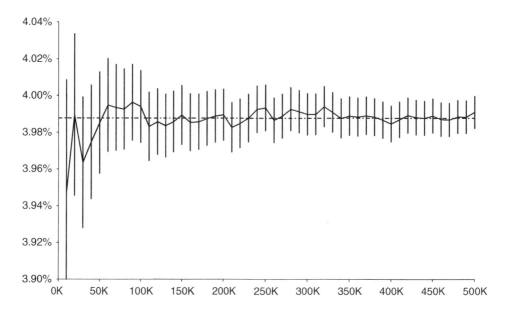

Figure 7.1 European call, $N_{\text{times}} = 10$: PV estimate and ± 1 s.d. error bars

Table 7.1   Standard errors halved by quadrupling N_{sims}

N_{sims}	$SE_{\bar{V}}$	SE/SE_{prev}
30 000	0.000 356 679	
120 000	0.000 179 301	0.502 694 273
480 000	$8.944\,42 \times 10^{-5}$	0.498 850 204

(see Table 7.1). Using this rule, one would expect that to halve them again would probably need about 480 000 simulations, and this is actually just about right.

A simple technique to verify that the convergence scales as $1/\sqrt{N_{sims}}$ is to extract the standard error from the Monte Carlo engine and to multiply it by $\sqrt{N_{sims}}$ to obtain a number that should be relatively constant over a wide range of N_{sims}. We tabulate these values in Table 7.2 and see that this certainly holds for this particular example.

As well as demonstrating that the convergence scales as $1/\sqrt{N_{sims}}$, it equivalently means that convergence scales as $1/\sqrt{T_{CPU}}$, where T_{CPU} is the amount of CPU time used to perform the Monte Carlo simulation, assuming other factors such as the number of timesteps N_{times} and CPU memory usage are held constant and only N_{sims} is changed. We therefore have another quantity we hope to keep constant:

$$\Theta = SE_{\bar{V}} * \sqrt{T_{CPU}}, \qquad (7.18)$$

which is tabulated in Table 7.3, with T_{CPU} measured in seconds.

In other words, the *best* we can do with Monte Carlo is to achieve convergence that scales as $1/\sqrt{T_{CPU}}$. That is as good as it gets for the standard Monte Carlo approach.

We can certainly do *worse* than this though. The above example shows the example of Monte Carlo simulation using 10 timesteps for a Black–Scholes model and a nonpath-dependent European option. Do we really need 10 timesteps? The answer is actually no, just one timestep would actually suffice. We can see this using the Θ number.

Decision rule for how to increase N_{sims} and N_{times} pragmatically

The Θ number gives us some idea of the most efficient way to balance the computational effort between increasing the number of simulations and the number of timesteps. If we tabulate Θ for x values of N_{sims} and y values of N_{times}, which I show in Table 7.4, we see that increasing the number of timesteps conveys little benefit whereas increasing the number of simulations reduces the standard error scaled by computational time. If you start at the top left corner and attempt to move away from it, while seeking out the valley of the tabulated two-dimensional surface, you end up moving out inexorably to the right. Consequently, the Θ decision rule tells us to increase the number of simulations but not the number of timesteps, at least for a European option with a Black–Scholes model and not taking into account term structure.

Table 7.2   Standard error multiplied by $100\sqrt{N_{sims}}$

10K	20K	30K	40K	50K	60K	70K	80K	90K	100K	110K
6.25	6.21	6.21	6.20	6.21	6.20	6.20	6.20	6.19	6.19	6.19

Table 7.3   European call: standard error multiplied by $100\,000\sqrt{N_{\text{CPU}}}$ for increasing N_{sims}

10K	20K	30K	40K	50K	60K	70K	80K	90K	100K	110K
5.67	5.72	5.73	5.60	5.70	5.65	5.62	5.62	5.71	5.63	5.77

The only caveat is that the standard error tells you how much variation your simulation has around the sample mean, being the point estimate for the price. It doesn't tell you whether that point estimate is biased or not. Consequently, it's a very good idea to check this against another independent pricing algorithm if possible. In Figure 7.2, we see that the prices for simulations with $N_{\text{times}} = 1$ appear to converge to the TV of 3.987% as N_{sims} increases from 10K to 500K. The TV mostly remains within one standard error of the MC price throughout, which is reassuring.

The utility of this approach is that we can use the exact same decision rule for either path-dependent options and/or more complex models than simple Black–Scholes to estimate the optimal balance between increasing N_{sims} and N_{times}.

7.3.3   Finding a balance between simulations and timesteps

We see above that we don't need that many timesteps for European options with a simple Black–Scholes model. As the price only depends on the distribution of logspot X_T at expiry, which is lognormally distributed under such a model, this is no surprise.

For path-dependent options, it's a different matter. Consider the example of a symmetric double no-touch binary option, with one year to expiry, and KO levels at $L = 0.9305$ and $U = 1.0695$, given the same Black–Scholes model as in Section 7.3.2. This is a simple product that pays 1 unit of cash, so long as the asset price process has *never* traded above 1.0695 nor below 0.9305 over the entire one year lifetime of the option.

This example has a TV of 9.9685% (I chose this example because the so-called 10% DNT is often of interest to traders, being particularly sensitive to stochastic and local volatility). As the barriers are continuously monitored, we cannot naively just check the spot level at the sample timepoints $\{t_0, t_1, \ldots, t_M\}$.

We can use one of two methods to get around this particular problem, both of which are well worth describing.

Table 7.4   European call: standard error multiplied by $100\,000\sqrt{N_{\text{CPU}}}$ for increasing N_{sims} and N_{times}

N_{times}	N_{sims}									
	10K	20K	30K	40K	50K	60K	70K	80K	90K	100K
1	1.68	1.80	1.83	1.80	1.80	1.84	1.83	1.82	1.81	1.96
5	3.97	4.05	4.10	4.11	4.09	4.08	4.07	4.11	4.15	4.14
10	5.67	5.72	5.73	5.60	5.70	5.65	5.62	5.62	5.71	5.63
15	7.04	7.00	6.97	7.00	7.02	7.01	7.02	7.06	7.07	7.11
20	8.12	8.18	8.30	8.04	8.10	8.13	8.19	9.75	8.26	8.13

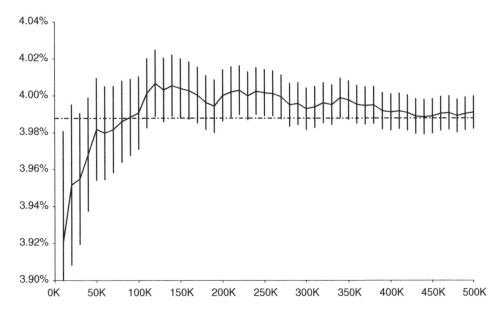

Figure 7.2   European call, $N_{\text{times}} = 1$: PV estimate and ± 1 s.d. error bars

The Broadie–Glassermann–Kou correction

As discussed in Broadie, Glassermann and Kou (1997), we can adjust the barrier level(s) inward by a factor of $\exp(\beta\sigma\sqrt{\Delta t})$, using the volatility[4] σ, with $\beta = -\zeta(\frac{1}{2})/\sqrt{2\pi} \approx 0.582\,597\,157\,939\,010\,67$, so the upper and lower levels U and L are adjusted to new values:

$$U' = U \exp(-\beta\sigma\sqrt{\Delta t}), \tag{7.19a}$$

$$L' = L \exp(\beta\sigma\sqrt{\Delta t}) \tag{7.19b}$$

respectively. The reason for this is that the Broadie, Glassermann and Kou correction as published tells us how to obtain the price of discretely monitored barrier options from a barrier option with a continuous knock-out feature. However, what we want to do in this case is the converse: to obtain a price estimate for a continuously monitored barrier option from the price of a suitably chosen discretely monitored barrier option, as we are using Monte Carlo simulation with discrete time-stepping.

Obviously, for single barrier products, only one of these adjustments is at all relevant. We then simulate the asset price process S_t at times $\{t_0, t_1, \ldots, t_M\}$ and check to see whether $S_{t_i} \leq L'$ or $S_{t_i} \geq U'$ for any of the t_i times – in which case, the product knocks out and the value at expiry for that particular simulation is zero.

Therefore, for a Monte Carlo simulation with 10 timesteps uniformly distributed over the interval from $t_0 = 0$ to $T = 1.0$, we have $\Delta t = 0.1$. Suppose $\sigma = 0.1$ for this example, in which case $\exp(\beta\sigma\sqrt{\Delta t}) = 1.018\,594\,2$. This factor means we transform the

---

[4] For a stochastic or local volatility model, we use the realised forward volatility driving the logspot process over the timeslice Δt, which will vary, simulation by simulation.

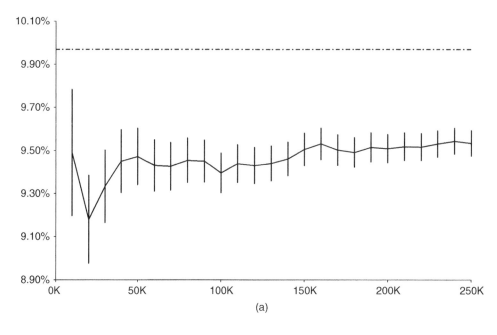

(a)

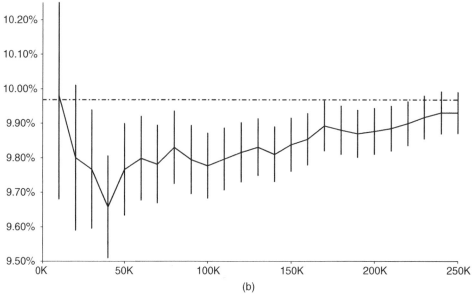

(b)

Figure 7.3   Double no-touch: PV estimate and ±1 s.d. error bars: (a) $N_{\text{times}} = 10$; (b) $N_{\text{times}} = 30$; (c) $N_{\text{times}} = 60$

original barrier levels $L = 0.9305$ and $U = 1.0695$ to $L' = 0.9305 \times 1.018\,594\,2 = 0.9478$ and $U' = 1.0695/1.018\,594\,2 = 1.0500$. Intuitively, this makes sense – imagine a particular Monte Carlo trajectory that attains realised points $\{1.0000, 0.9414, 0.9306, 0.9634, \dots\}$. None of these values, as observed on the discrete sample dates, is less than $L = 0.9305$, but it is

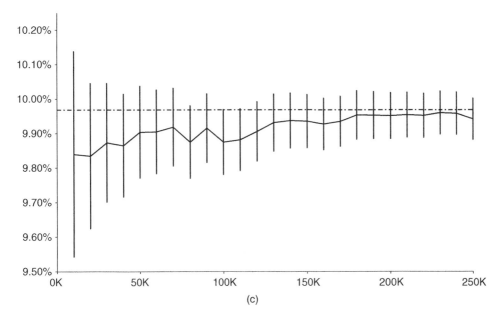

(c)

Figure 7.3 (continued)

very likely that the continuous trajectory *would* have made a deviation below L at some point, conditional on those discrete observations. We have therefore underestimated the probability of continuous knock-out by using the unadjusted barrier level L. The discrete barrier with adjusted level L', however, certainly knocks out at the $S_{t_2} = 0.9306$ observation and allows us to mimic continuously monitored barriers by suitably placed discrete barriers.

Figure 7.3 shows how a simple Monte Carlo engine with the Broadie–Glasserman–Kou correction eventually converges to the correct price, with N_{times} equal to 10, 30 or 60. For fewer timesteps, we see the convergence is far from good. This is not surprising because any Monte Carlo scheme that relies upon path histories either knocking out or not as a purely Boolean event has very coarse granularity. We're basically saying that for each path history, we simulate the process together with keeping track of an associated survival probability q_t that starts at unity ($q_0 = 1$) and ends up as either 1 or 0, depending on whether the asset price process at any timepoint is outside (L', U').

One can think of this as carrying along an auxiliary process for q_t with each simulation, and applying the transition rule that $q_{t_i} := 0$ if $S_{t_i} \leq L'$ or $S_{t_i} \leq U'$. At the end of the simulation, we compute the value function $q_T \times V_T$ (though, in practice, if q_t ever goes to zero, that particular simulation is terminated early).

Brownian bridge Monte Carlo

The other method for pricing continuously monitored barrier options uses the approach of making the survival probability q_t a continuous variable, which can smoothly decay from 1 downwards, to account for the likelihood that the spot process has made an excursion outside of the interval $[L, U]$ in between two timepoints t_i and t_{i+1}, conditional on the observed values S_{t_i} and $S_{t_{i+1}}$. Clearly, if $S_t \leq L$ or $S_t \geq U$, then the option knocks out at time t and q should be set to zero. The more interesting case is what happens if both S_t and S_{t+1} are inside (L, U). We will need an expression for the conditional probability that $u \in (t_i, t_{i+1})$ exists such that $S_u \notin (L, U)$, i.e. the probability of not hitting level L or level U in timeslice (t_i, t_{i+1}), conditioned on levels S_t and S_{t+1}. Let's denote this by $\ddot{\theta}_{t_i,t_{i+1}}(L, U)$, the two dots denoting the double barrier.

We compute this by an approximation

$$\ddot{\theta}_{t_i,t_{i+1}}(L, U) = \dot{\theta}_{t_i,t_{i+1}}(L) \times \dot{\theta}_{t_i,t_{i+1}}(U),$$

where we calculate the probabilities of not hitting L and not hitting U. The potential error in this approximation is that of hitting both barriers, and we assume that the probability of such an excursion is infinitesimal relative to the other three denumerable scenarios (remain within (L, U) throughout, make an excursion below L or make an excursion above U).

Using values for logspot instead, i.e. $X_t = \ln S_t$ and $X_{t+1} = \ln S_{t+1}$, we have

$$\dot{\theta}_{t_i,t_{i+1}}(B) = 1 - \exp\left[\frac{-2(\ln B - X_t)(\ln B - X_{t+1})}{\sigma^2 \Delta t}\right] \tag{7.20}$$

and then we can model q_t as a nonincreasing discrete time stochastic process on $\{t_0, t_1, \ldots, t_{N_{\text{times}}} = T\}$. We have $q_{t_0} = 1$ (assuming of course that $S_0 \in (L, U)$. Consider now S_{t_1}. If $S_{t_1} \notin (L, U)$, then we set $q_{t_1} = 0$ and terminate this particular simulation. If $S_{t_1} \in (L, U)$, however, we compute $\dot{\theta}_{t_0,t_1}$ and then have $q_{t_1} = q_{t_0} \times \dot{\theta}_{t_0,t_1}$. Evolution of subsequent values for q_{t_i} proceeds the same way by forward induction – we have $q_{ti+1} = q_{t_i} \times \dot{\theta}_{t_i,t_{i+1}}$. The survival probability q_{t_i} is a nonincreasing discrete time stochastic process. Eventually the simulation runs to time T and we then have both the asset value at expiry S_T together with the survival probability q_T. For a European product, we would use value at expiry $V_i = V_T(S_T)$, but for a knock-out product with the Brownian bridge approach we use $V_i = q_T \cdot V_T(S_T)$ instead.

7.3.4   Quasi Monte Carlo convergence *can* be as good as $1/N$

It is often noted that quasi-random number generators such as Halton, Faure, Sobol' and Niederreiter sequences can exhibit better convergence properties, potentially of order $1/N$ – see Niederreiter (1992) and Chapter 8 of Jäckel (2002). The problem is that pairwise independence is far from uniform, and actually degrades as one extracts increasingly many points from the sequence. This is particularly a problem for path-dependent options, and one would be strongly advised to take this into account when building simulation paths.

A sensible technique is to construct Brownian bridges, using the first quasi-random number to generate the asset price at time T from the starting value S_0 and then the second to generate the asset price at time $t = \frac{1}{2}T$ *conditional* on the values at $t = 0$ and $t = T$. The third and fourth quasi-random numbers can be used to determine the asset values at times $t = \frac{1}{4}T$ and $t = \frac{3}{4}T$, and so on. Further discussion can be found in Jung (1998) and Section 10.8.3 of Jäckel (2002).

It requires quite a lot of bookkeeping, however, to do this and to code it up, and from an FX practitioner's point of view, this class of simulation methods probably offers a much more tangible practical advantage for the valuation of non-path-dependent structures in higher dimensions, such as the European multicurrency baskets we encounter in Chapter 10, than it does for low-dimensional path-dependent options, which can be priced quite rapidly using low-dimensional PDE schemes.

7.3.5 Variance reduction

Variance reduction – antithetic sampling

Almost certainly the easiest mechanism to reduce the error of the Monte Carlo estimation is to employ the antithetic sampling technique. In its simplest form, for a one-dimensional Monte Carlo, this means that for each simulation where we use a stream $Z_1, \ldots, Z_{N_{times}} \sim N(0, 1)$ to simulate the asset price trajectory from today through to expiry, we build an additional parallel simulation where we use an antithetic stream $-Z_1, \ldots, -Z_{N_{times}}$, i.e. the arithmetic negative of all the deviates drawn from $N(0, 1)$, and use that to generate a second trajectory. In other words, using Euler time-stepping for a one-factor model, we obtain two realised simulations $X_t^{(j)}$ and $X_t^{(j+1)}$ of the asset price process from the same stream of pseudo-random numbers

$$X_{t_{i+1}}^{(j)} = X_{t_i}^{(j)} + \mu(t_i, X_{t_i}^{(j)})\Delta t + \sigma(t_i, X_{t_i}^{(j)})Z_i\sqrt{\Delta t}, \tag{7.21a}$$

$$X_{t_{i+1}}^{(j+1)} = X_{t_i}^{(j+1)} + \mu(t_i, X_{t_i}^{(j+1)})\Delta t - \sigma(t_i, X_{t_i}^{(j+1)})Z_i\sqrt{\Delta t}, \tag{7.21b}$$

with $\Delta t = t_{i+1} - t_i$. Note that this means that the instantanous logreturns of $X_t^{(j)}$ and $X_t^{(j+1)}$ are perfectly anticorrelated – and this is exactly why the technique reduces the error, because for every trajectory that goes up, there's an equivalent trajectory that goes down.

In higher dimensions, we refer back to (7.9) with $\mathbf{Z}_i = [Z_i^{(1)} \cdots Z_i^{(N)}]^\perp$ and obtain 2^N possible antithetic combinations:

$$\begin{bmatrix} \pm 1 & 0 & \cdots & 0 \\ 0 & \pm 1 & & 0 \\ \vdots & & 0 & \vdots \\ 0 & 0 & \cdots & \pm 1 \end{bmatrix} \begin{pmatrix} Z_i^{(1)} \\ Z_i^{(2)} \\ \vdots \\ Z_i^{(N)} \end{pmatrix},$$

each of which is fed into a separate simulation in the manner of (7.21).

The antithetic sampling technique is straightforward to implement and worth using at every opportunity, given its potential to improve convergence.

Variance reduction – control variate technique

If we are attempting to price a particular product $\mathbf{P}$ given a particular model $\mathbf{M}$ using Monte Carlo, then suppose that a similar model $\mathbf{M}'$ exists for which an exact price (or, at the least, a more exact price) can be found using a more exact pricing algorithm.

Denote the Monte Carlo prices by $V_{MC}(\mathbf{M}, \mathbf{P})$ and $V_{MC}(\mathbf{M}', \mathbf{P})$ respectively, and the exact price by $V_{exact}(\mathbf{M}', \mathbf{P})$. Since we know that the error introduced by the Monte Carlo estimation procedure is $\epsilon = V_{MC}(\mathbf{M}', \mathbf{P}) - V_{exact}(\mathbf{M}', \mathbf{P})$, if we reason that the Monte Carlo sampling error for the pricing problem $\{\mathbf{M}, \mathbf{P}\}$ is correlated with that for $\{\mathbf{M}', \mathbf{P}\}$, which we know to be ϵ, then we can subtract that estimated error from $V_{MC}(\mathbf{M}, \mathbf{P})$, giving our model control variate estimate

$$V_{MCCV}(\mathbf{M}, \mathbf{P}) = V_{MC}(\mathbf{M}, \mathbf{P}) - \left[V_{MC}(\mathbf{M}', \mathbf{P}) - V_{exact}(\mathbf{M}', \mathbf{P})\right].$$

Table 7.5 Importance sampling example

S_0	1.0	d_1	$-0.494\,68$
r^d	0%	d_2	$-1.014\,29$
r^f	0%	$N(d_1)$	0.310\,414
σ	30%	$N(d_2)$	0.155\,221
K	1.48	V_0	0.080\,686
T	3.0		

This is called the *model control variate*. One could use it for improving the Monte Carlo estimate for a price using local volatility by taking the Black–Scholes model as a control variate. Equivalently, one could use this for estimating the Monte Carlo price for a European option on LSV, using the Fourier transform price (not an exact price, but exact enough relative to Monte Carlo) for a pure stochastic volatility Heston model as the control variate.

Another equally useful idea is the *product control variate*. Suppose now that, relative to **P**, a similar product **P'** exists for which a more exact price can be found using a more exact pricing algorithm. We similarly have

$$V_{\text{MCCV}}(\mathbf{M}, \mathbf{P}) = V_{\text{MC}}(\mathbf{M}, \mathbf{P}) - \left[V_{\text{MC}}(\mathbf{M}, \mathbf{P'}) - V_{\text{exact}}(\mathbf{M}, \mathbf{P'}) \right].$$

The canonical example of this is pricing an Asian option with arithmetic averaging, using an Asian option with geometric averaging as the product control variate.

Variance reduction – importance sampling

Suppose we have a Black–Scholes model with an initial spot of unity, domestic and foreign interest rates both zero and a volatility of 30%, under which we attempt to price a deeply out-of-the-money call with strike $K = 1.48$ and time to expiry $T = 3$ (three years). Using (2.65), one computes the price as $V_0 = 0.080\,686$. The numbers in this example are shown in Table 7.5.

The strike of 1.48 is so far away, though, that the $N(d_2)$ term, which we know is the domestic risk-neutral probability $\mathbf{P}^d(S_T > K)$ of expiring in the money, is only $N(d_2) = 0.155\,221$. This means that, on average, for 100 000 simulations in a brute force Monte Carlo scheme, only about 15 000 will contribute any positive value to the sum (7.12).

Can we do better than this? The idea of importance sampling, as discussed in Kloeden and Platen (1992) and Glasserman (2004), is to shift the drift artificially to place more of the mass of the terminal distribution in the in-the-money region. This would of course introduce a bias, if it were not for the fact that we simultaneously adjust the pricing measure.

What measure can we shift to? Well, for starters, how about going from $\mathbf{P}^d$ to $\mathbf{P}^f$? As we know from Section 2.9, this is completely equivalent to pricing a European put in the flipped quote style: i.e. with $\hat{S}_0 = 1/S_0 = 1$ and $\hat{K} = 1/1.48 \approx 0.6756$ (and with r^d and r^f interchanged, except that both are zero in this particular example). Pricing the same option in either domestic or foreign risk-neutral measures analytically gives the same price using either (2.65) or (2.70).

However, from the point of view of Monte Carlo simulation, the choice of whether to price in the domestic or foreign risk-neutral measure makes a considerable difference. From the foreign investor's point of view, the risk-neutral probability of the European put with strike $\hat{K}$ expiring in the money is just the $N(d_1)$ computed earlier, which we see is 0.310 414 – basically

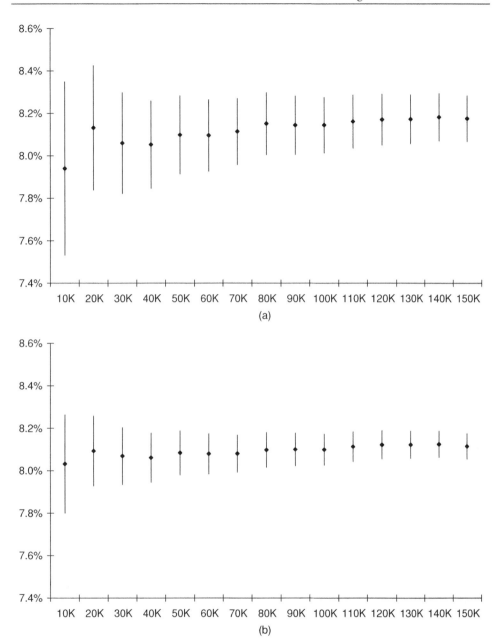

Figure 7.4 Monte Carlo in $\mathbf{P}^d$ and $\mathbf{P}^f$: PV estimate and ± 1 s.d. error bars: (a) Monte Carlo simulation in $\mathbf{P}^d$; (b) Monte Carlo simulation in $\mathbf{P}^f$

double the likelihood of $N(d_2)$. With this, we expect about 31 000 of our 100 000 simulations to make a positive value contribution to the sum (7.12) if we price a put on $\hat{S}_T$ under $\mathbf{P}^f$, where, in contrast, only about 15 000 simulations will make a positive contribution if we price a call on S_T under $\mathbf{P}^d$. We see this clearly in Figure 7.4.

The approach here is not the same as importance sampling as it is usually presented, as pricing from the foreign investor's point of view (as presented in Section 2.9) requires a call payout to be changed to a put payout and vice versa. Nevertheless, I illustrate it to convey the idea of changing measure. In fact, adjusting from a put payout to a call payout is actually unnecessary. We saw in Section 2.7.3 that the foreign risk-neutral measure could be characterised by supposing the FX spot rate to appreciate at $\mu^f = r^d - r^f + \sigma^2$, as given in (2.44). Since this exceeds $\mu^d = r^d - r^f$, more Monte Carlo simulations can be expected to be in the in-the-money region with $S_T \geq K$ at expiry T.

The question is, how to adjust for the change of measure? Usually, we attempt to compute $V_0 = e^{-r^d T} \mathbf{E}^d [V_T(S_T)]$. For the purposes of this exercise, however, we illustrate how importance sampling can be used to improve convergence by shifting measure (and therefore risk-neutral drift) to a measure in which more simulations will expire in the in-the-money region of the payoff. The example here is that of a European call, which benefits from an increase in drift from μ^d to μ^f. However, we have to adjust the measure in which the expectation is taken:

$$V_0 = e^{-r^d T} \mathbf{E}^d [V_T(S_T)]$$

$$= e^{r^d T} \mathbf{E}^f \left[\frac{d\mathbf{P}^d}{d\mathbf{P}^f} V_T(S_T) \right] \tag{7.22}$$

From (2.53) we have $d\mathbf{P}^f / d\mathbf{P}^d = \exp\left(\sigma W_T^d - \frac{1}{2}\sigma^2 T\right)$ and for W_T^d we use (2.57a) to write

$$\frac{d\mathbf{P}^f}{d\mathbf{P}^d} = \exp\left(\sigma W_T^d - \frac{1}{2}\sigma^2 T\right) = e^{-\mu^d T} \frac{S_T}{S_0},$$

from which we obtain

$$\frac{d\mathbf{P}^d}{d\mathbf{P}^f} = e^{\mu^d T} \frac{S_0}{S_T}. \tag{7.23}$$

Using (7.23) in (7.22) gives

$$V_0 = e^{r^d T} \mathbf{E}^f \left[e^{-\mu^d T} \frac{S_T}{S_0} V_T(S_T) \right]. \tag{7.24}$$

The reader can verify, for the simple example of a Black–Scholes model and a non-path-dependent option such as a European call, that this gives the same improved convergence as pricing the flipped European put on $\hat{S}_T$ under $\mathbf{P}^f$. Instead of having to translate the value at expiry into flipped terms, we only need to introduce a likelihood ratio.

The mathematical argument is less elegant and certainly less analytically feasible in the case where we have a more complex model than a pure Black–Scholes model and where we have a path-dependent option that depends on interim fixings S_{t^*} as well as the terminal spot rate S_T. For these reasons, importance sampling is not used very often in FX option pricing, at least not among the practitioner community.

It is easier and arguably more intuitive to change measure by shifting to the pricing numeraire under which the greatest number of simulations contribute to the final payoff. This achieves much the same objective as importance sampling and is more grounded in economic reality. Note that we can construct other synthetic numeraires to perform the risk-neutral pricing in, at the cost of having less of a real-world economic interpretation; this allows even greater flexibility in the choice of drift adjustment.

7.4   CONVECTION–DIFFUSION PDEs IN FINANCE

For a number of reasons, partial differential equations are especially popular among FX quants. Foreign currency option pricing is typically quite low dimensional (the examples given in this book are basically all one, two or three dimensional, though the models of Chapter 10 do extend to higher dimensions). Notably, for problems with dimensionality less than or equal to three, PDE methods such as encountered in real-world[5] engineering and applied mathematics problems are directly applicable. Further, the exotic options encountered in foreign currency often have a continuously monitored knock-in or knock-out feature, as described in Chapter 8, which PDE methods handle very naturally by imposition of a suitable Dirichlet condition. Finally, the calibration of a local stochastic volatility model as described in Chapter 6 requires the numerical solution of the Fokker–Planck PDE, coupled together with a forward bootstrapping procedure.

We attempt to present the general machinery required for the use and numerical solution of partial differential equations without restricting ourselves to any particular model, or indeed dimensionality, using the finite difference method.[6]

It is appropriate to use a similar notation to that in Section 5.2.2. We recognise that the backward partial differential equations we encounter for pricing, in the absence of jump diffusions, are all fundamentally convection–diffusion problems (Morton, 1996) in the realm of finance. Suppose coefficients b_{jk}, a_j and f (diffusion, convection and reaction terms respectively) can be found for which the backward partial differential equation describing the value $V = V(\mathbf{x}_t, t)$ of a derivative contract, expressed in terms of partial derivatives with respect to time t and state variables x_i (the tradeable factors can be represented in logspot or spot coordinates, as desired, and clearly this representation permits untradeable factors in the vector of state variables also), can be written

$$\frac{\partial V}{\partial t} + \sum_{j,k=1}^{m} b_{jk}(\mathbf{x}, t)\frac{\partial^2 V}{\partial x_j \partial x_k} + \sum_{j=1}^{m} a_j(\mathbf{x}, t)\frac{\partial V}{\partial x_j} + fV = 0. \qquad (7.25)$$

By analogy with applied mathematics, we refer to t as the temporal variable and x_j as the spatial variables. Since we shall be limiting ourselves to no more than three spatial variables at most when it comes to PDE schemes, we use x, y, z at various points to denote x_1, x_2 and x_3 – especially when it comes to setting up spatial mesh discretisations. Whether x_3 refers to the third spatial variable or point number 3 on a discretised mesh for x should be clear from the context.

For example, the simple Black–Scholes equation (2.17) admits the representation

$$b_{11} = \frac{1}{2}\sigma^2 x_1^2,$$

$$a_1 = (r^d - r^f)x_1,$$

$$f = -r^d,$$

---

[5] We live in three spatial dimensions and one temporal dimension, after all.
[6] Other methods are certainly possible, such as the finite element method (Topper, 2005).

where $x_1 = S$ denotes spot. Note that b_{11} and a_1 depend on x_1. When expressed in logspot coordinates $x_1 = \ln S = x$, as in (2.24), we have the simpler representation in which the diffusion and convection coefficients are homogeneous:

$$b_{11} = \frac{1}{2}\sigma^2,$$

$$a_1 = r^d - r^f - \frac{1}{2}\sigma^2,$$

$$f = -r^d.$$

For the Black–Scholes term structure model, we have the above but with instantaneous parameters r_t^d, r_t^f and σ_t, which depend on the temporal variable t. Similarly for the local volatility model of Chapter 5, the diffusion coefficient becomes a function of both x_1 and t, and one has

$$b_{11} = \frac{1}{2}\sigma_{loc}^2(x_1, t),$$

$$a_1 = r_t^d - r_t^f - \frac{1}{2}\hat{\sigma}_{loc}^2(x_1, t),$$

$$f = -r_t^d,$$

in logspot coordinates.

For multidimensional models, we have more coefficients, naturally. The multicurrency Black–Scholes models of Chapter 10 can be written similarly as

$$b_{jk} = \frac{1}{2}\rho_{jk}\sigma_j\sigma_k,$$

$$a_j = r^d - r^{f;j} - \frac{1}{2}\rho_{jk}\sigma_j\sigma_k,$$

$$f = -r^d.$$

For the Heston model and its LSV variant, write the appropriate pricing PDE – either (6.52) or (6.70) – as

$$b_{11} = \frac{1}{2}x_2 A^2(x_1, t),$$

$$b_{22} = \frac{1}{2}\alpha^2 x_2,$$

$$b_{12} = b_{21} = \frac{1}{2}\alpha\rho x_2 A(x_1, t),$$

$$a_1 = r^d - r^f - \frac{1}{2}x_2 A^2(x_1, t),$$

$$a_2 = \kappa[m - x_2] - \lambda V,$$

$$f = -r^d,$$

where the Heston case is read off by substituting $A(x, t) = 1$ into the above.

The three-factor pricing PDE (11.23) from Chapter 11 admits a similar representation, with

$$b_{11} = \frac{1}{2}[\hat{\sigma}^{fx}(x_1, t)]^2,$$

$$b_{22} = \frac{1}{2}[\sigma_t^d]^2,$$

$$b_{33} = \frac{1}{2}[\sigma_t^f]^2,$$

$$b_{12} = b_{21} = \frac{1}{2}\rho_t^{fx,d},$$

$$b_{13} = b_{31} = \frac{1}{2}\rho_t^{fx,f}, \tag{7.26}$$

$$b_{23} = b_{32} = \frac{1}{2}\rho_t^{d,f},$$

$$a_1 = \varphi_t^d + x_2 - \varphi_t^f - x_3 - \frac{1}{2}[\hat{\sigma}^{fx}(x_1, t)]^2,$$

$$a_2 = -\kappa_t^d x_2,$$

$$a_3 = -\kappa_t^f x_3 - \rho_t^{fx,f}\sigma_t^f \hat{\sigma}^{fx}(x_1, t),$$

$$f = -(x_2 + \varphi_t^d).$$

An important word is in order about the presence of various inhomogeneous terms in these coefficients, and how this relates to the numerical aspects of their solution. We shall see below that if the convection terms a_j are too large with respect to the corresponding diffusion terms b_{jj}, then this can cause numerical difficulties for a numerical scheme.

7.4.1 Visualising diffusion

Figure 7.5 shows schematically how the diffusion can be visualised for some of the models considered in this work. The backward pricing partial differential equations in this book, such as the Black–Scholes equation, describe how the future value of a derivative security diffuses back to today. I attempt to portray this visually in Figure 7.5 by portraying a spatial distribution of some physical quantity such as a chemical solute, temperature distribution or suchlike (I will stick to the chemical solute metaphor, as it's easier to visualise a chemical solute in a tank than to visually examine a temperature gradient). For the one-dimensional diffusion systems such as Black–Scholes and local volatility, we project the system uniformly into a second spatial dimension so we can visualise it easily, and compare it with two-dimensional diffusion systems such as stochastic volatility and local stochastic volatility. This is presented purely for expository purposes and is quite nonrigorous – this discussion is purely meant to help the reader gain some physical intuition regarding these models.

The meshes shown are notably *not* finite difference grids; they are schematically designed to represent how porous the medium is to the flow of the chemical solute. Where the mesh lines are packed in closely together, this is meant to illustrate less diffusivity, and where the mesh lines are sparse, the solute has more space to diffuse.

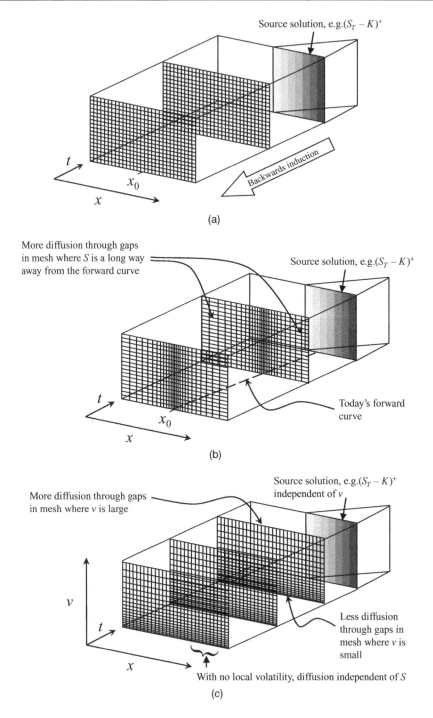

Figure 7.5 Schematic illustrations of one- and two-dimensional convection diffusion PDEs: (a) Black–Scholes diffusion; (b) local volatility diffusion; (c) stochastic volatility diffusion; (d) local stochastic volatility diffusion

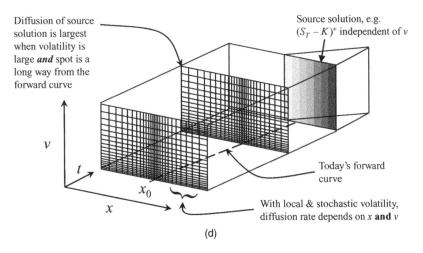

Diffusion of source
solution is largest
when volatility is
large *and* spot is a
long way from the
forward curve

Source solution, e.g.
$(S_T - K)^+$ independent of v

Today's forward
curve

With local & stochastic volatility,
diffusion rate depends on x **and** v

(d)

Figure 7.5   (continued)

Start with Figure 7.5(a), which shows how a terminal distribution of value diffuses back homogeneously to today, in the absence of any state-dependent terms in b_{11}. Compare this to Figure 7.5(b), which represents a pure local volatility model. In this case, the chemical solute is more likely to diffuse the further we are from the central part of the configuration region (basically, the diffusion is minimal around the centre of the local volatility function).

In both Figures 7.5(a) and (b), the y axis plays no role apart from allowing us to see what's going on. For the other two figures, we let y denote the untradeable factor corresponding to stochastic variance v. In Figure 7.5(c), we now see that the diffusivity is inhomogeneous in the second dimension and is greater where v is large, but goes to zero as v goes to zero. This is the effect of having a second factor driving the volatility of the tradeable asset. Finally, combining features from Figures 7.5(b) and (c), the local stochastic volatility model, pictured schematically in Figure 7.5(d), exhibits an inhomogeneous diffusivity that depends on both the tradeable factor x and the untradeable factor v.

7.4.2   Visualising convection

Convection–diffusion coefficients (7.26) corresponding to the longdated FX model of Chapter 11 are interesting, in that the spatial dependency is exhibited primarily in the convection terms a_j, and exclusively so if local volatility is neglected. The lower dimensional models we encounter are quite different in this regard.

The convection vector $\mathbf{a} = (a_1(x_1, \ldots, x_m), \ldots, a_m(x_1, \ldots, x_m))$ can be naturally thought of as a vector field in $\mathbb{R}^m$ and it will be interesting to see what it looks like, mapped in the state space $(x_1, \ldots, x_m) \in \mathbb{R}^m$.

Let us assume that domestic and foreign interest rates are comparable so that there is minimal convection due to any $r^d - r^f$ differential (we ignore the $\frac{1}{2}\sigma$ term due to working in logspot coordinates). Consequently, the one-dimensional models (Black–Scholes, Black–Scholes term structure and local volatility) are trivial.

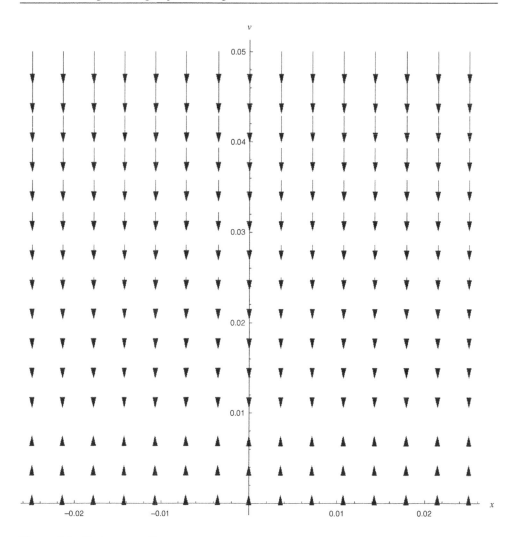

Figure 7.6 Heston convection

   In the two-dimensional model pantheon, we see convective terms of interest in the stochastic and LSV models, due to the presence of mean reversion in the second factor, pulling the chemical solute back towards an attractive level in the v direction. This is illustrated in Figure 7.6, where I have set $\kappa = 0.1$, $m = 0.01$ and $\lambda = 0$.
   As forewarned at the beginning, the three-dimensional model for longdated FX has a particularly demanding convection term to deal with. In Figures 7.7 and 7.8, I map the convection vector $\mathbf{a}(x, y, z) = (y - z, -\frac{1}{2}y, -\frac{1}{2}z)$, which adequately illustrated the problems one is likely to encounter. In purely the yz plane, the convection is mean reverting in both of these two state variables, hence the radial behaviour shown in Figure 7.8(a), but these factors also give rise to a third convective effect perpendicular to the yz plane, illustrated in

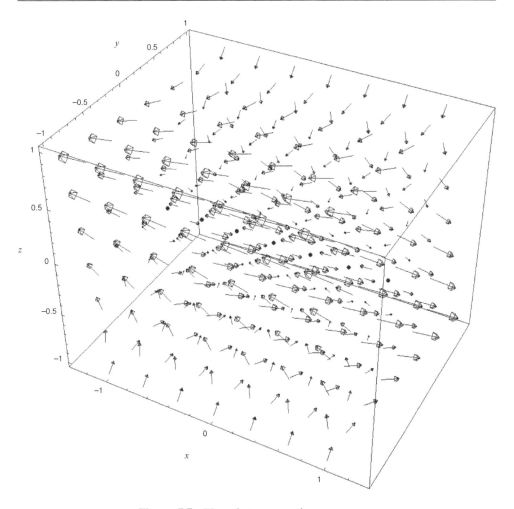

Figure 7.7   Three-factor convection

Figure 7.8(b), which gives a positive convection term in the x direction when $y > z$, shown as light colours in the heatmap, and negative when $z > y$ (shown in dark).

What this means, together with the discussion in Section 6.8.3 on LSV calibration, is that ideally we wish to equip ourselves with a PDE toolkit that permits:

- nonuniform spatial and temporal meshes;
- ability to handle mixed derivatives arising from correlation terms;
- schemes to handle convection-dominated problems;

7.5   NUMERICAL METHODS FOR PDEs

The first requirement is to shift to time-reversed coordinates in the standard manner, placing

$$\tau = T - t, \tag{7.27}$$

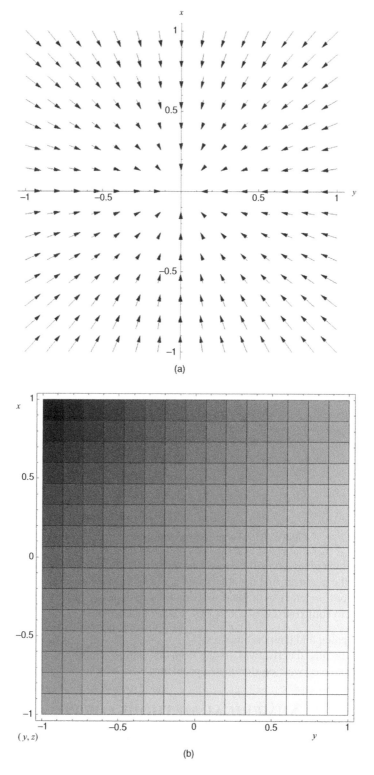

(a)

(b)

Figure 7.8 Cross-sectional representation of convection for the three-factor FX/IR model: (a) x component of convection for the three-factor FX/IR model as function of (y, z); (b) x component of the convention normal to the y, z plane for the three-factor FX/IR model as function of (y, z).

which transforms (7.25) into

$$\frac{\partial V}{\partial \tau} = \mathcal{L}V, \tag{7.28a}$$

where

$$\mathcal{L}V = \sum_{j,k=1}^{m} b_{jk}(\mathbf{x}, t) \frac{\partial^2 V}{\partial x_j \, \partial x_k} + \sum_{j=1}^{m} a_j(\mathbf{x}, t) \frac{\partial V}{\partial x_j} + f(\mathbf{x}, t)V, \tag{7.28b}$$

where $t = T - \tau$. For brevity, when we write $b_{jk}(\mathbf{x}, \tau)$ in the PDE with temporal coordinate τ, it will be understood that this means $b_{jk}(\mathbf{x}, T - \tau)$, and similarly for a_j and f. It would be more technically correct to use hatted coefficients, e.g. $\hat{b}_{jk}(\mathbf{x}, \tau) = b_{jk}(\mathbf{x}, T - \tau)$, but to the detriment of readability.

7.6 EXPLICIT FINITE DIFFERENCE SCHEME

Suppose that up to three spatial coordinates x_1, x_2 and x_3 exist, also denoted x, y and z, along with the time-reversed temporal coordinate τ, which is sampled at mesh points $\{\tau_1, \tau_2, \ldots, \tau_{N_t}\}$. Spatial meshes also exist, given by $\{x_1, x_2, \ldots, x_{N_x}\}$ $\{y_1, y_2, \ldots, y_{N_y}\}$ and $\{z_1, z_2, \ldots, z_{N_z}\}$. Due to stability restrictions, we can assume that the mesh spacings are constant, i.e. $h^\tau = \tau_i - \tau_{i-1}$, $h^x = x_i - x_{i-1}$, $h^y = y_i - y_{i-1}$ and $h^z = z_i - z_{i-1}$.

Let the values of $V(x, \ldots, \tau)$ on the mesh be denoted

$$V(x_i, y_j, z_k, \tau_l) = V^l_{i,j,k},$$

where the indices k and j are removed for lower dimensional PDEs in the natural manner. We sometimes write $V(x_i, \ldots, \tau_l) = V^l_{i,\ldots}$, where it is understood that other spatial variables and their mesh indices are included if necessary, depending on the dimensionality of the problem.

For an explicit PDE algorithm, we use the forward tau and central space (FTCS) method, making approximations:

$$\frac{\partial V(x_i, \ldots, \tau_l)}{\partial \tau} = \frac{V^{l+1}_{i,\ldots} - V^l_{i,\ldots}}{h^\tau}, \tag{7.29a}$$

$$\frac{\partial V(x_i, \ldots, \tau_l)}{\partial x} = \frac{V^l_{i+1,\ldots} - V^l_{i-1,\ldots}}{2h^x}, \tag{7.29b}$$

$$\frac{\partial^2 V(x_i, \ldots, \tau_l)}{\partial x^2} = \frac{V^l_{i+1,\ldots} - 2V^l_{i,\ldots} + V^l_{i-1,\ldots}}{[h^x]^2}. \tag{7.29c}$$

Partial derivatives with respect to y and z are obtained similarly, e.g.

$$\frac{\partial V(x_i, y_j, \ldots, \tau_l)}{\partial y} = \frac{V^l_{i,j+1,\ldots} - V^l_{i,j-1,\ldots}}{2h^y} \tag{7.30}$$

and by applying (7.30) to (7.29b) we obtain the mixed partial derivative terms such as

$$\frac{\partial^2 V(x_i, y_j, \ldots, \tau_l)}{\partial x \, \partial y} = \frac{1}{4h^x h^y} \left[V^l_{i+1,j+1,\ldots} - V^l_{i-1,j+1,\ldots} - V^l_{i+1,j-1,\ldots} + V^l_{i-1,j-1,\ldots} \right]. \tag{7.31}$$

Using (7.29) we write $\mathcal{L}V$ in (7.28) in the one-dimensional case:

$$\mathcal{L}V^l_i = \frac{b_{11}}{[h^x]^2} \left[V^l_{i+1} - 2V^l_i + V^l_{i-1} \right] + \frac{a_1}{2h^x} \left[V^l_{i+1} - V^l_{i-1} \right] + f V^l_i, \tag{7.32}$$

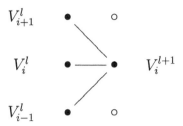

$$V_{i+1}^l \quad \bullet \qquad \circ$$

$$V_i^l \quad \bullet \!\!-\!\!\bullet \quad V_i^{l+1}$$

$$V_{i-1}^l \quad \bullet \qquad \circ$$

Figure 7.9 Explicit finite difference stencil

where it should be noted that b_{11}, a_1 and f may be functions of x and τ and therefore should really carry indices i and l. This would of course get confusing, so for notational convenience I will just assume that b_{jk}, a_j and f are evaluated at the appropriate point on the spatial and temporal grids.

In two dimensions we also use (7.31), writing

$$\mathcal{L}V_{i,j}^l = \frac{b_{11}}{[h^x]^2}\left[V_{i+1,j}^l - 2V_{i,j}^l + V_{i-1,j}^l\right] + \frac{b_{22}}{[h^y]^2}\left[V_{i,j+1}^l - 2V_{i,j}^l + V_{i,j-1}^l\right]$$
$$+ \frac{a_1}{2h^x}\left[V_{i+1,j}^l - V_{i-1,j}^l\right] + \frac{a_2}{2h^y}\left[V_{i,j+1}^l - V_{i,j-1}^l\right]$$
$$+ \frac{2b_{12}}{4h^x h^y}\left[V_{i+1,j+1}^l - V_{i-1,j+1}^l - V_{i+1,j-1}^l + V_{i-1,j-1}^l\right] + fV_{i,j}^l. \tag{7.33}$$

The FTCS scheme in three and higher dimensions follow similarly.

Clearly $\mathcal{L}V$, whether specified in (7.32), (7.33) or the three-dimensional case, only depends on values of $V_{i,\dots}^l$ at the lth tau mesh. We see a stencil in Figure 7.9 for the one-dimensional finite difference scheme. From (7.29a) and (7.28a), we have

$$V_{i,\dots}^{l+1} = V_{i,\dots}^l + h^\tau \mathcal{L}V_{i,\dots}^l = (1 + h^\tau \mathcal{L})V_{i,\dots}^l, \tag{7.34}$$

which means that mesh values at the $(l+1)$th tau mesh can be explicitly inferred from those at the lth tau mesh. Hence the name explicit PDE scheme.

How many points from the lth tau mesh are required to estimate $V_{i,\dots}^{l+1}$ though? In the one-dimensional case, we have a particularly simple representation

$$V_i^{l+1} = \frac{h^\tau b_{11}}{[h^x]^2}\left[V_{i+1}^l - 2V_i^l + V_{i-1}^l\right] + \frac{h^\tau a_1}{2h^x}\left[V_{i+1}^l - V_{i-1}^l\right] + (1 + fh^\tau)V_i^l.$$

This can be expressed as an inner product

$$V_i^{l+1} = \left[\frac{h^\tau b_{11}}{[h^x]^2} - \frac{h^\tau a_1}{2h^x}, \quad 1 + fh^\tau - \frac{2h^\tau b_{11}}{[h^x]^2}, \quad \frac{h^\tau b_{11}}{[h^x]^2} + \frac{h^\tau a_1}{2h^x}\right]\begin{pmatrix} V_{i-1}^l \\ V_i^l \\ V_{i+1}^l \end{pmatrix}. \tag{7.35}$$

Suppose we write an entire vector of mesh points at $\tau = \tau_l$, i.e. $\mathbf{V}^l = (V_1^l, V_2^l, \ldots, V_{N_x}^l)$. We can then write the explicit PDE as a tridiagonal matrix, giving the mesh points at $\tau = \tau_{l+1}$ as

$$\mathbf{V}^{l+1} = \begin{bmatrix} B_1 & C_1 & 0 & \cdots & \\ A_2 & B_2 & C_2 & \cdots & \\ & & \cdots & A_{N_x-1} & B_{N_x-1} & C_{N_x-1} \\ & & \cdots & 0 & A_{N_x} & B_{N_x} \end{bmatrix} \mathbf{V}^l, \qquad (7.36)$$

where, for i in the interior range $2 \leq i \leq N_x - 1$,

$$A_i = \frac{h^\tau b_{11}(x_i, \tau_l)}{[h^x]^2} - \frac{h^\tau a_1(x_i, \tau_l)}{2h^x}, \qquad (7.37a)$$

$$B_i = 1 + f(x_i, \tau_l)h^\tau - \frac{2h^\tau b_{11}(x_i, \tau_l)}{[h^x]^2}, \qquad (7.37b)$$

$$C_i = \frac{h^\tau b_{11}(x_i, \tau_l)}{[h^x]^2} + \frac{h^\tau a_1(x_i, \tau_l)}{2h^x}. \qquad (7.37c)$$

With this matrix representation, (7.35) can be written

$$V_i^{l+1} = \begin{bmatrix} A_i & B_i & C_i \end{bmatrix} \begin{pmatrix} V_{i-1}^l \\ V_i^l \\ V_{i+1}^l \end{pmatrix}.$$

7.6.1 Boundary conditions

When i is equal to 1 or N_x, however, the terms on the first or last row of the matrix in (7.36) require knowledge of the boundary conditions governing the PDE. Typical boundary conditions encountered or at least discussed in finance are (i) Dirichlet, (ii) intrinsic, (iii) Neumann (so the first spatial derivative vanishes on the boundary) and (iv) linearity, or the so-called 'natural' boundary condition, which ensures that the second spatial derivative vanishes on the boundary.

In the case of multiple spatial dimensions, these spatial derivatives should be understood to refer to the partial derivative normal to the boundary; i.e. we might conceivably require either $\partial V / \partial x$ or $\partial^2 V / \partial x^2$ to vanish on either or both of the spatial boundaries for x, i.e. $x = L_x$ or $x = U_x$.

It is well to note, however, that these boundary conditions can change during the course of the lifetime of an option pricing problem, e.g. windowed barrier options.

Dirichlet boundary condition

The Dirichlet condition is handled straightforwardly: we just set V_1^l or $V_{N_x}^l$ to zero, and in order to preserve this, we have $B_1 = 1$ and $C_1 = 0$ (for a left-hand Dirichlet boundary condition) or $A_{N_x} = 0$ and $B_{N_x} = 1$ (for the right-hand Dirichlet boundary condition). Dirichlet boundary conditions are completely standard for pricing knock-outs, no-touches, double knock-outs and double no-touches.

Intrinsic boundary condition

We handle this is much the same way as the Dirichlet condition. If $V(x_1, \tau) = F(\tau)$ for a prespecified function $F(\cdot)$, then we just have $B_1 = F(\tau_{l+1})/F(\tau_l)$ and $C_1 = 0$. In practice, we probably just set $V_1^{l+1} = F(\tau_{l+1})$ at each iteration. The same applies on the right-hand boundary, if required. An intrinsic boundary condition is not so common; one might see it for the example of an instant one-touch.

Neumann in x boundary condition

If $\partial V/\partial x = 0$ on the left-hand boundary $x = x_1$, then (7.28b) in one spatial dimension simplifies to

$$\left.\frac{\partial V}{\partial \tau}\right|_{x=x_1} = b_{11}(x_1, \tau)\left.\frac{\partial^2 V}{\partial x^2}\right|_{x=x_1} + f(x_1, \tau)V\big|_{x=x_1}. \tag{7.38}$$

How do we estimate $\partial^2 V/\partial x^2$ at $x = x_1$? It is standard to introduce a 'ghost point' x_0 outside of the configuration region, and as we are free to place it anywhere, we may as well choose it so that x_1 lies exactly midway between x_0 and x_2, i.e. $x_0 = 2x_1 - x_2$. If the first derivative vanishes at x_1, then by symmetry we must have $V(x_0, \tau) = V(x_2, \tau)$, i.e. $V_0^l = V_2^l$, which we can use in, (7.29c), i.e.

$$\left.\frac{\partial^2 V(x_1, \tau_l)}{\partial x^2}\right|_{x=x_1} = \frac{2[V_2^l - V_1^l]}{[h_2^x]^2} \tag{7.39}$$

Note that we specifically use $h_2^x = x_2 - x_1$ in the denominator, as this still holds even if the other mesh spacings are nonuniform. Using (7.39) in (7.38), we obtain

$$V_1^{l+1} = V_1^l + h^\tau \left[\frac{2b_{11}}{[h_2^x]^2}\left[V_2^l - V_1^l\right] + fV_1^l\right],$$

i.e.

$$B_1 = 1 + fh^\tau - \frac{2b_{11}h^\tau}{[h_2^x]^2} \quad \text{and} \quad C_1 = \frac{2b_{11}h^\tau}{[h_2^x]^2}. \tag{7.40a}$$

In the same manner, for a Neumann boundary condition at x_{N_x}, we have

$$A_{N_x} = -\frac{2b_{11}h^\tau}{[h_{N_x}^x]^2} \quad \text{and} \quad B_{N_x} = 1 + fh^\tau + \frac{2b_{11}h^\tau}{[h_{N_x}^x]^2}. \tag{7.40b}$$

Linearity in x boundary condition

Similarly, if $\partial^2 V/\partial x^2 = 0$ on the left-hand boundary $x = x_1$, then (7.28b) simplifies to

$$\frac{\partial V}{\partial \tau} = a_1(x_1, \tau)\frac{\partial V}{\partial x} + f(x_1, \tau)V. \tag{7.41}$$

There are two approaches to take to estimating $\partial V / \partial x$. The first is to use a one-sided difference scheme in place of (7.29b), such as one of

$$\frac{\partial V(x_1, \tau_l)}{\partial x} = \frac{V_2^l - V_1^l}{h_2^x} \tag{7.42a}$$

or

$$\frac{\partial V(x_{N_x}, \tau_l)}{\partial x} = \frac{V_{N_x}^l - V_{N_x-1}^l}{h_{N_x}^x}, \tag{7.42b}$$

to obtain

$$V_1^{l+1} = V_1^l + h^\tau \left[\frac{a_1}{h_2^x} \left[V_2^l - V_1^l \right], + f V_1^l \right],$$

i.e.

$$B_1 = 1 + f h^\tau - \frac{a_1 h^\tau}{h_2^x} \quad \text{and} \quad C_1 = \frac{a_1 h^\tau}{h_2^x}. \tag{7.43a}$$

Similarly, for a linear boundary condition at x_{N_x}, we have

$$A_{N_x} = -\frac{a_1 h^\tau}{h_{N_x}^x} \quad \text{and} \quad B_{N_x} = 1 + f h^\tau + \frac{a_1 h^\tau}{h_{N_x}^x}. \tag{7.43b}$$

The second approach is to use the 'ghost point' idea, as before. If x_1 is equidistant from x_0 and x_2, and $V(\cdot)$ is required to be linear at x_1, then $x_1 = \frac{1}{2}[x_0 + x_2]$ implies $V_1^l = \frac{1}{2}[V_0^l + V_2^l]$. We obtain the estimated value of $V(\cdot)$ satisfying the linearity condition at the ghost point $V_0^l = 2V_1^l - V_2^l$, which upon substitution into (7.29b) yields

$$\frac{\partial V(x_1, \tau_l)}{\partial x} = \frac{V_2^l - V_0^l}{2h_2^x} = \frac{2V_2^l - 2V_1^l}{2h_2^x} = \frac{V_2^l - V_1^l}{h_2^x}. \tag{7.44}$$

Comparing (7.44) with (7.42a), the two approaches turn out to be consistent.

Linearity in s boundary condition

Option payments are far more likely to be linear in spot than logspot. Note that $\partial^2 V / \partial S^2 = \frac{1}{S^2}[\partial^2 V / \partial x^2 - \partial V / \partial x]$. As a result, if convexity with respect to spot coordinates vanishes on the boundary, we impose $\partial^2 V / \partial x^2 = \partial V / \partial x$. This can be implemented by blending features from the previous two boundary conditions.

7.6.2   Von Neumann stability and the dimensionless heat equation

The benefits of the explicit scheme are that it is easy to code, handles correlations via mixed partial derivatives and is easy to understand. One major disadvantage, though, is that unless the time spacing is sufficiently small, the scheme will be numerically unstable.

In this section I will demonstrate how this arises, starting with the dimensionless heat equation for ease of understanding.

Consider (7.28). In the special case where $b_{ij} = \delta_{ij}$, $a_i = 0$ and $f = 0$, we have the dimensionless heat equation for $Q(x_1, \ldots, x_m, \tau)$ in several dimensions, with respect to spatial coordinates x_j and temporal[7] coordinate τ:

$$\frac{\partial Q}{\partial \tau} = \sum_{j=1}^{m} \frac{\partial^2 Q}{\partial x_j{}^2}. \tag{7.45}$$

Our analysis will commence with this.

Separation of variables

Write $Q(x_1, \ldots, x_m, \tau) = X_1(x_1) \cdots X_m(x_m) T(\tau)$, and since the various partial derivatives can be written

$$\frac{\partial Q}{\partial \tau} = X_1(x_1) \cdots X_m(x_m) T'(\tau)$$

$$\frac{\partial^2 Q}{\partial x_1^2} = X_1''(x_1) \cdots X_m(x_m) T(\tau)$$

$$\vdots$$

$$\frac{\partial^2 Q}{\partial x_m^2} = X_1(x_1) \cdots X_m''(x_m) T(\tau)$$

we write (7.45) as

$$\frac{T'(\tau)}{T(\tau)} = \sum_{j=1}^{m} \frac{X_j''(x_j)}{X_j(x_j)}. \tag{7.46}$$

Since the left-hand side of (7.46) only depends on τ while the right-hand side depends on the spatial variables x_j, both sides must simultaneously equal a separation constant (Duffy, 2006), such as

$$\frac{T'(\tau)}{T(\tau)} = -\lambda^2, \qquad \sum_{j=1}^{m} \frac{X_j''(x_j)}{X_j(x_j)} = -\lambda^2. \tag{7.47}$$

The choice of $-\lambda^2$ is to ensure that the separation constant is negative, which is required by boundedness considerations. For multidimensional problems, write $\lambda^2 = k_1^2 + \cdots + k_m^2$, obtaining

$$\frac{T'(\tau)}{T(\tau)} = -\sum_{j=1}^{m} k_j^2, \qquad \frac{X_j''(x_j)}{X_j(x_j)} = -k_j^2. \tag{7.48}$$

We assemble the components $k_1, \ldots, k_m$ into a vector $\mathbf{k} = (k_1, \ldots, k_m)$ with norm $|\mathbf{k}|$ defined by $|\mathbf{k}|^2 = \sum_{j=1}^{m} k_j^2 = \lambda^2$, which permits a compact representation of the solutions to (7.48) using the complex exponential[8]

$$T(\tau) = e^{-|\mathbf{k}|^2 \tau}, \qquad X_j(x_j) = e^{ik_j x_j},$$

---

[7] Though it is usual to use t in the literature, this has different meanings depending on whether a heat equation or an option pricing PDE is being considered, so to avoid confusion I use τ to denote the temporal direction of increasing diffusion.

[8] We will clearly have to stop using i, j and k as indices for the rest of this section, if $i = \sqrt{-1}$ for this purpose.

which enables fundamental solutions of the dimensionless heat equation to be written as a product of Fourier modes in each of the spatial dimensions

$$Q(x_1, \ldots, x_m, \tau) = e^{-|\mathbf{k}|^2 \tau} \prod_{j=1}^{m} e^{ik_j x_j} = e^{-|\mathbf{k}|^2 \tau} \exp\left(\sum_{j=1}^{m} ik_j x_j\right) = e^{-|\mathbf{k}|^2 \tau} e^{i\mathbf{k} \cdot \mathbf{x}} \qquad (7.49)$$

for any admissible wavevector $\mathbf{k}$, writing $\mathbf{x} = (x_1, \ldots, x_m)$.

Von Neumann stability criterion

This is well discussed in Morton and Mayers (2005) – the one-dimensional case in Section 2.7 and the two-dimensional case in Section 3.1. Including convective terms, Section 6.3.2 of Seydel (2004) discusses the von Neumann stability of a one-dimensional convection–diffusion system. For now, we stick to the dimensionless heat equation.

Basically, we recognise that no matter what spatial form we have for $\hat{Q}(x_1, \ldots, x_m) = Q(x_1, \ldots, x_m, \tau_0)$ at a particular $\tau = \tau_0$, $\hat{Q}$ can be decomposed using Fourier analysis into a sum of Fourier modes, of the form

$$\hat{Q}(x_1, \ldots, x_m) = \sum_{\omega} c_{\omega} e^{i\mathbf{k}_{\omega} \cdot \mathbf{x}}, \qquad (7.50)$$

where each Fourier mode is indexed and described using its wavenumber $\mathbf{k}_{\omega}$ and amplitude c_{ω}. Each of these constituent modes decays at the rate described in (7.49), i.e. $e^{-|\mathbf{k}_{\omega}|^2 \tau}$. Therefore, to check the numerical stability of any finite difference scheme, we construct the growth factor $G_{\mathbf{k}_{\omega}}$ for each mode and verify that it has absolute value less than unity at all mesh points. In fact we check all possible modes and make sure none have growth factor $G_{\mathbf{k}}$ with $|G_{\mathbf{k}}| > 1$.

Suppose uniformly spaced meshes for all spatial meshes, with mesh spacing h. The explicit finite difference scheme for the dimensionless heat equation in one, two and three spatial dimensions (describing the diffusion of $Q^l_{j_1}$, $Q^l_{j_1,j_2}$ and $Q^l_{j_1,j_2,j_3}$ respectively) is given by (7.34), i.e. $Q^{l+1}_{...} = Q^l_{...} + h^{\tau} \mathcal{L} Q^l_{...}$, with

$$\mathcal{L} Q^l_{j_1} = \frac{1}{h^2} \left[Q^l_{j_1+1} - 2Q^l_{j_1} + Q^l_{j_1-1} \right],$$

$$\mathcal{L} Q^l_{j_1,j_2} = \frac{1}{h^2} \left(\left[Q^l_{j_1+1,j_2} - 2Q^l_{j_1,j_2} + Q^l_{j_1-1,j_2} \right] + \left[Q^l_{j_1,j_2+1} - 2Q^l_{j_1,j_2} + Q^l_{j_1,j_2-1} \right] \right),$$

$$\mathcal{L} Q^l_{j_1,j_2,j_3} = \frac{1}{h^2} \left(\left[Q^l_{j_1+1,j_2,j_3} - 2Q^l_{j_1,j_2,j_3} + Q^l_{j_1-1,j_2,j_3} \right] \right.$$
$$+ \left[Q^l_{j_1,j_2+1,j_3} - 2Q^l_{j_1,j_2,j_3} + Q^l_{j_1,j_2-1,j_3} \right]$$
$$\left. + \left[Q^l_{j_1,j_2,j_3+1} - 2Q^l_{j_1,j_2,j_3} + Q^l_{j_1,j_2,j_3-1} \right] \right).$$

Note that each of the neighbouring interactions can be written with the following representation, e.g. with $\delta \mathbf{x} = (h, \ldots) = h \mathbf{e}_1$,

$$Q^l_{j_1+1,...} = e^{i\mathbf{k} \cdot (\mathbf{x}+\delta \mathbf{x})} = e^{i\mathbf{k} \cdot \delta \mathbf{x}} Q^l_{j_1,...} = e^{ihk \cdot \mathbf{e}_1} Q^l_{j_1,...}$$

$$Q^l_{j_1-1,...} = e^{i\mathbf{k} \cdot (\mathbf{x}-\delta \mathbf{x})} = e^{-i\mathbf{k} \cdot \delta \mathbf{x}} Q^l_{j_1,...} = e^{-ihk \cdot \mathbf{e}_1} Q^l_{j_1,...}$$

and similarly in other spatial dimensions, if applicable.

Note that these always occur in symmetric pairs, given a uniform mesh and a homogenous diffusion equation, and we may well note that

$$Q'_{j_1+1,\ldots} + Q'_{j_1-1,\ldots} = (e^{ih\mathbf{k}\cdot\mathbf{e}_1} + e^{-ih\mathbf{k}\cdot\mathbf{e}_1})Q'_{j_1,\ldots}$$
$$= 2\cos(h\mathbf{k}\cdot\mathbf{e}_1)Q'_{j_1,\ldots}.$$

We therefore have, in shorthand notation,

$$\mathcal{L}Q'_{j_1} = \frac{2}{h^2}\left[\cos(h\mathbf{k}\cdot\mathbf{e}_1) - 1\right]Q'_{j_1},$$

$$\mathcal{L}Q'_{j_1,j_2} = \frac{2}{h^2}\left[\cos(h\mathbf{k}\cdot\mathbf{e}_1) + \cos(h\mathbf{k}\cdot\mathbf{e}_2) - 2\right]Q'_{j_1,j_2},$$

$$\mathcal{L}Q'_{j_1,j_2,j_3} = \frac{2}{h^2}\left[\sum_{j=1}^{3}\cos(h\mathbf{k}\cdot\mathbf{e}_j) - 3\right]Q'_{j_1,j_2,j_3}.$$

Suppressing subscripts and letting N denote the number of spatial variables, we have

$$\mathcal{L}Q'_{\ldots} = \frac{2}{h^2}\left[\sum_{j=1}^{N}\cos(h\mathbf{k}\cdot\mathbf{e}_j) - N\right]Q'_{\ldots}$$

and therefore

$$Q^{l+1}_{\ldots} = \left[1 + \frac{2h^\tau}{h^2}\left(\sum_{j=1}^{N}\cos(h\mathbf{k}\cdot\mathbf{e}_j) - N\right)\right]Q'_{\ldots},$$

from which we obtain the growth factor

$$G_\mathbf{k} = 1 - 2\frac{h^\tau}{h^2}\left[N - \sum_{j=1}^{N}\cos(h\mathbf{k}\cdot\mathbf{e}_j)\right]. \tag{7.51}$$

Were it not for the $\mathbf{k}$ terms, this would look like $1 - 2Nh^\tau/h^2$ and no matter what the wavevector $\mathbf{k}$ is, this cannot be greater than unity.

The worst case for a stability point of view, as Morton and Meyers (2005) point out, is therefore when $\cos(h\mathbf{k}\cdot\mathbf{e}_j) = -1$ for all j, i.e. $\mathbf{k} = (1/h, \ldots, 1/h)$, which drives the growth factor down below unity, and possibly below -1. In other words, any instability is going to be an oscillatory instability in time, which grows in amplitude while simultaneously changing sign.

This corresponds to highly oscillatory spatial modes in (7.50), which alternate sign between adjacent meshpoints in each of the spatial directions. For this particularly toxic Fourier mode, we have $\cos(h\mathbf{k}\cdot\mathbf{e}_j) = -1 \;\forall j$ and the growth factor (7.51) becomes

$$G_\mathbf{k} = 1 - 4N\frac{h^\tau}{h^2}, \tag{7.52}$$

from which we obtain, by requiring $G_\mathbf{k} \geq -1$, the well-known *stability condition*

$$\frac{h^\tau}{h^2} \leq \frac{1}{2N}. \tag{7.53}$$

The extension of this von Neumann stability analysis for meshes that are uniformly spaced in each direction but with different mesh spacings along the different axes is presented in Section 3.1 or Morton and Mayers (2005) in the two-dimensional case; extension to higher dimensions is straightforward.

Note that this stability condition needs to hold at all mesh points, which effectively rules out any sensible use of nonuniform spatial meshes in a fully explicit PDE scheme. Any regions with a greater mesh concentration will need a smaller timestep to maintain stability in that region.

The von Neumann stability analysis is difficult, however, to extend to numerical schemes for partial differential equations with nonconstant coefficients. An alternative approach is the 'M-matrices' method, as discussed in Duffy (2001).

7.7 EXPLICIT FINITE DIFFERENCE ON NONUNIFORM MESHES

Instead of the forward tau and central space (FTCS) method, there is no reason why we can't use a backward tau and central space (BTCS) method, which I present in Section 7.8. Unlike the fully explicit scheme, an implicit scheme and its close friend the Crank–Nicolson scheme have no stability restriction on mesh spacing in the temporal direction, and therefore can be used with nonuniform spatial meshes. However, the Crank–Nicolson scheme, together with operator splitting techniques in higher dimensions, requires an explicit step, which may potentially be performed on a nonuniform mesh.[9] For that reason, we discuss how the coefficients of (7.36) are modified in the case of numerical solution of a convection–diffusion on a nonuniform mesh, using the explicit finite difference approach.

Suppose we have a mesh of N_x x-points $\{x_1, \ldots, x_N\}$. Mesh spacings are defined by $h_i^x = x_i - x_{i-1}$. Let the function $V(x, \ldots)$ depend on x, as well as other spatial and temporal variables. Our objective is to find approximate numerical expressions for the first and second partial derivatives of V at mesh point x_i, i.e. $\partial V/\partial x|_{x_i}$ and $\partial^2 V/\partial x|_{x^2}$. For brevity, let $V_i = V(x_i, \ldots)$, where the values of the other independent variables are fixed.

The parabola shown in Figure 7.10, generated by three points, is simply $y = ax^2 + bx + c$, with

$$
\begin{bmatrix} 1 & x_{i-1} & x_{i-1}^2 \\ 1 & x_i & x_i^2 \\ 1 & x_{i+1} & x_{i+1}^2 \end{bmatrix} \begin{bmatrix} c \\ b \\ a \end{bmatrix} = \begin{bmatrix} V_{i-1} \\ V_i \\ V_{i+1} \end{bmatrix}. \tag{7.54}
$$

This can easily be solved to yield

$$
a = \frac{h_i^x V_{i+1} + h_{i+1}^x V_{i-1} - [h_i^x + h_{i+1}^x] V_i}{h_i^x h_{i+1}^x [h_i^x + h_{i+1}^x]},
$$

$$
b = \frac{[h_i^x + h_{i+1}^x][x_{i+1} + x_{i-1}] V_i - h_{i+1}^x [x_i + x_{i+1}] V_{i-1} - h_i^x (x_{i-1} + x_i) V_{i+1}}{h_i^x h_{i+1}^x [h_i^x + h_{i+1}^x]},
$$

$$
c = \frac{x_i x_{i-1} h_i^x V_{i+1} + x_i x_{i+1} h_{i+1}^x V_{i-1} - x_{i+1} x_{i-1} [h_i^x + h_{i+1}^x] V_i}{h_i^x h_{i+1}^x [h_i^x + h_{i+1}^x]}.
$$

[9] I am grateful to Dr Nicolas Jackson for persuading me of the virtues of nonuniform meshes back in 2001 when we worked together at BNP Paribas.

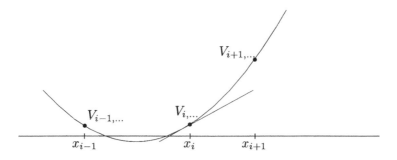

Figure 7.10 Calculation of spatial derivatives using fitted parabola

In fact, we only need the first two of these coefficients, since our objective is to estimate the first and second spatial derivatives evaluated at x_i, for which we shall use $f''(x) = 2a$ and $f'(x) = 2ax + b$.

We therefore calculate $f'(x_i)$ and $f''(x_i)$ to obtain the finite difference approximations

$$\frac{\partial V(x_i, \ldots, \tau_l)}{\partial x} \approx \frac{(h_i^x)^2 V_{i+1} - (h_{i+1}^x)^2 V_{i-1} + [(h_{i+1}^x)^2 - (h_i^x)^2] V_i}{h_i^x h_{i+1}^x [h_i^x + h_{i+1}^x]}, \tag{7.55a}$$

$$\frac{\partial^2 V(x_i, \ldots, \tau_l)}{\partial x^2} \approx 2 \frac{h_i^x V_{i+1} + h_{i+1}^x V_{i-1} - [h_i^x + h_{i+1}^x] V_i}{h_i^x h_{i+1}^x [h_i^x + h_{i+1}^x]}. \tag{7.55b}$$

These expressions are also given in (2.9b) and (2.10) of In t' Hout and Foulon (2010). Note that when $h_i^x = h_{i+1}^x = h^x$, these reduce to (7.29b) and (7.29c) respectively.

Using these instead, we have

$$\mathcal{L}V_i^l = \left[\frac{2b_{11}}{h_i^x(h_i^x + h_{i+1}^x)} - a_1 \frac{h_{i+1}^x}{h_i^x(h_i^x + h_{i+1}^x)} \right] V_{i-1}^l$$

$$+ \left[f + a_1 \frac{h_{i+1}^x - h_i^x}{h_i^x h_{i+1}^x} - 2 \frac{b_{11}}{h_i^x h_{i+1}^x} \right] V_i^l$$

$$+ \left[\frac{2b_{11}}{h_{i+1}^x(h_i^x + h_{i+1}^x)} + a_1 \frac{h_i^x}{h_{i+1}^x(h_i^x + h_{i+1}^x)} \right] V_{i+1}^l \tag{7.56}$$

and therefore equations (7.37) become, in the presence of a nonuniform spatial mesh,

$$A_i = \frac{2h^\tau b_{11}}{h_i^x(h_i^x + h_{i+1}^x)} - a_1 \frac{h_{i+1}^x}{h_i^x(h_i^x + h_{i+1}^x)}, \tag{7.57a}$$

$$B_i = 1 + fh^\tau + a_1 h^\tau \frac{h_{i+1}^x - h_i^x}{h_i^x h_{i+1}^x} - 2h^\tau \frac{b_{11}}{h_i^x h_{i+1}^x}, \tag{7.57b}$$

$$C_i = \frac{2h^\tau b_{11}}{h_{i+1}^x(h_i^x + h_{i+1}^x)} + a_1 \frac{h_i^x}{h_{i+1}^x(h_i^x + h_{i+1}^x)}, \tag{7.57c}$$

for i in the interior range $2 \leq i \leq N_x - 1$. We have already presented matrix elements corresponding to the specified boundary conditions in Section 7.6.1; these require no adaptation to work with nonuniform meshes.

7.7.1   Mixed partial derivative terms on nonuniform meshes

Equation (2.11) of In t' Hout and Foulon (2010) presents an expression for the mixed partial, which is obtained by applying (7.59) to (7.55a), much as in Section 7.6. Using a similar notation to theirs, we have

$$\frac{\partial V(x_i, y_j, \ldots, \tau_l)}{\partial x} \approx \beta_{i,-1}^x V_{i-1,j,\ldots}^l + \beta_{i,0}^x V_{i,j,\ldots}^l + \beta_{i,1}^x V_{i+1,j,\ldots}^l, \tag{7.58}$$

$$\frac{\partial V(x_i, y_j, \ldots, \tau_l)}{\partial y} \approx \beta_{j,-1}^y V_{i,j-1,\ldots}^l + \beta_{j,0}^y V_{i,j,\ldots}^l + \beta_{j,1}^y V_{i,j+1,\ldots}^l, \tag{7.59}$$

where

$$\beta_{i,-1}^x = \frac{-h_{i+1}^x}{h_i^x[h_i^x + h_{i+1}^x]}, \qquad \beta_{i,0}^x = \frac{h_{i+1}^x - h_i^x}{h_i^x h_{i+1}^x}, \qquad \beta_{i,1}^x = \frac{h_i^x}{h_{i+1}^x[h_i^x + h_{i+1}^x]},$$

$$\beta_{j,-1}^y = \frac{-h_{j+1}^y}{h_j^y[h_j^y + h_{j+1}^y]}, \qquad \beta_{j,0}^y = \frac{h_{j+1}^y - h_j^y}{h_j^y h_{j+1}^y}, \qquad \beta_{j,1}^y = \frac{h_j^y}{h_{j+1}^y[h_j^y + h_{j+1}^y]}.$$

Applying (7.59) to (7.58), much as in Section 7.6, we obtain

$$\frac{\partial^2 V(x_i, y_j, \ldots, \tau_l)}{\partial x \, \partial y} \approx \sum_{i',j'=-1}^{1} \beta_{i,i'}^x \beta_{j,j'}^y V_{i+i',j+j',\ldots}^l. \tag{7.60}$$

This can be used to generalise the multidimensional FTCS scheme, e.g. the two-dimensional case presented in (7.33), to nonuniform spatial meshes. The extension to a three-dimensional fully explicit FTCS scheme on nonuniform meshes is purely mechanical at this point.

One can verify that if x and y mesh spacings are uniform, i.e. if $h_i^x = h_{i+1}^x = h^x$ and $h_j^y = h_{j+1}^y = h^y$, then (7.60) reduces to (7.31).

7.8   IMPLICIT FINITE DIFFERENCE SCHEME

We construct a backward tau and central space [BTCS] method on a nonuniform spatial mesh in the following way. This illustration will only consider the one-dimensional case, for reasons that will become apparent.

Combine (7.55) with a backward difference approximation for $\partial V/\partial \tau$, obtaining

$$\left.\frac{\partial V}{\partial \tau}\right|_{x=x_i} = \frac{V_i^l - V_i^{l-1}}{h^\tau}, \tag{7.61a}$$

$$\left.\frac{\partial V}{\partial x}\right|_{x=x_i} = \frac{(h_i^x)^2 V_{i+1}^l - (h_{i+1}^x)^2 V_{i-1}^l + [(h_{i+1}^x)^2 - (h_i^x)^2]V_i^l}{h_i^x h_{i+1}^x[h_i^x + h_{i+1}^x]}, \tag{7.61b}$$

$$\left.\frac{\partial^2 V}{\partial x^2}\right|_{x=x_i} = 2\frac{h_i^x V_{i+1}^l + h_{i+1}^x V_{i-1}^l - [h_i^x + h_{i+1}^x]V_i^l}{h_i^x h_{i+1}^x[h_i^x + h_{i+1}^x]}. \tag{7.61c}$$

Using (7.61a) and (7.28a), we have

$$\frac{V_i^l - V_i^{l-1}}{h^\tau} = \mathcal{L}V_i^l,$$

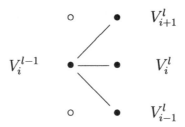

Figure 7.11   Implicit finite difference stencil

i.e.

$$(1 - h^\tau \mathcal{L})V_i^l = V_i^{l-1}, \tag{7.62}$$

which allows mesh values at τ_l to be obtained implicitly from those at τ_{l-1}. The stencil for the one-dimensional implicit finite difference scheme is shown in Figure 7.11. Note the contrast with (7.34). Using (7.63), we have

$$
\begin{aligned}
V_i^l - h^\tau \mathcal{L} V_i^l = &- h^\tau \left(\frac{2b_{11}}{h_i^x(h_i^x + h_{i+1}^x)} - a_1 \frac{h_{i+1}^x}{h_i^x(h_i^x + h_{i+1}^x)} \right) V_{i-1}^l \\
&+ \left[1 - h^\tau \left(f + a_1 \frac{h_{i+1}^x - h_i^x}{h_i^x h_{i+1}^x} - 2 \frac{b_{11}}{h_i^x h_{i+1}^x} \right) \right] V_i^l \\
&- h^\tau \left(\frac{2b_{11}}{h_{i+1}^x(h_i^x + h_{i+1}^x)} + a_1 \frac{h_i^x}{h_{i+1}^x(h_i^x + h_{i+1}^x)} \right) V_{i+1}^l.
\end{aligned}
\tag{7.63}
$$

Similarly to (7.36), this means we can write in matrix form

$$
\begin{bmatrix}
B_1 & C_1 & 0 & \cdots & & & \\
A_2 & B_2 & C_2 & \cdots & & & \\
& & \cdots & A_{N_x-1} & B_{N_x-1} & C_{N_x-1} \\
& & \cdots & 0 & A_{N_x} & B_{N_x}
\end{bmatrix}
\mathbf{V}^l = \mathbf{V}^{l-1},
\tag{7.64}
$$

where, for i in the interior range $2 \leq i \leq N_x - 1$,

$$A_i = -h^\tau \left(\frac{2b_{11}}{h_i^x(h_i^x + h_{i+1}^x)} - a_1 \frac{h_{i+1}^x}{h_i^x(h_i^x + h_{i+1}^x)} \right), \tag{7.65a}$$

$$B_i = 1 - h^\tau \left(f + a_1 \frac{h_{i+1}^x - h_i^x}{h_i^x h_{i+1}^x} - 2 \frac{b_{11}}{h_i^x h_{i+1}^x} \right), \tag{7.65b}$$

$$C_i = -h^\tau \left(\frac{2b_{11}}{h_{i+1}^x(h_i^x + h_{i+1}^x)} + a_1 \frac{h_i^x}{h_{i+1}^x(h_i^x + h_{i+1}^x)} \right). \tag{7.65c}$$

Boundary conditions are handled in the same way as in Section 7.6.1, so we can come up with sensible entries for B_1, C_1, A_{N_x} and B_{N_x}. This is a system of linear equations involving a tridiagonal matrix, and can be easily handled using the Thomas algorithm (Morton and Mayers, 2005, and Section 2.6.3 of Thomas, 1995) or numerical routines such as `tridag` in Press *et al.* (2002). Doing so enables us to solve an implicit tridiagonal system of linear equations to obtain meshpoints $\mathbf{V}_{i,\dots}^l$ from the preceding tau slice $\mathbf{V}_{i,\dots}^{l-1}$.

Importantly, the implicit finite difference scheme is unconditionally stable, no matter the choice of mesh parameters. Proofs of this are standard in the literature (Smith, 1985; Morton and Meyers, 2005).

Note that if we were dealing with more than one spatial dimension, it would not be possible to represent the implicit dependency of $V_{i,...}^l$ upon $V_{i,...}^{l-1}$ by a simple tridiagonal matrix. For even the simplest possible extension, to a two-dimensional convection–diffusion equation with no cross-derivative terms, a pentadiagonal matrix would be needed. Iterative matrix solution methods might offer some hope, but a two-dimensional system without correlation seems too restrictive. A much more commonly used technique to extend implicit solution methods to higher dimensions is operator splitting, which is often thought of as taking fractional timesteps in the journey from τ_l to τ_{l+1}; the easiest way to introduce this is via the well-known Crank–Nicolson technique.

7.9   THE CRANK–NICOLSON SCHEME

Suppose we imagine that we know the mesh points at τ_l and wish to infer them at τ_{l+1}, using (7.28a), i.e. $\partial V/\partial \tau = \mathcal{L}V$. The explicit and implicit finite difference schemes differ in which mesh points are used to estimate $\mathcal{L}V$. The explicit finite difference scheme uses $\mathcal{L}V^l$ whereas the implicit finite difference scheme uses $\mathcal{L}V^{l+1}$.

The idea of the Crank–Nicolson scheme, or its generalisation the theta method (Morton and Mayers, 2005), is to take an average of these two. We therefore have

$$\frac{V_i^{l+1} - V_i^l}{h^\tau} = \theta \mathcal{L}V_i^{l+1} + (1-\theta)\mathcal{L}V_i^l. \tag{7.66}$$

Note that $\theta = 0$ corresponds to the fully explicit scheme while $\theta = 1$ recovers the fully implicit scheme. Setting $\theta = 1/2$ gives the well-known Crank–Nicolson scheme, though θ can be any value in $[0, 1]$. For reasons that will become clear, set $\hat{\theta} = 1 - \theta$. Terms with respect to V_i^{l+1} can be gathered to the left, leaving terms with respect to V_i^l on the right, giving

$$(1 - \theta h^\tau \mathcal{L})V_i^{l+1} = (1 + \hat{\theta} h^\tau \mathcal{L})V_i^l. \tag{7.67}$$

Similarly to (19.8) in Wilmott *et al.* (1993), we introduce an interim term, which I denote $V_i^{l+\hat{\theta}}$, and then rewrite (7.67) as

$$V_i^{l+\hat{\theta}} = (1 + \hat{\theta} h^\tau \mathcal{L})V_i^l, \tag{7.68a}$$

$$(1 - \theta h^\tau \mathcal{L})V_i^{l+1} = V_i^{l+\hat{\theta}}. \tag{7.68b}$$

Compare (7.68a) to (7.34) and (7.68b) to (7.62), and it is readily apparent that the θ scheme can be readily implemented by taking an explicit step over a tau-step of size $\hat{\theta} h^\tau$, followed by an implicit step over a tau-step of size θh^τ. In other words, take the whole timestep h^τ and subdivide it into two components, a portion over which we apply the explicit method, followed by a portion over which we apply the implicit method. The stencil for the Crank–Nicolson method is shown in Figure 7.12; schematically, we have

$$E_X \rightarrow I_X \rightarrow E_X \rightarrow I_X \rightarrow \cdots.$$

Once this is understood, the choice of the boundary conditions to apply at the interim timepoint $\tau_l + \hat{\theta} h^\tau$ becomes much clearer – we just treat the boundary condition the same way as we would otherwise.

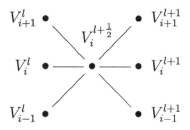

Figure 7.12   Crank-Nicolson finite difference stencil

One often cited advantage of the Crank–Nicolson scheme ($\theta = \frac{1}{2}$) is that it is $o([h^x]^2)$ accurate in space for the dimensionless heat equation on uniform meshes. As we work with more general partial differential equations, and may well not even be using uniform spatial meshes, this conveys less benefit in financial mathematics than in typical applications in applied mathematics. Indeed, one notable deficiency of Crank–Nicolson (Duffy, 2006) is that it can be prone to oscillatory behaviour near discontinuities in the value function or its first derivative, such as one finds at the strike or reverse KO barrier levels. For this reason, if a theta method such as Crank–Nicolson is used, it is quite common to use Rannacher stepping (Rannacher, 1984), where a purely implicit scheme is used for a small number of timesteps (four or so is typical) to allow these discontinuities to diffuse somewhat, after which we revert to the θ scheme as described. Note that any further injection of discontinuties, such as one may have with a derivative contract with several coupons, would ideally require Rannacher stepping to smooth out each of these discontinuities.

7.10   NUMERICAL SCHEMES FOR MULTIDIMENSIONAL PDEs

The benefit with implicit schemes, or methods using them such as the theta method, is that they obviate the stability restrictions on explicit schemes and work well in one dimension. Why? Basically, because it is easy to solve the system of tridiagonal linear equations they provide, in the one-dimensional case.

For PDEs in more than one dimension, implicit schemes become less well suited – and *much* less so once mixed partial derivatives are required, due to the presence of correlation in the driving asset dynamics.

In more than one dimension, we have (7.28) with $m > 1$. We decompose $\mathcal{L}V$ into operators solely along each of the coordinate axes, along with the mixed partial operator, i.e.

$$\mathcal{L}V = \sum_j \mathcal{L}_j V + \sum_{i \neq j}^{m} \mathcal{L}_{jk} V, \tag{7.69a}$$

with

$$\mathcal{L}_j V = \sum_j b_{jj}(\mathbf{x}, t) \frac{\partial^2 V}{\partial x_j^2} + \sum_j a_j(\mathbf{x}, t) \frac{\partial V}{\partial x_j} + \frac{1}{m} f(\mathbf{x}, t) V, \tag{7.69b}$$

$$\mathcal{L}_{jk} V = \sum_{j \neq k} b_{jk}(\mathbf{x}, t) \frac{\partial^2 V}{\partial x_j \, \partial x_k}, \tag{7.69c}$$

where the summations are from 1 to m. We often use x, y and z as indices in (7.69a), i.e. having in two dimensions $\mathcal{L}V = \mathcal{L}_x V + \mathcal{L}_y V + \mathcal{L}_{xy} V$ and in three dimensions $\mathcal{L}V = \mathcal{L}_x V + \mathcal{L}_y V + \mathcal{L}_z V + \mathcal{L}_{xy} V + \mathcal{L}_{xz} V + \mathcal{L}_{yz} V$.

7.10.1 Two-dimensional Crank–Nicolson scheme

This section and the following introduction to the Peaceman–Rachford scheme basically follow Section 3.2 of Morton and Meyers (2005). Consider a two-dimensional convection diffusion equation. Similarly to the one-dimensional Crank–Nicolson scheme (7.67), put

$$(1 - \theta h^\tau \mathcal{L})V_{i,j}^{l+1} = (1 + \hat{\theta} h^\tau \mathcal{L})V_{i,j}^l. \tag{7.70}$$

If the cross-derivative term b_{12} is zero, then $\mathcal{L}_{xy} V$ vanishes. We can put $\theta = \frac{1}{2}$ and (7.70) can be written

$$\left(1 - \frac{1}{2}h^\tau \mathcal{L}_x - \frac{1}{2}h^\tau \mathcal{L}_y\right) V_{i,j}^{l+1} = \left(1 + \frac{1}{2}h^\tau \mathcal{L}_x + \frac{1}{2}h^\tau \mathcal{L}_y\right) V_{i,j}^l. \tag{7.71}$$

This corresponds to an explicit step in both x and y, followed by an implicit step in both x and y. The first is straightforward; the second cannot be performed using our usual tridiagonal matrix machinery.

7.10.2 An early ADI scheme – Peaceman–Rachford splitting

An approach to deal with this was first suggested by Peaceman and Rachford (1955), in the context of modelling the heat equation relating to oil reservoirs.[10] Note that we can write

$$\left(1 + \frac{\phi}{2}h^\tau \mathcal{L}_x\right)\left(1 + \frac{\phi}{2}h^\tau \mathcal{L}_y\right) = \left(1 + \frac{\phi}{2}h^\tau \mathcal{L}_x + \frac{\phi}{2}h^\tau \mathcal{L}_y + \frac{1}{4}[h^\tau]^2 \mathcal{L}_x \mathcal{L}_y\right)$$

for $\phi \in \{-1, 1\}$. Consequently, adding the same term to both sides of (7.70) allows transformation to

$$\left(1 - \frac{1}{2}h^\tau \mathcal{L}_x\right)\left(1 - \frac{1}{2}h^\tau \mathcal{L}_y\right) V_{i,j}^{l+1} = \left(1 + \frac{1}{2}h^\tau \mathcal{L}_x\right)\left(1 + \frac{1}{2}h^\tau \mathcal{L}_y\right) V_{i,j}^l. \tag{7.72}$$

Introduce a fractional step level $V_{i,j}^{l+\frac{1}{2}}$ and (7.72) can be written

$$\left(1 - \frac{1}{2}h^\tau \mathcal{L}_x\right) V_{i,j}^{l+\frac{1}{2}} = \left(1 + \frac{1}{2}h^\tau \mathcal{L}_y\right) V_{i,j}^l, \tag{7.73a}$$

$$\left(1 - \frac{1}{2}h^\tau \mathcal{L}_y\right) V_{i,j}^{l+1} = \left(1 + \frac{1}{2}h^\tau \mathcal{L}_x\right) V_{i,j}^{l+\frac{1}{2}}. \tag{7.73b}$$

Note that this all presumes that terms of order $[h^\tau]^2 \mathcal{L}_x \mathcal{L}_y V_{i,j}^l$ can be neglected.

Examining the two components of (7.73) and comparing them to (7.68), we see the Peaceman–Rachford scheme can be represented as

$$E_Y \rightarrow I_X \rightarrow E_X \rightarrow I_Y \rightarrow \cdots.$$

---

[10] The hardware used was archaic by modern standards: the Card Programmed Calculator (CPC), which performed some five floating point operations per second. The method was first implemented on a 14×14 mesh, and alternating direction between x and y was performed by mechanical sorting of punched cards. This was state of the art back in 1955.

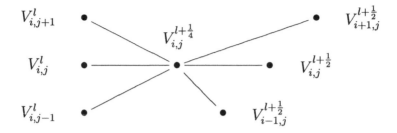

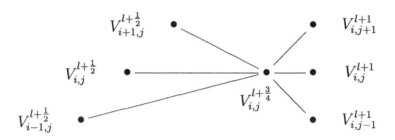

Figure 7.13 Peaceman–Rachford finite difference stencil

Note that while in the one-dimensional Crank–Nicolson method we split h^τ into two half-steps, the two-dimensional Peaceman–Rachford scheme splits h^τ into four quarter-steps. In (7.67), with $\theta = \frac{1}{2}$, we have $(1 - \frac{1}{2}h^\tau \mathcal{L})V_i^{l+1} = (1 + \frac{1}{2}h^\tau \mathcal{L})V_i^l$ and wrote this as

$$V_i^{l+\frac{1}{2}} = \left(1 + \frac{1}{2}h^\tau \mathcal{L}\right)V_i^l, \qquad \left(1 - \frac{1}{2}h^\tau \mathcal{L}\right)V_i^{l+1} = V_i^{l+\frac{1}{2}}. \tag{7.74}$$

However, each of the two equations in (7.73) takes a similar form to (7.67) and so we can write

$$V_{i,j}^{l+\frac{1}{4}} = \left(1 + \frac{1}{2}h^\tau \mathcal{L}_y\right)V_{i,j}^l, \tag{7.75a}$$

$$\left(1 - \frac{1}{2}h^\tau \mathcal{L}_x\right)V_{i,j}^{l+\frac{1}{2}} = V_{i,j}^{l+\frac{1}{4}}, \tag{7.75b}$$

$$V_{i,j}^{l+\frac{3}{4}} = \left(1 + \frac{1}{2}h^\tau \mathcal{L}_x\right)V_{i,j}^{l+\frac{1}{2}}, \tag{7.75c}$$

$$\left(1 - \frac{1}{2}h^\tau \mathcal{L}_y\right)V_{i,j}^{l+1} = V_{i,j}^{l+\frac{3}{4}}. \tag{7.75d}$$

While this fractional time-stepping idea is intuitively appealing and easy to picture (as depicted in Figure 7.13), two cautionary points are in order.

Firstly, we should consider where in the interval $[\tau_l, \tau_{l+1}]$ we should sample $b_{jk}(\mathbf{x}, t)$, $a_j(\mathbf{x}, t)$ and $f(\mathbf{x}, t)$, which appear as coefficients in the differential operator (7.69a). Since the Peaceman–Rachford scheme arises from splitting the two-dimensional Crank–Nicolson scheme, it is appropriate to sample the convection, diffusion and forcing terms at $\frac{1}{2}(\tau_l + \tau_{l+1})$, using these coefficients everywhere in (7.75), e.g. $b_{11}(\mathbf{x}, t)$ with $t = T - (\tau_l + h^\tau)$, and so on for the other coefficients.

Secondly, in the Crank–Nicolson scheme we split the entire timestep h^τ into two components of size $\frac{1}{2}h^\tau$, applying the same convection/diffusion operator over each half-step – the first using an explicit scheme to get the mesh points at $\tau_l + \frac{1}{2}h^\tau$ and the second time using an implicit scheme to obtain the mesh points at τ_{l+1}. The Peaceman–Rachford scheme has two separate operators – $\mathcal{L}_x$ and $\mathcal{L}_y$ – and applying these in the same manner only to the quarter timesteps of size $\frac{1}{4}h^\tau$ in which they apply will underestimate the total convection and diffusion. Basically, applying convection and diffusion in x to only half the entire timestep h^τ, and similarly for y, will give erroneous results unless the coefficients are boosted over those fractional timesteps over which they are used, by a factor of two.

Rewriting (7.75a) as $V_{i,j}^{l+\frac{1}{4}} = (1 + \frac{1}{4}h^\tau[2\mathcal{L}_y])V_{i,j}^l$, and similarly for the other components of (7.75), and comparing to (7.74) may help things to become a little clearer.

The Peaceman–Rachford scheme for the homogeneous two-dimensional diffusion problem with no cross-derivatives, convection or forcing terms is unconditionally stable (Thomas, 1995) and second-order accurate in h^τ, h^x and h^y. Regrettably, the same cannot be said for its three-dimensional counterpart, a result that Thomas poses as Exercise HW 4.4.11. A proof using the von Neumann stability criterion can be found in Gao and Wang (1996).

For completeness, we write the three-dimensional Peaceman–Rachford scheme, which has the following representation:

$$E_{Y;Z} \to I_X \to E_{X;Z} \to I_Y \to E_{X;Y} \to I_Z \to \cdots,$$

though we do *not* advise using this scheme on account of the potential for instability:

$$\left(1 - \frac{1}{3}h^\tau \mathcal{L}_x\right) V_{i,j,k}^{l+\frac{1}{3}} = \left(1 + \frac{1}{3}h^\tau[\mathcal{L}_y + \mathcal{L}_z]\right) V_{i,j,k}^l, \tag{7.76a}$$

$$\left(1 - \frac{1}{3}h^\tau \mathcal{L}_y\right) V_{i,j,k}^{l+\frac{2}{3}} = \left(1 + \frac{1}{3}h^\tau[\mathcal{L}_x + \mathcal{L}_z]\right) V_{i,j,k}^{l+\frac{1}{3}}, \tag{7.76b}$$

$$\left(1 - \frac{1}{3}h^\tau \mathcal{L}_z\right) V_{i,j,k}^{l+1} = \left(1 + \frac{1}{3}h^\tau[\mathcal{L}_x + \mathcal{L}_y]\right) V_{i,j,k}^{l+\frac{2}{3}}. \tag{7.76c}$$

7.10.3 Douglas–Rachford splitting

The Peaceman–Rachford method relies upon the approximate factorisation of the multidimensional Crank–Nicolson method. We could, of course, still assuming that the cross-derivative term is identically zero, start with the two-dimensional fully implicit method

$$(1 - h^\tau \mathcal{L}_x - h^\tau \mathcal{L}_y)V_{i,j}^{l+1} = V_{i,j}^l. \tag{7.77}$$

Adding $[h^\tau]^2 \mathcal{L}_x \mathcal{L}_y V_{i,j}^{l+1}$ to both the left and right sides of (7.77) and factorising, we have

$$(1 - h^\tau \mathcal{L}_x)(1 - h^\tau \mathcal{L}_y)V_{i,j}^{l+1} = V_{i,j}^l + [h^\tau]^2 \mathcal{L}_x \mathcal{L}_y V_{i,j}^{l+1}. \tag{7.78}$$

If we make the assumption that $[h^\tau]^2 \mathcal{L}_x \mathcal{L}_y V_{i,j}^{l+1} \approx [h^\tau]^2 \mathcal{L}_x \mathcal{L}_y V_{i,j}^l$, then we write (7.78) as what we now refer to as the Douglas–Rachford scheme:

$$(1 - h^\tau \mathcal{L}_x)(1 - h^\tau \mathcal{L}_y)V_{i,j}^{l+1} = [1 + [h^\tau]^2 \mathcal{L}_x \mathcal{L}_y]V_{i,j}^l. \tag{7.79}$$

as originally presented by Douglas and Rachford (1956). It is more usual to express this using an intermediate stage

$$(1 - h^\tau \mathcal{L}_x) V_{i,j}^{l+\frac{1}{2}} = \left(1 + h^\tau \mathcal{L}_y\right) V_{i,j}^l, \tag{7.80a}$$

$$\left(1 - h^\tau \mathcal{L}_y\right) V_{i,j}^{l+1} = V_{i,j}^{l+\frac{1}{2}} - h^\tau \mathcal{L}_y V_{i,j}^l. \tag{7.80b}$$

Notice that, unlike the Peaceman–Rachford scheme, this scheme requires knowledge of two preceding fractional meshes in (7.80b).

Extension of the Douglas–Rachford scheme to three dimensions is discussed in Section 3.3 of Morton and Mayers (2005), where the scheme is quoted as

$$(1 - h^\tau \mathcal{L}_x) V_{i,j,k}^{l+\frac{1}{3}} = \left(1 + h^\tau[\mathcal{L}_y + \mathcal{L}_z]\right) V_{i,j,k}^l, \tag{7.81a}$$

$$\left(1 - h^\tau \mathcal{L}_y\right) V_{i,j,k}^{l+\frac{2}{3}} = V_{i,j,k}^{l+\frac{1}{3}} - h^\tau \mathcal{L}_y V_{i,j,k}^l, \tag{7.81b}$$

$$(1 - h^\tau \mathcal{L}_z) V_{i,j,k}^{l+\frac{2}{3}} = V_{i,j,k}^{l+\frac{1}{3}} - h^\tau \mathcal{L}_z V_{i,j,k}^l. \tag{7.81c}$$

Note that both the two- and three-dimensional Douglas–Rachford schemes are unconditionally stable. Handling of boundary conditions is more complicated than for Peaceman–Rachford, as the fractional timeslices cannot be imbued with the same physical interpretation.

7.10.4   Craig–Sneyd splitting

We now have a method that works in two or three dimensions, but without incorporating cross-derivative terms. The imposition of correlation was investigated by McKee and Mitchell (1970) and Craig and Sneyd (1988) – we merely state the Craig–Sneyd method here. It is of interest to note that when the cross-derivatives vanish, then the schemes below recover the earlier Douglas–Rachford schemes if $\theta = 1$ and the Douglas (1962) schemes when $\theta = \frac{1}{2}$.

Craig–Sneyd in two dimensions

$$(1 - \theta h^\tau \mathcal{L}_x)V_{i,j}^{l+\frac{1}{2}} = \left(1 + h^\tau[(1 - \theta)\mathcal{L}_x + \mathcal{L}_y + \mathcal{L}_{xy}]\right)V_{i,j}^l,$$
$$(1 - \theta h^\tau \mathcal{L}_y)V_{i,j}^{l+1} = V_{i,j}^{l+\frac{1}{2}} - \theta h^\tau \mathcal{L}_y V_{i,j}^l. \tag{7.82}$$

Craig–Sneyd in three dimensions

$$(1 - \theta h^\tau \mathcal{L}_x)V_{i,j,k}^{l+\frac{1}{3}} = \left(1 + h^\tau[(1 - \theta)\mathcal{L}_x + \mathcal{L}_y + \mathcal{L}_z + \mathcal{L}_{xy} + \mathcal{L}_{xz} + \mathcal{L}_{yz}]\right)V_{i,j,k}^l,$$
$$(1 - \theta h^\tau \mathcal{L}_y)V_{i,j,k}^{l+\frac{2}{3}} = V_{i,j,k}^{l+\frac{1}{3}} - \theta h^\tau \mathcal{L}_y V_{i,j,k}^l, \tag{7.83}$$
$$(1 - \theta h^\tau \mathcal{L}_z)V_{i,j,k}^{l+1} = V_{i,j,k}^{l+\frac{2}{3}} - \theta h^\tau \mathcal{L}_z V_{i,j,k}^l.$$

7.11 PRACTICAL NONUNIFORM GRID GENERATION SCHEMES

There is a lot to be said for setting up a pricing library with the flexibility to use nonuniform meshes, not only for PDEs but also to allow Monte Carlo timestepping to be more concentrated around time intervals where there is more path dependency. Nonuniform spatial meshes are particularly useful for barrier bending, which we see in the next chapter.

The key reference in this area is Tavella and Randall (2000), to which I would now add the recent article by In t' Hout and Foulon (2010). The manifest advantage of setting up a PDE numerical framework in a generic fashion, which is capable of working with nonuniform meshes, is that one can effectively 'plug and play' with different meshes, depending on the nature of the pricing problem.

It is well worth having this flexibility at one's disposal. Let us suppose that we wish to generate a one-dimensional grid, from x_{min} to x_{max}, containing either N steps between mesh points or, equivalently, $N + 1$ meshpoints. In this section, I shall discuss how this can be achieved with various degrees of sophistication.

As this section is more computationally focused than other parts of this book, I use vectors with indices starting at zero, a notational convenience for this section only, for x_i.

7.11.1 Uniform grid generation

A trivial starting point is the mesh of points x_i, for $i \in \{0, N\}$, with

$$x_i = x_{min} + \frac{i}{N}(x_{max} - x_{min}). \tag{7.84}$$

7.11.2 Uniform grid generation with required levels

Suppose that we want to construct an almost uniform mesh, in logspot for example, but want to avoid the hassle of interpolating a value at $x_{initial} = \log(S_0)$ by forcing one of the nodes to lie on $x_{initial}$. Perhaps also we wish to force $x_{strike} = \log(K)$ to be one of the required points too. In general, presume we have a number of discrete levels $l_1, \ldots, l_M$ and require $\{l_1, \ldots, l_M\} \subseteq \{x_0, x_1, \ldots, x_N\}$. We presume without loss of generality that $x_{min} < l_i < x_{max}$, i.e. that all the required levels are interior points and that $l_i < l_j$ for $i < j$.

To give a concrete example, let's suppose we have a mesh from $x_{min} = 0$ to $x_{max} = 10$, with $N = 10$, and one required level $l_1 = 5$. It's clear that the unperturbed mesh $\{0, 1, 2, 3, 4, 5, 6, 7, 8, 9, 10\}$ already contains this point. If the required level l_1 was 5.1, however, then we would hope to construct $\{0, 1.02, 2.04, 3.06, 4.08, 5.1, 6.08, 7.06, 8.04, 9.02, 10\}$.

The approach I use is to look at the vector of completely uniform mesh points and to work out which is closest to the required level l_1 (in this case x_i with $i = 5$), and then to move that point. This is nothing more than building a monotonically increasing function $f(\cdot)$ mapping $[0, N] \subset \mathbb{R}$ into $[0, N] \subset \mathbb{R}$, which has $f(0) = 0$, $f(N) = N$ and, in this example, $f(5) = 5.1$. Building a piecewise linear interpolator $f(\cdot)$ from input points $(x, y) = \{(0, 0), (5, 5.1), (N, N)\}$ and setting

$$x_i = f\left(x_{min} + \frac{i}{N}(x_{max} - x_{min})\right) \tag{7.85}$$

achieves the desired objective.

We obtain the points that $f(\cdot)$ is required to pass through by looking for the inverse image of l_i under (7.84) and mapping that to the closest integer, i.e.

$$n_i = N\frac{l_i - x_{min}}{x_{max} - x_{min}}, \tag{7.86a}$$

$$z_i = \lfloor n_i + \tfrac{1}{2}\rfloor, \tag{7.86b}$$

where this is easily implemented in code such as by a statement like `z_i = static_cast<int>(n_i+0.5);` or similar.

A couple of important points need to be considered, though. If we had two required levels l_i and l_j very close to each other, then these could easily be mapped to the same value, i.e. $z_i = z_j$, which precludes the construction of $f(\cdot)$, as a function must be single valued. Secondly, even if l_i is sufficiently close to x_{min} or x_{max} that (7.86) would map them to $z_i = 0$ or $z_i = N$, this also has to be excluded.

We achieve both of these objectives by shuffling the raw $\{z_i\}$ grid positions, as obtained from (7.86), to adjusted levels $\{\hat{z}_i\}$ that meet these requirements. A forward shuffle

$$\tilde{z}_1 = \max(1, z_1)$$
$$\tilde{z}_2 = \max(\tilde{z}_1 + 1, z_2)$$
$$\vdots$$
$$\tilde{z}_M = \max(\tilde{z}_{M-1} + 1, z_M)$$

followed by a backward shuffle

$$\hat{z}_M = \min(N - 1, \tilde{z}_M)$$
$$\hat{z}_{M-1} = \min(\hat{z}_M - 1, \tilde{z}_{M-1})$$
$$\vdots$$
$$\hat{z}_1 = \min(\hat{z}_2 - 1, \tilde{z}_1)$$

has the desired effect. Having done this, build a piecewise linear interpolator $f(\cdot)$ from points $(x, y) = \{(0, 0), (\hat{z}_1, n_1), \ldots, (\hat{z}_M, n_M), \ldots, (N, N)\}$ and obtain mesh levels x_i from (7.85).

7.11.3 Spatial grid generation

The ideal grid generation scheme for spatial coordinates would allow nonuniform mesh points to be generated on $[x_{min}, x_{max}]$ with a maximal density concentrated around an interior value x_{conc}, with the optional ability to achieve concentration either in the interior neighbourhood of x_{min}, the neighbourhood of x_{max}, or both. For now, we present a scheme that achieves concentration around an interior point x_{conc}, which can be placed arbitrarily in $[x_{min}, x_{max}]$ – including the two endpoints. Extensions beyond this are left as an exercise for the practical reader.

The basic idea here is that if we have a monotonically increasing nonlinear function such as $x = f(u) = u^\alpha$ on $u > 0$, then a uniform mesh on u will be mapped to a nonuniform mesh in x (unless $\alpha = 1$). The grid density in the transformed variable will be greatest where the derivative is closest to zero – though one must be careful that the derivative is strictly positive. Candidates for such a function are u^3 and $\sinh(u)$. Following Tavella and Randall (2000), we use the hyperbolic sine.

Consider the domain and range of the hyperbolic sine function. If we map $[-1, 1]$ to $[-\sinh(1), \sinh(1)]$, then the nonuniform grid created will have maximal concentration directly in the middle of the interval. However, if we map $[0, 2]$ to $[0, \sinh(2)]$, then the concentration will be greatest at the leftmost point. Consequently, we need to determine a suitable interval over which to sample $\sinh(\cdot)$. The extent of the domain over which $\sinh(\cdot)$ is sampled is determined by the nonuniformity parameter β; the closer β is to zero, the more nonuniform the mesh. If we have a uniformly distributed mesh $u_i \in \{0, 1/N, \ldots, 1\}$, then a suitable nonuniform spatial mesh can be found using

$$x_i = x_{\text{conc}} + \beta \sinh(c_1 u_i + c_2(1 - u_i)) \tag{7.87}$$

We do need, however, to determine these constants c_1 and c_2, which are given straightforwardly by inverting (7.87). We obtain

$$c_1 = \sinh^{-1}\left(\frac{x_{\max} - x_{\text{conc}}}{\beta(x_{\max} - x_{\max})}\right),$$

$$c_2 = \sinh^{-1}\left(\frac{x_{\max} - x_{\text{conc}}}{\beta(x_{\max} - x_{\max})}\right).$$

Note that $\sinh^{-1}(x) = \log(x + \sqrt{1 + x^2})$.

If various important spatial levels l_i are required, we determine for each the required $\hat{l}_i$ point to include in the mesh of u_i values using the relationship

$$\hat{l}_i = \frac{1}{c_2 - c_1}\left[\sinh^{-1}\left(\frac{l_i - x_{\text{conc}}}{\beta(x_{\max} - x_{\min})}\right) - c_1\right].$$

Having done so, the method of Section 7.11.2 can be easily employed to force these $\hat{l}_i$ values to exist on the nearly uniform mesh spanning the unit interval $[0,1]$, which is then transformed to a nonuniform spatial mesh by use of (7.87).

7.11.4 Temporal grid generation

We present a scheme that allows concentration of points in the neighbourhood of $x_{\min} = 0$ and allows their temporal density to decrease as we move out towards $x_{\max}$. This is appropriate for LSV calibration and the forward Fokker–Planck equation; for backward pricing PDEs one would reverse the direction in the obvious manner.

Earlier we suggested a nonlinear function of the form $x = f(u) = u^\alpha$ to map a uniform mesh into a nonuniform mesh. The scheme we present actually has two exponents: α_s in the short end and α_l in the long end, coupled together by a mixing parameter λ. We have

$$x_i = x_{\max} u_i^{\alpha_s + (\alpha_l - \alpha_s)\exp(-\lambda u_i)}$$

$$= x_{\max} \exp\left(\log(u_i)\left(\alpha_s + (\alpha_l - \alpha_s)\exp(-\lambda u_i)\right)\right), \tag{7.88}$$

where u_i is a uniform (or nearly uniform) grid on the unit interval $[0,1]$ such as either $\{0, 1/N, \ldots, 1\}$ as described in Section 7.11.1 or the scheme in Section 7.11.2 if specified levels are required. Mapping required meshpoints l_j to their images $\hat{l}_i$ on $[0,1]$ is trivial by numerical inversion of (7.88).

Typical inputs for this scheme are $\alpha_s \approx 1$, $\alpha_l \approx 2.5$ and $\lambda \approx 0.2$, which seems to work well in practice.

7.12   FURTHER READING

The standard references to one-dimensional PDEs in finance are Wilmott, Dewynne and Howison (1993) and Wilmott (1998), and these books are certainly valuable keynote works in the area. Also useful for discussion of one-dimensional PDEs are Chapter 4 of Seydel (2004) and Section 5.3 of Kwok (1998). For numerical solution methods for multidimensional PDEs, a particularly informative source is Duffy (2006), who goes into considerably more depth than I have been able to cover in this chapter. Kohl-Landgraf (2007), despite the interest rate focus of his book, discusses ADI schemes such as Peaceman–Rachford and Craig–Sneyd in a financial context in Section 5.4, and his book is definitely worth consideration by practitioners in other asset classes also.

In recent literature, In t' Hout and Foulon (2010) discuss the Heston model with correlation and, motivated by these modelling considerations, describe two-dimensional operator splitting techniques including the Craig–Sneyd scheme together with more modern alternatives such as modified Craig–Sneyd (MCS) and the Hundsdorfer–Verwer scheme. Another useful reference is by Zvan, Vetzal and Forsyth (2000), who discuss PDEs and their applicability to pricing barrier options.

More academic books on the finite difference method are Morton and Mayers (2005), Smith (1985), Thomas (1995) and Strikwerda (1989), all from an applied mathematics background, and any of these are likely to be useful to the reader.

The greatest long-term benefit for the the reader, of course, will be obtained by getting stuck in and implementing some of these schemes in his or her own computer code, while being aware of the standard techniques such as presented here.

8

First Generation Exotics – Binary and Barrier Options

We now have the machinery to price European style options under models that provide a fuller description of the FX spot process than Black–Scholes. While European options are especially liquid, they are often seen as particularly expensive, and clients are often interested in cheaper alternatives.

One particularly common way to cheapen a European option in FX is to add a path-dependent barrier feature to it, so that the option can only be exercised if it expires in the money *and* has remained within a specified region of interest over its lifetime. Part of the reason these barrier options are popular in FX is that currency spot rates are often thought to be more range-bound or mean-reverting than stock prices, and clients sometimes feel that the price is unnecessarily high as a result of purchasing option protection for large but unlikely moves in the FX spot rate.

The price of a European option is just the discounted domestic risk-neutral expectation of the payout function at expiry. For a call option,

$$V_0 = \exp(-r^d T) \int_K^\infty f_{S_T}(u)(u - K)^+ du \tag{8.1}$$

Neglecting the discount factor for now, this is just the inner product of the PDF (for S_T) and the option payout. Though the option payout for a European call increases without bound beyond the strike K, the product of the PDF and the payout profile decays to zero beyond K, as the e^{-x^2} eventually dominates.

The price paid for a European option (8.1) therefore takes into account the payout at all possible future levels of S_T, including some potential future scenarios that the client may view as quite unlikely. From a client's point of view, therefore, if they have a view that the spot rate is unlikely to trade beyond a certain range, then they may be happy to consider an option that has a value at expiry function which goes abruptly from $(S_T - K)^+$ to zero, beyond a certain level H. This product is known as a European barrier option, and exists for both calls and puts. The European up-and-out call pays $(S_T - K)^+$ if $K < S_T < H$ (and zero otherwise), and its counterpart, the European down-and-out put (with barrier L), pays $(K - S_T)^+$ if $L < S_T < K$ (and zero otherwise). These products will be covered in Section 8.2.1.

Clearly the knock-out barrier is sampled only at time T; the asset price process can make any excursion whatsoever up to that time, without affecting the value at expiry. One can make the product even cheaper still by extending the barrier monitoring over the entire path history of the option.

In such a case, we have a continuously monitored barrier option, which depends on either the continuously monitored maximum M_T, the continuously monitored minimum m_T or potentially both (we introduce these in Section 8.3 below).

Even more simply, it is quite commonplace in FX to strip out the option payout $(S_T - K)^+$ entirely, and just have a path-dependent option, which pays one unit of either domestic or foreign currency at time T depending on whether M_t and/or m_t have remained entirely within

Table 8.1   American digitals/binaries

Product code	Name	Payout function V_T
OT1C	Foreign upside one-touch	$S_T \mathbf{1}_{\{M_T \geq U\}}$
OT1P	Foreign downside one-touch	$S_T \mathbf{1}_{\{m_T \leq L\}}$
OT2C	Domestic upside one-touch	$\mathbf{1}_{\{M_T \geq U\}}$
OT2P	Domestic downside one-touch	$\mathbf{1}_{\{m_T \leq L\}}$
DOT1	Foreign double-touch	$S_T \mathbf{1}_{\{m_T \leq L \cup M_T \geq U\}}$
DOT2	Domestic double-touch	$\mathbf{1}_{\{m_T \leq L \cup M_T \geq U\}}$
NT1C	Foreign upside no-touch	$S_T \mathbf{1}_{\{M_T < U\}}$
NT1P	Foreign downside no-touch	$S_T \mathbf{1}_{\{m_T > L\}}$
NT2C	Domestic upside no-touch	$\mathbf{1}_{\{M_T < U\}}$
NT2P	Domestic downside no-touch	$\mathbf{1}_{\{m_T > L\}}$
DNT1	Foreign double-no-touch	$S_T \mathbf{1}_{\{m_T > L\}} \mathbf{1}_{\{M_T < U\}}$
DNT2	Domestic double-no-touch	$\mathbf{1}_{\{m_T > L\}} \mathbf{1}_{\{M_T < U\}}$

particular ranges over the entire lifetime of the option. These are referred to as American digitals (or binaries) (see Table 8.1), and are basically just the path-dependent counterpart of the European digitals introduced in Section 2.12. Domestic corresponds to ccy2 and foreign corresponds to ccy1, in the manner introduced in Chapter 3.

Suppose the initial spot rate is 1.0, volatility is a flat 10 % and domestic and foreign interest rates are zero. In this example, we have a 1 year American cash-or-nothing digital that pays $1 in one year if an up-and-in barrier level of 1.1 is touched at *any* time during that year and a 1 year European digital that pays $1 if spot S_T at expiry exceeds the trigger level of 1.1 *on* the expiry date.

Clearly if the European condition is met, then the American option will have touched too – at time T (if not before). So the American digital must be worth *more* than the European digital. How much more? About twice as much – but capped at the one year discount factor.

We see this in Figure 8.1, where the TV prices of European and American style digitals are graphed as a function of the barrier level, with down-and-in digitals and up-and-in digitals

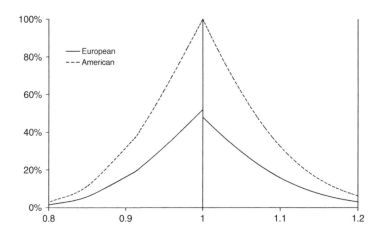

Figure 8.1   Digitals

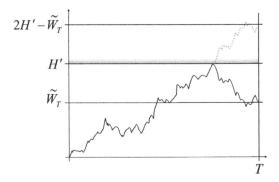

Figure 8.2 The reflection principle

separated either side of unity. Note the absence of symmetry, due to the presence of $-\frac{1}{2}\sigma^2$ in $N(d_2)$. For our particular example, the European digital is priced at 15.8 % whereas the American digital is worth about twice as much, at 32.4 %.

The rest of this chapter attempts to explain why, using the reflection principle, and to introduce the techniques required to price these first generation exotic options. It's never clear exactly what products fall in the remit of first generation products in FX, though binary and barrier options are always taken to fall into this category. I shall basically follow Wilmott (1998) and talk about the so-called weakly path-dependent products in this chapter, i.e. products that can be priced on one finite difference grid (in one tradeable factor, though possibly including other untradeable factors such as stochastic volatility). Strongly path-dependent options will be covered in Chapter 9.

8.1   THE REFLECTION PRINCIPLE

The reflection principle, as mentioned in Section 2.6 of Karatzas and Shreve (1991) basically states that for any driftless Brownian motion that hits a particular level H, we can construct a 'shadow path' that, upon arrival of the original trajectory at H', is thereafter just the mirror image of the original trajectory reflected about that level.

We have two possible paths: $\tilde{W}_t$, and $\tilde{W}_t^*$, where the second is defined by

$$\tilde{W}_t^* = \begin{cases} \tilde{W}_t, & t < \tau^{H'}, \\ 2H' - \tilde{W}_t, & \text{otherwise,} \end{cases}$$

where $\tau^{H'} = \inf\{t : \tilde{W}_t = H'\}$ is the hitting time.[1]

Somewhat heuristically, if we identify the trajectories shown in Figure 8.2 with possible asset price paths, and suppose that H' corresponds to the barrier level of $U = 1.10$, then both trajectories will cause the American one-touch to expire with value of unity, whereas only one

---

[1] Note that this is not the time-reversed τ, which is used in the PDE formulation of option pricing; it is a physical hitting time.

of $\tilde{W}_t$ and $\tilde{W}_t^*$ will correspond to the European digital being in the money at expiry (in this example, $\tilde{W}_t^*$). In other words, once the level H' has been touched, payment of the American digital is guaranteed, whereas the payment of the European digital is still indeterminate and depends on the probability of the asset pricing finishing with $S_T > U$ *conditional* on $S_\tau = U$. If the asset price process is driftless, then it is equally likely to drift up as it is to drift down; hence the European digital should be about half the price of the American digital.

8.2 EUROPEAN BARRIERS AND BINARIES

8.2.1 European barriers

A European up-and-out call with (upper) barrier U has the payout function (Figure 8.3)

$$V_T^{\text{EUOC}} = (S_T - K)^+ \mathbf{1}_{\{S_T < U\}} = (S_T - K)\mathbf{1}_{\{S_T \geq K \cap S_T < U\}}.$$

Depending on the knock-out (KO) level U, this will be cheaper than the equivalent European call. Similarly, a European down-and-out put with (lower) barrier L has the payout function (Figure 8.4)

$$V_T^{\text{EDOP}} = (K - S_T)^+ \mathbf{1}_{\{S_T > L\}} = (K - S_T)\mathbf{1}_{\{S_T \leq K \cap S_T > L\}}.$$

Pricing of these European barrier options (see Table 8.2) is straightforward, both in a Black–Scholes world and using the numerical methods introduced in Chapter 7. For the Black–Scholes

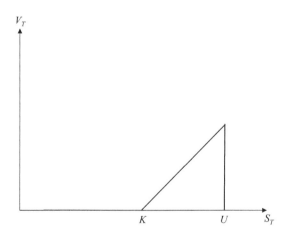

Figure 8.3 Payout function V_T for European up-and-out call

Table 8.2 Barrier options

Product code	Name	Payout function V_T
C,RKO or UOC	Up-and-out (reverse knock-out) call	$(S_T - K)^+ \mathbf{1}_{\{M_T \le U\}}$
C,KO or DOC	Down-and-out (regular knock-out) call	$(S_T - K)^+ \mathbf{1}_{\{m_T \ge L\}}$
P,KO or UOP	Up-and-out (regular knock-out) put	$(K - S_T)^+ \mathbf{1}_{\{M_T \le U\}}$
P,RKO or DOP	Down-and-out (reverse knock-out) put	$(K - S_T)^+ \mathbf{1}_{\{m_T \ge L\}}$
C,DKO or UODOC	Double knock-out call	$(S_T - K)^+ \mathbf{1}_{\{m_T > L\}} \mathbf{1}_{\{M_T < U\}}$
P,DKO or UODOP	Double knock-out put	$(K - S_T)^+ \mathbf{1}_{\{m_T > L\}} \mathbf{1}_{\{M_T < U\}}$
C,RKI or UIC	Up-and-in (reverse knock-in) call	$(S_T - K)^+ \mathbf{1}_{\{M_T \ge U\}}$
C,KI or DIC	Down-and-in (regular knock-in) call	$(S_T - K)^+ \mathbf{1}_{\{m_T \le L\}}$
P,KI or UIP	Up-and-in (regular knock-in) put	$(K - S_T)^+ \mathbf{1}_{\{M_T \ge U\}}$
P,RKI or DIP	Down-and-in (reverse knock-in) put	$(K - S_T)^+ \mathbf{1}_{\{m_T \le L\}}$
C,DKI or UIDIC	Double knock-in call	$(S_T - K)^+ \mathbf{1}_{\{m_T \le L \cup S_T \ge U\}}$
P,DKI or UIDIP	Double knock-in put	$(K - S_T)^+ \mathbf{1}_{\{m_T \le L \cup S_T \ge U\}}$

formula, we use the same risk-neutral expectation approach in Section 2.8 and compute for the European up-and-out call

$$
\begin{aligned}
V_0^{\text{EUOC}} &= e^{-r^d T} \mathbf{E}^d \left[V_T^{\text{EUOC}} \right] \\
&= e^{-r^d T} \mathbf{E}^d \left[(S_T - K) \mathbf{1}_{\{S_T \ge K \cap S_T < U\}} \right] \\
&= e^{-r^d T} \mathbf{E}^d \left[S_T \mathbf{1}_{\{S_T \ge K \cap S_T < U\}} - K \mathbf{1}_{\{S_T \ge K \cap S_T < U\}} \right] \\
&= e^{-r^d T} \mathbf{E}^d \left[S_T \mathbf{1}_{\{S_T \ge K \cap S_T < U\}} \right] - K e^{-r^d T} \mathbf{E}^d \left[\mathbf{1}_{\{S_T \ge K \cap S_T < U\}} \right] \\
&= e^{-r^d T} \mathbf{E}^d \left[S_T \mathbf{1}_{\{S_T \ge K \cap S_T < U\}} \right] - K e^{-r^d T} \mathbf{P}^d \left[S_T \ge K \cap S_T < U \right] \\
&= S_0 e^{-r^f T} \mathbf{E}^d \left[\frac{d\mathbf{P}^f}{d\mathbf{P}^d} \mathbf{1}_{\{S_T \ge K \cap S_T < U\}} \right] - K e^{-r^d T} \mathbf{P}^d \left[S_T \ge K \cap S_T < U \right] \\
&= S_0 e^{-r^f T} \mathbf{P}^f \left[S_T \ge K \cap S_T < U \right] - K e^{-r^d T} \mathbf{P}^d \left[S_T \ge K \cap S_T < U \right].
\end{aligned}
$$

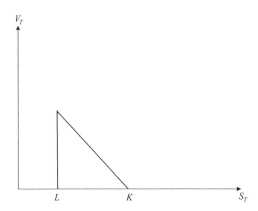

Figure 8.4 Payout function V_T for European down-and-out put

Note the similarity to (2.62). From (2.60), we have $\mathbf{P}^{X(i)}[S_T \geq K] = N(d_i)$ – recall $X(1;2) \equiv f;d$.

Using the generalised moneyness notation introduced in (2.82), we can write this in terms of probabilities involving S_T exceeding not the strike K but an arbitrary level X, as $\mathbf{P}^{X(i)}[S_T \geq X] = N(d_i(X))$ with

$$d_{1;2}(S_0, X) = \frac{\ln(S_0/X) + \left(r^d - r^f \pm \sigma^2\right) T}{\sigma \sqrt{T}}. \tag{8.2}$$

We can therefore write

$$\mathbf{P}^{X(i)}[S_T \geq K \cap S_T < U] = N(d_i) - N(d_i(S_0, U)),$$

obtaining

$$V_0^{\text{EUOC}} = S_0 e^{-r^f T}\left[N(d_1) - N(d_1(S_0, U))\right] - K e^{-r^d T}\left[N(d_2) - N(d_2(S_0, U))\right].$$

Similarly, we adapt the price for a European put to account for the down-and-out European barrier, obtaining

$$V_0^{\text{EDOP}} = K e^{-r^d T}\left[N(-d_2) - N(-d_2(S_0, L))\right] - S_0 e^{-r^f T}\left[N(-d_1) - N(-d_1(S_0, L))\right].$$

Valuation of the European barrier products using PDE and Monte Carlo methods proceeds in the same way as for Europeans, using the value at expiry function $V_T(S_T)$, but with a Dirichlet condition wherever a knock-out barrier is placed. For a knock-in barrier option, we obtain the price by subtracting the price of a knock-out from that of an equivalent European (both with the same strike K).

From a mesh concentration point for PDEs, taking as an example the European up-and-out call, since diffusion is maximal both at the strike $S_T = K$ and at the barrier $S_T = U$ it makes sense to concentrate spatial points in the vicinity of both $x = \ln K$ and $x = \ln U$ and temporal points in the vicinity of $t = T$, i.e. $\tau = 0$.

8.2.2   Barrier parity relationships

One can construct up-and-in and down-and-in barriers by barrier parity. A European up-and-in call is also a call, but one that only expires in the money if the spot rate *exceeds* U. Similarly, the European down-and-in put only pays if the spot rate is less than L:

$$V_T^{\text{EUIC}} = (S_T - K)^+ \mathbf{1}_{\{S_T > U\}}, \tag{8.3a}$$

$$V_T^{\text{EDIP}} = (K - S_T)^+ \mathbf{1}_{\{S_T < L\}}. \tag{8.3b}$$

Since $\mathbf{1}_{\{S_T < x\}} + \mathbf{1}_{\{S_T > x\}} = \mathbf{1}_{\{S_T \neq x\}}$ and $S_T \neq x$ almost surely (a.s.), i.e. with probability one, we have

$$V_0^{\text{EUIC}} + V_0^{\text{EUOC}} = V_0^{\text{C}}, \tag{8.4a}$$

$$V_0^{\text{EDIP}} + V_0^{\text{EDOP}} = V_0^{\text{P}}. \tag{8.4b}$$

The same barrier parity relationships apply to American style barriers.

8.2.3 European digitals

Numerical valuation of these instruments, originally presented in Section 2.12, but using PDE and Monte Carlo methods, proceeds in the same way as for Europeans, using the value at expiry function $V_T(S_T)$ from Table 2.1. From a mesh concentration point for PDEs, since diffusion is maximal at $S_T = K$, where we have the discontinuity in the value function $V_T(S_T)$, it makes sense to concentrate spatial points in the vicinity of $x = \ln U$ or $x = \ln L$ (for up-and-in and down-and-in respectively) and temporal points in the vicinity of $t = T$, i.e. $\tau = 0$.

8.3 CONTINUOUSLY MONITORED BINARIES AND BARRIERS

One can certainly add a European style knock-out barrier to cheapen the price of a European option, as discussed above. However, the price can only be reduced by so much while keeping the call/put payout intact at expiry. Additionally, the barrier can only be placed in the in-the-money payout region.

An alternative approach is to introduce an American style barrier that knocks out the value of the underlying European option if a barrier level is crossed at *any* time during the lifetime of the option. As this depends on the continuously monitored minimum and maximum, we let m_t and M_T denote the minimum and maximum values achieved by the spot process S_t over the interval $[0, T]$, i.e.

$$m_t = \inf [S_u : 0 \le u \le t],$$

$$M_t = \sup [S_u : 0 \le u \le t].$$

We introduce a convenient notation for stopping and exit times.

Stopping times

$$\tau^U \equiv \tau^U_{-\infty} = \inf \{t : S_t \ge U\},$$

$$\tau_L \equiv \tau^\infty_L = \inf \{t : S_t \le L\}.$$

Exit time

$$\tau^U_L = \inf \{t : S_t \notin [L, U]\}.$$

For brevity, we let τ denote one of the three exit/stopping times above without loss of generality. Similarly to European binaries, we have the following for American style binaries (where τ bears either a superscript H, a subcript L, or potentially both):

$$V_0^{\text{foreign touch}} = S_0 e^{-r^f T} \mathbf{P}^f [\tau \le T], \tag{8.5a}$$

$$V_0^{\text{foreign no-touch}} = S_0 e^{-r^f T} \mathbf{P}^f [\tau > T], \tag{8.5b}$$

$$V_0^{\text{domestic touch}} = e^{-r^d T} \mathbf{P}^d [\tau \le T], \tag{8.5c}$$

$$V_0^{\text{domestic no-touch}} = e^{-r^d T} \mathbf{P}^d [\tau > T]. \tag{8.5d}$$

The task, therefore, is to calculate the probabilities of the barrier(s) being touched, in both the domestic and foreign risk-neutral measures. It will be more useful later (when pricing barrier options) to obtain general risk-neutral joint probabilities of the form

$$\mathbf{P}^{X(i)}\left[S_T \in [A, B] \cap \tau_L^H \leq T\right] \quad \text{with} \quad A, B, L, U \in [0, \infty].$$

This will be sufficient to price the American binaries, since for a no-touch

$$
\begin{aligned}
c &= \mathbf{P}^{X(i)}\left[S_T \in [L, H] \cap \tau_L^H > T\right] \\
  &= \mathbf{P}^{X(i)}\left[S_T \in [L, H]\right] - \mathbf{P}^{X(i)}\left[S_T \in [L, H] \cap \tau_L^H \leq T\right],
\end{aligned}
$$

as we require the probability for S_t to be within $[L, U]$ for all $t \leq T$ *including* T. For a touch we have

$$
\begin{aligned}
\mathbf{P}^{X(i)}\left[\tau_L^U \leq T\right] &= 1 - \mathbf{P}^{X(i)}\left[\tau_L^U > T\right] \\
&= 1 - \mathbf{P}^{X(i)}\left[S_T \in [L, H]\right] + \mathbf{P}^{X(i)}\left[S_T \in [L, H] \cap \tau_L^H \leq T\right] \quad (8.6)
\end{aligned}
$$

From (2.41) and (2.45), we have expressions for the spot rate process S_t driven by Brownian motions W_t^d and W_t^f, which are driftless Brownian motions under $\mathbf{P}^d$ and $\mathbf{P}^f$ respectively:

$$S_T = S_0 \exp\left(\left(\mu^{X(i)} - \frac{1}{2}\sigma^2\right)T + \sigma W_T^{X(i)}\right).$$

To make it easier to check the maximum and minimum conditions, we write the spot rate process as the exponential of a Brownian motion $\tilde{W}_t$ with drift (it will, in general, have drift in either measure). Then, the condition that the spot rate is above a lower bound is equivalent to the condition that the driving Brownian motion $\tilde{W}_t$ is above an equivalent lower bound in logspot space, and similarly for upper bounds.

We obtain

$$\tilde{W}_t = W_t^{d;f} + v^{d;f}t, \quad (8.7)$$

where

$$v^{d;f} = \frac{\mu^{d;f}}{\sigma}t - \frac{\sigma}{2} \quad (8.8)$$

with

$$S_t = S_0 \exp(\sigma \tilde{W}_t),$$

where $\tilde{W}_t = v^{d;f}t + \sqrt{t}\xi$ with $\xi \sim N(0, 1)$ under $\mathbf{P}^{d;f}$. Note that

$$v^d = \frac{r^d - r^f}{\sigma} - \frac{1}{2}\sigma, \quad (8.9a)$$

$$v^f = \frac{r^d - r^f}{\sigma} + \frac{1}{2}\sigma. \quad (8.9b)$$

It is illustrative to check that this recovers the existing risk-neutral probabilities we used earlier for Europeans and digitals. Consider first a cash-or-nothing European call digital:

$$\mathbf{P}^d \left[S_T \geq K \right] = \mathbf{P}^d \left[S_0 \exp(\sigma \tilde{W}_T) \geq K \right]$$

$$= \mathbf{P}^d \left[\exp(\sigma \tilde{W}_T) \geq K/S_0 \right]$$

$$= \mathbf{P}^d \left[\tilde{W}_T > \sigma^{-1} \ln(K/S_0) \right]$$

$$= \mathbf{P}^d \left[v^d T + \sqrt{T} \xi \geq \sigma^{-1} \ln(K/S_0) \right]$$

$$= \mathbf{P}^d \left[\left(r^d - r^f - \frac{1}{2}\sigma^2 \right) T + \sigma \sqrt{T} \xi \geq \ln(K/S_0) \right]$$

$$= \mathbf{P}^d \left[\xi \geq \frac{\ln(K/S_0) - \left(r^d - r^f - \frac{1}{2}\sigma^2 \right) T}{\sigma \sqrt{T}} \right]$$

$$= \mathbf{P}^d \left[\xi \leq \frac{\ln(S_0/K) + \left(r^d - r^f - \frac{1}{2}\sigma^2 \right) T}{\sigma \sqrt{T}} \right]$$

$$= N(d_2).$$

This is exactly as one would expect and gives the same price for a cash-or-nothing European call digital as (2.88c) once the domestic discount factor is included. The same analysis, but for the case of an asset-or-nothing digital, holds in the foreign risk-neutral measure. Finally, since a European option can be decomposed into a sum of European cash-or-nothing and asset-or-nothing digitals, the result holds for Europeans.

The advantage now is that it is easier to consider the joint probability under conditions on the maximum and/or minimum of the spot rate, by use of

$$\tilde{M}_t = \sup \left[\tilde{W}_u : 0 \leq u \leq t \right], \tag{8.10a}$$

$$\tilde{m}_t = \inf \left[\tilde{W}_u : 0 \leq u \leq t \right]. \tag{8.10b}$$

The required expression is $\mathbf{P}^{X(i)} \left[S_T \in [A, B] \cap \tau_L^H \leq T \right]$, which we will evaluate first for a single upper barrier, i.e. $\mathbf{P}^{X(i)} \left[S_T \in [A, B] \cap \tau^H \leq T \right]$. We have

$$\mathbf{P}^{X(i)} \left[S_T \in [A, B] \cap \tau^H \leq T \right]$$

$$= \mathbf{P}^{X(i)} \left[S_0 \exp(\sigma \tilde{W}_T) \in [A, B] \cap \tau^H \leq T \right]$$

$$= \mathbf{P}^{X(i)} \left[\left\{ \sigma^{-1} \ln(A/S_0) \leq \tilde{W}_T \leq \sigma^{-1} \ln(B/S_0) \right\} \cap \tau^H \leq T \right]$$

$$= \mathbf{P}^{X(i)} \left[\left\{ \sigma^{-1} \ln(A/S_0) \leq \tilde{W}_T \leq \sigma^{-1} \ln(B/S_0) \right\} \cap \max\{S_t :\leq t \leq T\} \geq H \right]$$

$$= \mathbf{P}^{X(i)} \left[A' \leq \tilde{W}_T \leq B' \cap \tilde{M}_T \geq H \right],$$

where $A' = \sigma^{-1} \ln(A/S_0)$, $B' = \sigma^{-1} \ln(B/S_0)$ and $H' = \sigma^{-1} \ln(H/S_0)$.

We aim to use the reflection principle, which involves reflecting the Brownian motion around H' after the first point of contact with H', as depicted in Figure 8.2. In order to utilise this, the Brownian motion $\tilde{W}_t$ must be driftless with respect to the measure $\mathbf{P}^{X(i)}$ with which we

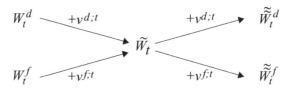

Figure 8.5 Measure change for application of the reflection principle

calculate the probability. As $\tilde{W}_t = W_t^{d;f} + v^{d;f}t$, we see that this is not satisfied. Therefore we need to change to the measure $\tilde{\tilde{P}}$ under which $\tilde{W}_t$ is driftless, using Girsanov's theorem.

For an arbitrary event ε, we have

$$\mathbf{P}^{X(i)}[\varepsilon] = \mathbf{E}^{X(i)}[\mathbf{1}_\varepsilon] = \tilde{\mathbf{E}}\left[\frac{d\mathbf{P}^{X(i)}}{d\tilde{\mathbf{P}}}\mathbf{1}_\varepsilon\right],$$

and since $\tilde{W}_t = W_t^{d;f} + v^{d;f}t$ we have

$$\frac{d\mathbf{P}^{X(i)}}{d\tilde{\mathbf{P}}} = \exp\left(v^{X(i)}\tilde{W}_T - \frac{1}{2}\left(v^{X(i)}\right)^2 T\right).$$

Therefore, let $E = \left\{A' \leq \tilde{W}_T \leq B' \cap \tilde{M}_T \geq H\right\}$ and then calculate

$$\mathbf{P}^{X(i)}[E] = \mathbf{E}^{X(i)}[\mathbf{1}_E]$$

$$= \tilde{\mathbf{E}}\left[\frac{d\mathbf{P}^{X(i)}}{d\tilde{\mathbf{P}}}\mathbf{1}_E\right]$$

$$= \tilde{\mathbf{E}}\left[\exp\left(v^{X(i)}\tilde{W}_T - \frac{1}{2}\left(v^{X(i)}\right)^2 T\right)\mathbf{1}_E\right].$$

It is at this point that we can apply the reflection principle (see Figure 8.5):

$$\tilde{\mathbf{E}}\left[\exp\left(v^{X(i)}\tilde{W}_T - \frac{1}{2}\left(v^{X(i)}\right)^2 T\right)\mathbf{1}_{\{A' \leq \tilde{W}_T \leq B' \cap \tilde{M}_T \geq H\}}\right]$$

$$= \tilde{\mathbf{E}}\left[\exp\left(v^{X(i)}[2H' - \tilde{W}_T] - \frac{1}{2}\left(v^{X(i)}\right)^2 T\right)\mathbf{1}_{\{2H' - B' \leq \tilde{W}_T \leq 2H' - A'\}}\right].$$

Now let's recap what we've done. We've taken Brownian motions W_t^d and W_t^f under the domestic and foreign risk-neutral measures respectively. By adding on drift terms $v^d t$ and $v^f t$ respectively, we obtained a Brownian motion $\tilde{W}_T$ that has a one to-one mapping on to S_t and now we try adding on the drift terms a *second* time. Then we have

$$\frac{d\overset{\approx}{\mathbf{P}}^{X(i)}}{d\tilde{\mathbf{P}}} = \exp\left(-v^{X(i)}\tilde{W}_T - \frac{1}{2}\left[v^{X(i)}\right]^2 T\right),$$

which gives

$$
\begin{aligned}
\mathbf{P}^{X(i)}[E] &= \tilde{\mathbf{E}}\left[\exp\left(v^{X(i)}[2H' - \tilde{W}_T] - \frac{1}{2}\left(v^{X(i)}\right)^2 T\right) \mathbf{1}_{\{2H' - B' \le \tilde{W}_T \le 2H' - A'\}}\right] \\
&= e^{2v^{X(i)}H'} \cdot \tilde{\mathbf{E}}\left[\exp\left(-v^{X(i)}\tilde{W}_T - \frac{1}{2}\left(v^{X(i)}\right)^2 T\right) \mathbf{1}_{\{2H' - B' \le \tilde{W}_T \le 2H' - A'\}}\right] \\
&= e^{2v^{X(i)}H'} \cdot \tilde{\mathbf{E}}\left[\frac{d\overset{\approx X(i)}{\mathbf{P}}}{d\tilde{\mathbf{P}}} \mathbf{1}_{\{2H' - B' \le \tilde{W}_T \le 2H' - A'\}}\right] \\
&= e^{2v^{X(i)}H'} \cdot \overset{\approx X(i)}{\mathbf{P}}\left[2H' - B' \le \tilde{W}_T \le 2H' - A'\right] \\
&= e^{2v^{X(i)}H'} \cdot \overset{\approx X(i)}{\mathbf{P}}\left[2H' - B' \le \tilde{W}_T - v^{X(i)}T \le 2H' - A'\right] \\
&= e^{2v^{X(i)}H'} \cdot \overset{\approx X(i)}{\mathbf{P}}\left[2H' - B' + v^{X(i)}T \le \tilde{W}_T^{X(i)} \le 2H' - A' + v^{X(i)}T\right] \\
&= \left(\frac{H}{S_0}\right)^{2v^{X(i)}/\sigma} \cdot \overset{\approx X(i)}{\mathbf{P}}\left[2H' - B' + v^{X(i)}T \le \tilde{W}_T^{X(i)} \le 2H' - A' + v^{X(i)}T\right].
\end{aligned}
$$

We can then use the fact that $\overset{\approx X(i)}{W}_T \sim N(0, T)$ under $\overset{\approx X(i)}{\mathbf{P}}$ to obtain

$$
\begin{aligned}
&\mathbf{P}^{X(i)}[S_T \in [A, B] \cap \tau^H \le T] \\
&\quad = \left(\frac{H}{S_0}\right)^{2v^{X(i)}/\sigma}\left[N\left(\frac{2H' - A' + v^{X(i)}T}{\sqrt{T}}\right) - N\left(\frac{2H' - B' + v^{X(i)}T}{\sqrt{T}}\right)\right]
\end{aligned}
$$

and similarly

$$
\begin{aligned}
&\mathbf{P}^{X(i)}[S_T \in [A, B] \cap \tau_L \le T] \\
&\quad = \left(\frac{L}{S_0}\right)^{2v^{X(i)}/\sigma}\left[N\left(\frac{2L' - A' + v^{X(i)}T}{\sqrt{T}}\right) - N\left(\frac{2L' - B' + v^{X(i)}T}{\sqrt{T}}\right)\right],
\end{aligned}
$$

which, in conjunction with

$$
\mathbf{P}^{X(i)}\left[S_T \in [A, B]\right] = N\left(\frac{B' - v^{X(i)}T}{\sqrt{T}}\right) - N\left(\frac{A' - v^{X(i)}T}{\sqrt{T}}\right),
$$

are enough to price all the single barrier type binary options. We restrict ourselves to a few representative examples, recalling the generalised moneyness formula from (2.82). A fuller list of all the relevant formulae can be found in the excellent compendia by Zhang (1997) and Section 4.19.5 of Haug (2007), which details 28 possibilities for American binary options alone. I do not intend to detail all of these cases. The aim here is merely to present how these equations can be derived using the machinery of this book.

8.3.1   Domestic binaries

Domestic upside no-touch

We have $V_0^{\text{NT2C}} = e^{-r^d T} \mathbf{P}^d[\tau^H > T]$. Then

$$\mathbf{P}^d[\tau^H > T] = \mathbf{P}^d\left[S_T \in [0, H]\right] - \mathbf{P}^d\left[S_T \in [0, H] \cap \tau^H \le T\right]$$

$$= N\left(\frac{H' - v^d T}{\sqrt{T}}\right) - \left(\frac{H}{S_0}\right)^{2v^d/\sigma}\left[1 - N\left(\frac{2H' - H' + v^d T}{\sqrt{T}}\right)\right]$$

$$= N\left(\frac{H' - v^d T}{\sqrt{T}}\right) - \left(\frac{H}{S_0}\right)^{2v^d/\sigma} N\left(\frac{-H' - v^d T}{\sqrt{T}}\right)$$

$$= N\left(\frac{\ln(H/S_0) - \left(r^d - r^f - \frac{1}{2}\sigma^2\right)T}{\sigma\sqrt{T}}\right)$$

$$- \left(\frac{H}{S_0}\right)^{2v^d/\sigma} N\left(\frac{\ln(S_0/H) - \left(r^d - r^f - \frac{1}{2}\sigma^2\right)T}{\sigma\sqrt{T}}\right).$$

We therefore have

$$V_0^{\text{NT2C}} = e^{-r^d T}\left(N(-d_2(S_0, H)) - \left(\frac{H}{S_0}\right)^{2(r^d - r^f)/\sigma^2 - 1} N(-d_2(H, S_0))\right).$$

D-omestic downside no-touch

We have $V_0^{\text{NT2P}} = e^{-r^d T} \mathbf{P}^d[\tau_L > T]$. Then

$$\mathbf{P}^d[\tau_L > T] = \mathbf{P}^d\left[S_T \in [L, \infty]\right] - \mathbf{P}^d\left[S_T \in [L, \infty] \cap \tau_L \le T\right]$$

$$= 1 - N\left(\frac{L' - v^d T}{\sqrt{T}}\right) - \left(\frac{L}{S_0}\right)^{2v^d/\sigma}\left[N\left(\frac{2L' - L' + v^d T}{\sqrt{T}}\right)\right]$$

$$= N\left(\frac{-L' + v^d T}{\sqrt{T}}\right) - \left(\frac{L}{S_0}\right)^{2v^d/\sigma}\left[N\left(\frac{L' + v^d T}{\sqrt{T}}\right)\right]$$

$$= N\left(\frac{\ln(S_0/L) + \left(r^d - r^f - \frac{1}{2}\sigma^2\right)T}{\sigma\sqrt{T}}\right)$$

$$- \left(\frac{L}{S_0}\right)^{2v^d/\sigma} N\left(\frac{\ln(L/S_0) + \left(r^d - r^f - \frac{1}{2}\sigma^2\right)T}{\sigma\sqrt{T}}\right),$$

which can be written more concisely as

$$V_0^{\text{NT2P}} = e^{-r^d T}\left(N(d_2(S_0, L)) - \left(\frac{L}{S_0}\right)^{2(r^d - r^f)/\sigma^2 - 1} N(d_2(L, S_0))\right).$$

Prices for the corresponding one-touches, which pay in domestic currency at time T, follow directly.

Domestic upside one-touch

$$V_0^{\text{OT2C}} = e^{-r^d T} \mathbf{P}^d [\tau^H \le T]$$

$$= e^{-r^d T} \left(N(d_2(S_0, H)) + \left(\frac{H}{S_0} \right)^{2(r^d - r^f)/\sigma^2 - 1} N(-d_2(H, S_0)) \right).$$

Domestic downside one-touch

$$V_0^{\text{OT2P}} = e^{-r^d T} \mathbf{P}^d [\tau_L \le T]$$

$$= e^{-r^d T} \left(N(-d_2(S_0, L)) + \left(\frac{L}{S_0} \right)^{2(r^d - r^f)/\sigma^2 - 1} N(d_2(L, S_0)). \right)$$

8.3.2 Foreign binaries

Foreign upside no-touch

We have $V_0^{\text{NT1C}} = S_0 e^{-r^f T} \mathbf{P}^f [\tau^H > T]$. Then

$$\mathbf{P}^f [\tau^H > T] = N \left(\frac{H' - v^f T}{\sqrt{T}} \right) - \left(\frac{H}{S_0} \right)^{2v^f/\sigma} N \left(\frac{-H' - v^f T}{\sqrt{T}} \right)$$

$$= N \left(\frac{\ln(H/S_0) - \left(r^d - r^f + \frac{1}{2}\sigma^2 \right) T}{\sigma \sqrt{T}} \right)$$

$$- \left(\frac{H}{S_0} \right)^{2v^f/\sigma} N \left(\frac{\ln(S_0/H) - \left(r^d - r^f + \frac{1}{2}\sigma^2 \right) T}{\sigma \sqrt{T}} \right)$$

and so

$$V_0^{\text{NT1C}} = S_0 e^{-r^f T} \left(N(-d_1(S_0, H)) - \left(\frac{H}{S_0} \right)^{2(r^d - r^f)/\sigma^2 + 1} N(-d_1(H, S_0)) \right).$$

Foreign downside no-touch

We have $V_0^{\text{NT1P}} = S_0 e^{-r^f T} \mathbf{P}^f [\tau_L > T]$. Then

$$\mathbf{P}^f [\tau_L > T] = N \left(\frac{-L' + v^f T}{\sqrt{T}} \right) - \left(\frac{L}{S_0} \right)^{2v^f/\sigma} \left[N \left(\frac{L' + v^f T}{\sqrt{T}} \right) \right]$$

$$= N \left(\frac{\ln(S_0/L) + \left(r^d - r^f + \frac{1}{2}\sigma^2 \right) T}{\sigma \sqrt{T}} \right)$$

$$- \left(\frac{L}{S_0} \right)^{2v^f/\sigma} N \left(\frac{\ln(L/S_0) + \left(r^d - r^f + \frac{1}{2}\sigma^2 \right) T}{\sigma \sqrt{T}} \right).$$

From this we immediately obtain

$$V_0^{\text{NTIP}} = S_0 e^{-r^f T} \left(N(d_1(S_0, L)) - \left(\frac{L}{S_0} \right)^{2(r^d - r^f)/\sigma^2 + 1} N(d_1(L, S_0)) \right).$$

Foreign upside one-touch

$$V_0^{\text{OT1C}} = S_0 e^{-r^f T} \mathbf{P}^f [\tau^H \leq T]$$

$$= S_0 e^{-r^f T} \left(N(d_1(S_0, H)) + \left(\frac{H}{S_0} \right)^{2(r^d - r^f)/\sigma^2 + 1} N(-d_1(H, S_0)) \right).$$

Foreign downside one-touch

$$V_0^{\text{OT1P}} = S_0 e^{-r^f T} \mathbf{P}^f [\tau_L \leq T]$$

$$= S_0 e^{-r^f T} \left(N(-d_1(S_0, L)) + \left(\frac{L}{S_0} \right)^{2(r^d - r^f)/\sigma^2 + 1} N(d_1(L, S_0)) \right).$$

8.3.3 Instant one-touch products

One difference between one-touches and other first generation exotics is that one-touches are the only product that can meaningfully pay instantly upon hitting the barrier. For no-touch binaries, one always has to wait until time T to know if the barriers have been untouched. Even if you get to one week from expiry without hitting the barrier, there's always a chance that the barrier might hit in the final week of trading. In contrast, once a barrier has been hit, then the knock-in/knock-out state for that product is determined. For barrier options with a call or put payout, even if you know that the product has knocked in, the payout $(\omega(S - K))^+$ requires us to wait until S_T to know the terminal value.

In contrast, an instant one-touch (or instant-double touch) can in principle pay the one unit of cash (in foreign or domestic currency) as soon[2] as the barrier is touched. Payoffs for these products are given by

$$V_0^{\text{IOT1C}} = S_0 \mathbf{E}^f \left[e^{-r^f \tau^H} \mathbf{1}_{\{\tau^H \leq T\}} \right],$$

$$V_0^{\text{IOT1P}} = S_0 \mathbf{E}^f \left[e^{-r^f \tau_L} \mathbf{1}_{\{\tau_L \leq T\}} \right],$$

$$V_0^{\text{IDT1}} = S_0 \mathbf{E}^f \left[e^{-r^f \tau_L^H} \mathbf{1}_{\{\tau_L^H \leq T\}} \right],$$

$$V_0^{\text{IOT2C}} = \mathbf{E}^d \left[e^{-r^d \tau^H} \mathbf{1}_{\{\tau^H \leq T\}} \right],$$

$$V_0^{\text{IOT2P}} = \mathbf{E}^d \left[e^{-r^d \tau_L} \mathbf{1}_{\{\tau_L \leq T\}} \right],$$

$$V_0^{\text{IDT2P}} = \mathbf{E}^d \left[e^{-r^d \tau_L^H} \mathbf{1}_{\{\tau_L^H \leq T\}} \right].$$

---

[2] In practice, probably on the spot date thereafter – usually $T + 2$.

These products do not admit the same techniques as normal binary options with expiry time T, and are priced by constructing the risk-neutral distribution for the appropriate hitting time τ and then numerically integrating its probability density function multiplied by $e^{-r^{d;f}\tau}$ from 0 to T. Note that if the interest rate for the currency in which the instant one-touch is paid is zero, then the price equates to that for the equivalent one-touch.

These products are encountered much less often than the standard one-touches, which pay one unit of cash at T conditional on whether a particular barrier level has been touched or not by then, irrespective of when.

8.3.4 Barrier products

As mentioned at the start of this chapter, the original rationale for barrier products was to find a way to offer a European style option payout more cheaply than the non-path-dependent European. We denumerate the possibilities below.

Note that for single barrier products, the KI/KO barrier level can either be in the in-the-money (ITM) region or in the out-of-the-money (OTM) region. Where the barrier level is in the ITM region, there is a value discontinuity and the product is said to be a reverse knock-in or reverse knock-out (as opposed to the regular knock-in and regular knock-out products). In an example of confusing market terminology, KI and KO often denote a regular knock-in and a regular knock-out respectively, whereas RKI and RKO denote the reverse knock-in and reverse knock-out. DKI and DKO always denote double knock-in and double knock-out options, however.

One would generally imagine $L < K < U$, but this is actually not always so. It is perfectly feasible, though unusual, to construct an example of a down-and-out call option where the option is sufficiently in the money that $K < L < S_0$.

Pricing of these products follows by the same principle of decomposition. Just as we can decompose a European option with payout $(S_T - K)^+$ into two European digitals (asset-or-nothing and cash-or-nothing), we can do exactly the same with path dependency added.

We limit ourselves mathematically to one example here, to demonstrate the method.

Down-and-in call

We consider here only the case where $K \in (L, S_0)$, as in that case the knock-in is triggered when the barrier L is touched and at that point becomes an out-of-the-money option with strike K. In the case where $K < L$, the option becomes immediately active and in-the-money when the level L becomes touched, which complicates the analysis.

We have

$$V_0^{DIC} = e^{-r^d T} \mathbf{E}^d[(S_T - K)^+ \mathbf{1}_{\{\tau_L \leq T\}}]$$

$$= S_0 e^{-r^f T} \mathbf{P}^f[S_T > K \cap \tau_L \leq T] - K e^{-r^d T} \mathbf{P}^d[S_T > K \cap \tau_L \leq T]$$

$$= S_0 e^{-r^f T} \left(\frac{L}{S_0}\right)^{2v^f/\sigma} N\left(\frac{2L' - K' + v^f T}{\sqrt{T}}\right)$$

$$- K e^{-r^d T} \left(\frac{L}{S_0}\right)^{2v^d/\sigma} N\left(\frac{2L' - K' + v^d T}{\sqrt{T}}\right)$$

$$= S_0 e^{-r^f T} \left(\frac{L}{S_0} \right)^{2(r^d - r^f)/\sigma^2 + 1} N \left(\frac{\ln\left(L^2/(S_0 K)\right) + \left(r^d - r^f + \frac{1}{2}\sigma^2\right) T}{\sigma\sqrt{T}} \right)$$

$$- K e^{-r^d T} \left(\frac{L}{S_0} \right)^{2(r^d - r^f)/\sigma^2 - 1} N \left(\frac{\ln\left(L^2/(S_0 K)\right) + \left(r^d - r^f - \frac{1}{2}\sigma^2\right) T}{\sigma\sqrt{T}} \right),$$

where we note that $2L' - K' = (2/\sigma)\ln(L/S_0) - (1/\sigma)\ln(K/S_0) = (1/\sigma)\ln(L^2/(S_0 K))$. This gives

$$V_0^{DIC} = S_0 e^{-r^f T} \left(\frac{L}{S_0} \right)^{2(r^d - r^f)/\sigma^2 + 1} N(d_1(L^2, S_0 K))$$

$$- K e^{-r^d T} \left(\frac{L}{S_0} \right)^{2(r^d - r^f)/\sigma^2 - 1} N(d_2(L^2, S_0 K)).$$

The price for an up-and-in put (with $U > K$) is obtained using the same approach:

$$V_0^{UIP} = K e^{-r^d T} \left(\frac{U}{S_0} \right)^{2(r^d - r^f)/\sigma^2 - 1} N(-d_2(U^2, S_0 K))$$

$$- S_0 e^{-r^f T} \left(\frac{U}{S_0} \right)^{2(r^d - r^f)/\sigma^2 + 1} N(-d_1(U^2, S_0 K)).$$

Given such formulae for regular knock-in options, the price for a regular knock-out is easily obtained by subtracting the knock-in price from the equivalent vanilla.

Note that reverse knock-out and reverse knock-in options are slightly more complicated to price using the reflection principle, on account of the discontinuity in the value at the expiry function. In fact, both the down-and-in and the up-and-in calls are easy to value in the case where the strike K is between the barrier and the current spot level. We priced the first of these above. The second, an up-and-in call with $S_0 < U < K$, has exactly the same price as a non-path-dependent European call, because if the call expires in the money, then the spot rate process must have crossed U at some time.

Details of valuing barrier options where the barrier level is in the ITM region can be found in Rubinstein and Reiner (1991) and Rich (1994), the results of which are summarised in Zhang (1998) and Haug (2007). I relate them here for ease of reference, leaving out the rebate feature, which is rarely encountered in FX and is priceable as a separate one-touch in any case if desired.

In order to do so efficiently, we let H denote either U or L as appropriate (for down and up barriers respectively) and use the following symbols to be consistent with A10.3 of Zhang (1998), from which this algebraic simplification is taken:

$$\upsilon = r^d - r^f - \frac{1}{2}\sigma^2,$$

$$V_0^{C;P}(S, K; \omega) = \omega \left[S e^{-r^f T} N(\omega d_1(S, K)) - K e^{-r^d T} N(\omega d_2(S, K)) \right],$$

$$C_{x,y}^\omega = \omega \times \max(\omega x, \omega y).$$

A word of explanation: $C^{\omega}_{x,y}$ is the comparative operator, defined by

$$C^{\omega}_{x,y} = \begin{cases} \max(x,y), & \omega = +1, \\ \min(x,y), & \omega = -1. \end{cases}$$

With this we can unify V_0^{DIC} and V_0^{UIP} and include the additional terms required if the $K > L$ or $K < U$ condition fails to be satisfied, obtaining

$$
\begin{aligned}
V_0^{\text{DIC;UIP}}(\omega,\theta) &= \left(\frac{H}{S_0}\right)^{2\upsilon/\sigma^2} \left[V_0^{\text{C;P}}\left(\frac{H^2}{S}, C^{\omega}_{H,K}; \omega\right) \right. \\
&\quad \left. + \theta[C^{\omega}_{H,K} - K]e^{-r^d T} N\left(\omega d_2\left(\frac{H^2}{S_0}, C^{\omega}_{H,K}\right)\right) \right] \\
&\quad + \left\{ V_0^{\text{C;P}}(S,K;-\theta) - V_0^{\text{C;P}}(S,H;-\theta) \right. \\
&\quad \left. + \theta[H - K]e^{-r^d T} N\left(\theta d_2(S,H)\right) \right\} \mathbf{1}_{\{\theta H > \theta K\}}.
\end{aligned}
$$

The other formula required is for the up-and-in call or the down-and-in put, which we merely quote here:

$$
\begin{aligned}
V_0^{\text{UIC;DIP}}(\omega,\theta) &= \left(\frac{H}{S_0}\right)^{2\upsilon/\sigma^2} \left[V_0^{\text{C;P}}\left(\frac{H^2}{S}, K;\theta\right) - V_0^{\text{C;P}}\left(\frac{H^2}{S}, H;\theta\right) \right. \\
&\quad \left. + \omega[H - K]e^{-r^d T} N(\theta d_2(H,S)) \right] \mathbf{1}_{\{\omega K > \omega H\}} \\
&\quad + V_0^{\text{C;P}}\left(S, C^{\omega}_{H,K}; -\theta\right) + \omega C^{\omega}_{H,K} - Ke^{-r^d T} N(\omega d_2(S, C^{\omega}_{H,K})).
\end{aligned}
$$

While these are quite formidable, they allow closed-form expressions for Black–Scholes prices for all the single barrier options to be written

$$
\begin{aligned}
V_0^{\text{DIC}} &= V_0^{\text{DIC;UIP}}(+1,+1), \\
V_0^{\text{UIP}} &= V_0^{\text{DIC;UIP}}(-1,-1), \\
V_0^{\text{UIC}} &= V_0^{\text{UIC;DIP}}(+1,-1), \\
V_0^{\text{DIP}} &= V_0^{\text{UIC;DIP}}(-1,+1), \\
V_0^{\text{DOC}} &= V_0^{\text{C}} - V_0^{\text{DIC;UIP}}(+1,+1), \\
V_0^{\text{UOP}} &= V_0^{\text{P}} - V_0^{\text{DIC;UIP}}(-1,-1), \\
V_0^{\text{UOC}} &= V_0^{\text{C}} - V_0^{\text{UIC;DIP}}(+1,-1), \\
V_0^{\text{DOP}} &= V_0^{\text{P}} - V_0^{\text{UIC;DIP}}(-1,+1).
\end{aligned}
$$

In the case where the single barrier is only active for a subinterval of $[0, T]$, Heynen and Kat (1994) derived similar but more complicated closed-form pricing formulae for the case of partial barrier options (where the barrier is effective from $t = 0$ to $t = t^*$) and forward barrier options (where the barrier is effective from $t = t^*$ to $t = T$). One should be careful with the forward barrier options in particular as they can be rather sensitive to the forward volatility skew.

Strike-out products

A particularly interesting type of single barrier product[3] is one for which the barrier is placed at the strike and the option is in-the-money at inception, e.g. a USDJPY down-and-out call with $S_0 = 100$, $K = 90$ and continuous extinguishing barrier at $L = 90$. Assume that the interest rates are zero in USD and JPY. In that case, both convection and reaction terms in the option pricing PDE expressed with respect to S vanish. Hence it is purely a diffusive equation. Because the option payout is linear above K and this linearity is maintained indefinitely by the presence of the Dirichlet condition at L, the diffusion also has no effect. Therefore, the option is *always* worth the intrinsic value of 10 JPY pips, no matter what the maturity is. The same is *not* true once interest rates are presumed to be stochastic, however.

If you are being asked to quote a price on such a product, it is therefore very likely indeed that the counterparty is trying to assess whether you have a working longdated FX model.

8.3.5 KIKOs and ONTOs

Various other barrier type products that are peculiar to FX may be encountered from time to time. One that is quite common for taking a directional view is the KIKO, or the knock-in on a knock-out. This is a product that differs from a conventional knock-in, in that if the KI level is touched, then instead of transforming into a vanilla, it transforms into a KO with an extinguishing barrier. These can be priced using simple parity relationships; for example, if the KI barrier is to the upside at U and the KO barrier is to the downside at L, then this KIKO plus a double KO must sum to a downside KO. Hence the KIKO can be priced as

$$V_0^{\text{KIKO}} = V_0^{\text{KO}} - V_0^{\text{DKO}}.$$

The same applies for digitals with payout of one unit of cash, for which these instruments are called a one-touch on a no-touch:

$$V_0^{\text{OTNT}} = V_0^{\text{NT}} - V_0^{\text{DNT}}.$$

Note that in both cases, if the knock-out barrier hits first, then all bets are off and the contract expires worthless. It is possible to construct a variant of this product where the KO feature only comes into existence after the KI barrier is touched, but this introduces an asymmetry between the hitting times for the upper and lower barriers, and is considerably more complicated to deal with.

8.4   DOUBLE BARRIER PRODUCTS

The intuitive appeal of the reflection principle sadly fails to help when it comes to pricing products with barriers either side of the current spot level S_0. We shall consider only the case of the domestic double no-touch here. Extension to the foreign double no-touch is a matter of a simple measure change, and pricing the European style products with double barriers can be obtained by extension:

$$\mathbf{P}^d\left[S_t \in [L, U]\ \forall t \in [0, T]\right] = \mathbf{P}^d\left[S_0 \exp(\sigma \tilde{W}_t) \in [L, U]\ \forall t \in [0, T]\right]$$
$$= \mathbf{P}^d\left[\sigma \tilde{W}_t \in [\ln(L/S_0), \ln(U/S_0)]\ \forall t \in [0, T]\right].$$

---

[3] I am grateful to Tim Sharp for this example, which made rather a good interview question back in 2003.

Assume that $b < x < a$. We follow (78) of Section 5.7 of Cox and Miller (1965), which is described in Section 11.10 of Zhang (1998), and write

$$P_{db}(x,t) = \sum_{n=-\infty}^{\infty} p_n(x,t)$$

with

$$f(x,t) = \frac{1}{\sigma\sqrt{2\pi t}} \exp\left(\frac{-(x-\upsilon t)^2}{2\sigma^2 t}\right),$$
$$p_n(x,t) = \exp\left(x_n'\upsilon/\sigma^2\right) f(x - x_n', t) - \exp\left(x_n''\upsilon/\sigma^2\right) f(x - x_n'', t),$$
$$x_n' = 2n(a-b),$$
$$x_n'' = 2a - x_n' = 2a - 2n(a-b),$$
$$a = \ln\left(\frac{U}{S_0}\right),$$
$$b = \ln\left(\frac{L}{S_0}\right),$$
$$\upsilon = r^d - r^f - \frac{1}{2}\sigma^2.$$

Calculation of

$$V_0^{\text{DNT2}} = e^{-r^d T} \mathbf{P}^d \left[\tau_L^U > T\right]$$

can be shown to reduce to the following expression:

$$V_0^{\text{DNT2}} = e^{-r^d T} \sum_{n=-\infty}^{\infty} \left[\left(\frac{U}{L}\right)^{2n\upsilon/\sigma^2} \left(N(d_1^{\text{DNT}}) - N(d_2^{\text{DNT}})\right)\right.$$
$$\left. - \left(\frac{U}{S_0}\right)^{2\upsilon/\sigma^2} \left(\frac{L}{U}\right)^{2n\upsilon/\sigma^2} \left(N(d_3^{\text{DNT}}) - N(d_4^{\text{DNT}})\right)\right],$$

where

$$x_n' = 2n \ln\left(\frac{U}{L}\right), \qquad x_n'' = 2\ln\left(\frac{U}{S_0}\right) - 2n\ln\left(\frac{U}{L}\right),$$
$$d_1^{\text{DNT}} = \frac{\ln(U/S_0) - \upsilon T - x_n'}{\sigma\sqrt{T}}, \qquad d_2^{\text{DNT}} = \frac{\ln(L/S_0) - \upsilon T - x_n'}{\sigma\sqrt{T}},$$
$$d_3^{\text{DNT}} = \frac{\ln(U/S_0) - \upsilon T - x_n''}{\sigma\sqrt{T}}, \qquad d_4^{\text{DNT}} = \frac{\ln(L/S_0) - \upsilon T - x_n''}{\sigma\sqrt{T}}.$$

8.5   SENSITIVITY TO LOCAL AND STOCHASTIC VOLATILITY

Unfortunately, in the same way that the Black–Scholes model fails to provide an accurate representation of the market price of Europeans, barrier and binary options are similarly mispriced by a pure Black–Scholes model. Whereas we can get a visual idea of how the price

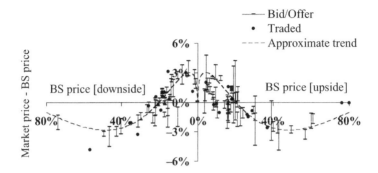

Figure 8.6 The moustache graph

of various Europeans deviates from a pure Black–Scholes model by examining the implied volatility surface, a different approach is needed for binaries.

The graphs presented here are a popular way of visualising the systematic deviation of either market prices or model prices from the Black–Scholes TV prices for both single barrier and double barrier binary options. Similar graphs can be found in Jex *et al.* (1999), but with different axes.

In constructing the moustache graph[4] in Figure 8.6, I collected both bid/offer and actual traded prices from the trading desk at one of the institutions where I worked over a period of time, for a variety of major currency pairs.[5] I then tabulated how those market prices compared to the TV prices. The x axis is the TV, or the Black–Scholes price, where downside one-touches are gathered to the left and upside one-touches to the right, and the y axis shows the arithmetic difference between the market price and the TV price.

What we see here is sensible and plausible – any one-touch that is either guaranteed to hit or guaranteed not to hit in a Black–Scholes world attains the same value in a realistic market, due to limiting behaviour. However, for a cheap one-touch, typically with a TV of about 10 % (recall this means that the implied probability of the barrier level being touched is 0.1 under the domestic risk-neutral measure), the market will price this in excess of 10 %, at around 12 or 13 % in this example. There is an interesting crossover at about 20 %, and for one-touches that have a TV of close to 50 %, the market price is actually less. This is characteristic of a leptokurtic distribution, due to the fat tails and the narrow shoulders.

Figure 8.7 shows how a pure local volatility model, a pure stochastic volatility model, and two intermediate local-stochastic volatility models numerically price one-touches relative to a Black–Scholes benchmark, the y axis being the arithmetic spread of the *model* price over the TV this time. Figure 8.8 for the double no-touch (DNT) similarly shows how the model implied prices, graphed as a spread over the TV, relate to the TV for symmetric double no-touches.

It is interesting that the most liquid double no-touches in the market are generally at about the 10 % TV level, which we clearly see makes them the most sensitive instrument to the tuning between local and stochastic volatility.

---

[4] The name is both a visual descriptor, perhaps reminiscent of Salvador Dali, and is something to deal with on top of the smile, as it were....

[5] In retrospect, it would have been preferable to split these up and analyse each currency pair separately. Nevertheless, the pattern is still clear.

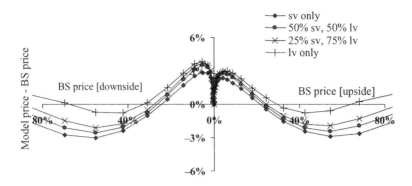

Figure 8.7 The model implied moustache graph

8.6 BARRIER BENDING

One problem we have with reverse knock-outs in particular is that the discontinuity gives rise to very large risk exposure in the event that the spot rate is close to the barrier near to expiry.

We give the example here of an option with strike $K = 1$, up-and-out level $U = 1.10$, domestic and foreign rates of zero, and $\sigma = 10\%$. Clearly, Figure 8.9 shows how the presence of the KO barrier causes the option position to have a very large negative delta for spot values S_t just below 1.10, and particularly so for a short period of time just before expiry. Even worse from a trading point of view, the delta goes from this very large negative value to zero if the barrier is touched, meaning the delta position needs to be unwound as soon as possible if the barrier is touched.

This section details some fairly useful barrier adjustments that are used in the industry to manage these risks.

The same approach is applicable to double knock-outs, where the techniques described herein are employed with respect to the barrier which is in the in-the-money region.

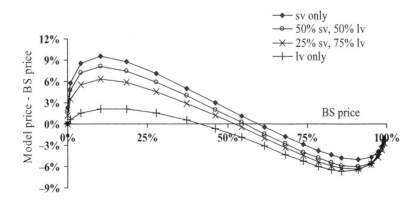

Figure 8.8 The model implied DNT profile

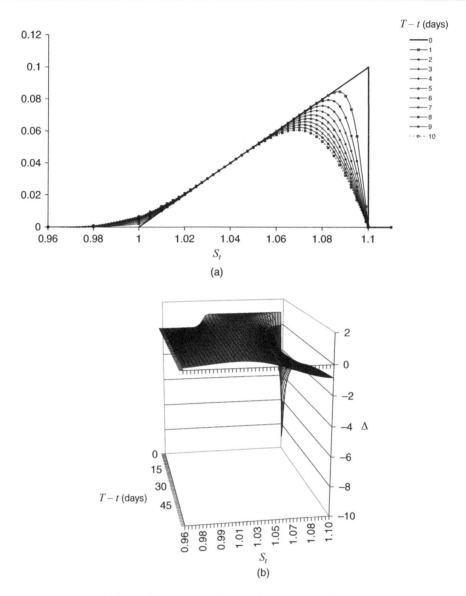

Figure 8.9   Value and delta profile for RKO call: (a) value profile; (b) delta profile; (c) delta heatmap

Firstly, note that we can certainly cap the absolute value of the delta[6] at a specified level Δ_{max} by just building a tight RKO call spread, long one RKO with the original strike K and short N units of an RKO with strike equal to $u - 1/N$. This has a delta between $K - \epsilon$ and K of $1 - N$ and by choosing N suitably, we can ensure that the delta of this product never departs from a prespecified region of manageable delta. This is shown in Figure 8.10.

---

[6] Deltas in this section are purely spot pips deltas; the extension to other deltas is straightforward.

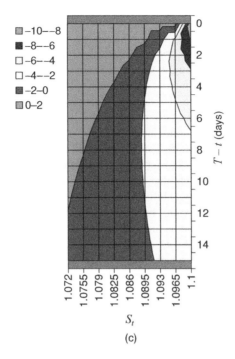

(c)

Figure 8.9   (cont.)

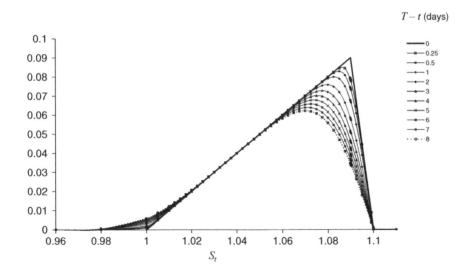

Figure 8.10   Value profile for tight RKO call spread

This product is of course an imperfect approximation to the original RKO call, but, being cheaper, it provides a sensible bid price.

How should we obtain an offer price for such a security, subject to constraints on the maximal size of delta we are willing to expose ourselves to over the lifetime of the option? Clearly we need to make the option more expensive for the counterparty, and need to do so in such a way that removes the region of excessive negative delta from our concern. The easiest way to do so is to price the security after imposing a parallel shift of the KO barrier from the original level U outwards by some amount. In this example, we move the barrier from $U = 1.10$ to a new level $U' = 1.1035$. This is illustrated in Figure 8.11. Note that the region of large negative delta, such as the cluster with delta below -8, remains stuck to the barrier and pulled out towards 1.1035. Note that this will make the product more expensive for the counterparty, and at the same time it shifts the region of excessively large deltas (below -8) out completely into the 'shadow region' between 1.10 and 1.1035.

We do not quote this barrier adjustment to the counterparty, however, who is given to understand that they have entered into a trade involving the original barrier product with barrier level U. The barrier shifting technique (like the barrier bending technique to follow) is purely an internal risk management device used to skew the price to the offer in such a way that we can manage the discontinuity risk.

The shadow region is interesting, in that if the spot process enters this zone, then the counterparty believes the barrier option has knocked out, but the trade as booked does not unless U' touches. Consequently, we have the possibility of a windfall profit if the quoted barrier level $U = 1.10$ is breached but the internal shifted barrier level $U' = 1.10135$ is not.

The parallel barrier shift technique is effective but somewhat heavy handed. The original barrier level of $U = 1.10$ is innocuous for most of the lifetime of the contract and it seems quite unnecessary to move the entire barrier just to handle a small region of excessive risk near to expiry.

One possible refinement is to use a piecewise constant barrier specification, such as having the barrier set to $U = 1.10$ for most of the lifetime of the trade, but then moving out to $U = 1.1035$ for n days before expiry (with n to be determined). The time at which the barrier shifts, then, can be written $t^* = T - n/365$ and we have

$$U(t) = \begin{cases} U, & t < t^*, \\ U', & \text{otherwise.} \end{cases}$$

A better idea is to allow the barrier to exist at $U = 1.10$ for most of the lifetime of the trade, but then moving out smoothly to $U = 1.1035$ at expiry as a linear function of the number of days remaining. In other words,

$$U(t) = \begin{cases} U, & t < t^*, \\ U + \dfrac{\delta U}{T - t*}(t - t^*), & \text{otherwise.} \end{cases}$$

where $\delta U = U' - U$.

We show this in Figure 8.12, where once again the region of excessive delta remains anchored to the barrier, but where this barrier level is effectively a moving level in spacetime. Note that, once again, the entire region of large delta (less than -8 in this example) remains anchored to the bent barrier, and is insulated from the client within the shadow region out beyond the quoted barrier level of 1.10.

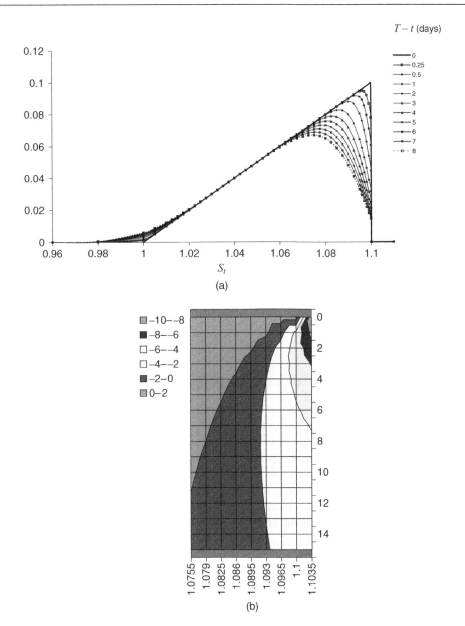

Figure 8.11 Value and delta profile for RKO call with $U' = 1.1035$: (a) value profile; (b) delta heatmap

Pricing of these bent barrier structures requires careful attention to grid generation, to allow the barrier level $U(t)$ for each physical time t (or $\tau = T - t$ in a PDE framework) to be specified as a required spatial level. Using the techniques of Section 7.11, one has the machinery to do this.

In summary, we can effectively manage discontinuity risk for reverse knock-out options by using a tight RKO spread to quote a bid price and using barrier bending techniques to quote an offer price.

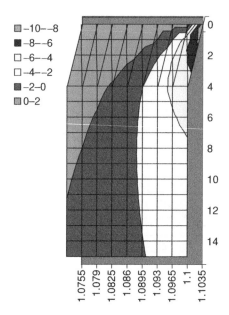

Figure 8.12 Delta heatmap for RKO call with barrier bend from $U = 1.10$ to $U' = 1.1035$

8.7   VALUE MONITORING

The final technique I wish to describe is that of monitoring the value $V(S, t)$ of an option when being priced on a PDE scheme, in order to assess whether it might be optimal to exercise it early. Similar schemes to assess the effect of early exercisability are possible for Monte Carlo simulation methods using regression methods, as discussed in Longstaff and Schwartz (2001) and Chapter 8 of Glasserman (2004). We discuss only the PDE approach here.

For clarity I presume that the spatial coordinate is spot, but it may well be represented as logspot within the finite difference engine. The valuation principle is the same, either way.

The canonical example is that of an American, but I shall introduce a simpler example first.

8.7.1   Compounds

Suppose we have the right to buy, at time $t_1 < T$, a call option with strike K and expiry T, i.e. a call on a call. However, in order to exercise this option at t_1, we need to pay K_C to do so. The payoff of this product at time T, if exercised at t_1, is

$$V_T = (S_T - K)^+ \tag{8.11a}$$

and consequently the value at time t_1 is just

$$V_{t_1} = \max\left(e^{r^d[T - t_1]} \mathbf{E}^d[V_T | S_{t_1}] - K_C, 0\right). \tag{8.11b}$$

This allows us to use backward induction from T to t_1 to obtain the conditional expectation of the value of the underlying option at t_1, which will have a convex profile $V(S_{t_1}, t_1)$, and then we use (8.11b) to price the compound at time t_1 and similarly use backward induction from

t_1 back to $t = 0$ to value the compound option. We can represent this as a value monitoring condition at t_1, which we use to infer the value at time t_1^- from time t_1^+ (just before and just after t_1, where t represents physical forward-stepping time):

$$V(S, t_1^-) = \max(V(S, t_1^+) - K_C, 0). \tag{8.12}$$

8.7.2 Americans

Suppose we have an early exercisable option, which unlike a compound can be exercised at any time between $t = 0$ and $t = T$. This can straightforwardly be handled by using a similar value monitoring condition on a PDE scheme; just compare the value $V(S, t)$ on the finite difference mesh against the intrinsic value, e.g. $(S - K)^+$ for a call and $(K - S)^+$ for a put, and choose the maximum of these two quantities at each iteration. Note that American style options are quite uncommon in FX:

$$V(S, t^-) = \max(V(S, t^+) - K_C, (\omega(S_t - K)^+)). \tag{8.13}$$

8.7.3 Bermudans

Extension to Bermudan type structures is even easier on PDEs – one just applies jump condition (8.13) at the Bermudan exercise dates, and nowhere else. Clearly this requires the temporal grid to include τ points corresponding to these days. Suppose the possible future exercise dates are $t_1, \ldots, t_N$; in that case the value monitoring condition is

$$V(S, t_i^-) = \max(V(S, t_i^+) - K_C, (\omega(S_{t_i} - K)^+)). \tag{8.14}$$

9

Second Generation Exotics

The products introduced above in Chapter 8, while heavily traded in FX, all have a value at expiry V_T that depends on some nontrivial combination of either the asset price at expiry S_T or the continuously monitored minimum m_T or maximum M_T over the interval $[0, T]$.

More correctly, we should say that we can handle an indicator function $\mathbf{1}_\epsilon$ on m_T and/or M_T by imposition of a suitable Dirichlet boundary condition on a backward time-stepping finite difference PDE scheme or a suitable extinguishing condition for a forward time-stepping Monte Carlo scheme. This means that we can price barriers, such as a double knock-out, with the value at expiry given by $V_T = (S_T - K)^+ \mathbf{1}_{\{m_T > L\}} \mathbf{1}_{\{M_T < U\}}$. The use of Dirichlet boundary conditions to handle KO barriers, which we may call weakly path-dependent products after the fashion of Wilmott (1998), extends to partial, forward and windowed barriers, as well as barriers with discretely observed fixings.

However, if we are asked to price up a fixed/floating strike lookback call or put, with payoff given by $V_T = (\omega(M_T - K))^+$ or $V_T = (\omega(M_T - S_T))^+$ for $\omega = \pm 1$, then the methods from Chapter 8 are inapplicable. We've basically reached the limits of how far we can go with a simple PDE with appropriately chosen boundary conditions.

All is not lost, however. As well as being amenable to Monte Carlo methods, there are a number of numerical techniques that rely upon using an augmented state variable as effectively as an additional dimension in the PDE formulation. This technique is suitable for strongly path-dependent products such as lookbacks, Asian options, range accruals, target redemption notes and the like.

I shall restrict myself to the case where the strong path dependency is due to discrete monitoring, as the technique will always be implemented numerically on a scheme with a finite number of timepoints, and most strongly path-dependent options only are sampled with a discrete frequency (daily at most).

The use of partial differential equations with auxiliary state variables, and the handling of discrete fixings using jump conditions, has been known for many years now, but practitioners often tend to meet with difficulty when putting these schemes into practice. In this chapter, I will suggest an incremental approach that I believe will take the reader from being able to price very simple options using a small number of pricing meshes to being able to price the more interesting products such as discretely sampled Asian options.

The technique of auxiliary state variables is discussed quite extensively in Chapters 16 to 18 of Wilmott (1998), Chapter 6 of Kwok (1998) and Section 6.2 of Seydel (2004), as well as more recently in Kwok (2009).

The basic idea here is that we suppose we have a number of future times, denoted $t_1, \ldots, t_N < T$, strictly between $t = 0$ and $t = T$, which affect the value of the product. If we can use backward induction on a denumerable number of possible states of the world, and "glue" them together in an appropriate way at each of these times, then we may be able to synthesise a backward pricing scheme that works.

It is somewhat tricky to understand and intricate to implement, but when done correctly is a rather powerful technique. We begin our introduction with two simple examples of products that require two PDE meshes, not one, to value. We then consider systems that require a larger number of PDE meshes, corresponding to an auxiliary state variable such as discrete arithmetic average, discrete maximum, or discrete minimum.

9.1   CHOOSER OPTIONS

Suppose we have an option, similar in a way to a compound, that allows us to elect to receive at t_1 (with $t_1 < T$) either a call or a put, with fixed strike K and expiry T. As discussed in Section 13.9 of Wilmott (1998), this means we have to value both the call and the put (each with strike K and expiry T) at time t_1. In order to preserve the convexity of each payout separately, we value these on two separate finite difference meshes, denoted $V^{\|}(S, t; \omega = 1)$ and $V^{\|}(S, t; \omega = 2)$ for the call and the put respectively.

Thus, we have two parallel PDE meshes and hence the notation $V^{\|}$, where each parallel PDE is indexed using a notation after the semicolon. Each have the same convection/diffusion/reaction terms, but with different payout functions

$$V^{\|}(S, T; \omega = 1) = \max(S - K, 0), \tag{9.1a}$$

$$V^{\|}(S, T; \omega = 2) = \max(K - S, 0). \tag{9.1b}$$

Each of these parallel PDEs is solved backwards from expiry time T to the exercise date t_1.

On the exercise date t_1, much as in Section 8.7.1, we apply a value monitoring condition but this time comparing two meshes:

$$V(S, t_1^-) = \max\left(V^{\|}(S, t_1^+; \omega = 1), V^{\|}(S, t_1^+; \omega = 2)\right). \tag{9.2}$$

Crucially, notice at this point that we have no further need of maintaining the parallel PDE meshes. The problem collapses to a standard PDE pricing problem such as we are used to, and therefore I refer to this as a *collapse condition*, by analogy with the collapse of the state vector into a single state in quantum mechanics.[1]

Basically, the two possible future states of the world (where we exercise into a call or a put respectively) collapse into one, and we then continue the backward induction on $V(S, t)$ from t_1 back to $t = 0$ and read off the present value, in the standard manner.

9.2   RANGE ACCRUAL OPTIONS

Another example of an interesting path-dependent product is the range accrual, which has a schedule of fixing dates $t_1, \ldots, t_N$ and a range – call it $[L, U]$. If the product has a standard value at expiry function of the form $V_T(S_T)$, then the range accrual feature links the notional to the proportion of these N fixings that were observed to lie in the range $[L, U]$.

Symbolically, we have

$$V_0 = e^{-r^d T} \frac{1}{N} \mathbf{E}^d \left[V_T(S_T) \sum_{i=1}^{N} \mathbf{1}_{\{S_{t_i} \in [L, U]\}} \right]. \tag{9.3}$$

---

[1] Physicists among you can visualise states of the world: $\omega = 1$ where the cat is alive and $\omega = 2$ where the cat is dead. It's basically the same idea.

This can also be priced using the two-mesh technique. Let the $\omega = 2$ mesh handle the pricing problem for the underlying product and the $\omega = 1$ mesh correspond to the pricing problem for the range accrual. At expiry, we have

$$V^{\|}(S, T; \omega = 2) = V_T(S), \tag{9.4a}$$

$$V^{\|}(S, T; \omega = 1) = 0. \tag{9.4b}$$

At each of the range accrual monitoring dates, a certain fraction $1/N$ of the value of the underlying product is allowed to propagate down into the $\omega = 1$ mesh for the range accrual, but only for values of spot in the range $[L, U]$ (or equivalently, for values of logspot in the range $[\ln L, \ln U]$). Boundary conditions for the two products are determined by the underlying product and are common to both meshes – so we can handle a range accrual on barrier options quite easily.

We represent the coupling of this two-mesh system up to but not including the first future fixing by the *jump condition*:

$$V^{\|}(S, t_i^-; \omega = 1) = V^{\|}(S, t_i^+; \omega = 1) + \frac{1}{N} V^{\|}(S, t_i^+; \omega = 2), \tag{9.5}$$

which maintains both meshes. In this case, it allows value from mesh 2 to fall through into mesh 1, conditional on whether the spot rate at that time is in the accrual range $[L, U]$.

Finally, as we cross back from the first future fixing date, the collapse condition is

$$V(S, t_1^-) = V^{\|}(S, t_1^+; \omega = 1) + \frac{1}{N} V^{\|}(S, t_1^+; \omega = 2), \tag{9.6}$$

which is basically the same as (9.5) except that we can throw the $\omega = 2$ mesh away thereafter and rename $V^{\|}(S, t; \omega = 1)$ as $V(S, t)$.

9.3   FORWARD START OPTIONS

Suppose we have a forward starting call[2] option that has the strike set at time t_1, rather than being set to a known value K today, as is usually the case. Most commonly, the strike will be set to the spot price S_{t_1} at t_1, though it can be easily set to a multiple αS_{t_1}. In that case, the value at expiry is

$$V_T(S_T) = \max(S_T - \alpha S_{t_1}, 0).$$

We can value this on a system of stacked PDEs by conditioning on the asset value at the fixing time t_1. This is described in Section 18.2 of Wilmott (1998).

If we had a regular European option with strike K, then we could set up a mesh of various points for spot S, denoted $\{S_i\}_{i=1}^{N_x}$, or equivalently mesh points $\{x_i\}_{i=1}^{N_x}$ for logspot, and value the option accordingly. However, we don't know the strike yet.

What can be done, though, is to introduce an auxiliary state variable $\mathcal{S}$ that denotes the value of spot S_{t_1} at the interim fixing t_1. In that case, the value at expiry can be expressed as

$$V_T(S_T) = \max(S_T - \alpha \mathcal{S}, 0).$$

In a forward time-stepping framework, we have the update rule at time t_1:

$$\mathcal{S}_1 = S_{t_1},$$

---

[2] The extension to a forward starting put or straddle is trivial.

where, importantly, S_0 doesn't exist; i.e. $\mathcal{S}$ is indeterminate for times before t_1. It can only be fixed after the observation. However, the aim is to use backward induction, using a network of PDEs. If we suppose the same number of mesh points for $\mathcal{S}$ as for S, then we have N_x possible states of the world, each corresponding to a possible future level for S_{t_1} at time t_1. Therefore, $\omega = 1$ is the $\mathcal{S} = S(t_1) = S_1$ state of the world, up to $\omega = N_x$, which denotes the $\mathcal{S} = S(t_1) = S_{N_x}$ state of the world. We adopt the notational convenience

$$V^\|(S, T; \omega = i) \equiv V^\|(S, T; \mathcal{S} = S_i).$$

The value at expiry for each of these pricing problems on the stacked PDEs is therefore

$$V^\|(S, T; \omega = 1) = \max(S - S_1, 0)$$

$$\vdots \tag{9.7}$$

$$V^\|(S, T; \omega = N_x) = \max(S - S_{N_x}, 0),$$

which can be stated more compactly as

$$V^\|(S, T; \mathcal{S}) = \max(S - \mathcal{S}, 0).$$

We value the option payouts from (9.14) back from $t = T$ to $t = t_1$ separately and independently, using our PDE machinery from Chapter 7, to t_1.

At time t_1, we use the collapse condition

$$V(S, t_1^-) = V^\|(S, t_1^+; \mathcal{S}), \tag{9.8}$$

which can be expressed for each of the points on the spatial mesh

$$V(S_i, t_1) = V^\|(S, t_1^+; \omega = i). \tag{9.9}$$

In other words, let's suppose we have a stack of auxiliary PDEs, indexed by ω_i, each corresponding to one of N_x possible states of the world where the value of S_{t_1} is determined, but at a different level, which we denote in the abstract by R. At time t_1, we glue these future states of the world together. How? We use the knowledge that if $S_{t_1} = S_i$, then $\mathcal{S}$ must be equal to S_i thereafter, and hence the option pricing problem that contributes to the value of the forward start option in the $S_{t_1} = S_i$ state of the world is $V^\|(S, t; \omega = i)$.

The collapse condition means that if we have a stack of N_x PDEs, each with N_x spatial points in the finite difference mesh, then at time t_1 we extract one value point from each and propagate that on to a single PDE mesh $V(S, t)$. We are effectively taking diagonal entries on the matrix of (S_i, S_j) entries, and this requires no interpolation. Since it requires no interpolation, it makes no difference whether these points are represented using spot or logspot spatial coordinates. However, since the various PDEs in the system of stacked PDEs each have different strikes, there is much less benefit in using nonuniform meshes for these strongly path-dependent products.[3]

While I illustrate the approach by presuming that S and $\mathcal{S}$ share the same meshpoints, this is not strictly necessary. In fact, the forward starting option has no dependence on the interim fixing in any case (at least in a Black–Scholes world) so one can easily get by with a much

---

[3] The only smart thing I can see to do is to prescribe a common mesh framework for all the separate PDE layers, but allow each in turn to impose additional nonuniform spatial points, specific to that layer and concentrated around the particular discontinuity for that pricing problem, but only for a small period of time near expiry T, and then to impose restriction of the finite difference schemes on to a coarse spatial grid that is common to all of the PDE layers. This may remind some readers of multigrid methods; see Wesseling (1992).

coarser mesh for S, and then building an interpolator for the points on the (S, S) diagonal and using that to apply the collapse condition. There is definitely scope for improving the efficiency of these schemes, but it's best to keep it simple to start with.

It is easy to check the price, at least in a Black–Scholes world. Since the contract only has any optionality between t_1 and T, if α is chosen so that the option will be struck at the money forward (e.g. $\alpha = D_T^f(t_1)/D_T^d(t_1)$), then the price should be approximately $0.04 D_T^d(0)\sigma\sqrt{T - t_1}$.

In addition, Haug (2007) provides closed-form pricing formulae in Section 4.6 of his book, which one can use to check one's stacked PDE implementation against the case of a more general α.

9.3.1   Strike reset options

An extension to the forward starting option is one where the strike is specified today, as K, but where the holder has the option to renegotiate the strike at time t_1 to αS_{t_1}, if he or she perceives it to be advantageous to do so. This is a simple extension of the forward start option detailed above; all we need to do is add a new state of the world ω_K (we may be able to reuse one of the $\{\omega_i\}$ cases in the analysis above if an S_i exists that is equal to K/α). The payout at expiry for this state of the world, corresponding to the scenario where the option does not have its strike renegotiated, is

$$V^{\parallel}(S, T; \omega = \omega_K) = \max(S - K, 0)$$

and the collapse condition is one that just combines features from the forward start option and the chooser

$$V(S, t_1^-) = \max\left(V^{\parallel}(S, t_1^+; S), V^{\parallel}(S, t_1^+; \omega = \omega_K)\right). \tag{9.10}$$

9.4   LOOKBACK OPTIONS

While relatively uncommon in FX, the lookback is probably the simplest of the multiperiod strongly path-dependent options to consider. We consider the example of a lookback call floating strike, which in the continuous case has value at expiry

$$V_T(S_T) = M_T - S_T$$

with M_T being the continuous maximum defined in Chapter 8. In the case of discrete observations, this becomes

$$V_T(S_T) = \max(M_T - S_T, 0)$$

with $M_T = \max\{S_{t_1}, \ldots, S_{t_N}\}$. Note that we need to include the max because the auxiliary state variable framework requires $t_1 > 0$ and $t_N < T$, and it's certainly possible that the final spot observation S_T may be above the maximum of all prior observations. In practice, the difference is minimal, for reasons we see later.

Similarly to the forward start option example, we introduce an auxiliary state variable for the discretely observed maximum M_t or the discretely observed minimum m_t, observed at time t taking into account all fixings up to and including time t. In a forward time-stepping framework, we have the update rule at time t_i:

$$M_i = \begin{cases} \max(S_{t_i}, M_{i-1}), & i > 1, \\ S_{t_1}, & i = 1, \end{cases} \qquad (9.11a)$$

$$m_i = \begin{cases} \min(S_{t_i}, m_{i-1}), & i > 1, \\ S_{t_1}, & i = 1, \end{cases} \qquad (9.11b)$$

with corresponding jump conditions

$$V^{\|}(S, t_i^-; M) = V^{\|}(S, t_i^+; \max(S, M)), \qquad (9.12a)$$

$$V^{\|}(S, t_i^-; m) = V^{\|}(S, t_i^+; \min(S, m)), \qquad (9.12b)$$

and collapse conditions

$$V(S, t_1^-) = V^{\|}(S, t_1^+; S), \qquad (9.13a)$$

$$V(S, t_1^-) = V^{\|}(S, t_1^+; S). \qquad (9.13b)$$

The value at expiry is set, for each of the parallel PDEs, by

$$V^{\|}(S, T; \omega = 1) = \max(M_1 - S, 0)$$

$$\vdots \qquad (9.14)$$

$$V^{\|}(S, T; \omega = N_x) = \max(M_{N_x} - S, 0),$$

which can be stated more compactly as

$$V^{\|}(S, T; M) = \max(M - S, 0).$$

The meshes we use are basically the same as we would use for the forward start option, i.e. for every meshpoint for S_i, we have an equivalent meshpoint for M_i. So, to be clear we have spot S_0 and logspot x_0 if we use a spatial mesh $x_1 = x_{\min}, \ldots, x_{N_x} = x_{\max}$.

Perhaps counterintuitively, this means we have mesh points for possible levels of the discretely observed maximum below today's level of spot. This is because the auxiliary state variable approach is purely for indeterminate timepoints $t_1, \ldots, t_N$ in the future, and we have no way of knowing what values we may encounter there.

Just as the collapse condition for the forward state option takes the diagonal elements of (S, R) and constructs a single value profile $V(S, t_1)$ at time t_1, the collapse condition for any lookback product priced using the auxiliary state variable approach does the same. This makes sense, as a lookback option with only one interim fixing is in fact just a forward start option.

What differs is the jump condition for fixings $t_2, \ldots$. Basically, for the case of the discretely monitored maximum, this says that no matter what the value $V^{\|}(S, t_i; M)$ is for pairs of (S, M), if at time t_i^+ the value of the spot coordinate S exceeds the value of the auxiliary state variable M, then this is physically unattainable and the value at that point is replaced by the value from the diagonal, i.e. $V^{\|}(S, t_i; S)$. We preclude any future information to flow back from states of the world where $M < S$, as this is unattainable. Note that if we impose this condition immediately at $t = T$ upon commencement of pricing a lookback on a system of PDEs, this renders $V_T = M - S$ and $V_t = \max(M_T - S_t, 0)$ completely equivalent, as the diagonal entries are just zero at that time and the jump condition propagates that zero value down over the top of any negative entries.

Visually, this means that if we have a stack of N_x PDEs, each with N_x spatial points in the finite difference mesh corresponding to possible observations of the discrete maximum, then at time t_1 we take all the values on the (S_i, M_i) diagonal and propagate that down every column, below the diagonal, to overwrite (S_i, M_j) entries for which $S_i > M_j$. Once again, no interpolation is required if the meshes are common to S and M.

In the case of an auxiliary state variable for the discretely observed minimum, with pairs of (S, m), it is the elements with $m > S$ that are replaced with value entries from the (S_i, m_i) diagonal, i.e. where $m = S$, and visually this means elements above the diagonal are overwritten.

Typical lookback products that may be encountered, together with their payout profiles at expiry in the auxiliary state variable framework, are now given.

Floating strike lookback call
$$V^{\|}(S, T; m) = \max(S - m, 0).$$

Floating strike lookback put
$$V^{\|}(S, T; M) = \max(M - S, 0).$$

Fixed strike lookback call
$$V^{\|}(S, T; M) = \max(M - K, 0).$$

Fixed strike lookback put
$$V^{\|}(S, T; m) = \max(K - m, 0).$$

Note that apart from the different specifications of the value at expiry, these are all handled in the same way for pricing, using the same jump and collapse conditions.

Pricing formulae for comparison in the Black–Scholes case can be found in Proposition 9.7.1 of Musiela and Rutkowski (1997), page 215, and Section 4.15 of Haug (2007), which are useful for checking the implementation.

9.4.1 Double lookback options

An uncommon but interesting product is one that pays the difference of the realised maximum and minimum, i.e.

$$V_T = M_t - m_t.$$

This can be handled using not one but *two* auxiliary state variables, and a terminal value specification of the form

$$V^{\|}(S, T; M, m) = M - m.$$

We then backward induct and apply the jump condition appropriately

$$V^{\|}(S, t_i^-; M, m) = V^{\|}(S, t_i^+; \max(S, M), \min(S, m)),$$

together with the collapse condition at the first future fixing (i.e. the final τ)

$$V(S, t_1^-) = V^{\parallel}(S, t_1^+; \max(S, M), \min(S, m)).$$

This product is of little use in itself but it would be a good starting point before tackling more practical examples that require two auxiliary state variables, such as volatility swaps.

9.5   ASIAN OPTIONS

One interesting aspect of lookback put options, which depend on the discretely monitored maximum, is that they are actually a very specific form of average rate option, where the fixings are averaged, but using the infinity norm, scaled by $1/N$:

$$\|\mathbf{x}\|_\infty = \max\{x_1, \ldots, x_N\} = \lim_{p \to \infty} \|\mathbf{x}\|_p,$$

where

$$\|\mathbf{x}\|_p = \left(\sum_{i=1}^N |x_i|^p\right)^{1/p}.$$

A typical arithmetic average rate option uses the more conventional 1-norm $\|\mathbf{x}\|_1 = \sum_{i=1}^n |x_i|$, from which we have $A = (1/N)\|\mathbf{S}\|_1$, with $\mathbf{S} = \{S_{t_1}, \ldots, S_{t_N}\}$ being a vector of all the future observations before but not including the expiry time T.

Clearly this can be put into the auxiliary state variable framework too. Following Wilmott (1998), note that we can write the running (arithmetic) average in the following manner:

$$A_1 = S_{t_1}$$

$$A_2 = \frac{1}{2}A_1 + \frac{1}{2}S_{t_2} = \frac{1}{2}[S_{t_1} + S_{t_2}]$$

$$A_3 = \frac{2}{3}A_2 + \frac{1}{3}S_{t_3} = \frac{1}{3}[S_{t_1} + S_{t_2} + S_{t_3}]$$

$$\vdots$$

$$A_j = \frac{j-1}{j}A_{j-1} + \frac{1}{j}S_{t_j}.$$

We therefore have the jump condition

$$V^{\parallel}(S, t_i^-; A) = V^{\parallel}\left(S, t_i^+; \frac{j-1}{j}A + \frac{1}{j}S\right) \tag{9.15}$$

and the collapse condition for t_1

$$V(S, t_1^-) = V^{\parallel}(S, t_1^+; S). \tag{9.16}$$

The collapse condition must be the same as for the forward start or the lookbacks, because an average strike option with only one fixing, which pays $V_T = (S_T - A_T)^+$, is just a forward starting option.

Note that while the jump conditions for the discretely observed maximum and minimum flood the half of the (S, M) or (S, m) configuration space respectively with terms from the diagonal, the jump condition for the arithmetic average performs a rotation of sorts. We can see this most clearly in the case when $j = 2$. In that case, the jump condition is

$$V^{\parallel}(S, t_2^-; A) = V^{\parallel}(S, t_2^+; \tfrac{1}{2}A + \tfrac{1}{2}S).$$

As Section 6.2.4 of Seydel (2004) describes very nicely, this is basically a clockwise rotation in the (S, A) configuration space. The same is true for other future fixing dates, with different weights in the linear combination. As a result, the meshpoints that are used for A are determined by the same upper and lower limits for the mesh for spot. We can equivalently use logspot and logaverage coordinates if we wish; the difference is negligible. All we really have is a network of convection–diffusion equations with different terminal conditions, which are allowed to rotate their value profiles into each other at a number of fixing dates.

This means that from an implementation point of view, for each S_i, we need to build an interpolator $f(A)$ from the observed values of $V^{\parallel}(S_i, t_2^+; A)$ that satisfies $f(A) = V^{\parallel}(S_i, t_2^+; A)$, and then set $V^{\parallel}(S_i, t_2^-; A_j) = f(\tfrac{1}{2}[S_i + A_j])$. Since this scheme naturally requires interpolation, it is very amenable to a relatively small number of auxiliary state mesh points for A.

Weighted averages can easily be incorporated into this scheme too, at the expense of slightly more involved arithmetic.

Types of Asian options that might well be encountered in practice are now given.

Average strike call

$$V^{\parallel}(S, T; A) = \max(S - A, 0).$$

Average strike put

$$V^{\parallel}(S, T; A) = \max(A - S, 0).$$

Average rate call

$$V^{\parallel}(S, T; A) = \max(A - K, 0).$$

Average rate put

$$V^{\parallel}(S, T; A) = \max(K - A, 0).$$

The same jump and collapse conditions apply to all four of these instruments.

9.5.1   Notes on seasoned Asians and fixing at expiry

The thing about Asian options is that, once they are booked, they accumulate historical fixings, which affect the pricing of the contract. In order to price these seasoned Asian options, we need to strip out the historical fixings. In fact, if the average also contains the fixing on the expiry date, this must be removed also.

Let us suppose that the average, for purposes of computing the value at expiry, is

$$A_{\text{seasoned}} = \frac{1}{M + N + \phi}[S_{t_{-M}} + \cdots + S_{t_{-1}} + S_{t_1} + S_{t_2} + \cdots + S_{t_N} + \phi S_T], \tag{9.17}$$

where $t_{-M} < \cdots < t_{-1} < 0 < t_1 < t_2 < \cdots < t_N < T$ and historical fixings have already been recorded for $S_{T_{-M}} \ldots S_{t_{-1}}$. I include a $\phi \in \{0, 1\}$ variable so we can optionally include the expiry date in the average or not, as desired. We have the auxiliary state variable $A_N = (1/N)[S_{t_1} + S_{t_2} + \cdots + S_{t_N}]$ and, therefore, if the value at expiry in terms of the actual average is $f(S, A)$, where A now has M historical observations, then we can express it in terms of the auxiliary state variable A_N as

$$A_{\text{seasoned}} = \frac{1}{M + N + \phi}[S_{t_{-M}} + \cdots + S_{t_{-1}} + N A_N + \phi S_T].$$

Consequently, the value at expiry is given by

$$V^{\parallel}(S, T; A) = f\left(S, \tfrac{1}{M+N+\phi}\left[NA + \sum_{i=1}^{M} S_{t_{-i}} + \phi S\right]\right).$$

9.6 TARGET REDEMPTION NOTES

Other interesting strongly path-dependent products can be handled in this framework. Target redemption notes, which are basically a strip of structured coupons that terminate after a certain aggregate coupon has been paid out in total to the holder, are amenable to this technique using the coupon paid to date as the auxiliary state.

A typical example of a target redemption note is the *target redemption forward*, which is a strip of N forwards with coupons expressible as $V_{t_1}, \ldots, V_{t_N}$. Each coupon has payout $V_{t_i} = (S_{t_i} - K)$, but the total structure is limited by the requirement that once the total payout exceeds a target level V_{cap}, then the structure ceases to exist.

Note that there are two flavours of target redemption notes. The first case is where we get the entire payout of the final coupon V_{t_n}, which takes the accumulated coupon over V_{cap}, in which case $\sum_{i=1}^{n} V_{t_i} \geq V_{\text{cap}}$ and the second in which the final coupon is truncated so that $\sum_{i=1}^{n} V_{t_i} = V_{\text{cap}}$. Similarly to the average rate option case discussed above, we introduce an auxiliary state variable A, which denotes the running sum of the coupon obtained to date. For further details we refer the reader to Chu and Kwok (2007).

9.7 VOLATILITY AND VARIANCE SWAPS

Volatility swaps, or realised volatility products in general, take into account the logreturns realised between each of the future timepoints t_i. The realised volatility is given by

$$\sigma_{\text{realised}} = \sqrt{\frac{1}{N + 1} \sum_{k=1}^{N} \frac{[\log(S_{t_k}) - \log(S_{t_{k-1}})]^2}{t_k - t_{k-1}}},$$

where we have the notational convenience that $t_0 = 0$ and $tN + 1 = T$, so that the future fixings $t_1, \ldots, t_N$ can be interpreted as auxiliary state variables. As described in Section 18.6 of Wilmott (1998), this can be handled using not one but two auxiliary states:

$$I_j = \sqrt{\frac{1}{j + 1} \sum_{k=1}^{j} \frac{[\log(S_{t_k}) - \log(S_{t_{k-1}})]^2}{t_k - t_{k-1}}}, \tag{9.18a}$$

$$\mathcal{S}_j = S(t_{j-1}), \tag{9.18b}$$

where I_j represents the realised volatility determined so far and R represents the previous sampled level for spot.

With this, we have the jump condition

$$V^{\parallel}(S, t_i^-; \mathcal{S}, I) = V^{\parallel}\left(S, t_i^+; \mathcal{S}, \sqrt{\frac{i}{i-1}I^2 + \frac{1}{i-1}\frac{[\log(S_{t_k}) - \log(S_{t_{k-1}})]^2}{t_k - t_{k-1}}}\right) \qquad (9.19)$$

and collapse condition

$$V(S, t_1^-) = V^{\parallel}\left(S, t_1^+; \mathcal{S}, 0\right). \qquad (9.20)$$

This is not actually as fearsome as it looks, as it only requires interpolation in the I auxiliary factor.

Possible product types that might be encountered are as follows.

Variance swap

$$V_T = \sigma_{\text{realised}}^2 - K^2.$$

Volatility swap

$$V_T = \sigma_{\text{realised}} - K.$$

9.7.1 Volatility observation

Both volatility and variance swaps are characterised by having a fixed discrete set $\{t_i : i = 0, 1, \ldots, N\}$ of observation dates, where the quantity of interest is a functional of the logreturns evaluated across each discrete period:

$$R_i = \ln\left(S_{t_i}/S_{t_{i-1}}\right) = X_{t_i} - X_{t_{i-1}}, \quad i = 1, \ldots, N. \qquad (9.21)$$

Of course some of these observation dates may well be in the past, so we denote by n_0 the index of the most recently elapsed sample

$$t_0 < t_1 < \cdots < t_{n_0} \leq 0 < t_{n_0+1} < \cdots < T_N. \qquad (9.22)$$

The corresponding values at these timepoints for spot and logspot processes are respectively denoted by $\{S_{t_0}, S_{t_1}, \ldots, S_{t_{n_0}}, S_0, S_{t_{n_0+1}}, \ldots, S_{t_N}\}$ and $\{X_{t_0}, X_{t_1}, \ldots, X_{t_{n_0}}, X_0, X_{t_{n_0+1}}, \ldots, X_{t_N}\}$.

By integrating (2.74), we have for the first future fixing

$$X_{t_{n_0+1}} - X_0 = \int_0^{t_{n_0+1}}\left(r_s^d - r_f(s) - \frac{1}{2}\sigma^2(s)\right)ds + \int_0^{t_{n_0+1}}\sigma(s)dW_s \qquad (9.23)$$

and for subsequent fixings

$$X_{t_i} - X_{t_{i-1}} = \int_{t_{i-1}}^{t_i}\left(r_s^d - r_f(s) - \frac{1}{2}\sigma^2(s)\right)ds + \int_{t_{i-1}}^{t_i}\sigma(s)dW_s. \qquad (9.24)$$

For some forms of variance and volatility swaps, we shall be concerned with the central moment $\bar{R}$, defined straightforwardly by

$$\bar{R} = \frac{1}{N}\sum_{i=1}^{N}R_i. \qquad (9.25)$$

In order to clarify the notation, we shall use 'hatted' returns $\hat{R}$ to denote logreturns that are deterministic at time $t = 0$, i.e.

$$\hat{R}_i \equiv R_i = X_{t_i} - X_{t_{i-1}}, \quad i \in \{1, \ldots, n_0\}.$$

We therefore have

$$R_i = \begin{cases} \int_{t_{i-1}}^{t_i} \left(r_s^d - r_s^f - \frac{1}{2}\sigma^2(s) \right) ds + \int_{t_{i-1}}^{t_i} \sigma(s) dW_s, & i > n_0 + 1, \\ \int_0^{t_{n_0+1}} \left(r_s^d - r_s^f - \frac{1}{2}\sigma^2(s) \right) ds + \int_0^{t_{n_0+1}} \sigma(s) dW_s + X_0 - X_{t_{n_0}}, & i = n_0 + 1, \\ \hat{R}_i, & i \leq n_0. \end{cases} \quad (9.26)$$

9.7.2 Product specification and value at expiry

Let V_{Realised} denote the final realised variance at time T. It is given by

$$V_{\text{Realised}} = \frac{\beta}{N} \sum_{i=1}^{N} (R_i - \phi \bar{R})^2, \quad (9.27)$$

where β is an annualisation factor, to convert the realised variance into an annualised variance, and ϕ is an argument that enables the realised drift of the asset price returns to be excluded from the computation:

$$\phi = \begin{cases} 1, & \text{to exclude the central moment of asset logreturns,} \\ 0, & \text{otherwise.} \end{cases}$$

With this, the values at expiry of the volatility and variance swaps can be simply written

$$\text{VarSwap}(T) = V_{\text{Realised}} - K^2 \quad (9.28)$$

and

$$\text{VolSwap}(T) = \sqrt{V_{\text{Realised}}} - K. \quad (9.29)$$

9.7.3 Variance swap product valuation

Let E_{Variance} denote the conditional expectation at time $t = 0$ of the realised variance

$$E_{\text{Variance}} = \mathbf{E}\left[V_{\text{Realised}} \middle| \mathcal{F}_0 \right] = \mathbf{E}\left[\frac{\beta}{M} \sum_{i=1}^{N} (R_i - \phi \bar{R})^2 \middle| \mathcal{F}_0 \right]. \quad (9.30)$$

We choose

$$M = \begin{cases} N - 1, & \text{for unbiased estimator of variance,} \\ N, & \text{otherwise.} \end{cases} \quad (9.31)$$

Now since ϕ is either 0 or 1, $\phi^2 = \phi$ and therefore

$$\sum_{i=1}^{N} (R_i - \phi \bar{R})^2 = \sum_{i=1}^{N} R_i^2 + \phi^2 N \bar{R}^2 - 2\phi \bar{R} \sum_{i=1}^{N} R_i = \sum_{i=1}^{N} R_i^2 - \phi N \bar{R}^2.$$

Since we may have historical fixings, decompose this into

$$\sum_{i=1}^{n_0} R_i^2 + R_{n_0+1}^2 + \sum_{i=n_0+2}^{N} R_i^2 - \phi N \bar{R}^2,$$

where $\sum_{i=1}^{n_0} R_i^2$ is deterministic. So therefore

$$E_{\text{Variance}} = \frac{\beta}{M} \mathbf{E} \left[\sum_{i=1}^{N} (R_i - \phi \bar{R})^2 \middle| \mathcal{F}_0 \right]$$

$$= \frac{\beta}{M} \left\{ \sum_{i=1}^{n_0} R_i^2 + \mathbf{E} \left[R_{n_0+1}^2 \middle| \mathcal{F}_0 \right] + \mathbf{E} \left[\sum_{i=n_0+2}^{N} R_i^2 \middle| \mathcal{F}_0 \right] - \phi N \mathbf{E} \left[\bar{R}^2 \middle| \mathcal{F}_0 \right] \right\}. \quad (9.32)$$

We therefore have three expectations to compute. Firstly, we shall need the results

$$\mathbf{E} \left[\ln \frac{S_{t_j}}{S_{t_i}} \middle| \mathcal{F}_0 \right] = \int_{t_i}^{t_j} \left[r_s^d - r_s^f - \frac{1}{2} \sigma^2(s) \right] ds, \quad (9.33)$$

$$\mathbf{E} \left[\left(\ln \frac{S_{t_j}}{S_{t_i}} \right)^2 \middle| \mathcal{F}_0 \right] = \left(\int_{t_i}^{t_j} \left[r_s^d - r_s^f - \frac{1}{2} \sigma^2(s) \right] ds \right)^2 + \int_{t_i}^{t_j} \sigma^2(s) ds. \quad (9.34)$$

We can now compute the expectations in (9.32). Starting with the first term

$$R_{n_0+1} = \ln \frac{S_{t_{n_0+1}}}{S_{t_{n_0}}} = \ln \frac{S_0}{S_{t_{n_0}}} + \ln \frac{S_{t_{n_0+1}}}{S_0},$$

where $\ln S_0 / S_{t_{n_0}}$ is deterministic and $\ln S_{t_{n_0+1}} / S_0$ is the stochastic quantity of interest. Consequently,

$$R_{n_0+1}^2 = \left(\ln \frac{S_0}{S_{t_{n_0}}} \right)^2 + 2 \ln \frac{S_0}{S_{t_{n_0}}} \ln \frac{S_{t_{n_0+1}}}{S_0} + \left(\ln \frac{S_{t_{n_0+1}}}{S_0} \right)^2,$$

and therefore

$$\mathbf{E} \left[R_{n_0+1}^2 \middle| \mathcal{F}_0 \right] = \left(\ln \frac{S_0}{S_{t_{n_0}}} \right)^2 + 2 \ln \frac{S_0}{S_{t_{n_0}}} \mathbf{E} \left[\ln \frac{S_{t_{n_0+1}}}{S_0} \right] + \mathbf{E} \left[\left(\ln \frac{S_{t_{n_0+1}}}{S_0} \right)^2 \right]$$

$$= \left(\ln \frac{S_0}{S_{t_{n_0}}} \right)^2 + 2 \ln \frac{S_0}{S_{t_{n_0}}} \int_0^{t_{n_0+1}} \left[r_s^d - r_s^f - \frac{1}{2} \sigma^2(s) \right] ds$$

$$+ \left(\int_0^{t_{n_0+1}} \left[r_s^d - r_s^f - \frac{1}{2} \sigma^2(s) \right] ds \right)^2 + \int_0^{t_{n_0+1}} \sigma^2(s) ds. \quad (9.35)$$

The second expectation in (9.32) is easier to compute because of additivity:

$$\mathbf{E} \left[\sum_{i=n_0+2}^{N} R_i^2 \middle| \mathcal{F}_0 \right] = \sum_{i=n_0+2}^{N} \mathbf{E} \left[R_i^2 \middle| \mathcal{F}_0 \right],$$

where

$$\mathbf{E}\left[R_i^2\middle|\mathcal{F}_0\right] = \left(\int_{t_{i-1}}^{t_i}\left[r_s^d - r_s^f - \frac{1}{2}\sigma^2(s)\right]ds\right)^2 + \int_{t_{i-1}}^{t_i}\sigma^2(s)ds,$$

so

$$\mathbf{E}\left[\sum_{i=n_0+2}^{N} R_i^2\middle|\mathcal{F}_0\right] = \sum_{i=n_0+2}^{N}\left(\int_{t_{i-1}}^{t_i}\left[r_s^d - r_s^f - \frac{1}{2}\sigma^2(s)\right]ds\right)^2 + \int_{t_{n_0+1}}^{t_N}\sigma^2(s)ds. \qquad (9.36)$$

The third expectation follows from the definition of $\bar{R}$. We can easily obtain

$$\bar{R} = \frac{1}{N}\ln\frac{S_{t_N}}{S_{t_0}}.$$

This is fine for volatility and variance swaps at/before initiation (i.e. if $t_0 > 0$), but after one or several fixings have gone through, we need to account for the deterministic fixings. As above, we do this by introducing S_0 in the algebra:

$$\bar{R} = \frac{1}{N}\left[\ln\frac{S_{t_N}}{S_0} + \ln\frac{S_0}{S_{t_0}}\right].$$

$\bar{R}^2$ is, therefore, if $t_0 \le 0$,

$$\bar{R}^2 = \frac{1}{N^2}\left[\left(\ln\frac{S(0)}{S(t_{n_0})}\right)^2 + 2\ln\frac{S(0)}{S(t_{n_0})}\ln\frac{S_{t_N}}{S_0} + \left(\ln\frac{S_{t_N}}{S_0}\right)^2\right], \quad t_0 \le 0,$$

and

$$\bar{R}^2 = \frac{1}{N^2}\left(\ln\frac{S_{t_N}}{S_{t_0}}\right)^2, \quad t_0 > 0.$$

The expectations of these quantities are obtained using the identities above:

$$\mathbf{E}\left[\bar{R}^2\middle|\mathcal{F}_0\right] = \frac{1}{N^2}\left[\left(\int_0^{t_N}\left[r_s^d - r_s^f - \frac{1}{2}\sigma^2(s)\right]ds\right)^2 + \int_{t_0}^{t_N}\sigma^2(s)ds\right], \quad t_0 > 0, \qquad (9.37)$$

and if $t_0 \le 0$,

$$\mathbf{E}\left[\bar{R}^2\middle|\mathcal{F}_0\right] = \frac{1}{N^2}\left[\left(\ln\frac{S_0}{S_{t_0}}\right)^2 + \left(\int_0^{t_N}\left[r_s^d - r_s^f - \frac{1}{2}\sigma^2(s)\right]ds\right)^2 \right.$$
$$\left. + 2\ln\frac{S_0}{S_{t_0}}\int_0^{t_N}\left[r_s^d - r_s^f - \frac{1}{2}\sigma^2(s)\right]ds + \int_0^{t_N}\sigma^2(s)ds\right].$$

Assembling these terms in (9.32), we obtain

$$E_{\text{Variance}} = \frac{\beta}{M}[c_1 + c_2 + c_3 - \phi c_4], \qquad (9.38)$$

using (9.35), (9.36) and (9.37), where

$$c_1 = \sum_{i=1}^{n_0} R_i^2, \tag{9.39}$$

$$c_2 = \mathbf{E}\left[R_{n_0+1}^2 \middle| \mathcal{F}_0 \right], \tag{9.40}$$

$$c_3 = \mathbf{E}\left[\sum_{i=n_0+2}^{N} R_i^2 \middle| \mathcal{F}_0 \right], \tag{9.41}$$

$$c_4 = \mathbf{E}\left[\bar{R}^2 \middle| \mathcal{F}_0 \right]. \tag{9.42}$$

These quantities are easily computed on a lattice of discrete tenor points, by consideration of forward volatility and a term structure of drift.

With this, the values at time $t = 0$ of the volatility and variance swaps can be simply written as

$$\text{VarSwap}(0) = D_{0,T}^d \left[E_{\text{Variance}} - K^2 \right]. \tag{9.43}$$

9.7.4   Volatility swap product valuation

I present a scheme below that can be used to value volatility derivatives, in the presence of discretely observed fixings, under simple Black–Scholes or Black–Scholes term structure models. It can be used to check the implementation of an auxiliary state variable PDE pricer for realised volatility products, before attempting to price these instruments on a more complicated model.

Let $E_{\text{Volatility}}$ denote the conditional expectation at time $t = 0$ of the realised volatility

$$E_{\text{Volatility}} = \mathbf{E}\left[\sqrt{V_{\text{Realised}}} \middle| \mathcal{F}_0 \right] = \mathbf{E}\left[\sqrt{\frac{\beta}{M} \sum_{i=1}^{N} (R_i - \phi\bar{R})^2} \middle| \mathcal{F}_0 \right]. \tag{9.44}$$

We can use Jensen's inequality

$$\mathbf{E}\left[\sqrt{V_{\text{Realised}}} \middle| \mathcal{F}_0 \right] \le \sqrt{\mathbf{E}\left[V_{\text{Realised}} \middle| \mathcal{F}_0 \right]} = \sqrt{E_{\text{Variance}}} \tag{9.45}$$

to provide an upper bound on the price of a volatility swap. We obtain, as a rather rough upper bound,

$$\text{VolSwap}(0) \approx D_{0,T}^D \left[\sqrt{E_{\text{Variance}}} - K \right]. \tag{9.46}$$

Even though this estimate is coarse, it is quite reasonable if a large number of fixings exist.

Badescu *et al.* (2002) suggest a more accurate approach to estimate the fair value of a discretely monitored volatility swap. As we are trying to compute $\sqrt{V_{\text{Realised}}}$, consider a second-order Taylor series expansion of $f(x) = \sqrt{x}$ around x_0:

$$f(x) \approx f(x_0) + (x - x_0) f'(x_0) + \frac{1}{2}(x - x_0)^2 f''(x_0)$$

with $f'(x) = \frac{1}{2}x^{-1/2}$ and $f''(x) = -\frac{1}{4}x^{-3/2}$. So

$$\sqrt{x} \approx \sqrt{x_0} + \frac{1}{2}\frac{x - x_0}{x_0^{1/2}} - \frac{1}{8}\frac{(x - x_0)^2}{x_0^{3/2}}.$$

Therefore, with $x = V_{\text{Realised}}$ and $x_0 = E_{\text{Variance}}$ we have

$$\sqrt{V_{\text{Realised}}} \approx \sqrt{x_0} + \frac{1}{2}\frac{V_{\text{Realised}} - x_0}{x_0^{1/2}} - \frac{1}{8}\frac{(V_{\text{Realised}} - x_0)^2}{x_0^{3/2}}$$

$$= \frac{3}{8}x_0^{1/2} + \frac{3}{4}x_0^{-1/2}V_{\text{Realised}} - \frac{1}{8}x_0^{-3/2}V_{\text{Realised}}^2$$

and thus

$$\mathbf{E}\left[\sqrt{V_{\text{Realised}}}\,\Big|\,\mathcal{F}_0\right] \approx \mathbf{E}\left[\frac{3}{8}x_0^{1/2} + \frac{3}{4}x_0^{-1/2}V_{\text{Realised}} - \frac{1}{8}x_0^{-3/2}V_{\text{Realised}}^2\,\Big|\,\mathcal{F}_0\right]$$

$$= \frac{3}{8}x_0^{1/2} + \frac{3}{4}x_0^{-1/2}\mathbf{E}\left[V_{\text{Realised}}\,\Big|\,\mathcal{F}_0\right] - \frac{1}{8}x_0^{-3/2}\mathbf{E}\left[V_{\text{Realised}}^2\,\Big|\,\mathcal{F}_0\right]$$

$$= \frac{9}{8}x_0^{1/2} - \frac{1}{8}x_0^{-3/2}\mathbf{E}\left[V_{\text{Realised}}^2\,\Big|\,\mathcal{F}_0\right]$$

$$= \frac{9}{8}\sqrt{E_{\text{Variance}}} - \frac{1}{8E_{\text{Variance}}^{3/2}}\mathbf{E}\left[V_{\text{Realised}}^2\,\Big|\,\mathcal{F}_0\right].$$

More succinctly,

$$\mathbf{E}\left[\sqrt{V_{\text{Realised}}}\,\Big|\,\mathcal{F}_0\right] \approx \sqrt{E_{\text{Variance}}}\left[\frac{9}{8} - \frac{1}{8}\frac{\mathbf{E}\left[V_{\text{Realised}}^2\,\Big|\,\mathcal{F}_0\right]}{E_{\text{Variance}}^2}\right]. \tag{9.47}$$

We therefore need to estimate $\mathbf{E}[V_{\text{Realised}}^2|\mathcal{F}_0]$.

Suppose X is a random variable (r.v.) with mean μ and standard deviation σ and we are trying to estimate $\mathbf{E}[\sqrt{X}]$ using this technique. We have $\mathbf{E}[X] = \mu$ and $\mathbf{E}[X^2] = \mu^2 + \sigma^2$. From the Taylor series expansion above we have

$$\mathbf{E}\left[\sqrt{X}\right] \approx \sqrt{\mu}\left[\frac{9}{8} - \frac{1}{8}\frac{\mathbf{E}\left[X^2\right]}{\mu^2}\right]$$

$$= \sqrt{\mu}\left[\frac{9}{8} - \frac{1}{8}\frac{\mu^2 + \sigma^2}{\mu^2}\right]$$

$$= \sqrt{\mu}\left[1 - \frac{1}{8}\frac{\sigma^2}{\mu^2}\right]$$

$$< \sqrt{\mu} \quad \text{for } \sigma > 0, \text{ as expected.}$$

Thus

$$E_{\text{Volatility}} = \mathbf{E}\left[\sqrt{V_{\text{Realised}}}\,\Big|\,\mathcal{F}_0\right] \approx \sqrt{E_{\text{Variance}}}\left[1 - \frac{1}{8}\frac{\sigma_{\text{Variance}}^2}{E_{\text{Variance}}^2}\right], \tag{9.48}$$

where

$$\sigma_{\text{Variance}}^2 = \mathbf{E}\left[V_{\text{Realised}}^2\,\Big|\,\mathcal{F}_0\right] - E_{\text{Variance}}^2$$

denotes the square of the standard deviation of the realised variance.

Firstly, to demonstrate the technique and build intuition, we shall derive the convexity correction for the case of a volatility swap at initiation (i.e. at $t = 0$, so there are no historical fixings), in the absence of rates (so $r^d = r^f = 0$), with no term structure of volatility (so σ is constant) and without the central moment included (so $\phi = 0$). Suppose also that all time increments are equal, so $t_i - t_{i-1} = \Delta t$:

$$V_{\text{Realised}} = \frac{\beta}{N}\sum_{i=1}^{N} R_i^2. \tag{9.49}$$

Then

$$E_{\text{Variance}} = \mathbf{E}\left[V_{\text{Realised}}\,\Big|\,\mathcal{F}_0\right] = \frac{\beta}{M}\sum_{i=1}^{N}\mathbf{E}\left[R_i^2\,\Big|\,\mathcal{F}_0\right] = \frac{\beta N}{M}\sigma^2\Delta t, \tag{9.50}$$

as we know that

$$\mathbf{E}\left[R_i^2\,\Big|\,\mathcal{F}_0\right] = \sigma^2\Delta t \qquad \text{and} \qquad \mathbf{E}\left[R_i^4\,\Big|\,\mathcal{F}_0\right] = 3\sigma^4(\Delta t)^2.$$

What of $\sigma_{\text{Variance}}^2$? Consider firstly $\mathbf{Var}(R_i^2) = \mathbf{E}[R_i^4|\mathcal{F}_0] - \left(\mathbf{E}[R_i^2|\mathcal{F}_0]\right)^2 = 2\sigma^4(\Delta t)^2$. Therefore

$$\sigma_{\text{Variance}}^2 = \left(\frac{\beta}{M}\right)^2 2N\sigma^4(\Delta t)^2.$$

We then construct the ratio $\sigma_{\text{Variance}}^2/E_{\text{Variance}}^2$, obtaining

$$\frac{\sigma_{\text{Variance}}^2}{E_{\text{Variance}}^2} = \frac{(\beta/M)^2\,2N\sigma^4(\Delta t)^2}{[(\beta N/M\sigma^2)\Delta t]^2} = \frac{2}{N}.$$

Substituting this into (9.48) we obtain

$$\mathbf{E}\left[\sqrt{V_{\text{Realised}}}\,\Big|\,\mathcal{F}_0\right] \approx \sqrt{E_{\text{Variance}}}\left[1 - \frac{1}{8}\frac{2}{N}\right] = \sqrt{E_{\text{Variance}}}\left[1 - \frac{1}{4N}\right]. \tag{9.51}$$

We then conclude by estimating the convexity correction for the volatility swap in general. The task remaining is to estimate σ_{Variance}, the standard deviation of the realised variance, which of course will only obtain any measure of dispersion around its mean value from indeterminate future fixings. We have

$$\sigma^2_{\text{Variance}} = \frac{\beta^2}{M^2} \text{Var} \left[\sum_{i=1}^{N} (R_i - \phi \bar{R})^2 \right]$$

$$= \frac{\beta^2}{M^2} \left[\sum_{i=1}^{N} \text{Var}(R_i^2) - 2\phi \sum_{i=1}^{N} \text{Var}(R_i \bar{R}) + N\phi \text{Var}(\bar{R}^2) \right]. \qquad (9.52)$$

As before we have

$$\text{Var}(R_i^2) = \begin{cases} 2 \left(\int_{t_{i-1}}^{t_i} \sigma^2(s) \mathrm{d}s \right)^2, & i > n_0 + 1, \\ 2 \left(\int_{0}^{t_i} \sigma^2(s) \mathrm{d}s \right)^2, & i = n_0 + 1, \\ 0, & i \le n_0. \end{cases} \qquad (9.53)$$

As for the terms involving $\bar{R}$, recall that $\bar{R} = \sum_{i=1}^{N} R_i$. Consequently,

$$\text{Var} \left(R_i \bar{R} \right) = \frac{1}{N^2} \text{Var} \left(R_i \sum_{j=1}^{N} R_j \right) = \frac{1}{N^2} \text{Var} \left(R_i^2 \right) \qquad (9.54)$$

and

$$\text{Var} \left(\bar{R}^2 \right) = \frac{1}{N^4} \text{Var} \left(\sum_{i,j=1}^{N} R_i R_j \right) = \frac{1}{N^4} \sum_{i=1}^{N} \text{Var} \left(R_i^2 \right). \qquad (9.55)$$

Under the same simplifying assumptions as earlier, we have $\text{Var}(R_i^2) = 2\sigma^4(\Delta t)^2$, $\text{Var}(R_i \bar{R}) = 2\sigma^4(\Delta t)^2/N^2$ and $\text{Var}(\bar{R}^2) = 2\sigma^4(\Delta t)^2/N^3$. Substituting these into (9.52) we obtain

$$\sigma^2_{\text{Variance}} = \frac{2\beta^2}{M^2} \sigma^4(\Delta t)^2 \left[N + \phi - \frac{2\phi}{N} \right]. \qquad (9.56)$$

We then once again construct the ratio $\sigma^2_{\text{Variance}}/E^2_{\text{Variance}}$, obtaining

$$\frac{\sigma^2_{\text{Variance}}}{E^2_{\text{Variance}}} = \frac{(2\beta^2/M^2)\sigma^4(\Delta t)^2 [N + \phi - 2\phi/N]}{[(\beta N/M)\sigma^2 \Delta t]^2} = \frac{2}{N} \left[1 + \frac{\phi}{N} - \frac{2\phi}{N^2} \right].$$

Substituting this into (9.48) we obtain

$$E \left[\sqrt{V_{\text{Realised}}} \middle| \mathcal{F}_0 \right] \approx \sqrt{E_{\text{Variance}}} \left[1 - \frac{1}{8} \frac{2}{N} \left(1 + \frac{\phi}{N} - \frac{2\phi}{N^2} \right) \right]$$

$$= \sqrt{E_{\text{Variance}}} \left[1 - \frac{1}{4N} \left(1 + \frac{\phi}{N} - \frac{2\phi}{N^2} \right) \right]. \qquad (9.57)$$

Finally, we express the convexity correction in the case where a term structure of volatility exists. From (9.52) we have

$$\sigma^2_{\text{Variance}} = \frac{\beta^2}{M^2} \left[\sum_{i=1}^{N} \mathbf{Var}(R_i^2) - 2\phi \sum_{i=1}^{N} \mathbf{Var}(R_i \, \bar{R}) + N\phi \mathbf{Var}(\bar{R}^2) \right].$$

Using (9.53), (9.54) and (9.55) we obtain

$$\sigma^2_{\text{Variance}} = \frac{\beta^2}{M^2} \left[\sum_{i=1}^{N} \mathbf{Var}(R_i^2) \right] \left[1 + \frac{\phi}{N} - \frac{2\phi}{N^2} \right]$$

$$= \frac{2\beta^2}{M^2} \left[\left(\int_0^{t_{n_0+1}} \sigma^2(s)ds \right)^2 + \sum_{i=n_0+2}^{N} \left(\int_{t_{i-1}}^{t_i} \sigma^2(s)ds \right)^2 \right] \left[1 + \frac{\phi}{N} - \frac{2\phi}{N^2} \right], \quad (9.58)$$

which we then substitute into (9.48) to obtain $E_{\text{Volatility}}$.

Summary

We present the equations derived in this section for ease of reference:

$$c_1 = \sum_{i=1}^{n_0} \hat{R}_i^2,$$

$$c_2 = \mathbf{E}\left[R_{n_0+1}^2 \middle| \mathcal{F}_0 \right]$$

$$= \left(\ln \frac{S_0}{S_{t_{n_0}}} \right)^2 + 2 \ln \frac{S_0}{S_{t_{n_0}}} \int_0^{t_{n_0+1}} \left[r_s^d - r_s^f - \frac{1}{2}\sigma^2(s) \right] ds$$

$$+ \left(\int_0^{t_{n_0+1}} \left[r_s^d - r_s^f - \frac{1}{2}\sigma^2(s) \right] ds \right)^2 + \int_0^{t_{n_0+1}} \sigma^2(s)ds,$$

$$c_3 = \mathbf{E}\left[\sum_{i=n_0+2}^{N} R_i^2 \middle| \mathcal{F}_0 \right]$$

$$= \sum_{i=n_0+2}^{N} \left(\int_{t_{i-1}}^{t_i} \left[r_s^d - r_s^f - \frac{1}{2}\sigma^2(s) \right] ds \right)^2 + \int_{t_{n_0+1}}^{t_N} \sigma^2(s)ds,$$

$$c_4 = \mathbf{E}\left[\bar{R}^2 \middle| \mathcal{F}_0 \right]$$

$$= \begin{cases} \dfrac{1}{N^2} \left[\left(\displaystyle\int_0^{t_N} \left[r_s^d - r_s^f - \frac{1}{2}\sigma^2(s) \right] ds \right)^2 + \displaystyle\int_{t_0}^{t_N} \sigma^2(s)ds \right], & t_0 > 0, \\[2ex] \dfrac{1}{N^2} \left[\left(\ln \dfrac{S_0}{S_{t_0}} \right)^2 + \left(\displaystyle\int_0^{t_N} \left[r_s^d - r_s^f - \frac{1}{2}\sigma^2(s) \right] ds \right)^2 \right. \\[2ex] \qquad \left. + 2 \ln \dfrac{S_0}{S_{t_0}} \displaystyle\int_0^{t_N} \left[r_s^d - r_s^f - \frac{1}{2}\sigma^2(s) \right] ds + \displaystyle\int_0^{t_N} \sigma^2(s)ds \right], & t_0 \le 0, \end{cases}$$

$$E_{\text{Variance}} = \frac{\beta}{M}[c_1 + c_2 + c_3 - \phi c_4],$$

$$\sigma^2_{\text{Variance}} = \frac{2\beta^2}{M^2}\left[\left(\int_0^{t_{n_0+1}} \sigma^2(s)ds\right)^2 + \sum_{i=n_0+2}^{N}\left(\int_{t_{i-1}}^{t_i} \sigma^2(s)ds\right)^2\right]\left[1 + \frac{\phi}{N} - \frac{2\phi}{N^2}\right],$$

$$E_{\text{Volatility}} \approx \sqrt{E_{\text{Variance}}}\left[1 - \frac{1}{8}\frac{\sigma^2_{\text{Variance}}}{E^2_{\text{Variance}}}\right],$$

$$\text{VarSwap}(0) = D^d_{0,T}\left[E_{\text{Variance}} - K^2\right],$$

$$\text{VolSwap}(0) = D^d_{0,T}\left[E_{\text{Volatility}} - K\right].$$

10

Multicurrency Options

Most FX options that trade are single currency products, but there is a definite demand for options that depend upon a number of FX spot rates. Whereas single currency pair exotics often trade in the interbank market, or with hedge funds, multicurrency FX options are more often tailored to the needs of a corporate client – either due to a structuring request or as an embedded product within a trade note.

The typical example is a basket option, which a client can use to hedge the FX risk of a number of different currency exposures simultaneously and more cheaply than by buying an FX option for each of the FX rates separately.

An example may make this clearer. Consider a hypothetical Japanese sporting goods exporter, who sells athletic equipment (running shoes, athletics wear, etc.) both in their domestic market and internationally. On the basis of prior sales and internal forecasts, they expect to realise first quarter revenues of about 3 billion yen in Europe and 8 billion yen in their North American sales region.

To make the arithmetic easier, let's suppose that USDJPY is trading at 90.00 and EURJPY is trading at 110.00. This fixes EURUSD at 1.2222 in order to avoid arbitrage, and the expected revenues in units of local currency are EUR 27.3 million and USD 88.9 million respectively.

The goods for sale are obviously priced in EUR and USD in the local markets, thus giving rise to currency risk in each of the two factors EURJPY and USDJPY. Clearly our Japanese exporter could hedge this risk by buying puts on EURJPY and USDJPY with notionals indicated above.

From the exporter's point of view, they have a long position in both EUR and USD, regarded as risky assets, and instead of hedging the two exposures separately, they can think of this as a diversified portfolio. We already know from modern portfolio theory that this is highly sensitive to the correlation between EUR and USD (viewed from a JPY numeraire) and therefore the optimal hedge for such a two-asset portfolio is not in fact two separate FX options in EURJPY and USDJPY, but a combined basket option – which will in general be cheaper than buying protection on each currency exposure separately.

Consider two limiting cases. If the correlation between EURJPY and USDJPY is 1.0, then the hedge for this basket will indeed be the sum of the two options – the two risky assets necessarily move in lockstep and the total currency risk from the Japanese exporter's point of view is 11 billion yen. However, if the correlation between EURJPY and USDJPY is −1.0, then if the US dollar strengthens, the Euro will weaken, and vice versa. Consequently, the net currency risk in this scenario is only 5 billion yen, and hedging the currency risk in this case will be equally effective for less than half the cost.

Basically, if two assets are completely anticorrelated, one wants to avoid buying two options and always throwing one away.

For intermediate values of correlation between −1 and +1, such as is realistic in the markets, we can still realise some practical benefits from tailoring multicurrency options such as this, to meet the needs of clients.

In order to do so, we need to understand correlation.

Table 10.1   Arbitrage trade for inconsistent currency triangle

Trade	JPY notional	EUR notional	USD notional
Buy EURJPY	−1 bio	+9.09 mio	
Sell USDJPY	+1 bio		−11.1 mio
Sell EURUSD		−9.09 mio	+11.8 mio
NET	−	−	+707 070.70

10.1   CORRELATIONS, TRIANGULATION AND ABSENCE OF ARBITRAGE

At the start we stated that if EURJPY was 110 and USDJPY was 90, then EURUSD *must* be 1.2222. This is required in order to avoid arbitrage. The argument below applies to FX forwards as well as spot.

Example.   Suppose the current spot rate for EURJPY is 110, USDJPY is 90 and EURUSD is 1.30. This indicates that the EURUSD leg is overvalued relative to the {EUR, USD, JPY} triangle, which an arbitrageur would want to sell and fund using the EURJPY and USDJPY spot rates to build a riskless portfolio.

They could therefore simultaneously buy EURJPY with notional of 1 billion yen (i.e. sell 1 billion yen and buy 9.09 million EUR) and sell USDJPY with notional of 1 billion yen (i.e. buy 1 billion yen and sell 11.1 million USD). As a net result, they have entered into a spot trade that effectively involves the exchange of +9.09 million EUR for −11.1 million USD, i.e. a long EURUSD position.

However, the same trade can be performed at a different rate of exchange on the EURUSD cross. Simultaneously, they sell 9.09 million euros and buy 11.8 million US dollars, using the EURUSD spot rate of 1.30, i.e. *selling* EURUSD at this overvalued 1.30 level. The yen and euro amounts net out, and a riskless profit of $707 070.70 remains. Nice work if you can get it.[1]

We illustrate the cashflows in Table 10.1.

As described in Chapter 14 ('How the Greeks would have Hedged Correlation Risk of Foreign Exchange Options') of Hakala and Wystup (2002), these three FX rates form a natural currency triangle, which I schematically illustrate in Figure 10.1. Starting with Figure 10.1(a), which is meant to show an initial FX market consisting of three FX rates that triangulate, Figure 10.1(b) then shows the effect of a strengthening of the USD and Figure 10.1(c) shows an effect of a strengthening of the euro.

We can therefore suppose a multicurrency[2] Black–Scholes market with a common base currency (ccy_0) and two risky currencies (ccy_1 and ccy_2), for which we have SDEs

$$dS_t^{(1)} = [r^d - r^{f;1}]S_t^{(1)}\,dt + \sigma^{(1)}S_t^{(1)}\,dW_t^{(1;d)}, \tag{10.1a}$$

$$dS_t^{(2)} = [r^d - r^{f;2}]S_t^{(2)}\,dt + \sigma^{(2)}S_t^{(2)}\,dW_t^{(2;d)}, \tag{10.1b}$$

---

[1] Not particularly likely. Note that arbitrage can theoretically exist for short periods of time in market quotes if there was no liquidity in the cross. This can be seen from time to time in minor currency pairs, especially if the spot rates are updated less frequently.

[2] Note that in the world of multicurrency options, the ccy_i specifiers have completely different meanings to ccy1 and ccy2 as introduced in Chapter 1.

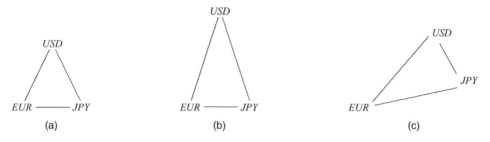

Figure 10.1 Currency triangles: (a) simple initial triangle; (b) currently triangle after appreciation of USD against both EUR and JPY (EURJPY unchanged; (c) currently triangle after appreciation of USD against both EUR and JPY (EURJPY unchanged)

with the two Brownian motions subject to correlation $< \mathrm{d}W_t^{(1;d)}, \mathrm{d}W_t^{(2;d)} > = \rho_{12;d}\, \mathrm{d}t$. The Brownians are superscripted with d to indicate they are Brownians with respect to the domestic risk-neutral measure corresponding to the ccy_0 numeraire.[3]

Note that the cross rate can be inferred either by multiplication or division, depending on the quote style; e.g. S[EURJPY] is equal to S[EURUSD] times S[USDJPY], but S[USDJPY] is equal to S[EURJPY] divided by S[EURUSD]. So the cross rate might be $S_t^{(12)} = S_t^{(1)} S_t^{(2)}$, $S_t^{(1;2)} = S_t^{(1)}/S_t^{(2)}$, $S_t^{(2;1)} = S_t^{(2)}/S_t^{(1)}$ or even $S_t^{(;12)} = [S_t^{(1)} S_t^{(2)}]^{-1}$. A word on the choice of notation: $S_t^{(2;1)}$ is the cross rate for ccy_2 expressed in units of ccy_1. It is the value in ccy_1 of a single unit of ccy_2, and therefore is a ccy_1 per ccy_2 price.[4]

Inferring cross rates is just a straightforward application of the stochastic product formula $\mathrm{d}(X_t Y_t) = X_t\, \mathrm{d}Y_t + Y_t\, \mathrm{d}X_t + < \mathrm{d}X_t, \mathrm{d}Y_t >$, which we find as Exercise 4.3 in Øksendal (1998). We illustrate with the $S_t^{(2;1)}$ example; the others follow straightforwardly. Constructing the reciprocal of $S_t^{(1)}$ and denoting it $\hat{S}_t^{(1)} = 1/S_t^{(1)}$, we have $S_t^{(2;1)} = S_t^{(2)} \hat{S}_t^{(1)}$ and therefore need

$$\mathrm{d}\left[\hat{S}_t^{(1)}\right] = \left[r^{f;1} - r^d + [\sigma^{(1)}]^2\right] \hat{S}_t^{(1)}\, \mathrm{d}t - \sigma^{(1)} \hat{S}_t^{(1)}\, \mathrm{d}W_t^{(1;d)}.$$

Applying the product formula, we have

$$\begin{aligned}
\mathrm{d}S_t^{(2;1)} &= \mathrm{d}\left[S_t^{(2)} \hat{S}_t^{(1)}\right] \\
&= S_t^{(2)}\, \mathrm{d}\hat{S}_t^{(1)} + \hat{S}_t^{(1)}\, \mathrm{d}S_t^{(2)} + \mathrm{d}S_t^{(2)}\, \mathrm{d}\hat{S}_t^{(1)} \\
&= S_t^{(2)} \hat{S}_t^{(1)} \left[r^{f;1} - r^d + [\sigma^{(1)}]^2\right]\, \mathrm{d}t - \sigma^{(1)} S_t^{(2)} \hat{S}_t^{(1)}\, \mathrm{d}W_t^{(1;d)} \\
&\quad + \hat{S}_t^{(1)} \left[\left[r^d - r^{f;2}\right] S_t^{(2)}\, \mathrm{d}t + \sigma^{(2)} S_t^{(2)}\, \mathrm{d}W_t^{(2;d)}\right] - \sigma^{(2)} S_t^{(2)} \sigma^{(1)} \hat{S}_t^{(1)} \rho_{12;d}\, \mathrm{d}t \\
&= S_t^{(2,1)} \left(\left[r^{f;1} - r^{f;2} + [\sigma^{(1)}]^2 - \rho_{12;d}\sigma^{(1)}\sigma^{(2)}\right]\, \mathrm{d}t - \sigma^{(1)}\, \mathrm{d}W_t^{(1;d)} + \sigma^{(2)}\, \mathrm{d}W_t^{(2;d)}\right),
\end{aligned}$$

from which we obtain the process for the logspot of the cross rate:

$$\mathrm{d}X_t^{(2;1)} = \left[r^{f;1} - r^{f;2} + \frac{1}{2}[\sigma^{(1)}]^2 - [\sigma^{(2)}]^2\right]\, \mathrm{d}t - \sigma^{(1)}\, \mathrm{d}W_t^{(1;d)} + \sigma^{(2)}\, \mathrm{d}W_t^{(2;d)}$$

---

[3] More correctly, quasi-numeraire, as we factor out the relevant discount factors.

[4] And *that* is why I denote it as $S_t^{(2;1)}$ not $S_t^{(2/1)}$. Pedantic? It all depends on what you mean by pedantic.

in the domestic risk neutral measure. Whichever way things are quoted, we can obtain the volatility of the cross rate. For example, neglecting the drift terms for brevity, as we are only interested in the volatility term for now, we have

$$dX_t^{(2;1)} = [\ldots] dt + \sigma^{(2)} dW_t^{(2;d)} - \sigma^{(1)} dW_t^{(1;d)}$$

$$= [\ldots] dt + \sigma^{(2)} \left[\rho_{12;d} dW_t^{(1;d)} + \sqrt{1 - \rho_{12;d}^2} dW_t^{(1\perp;d)} \right] - \sigma^{(1)} dW_t^{(1;d)}$$

$$= [\ldots] dt + [\rho_{12;d}\sigma^{(2)} - \sigma^{(1)}] dW_t^{(1;d)} + \sqrt{1 - \rho_{12;d}^2}\sigma^{(2)} dW_t^{(1\perp;d)}$$

$$= [\ldots] dt + \sigma^{(2;1)} dW_t^{(*;d)},$$

using Cholesky decomposition to represent $W_t^{(2;d)}$ in terms of independent Brownian motions $W_t^{(1;d)}$ and $W_t^{(1\perp;d)}$, and writing

$$[\sigma^{(2;1)}]^2 = [\rho_{12;d}\sigma^{(2)} - \sigma^{(1)}]^2 + [1 - \rho_{12;d}^2][\sigma^{(2)}]^2$$

$$= [\sigma^{(1)}]^2 + [\sigma^{(2)}]^2 - 2\rho_{12;d}\sigma^{(1)}\sigma^{(2)}. \qquad (10.2)$$

We therefore see that the volatility of the FX cross is directly determined by the volatilities of the other two spot rate processes, together with the correlation between the two Brownian motions.

In the case where the cross rate is obtained by multiplication and not division of the two spot rates, we straightforwardly obtain $[\sigma^{(1*2)}]^2 = [\sigma^{(1)}]^2 + [\sigma^{(2)}]^2 + 2\rho_{12;d}\sigma^{(1)}\sigma^{(2)}$. This means that correlations can be obtained from implied volatility quotes for the three FX spot rates comprising the currency triangle

$$\rho^{(1*2)} = \frac{[\sigma^{(1*2)}]^2 - [\sigma^{(1)}]^2 - [\sigma^{(2)}]^2}{2\sigma^{(1)}\sigma^{(2)}}, \qquad (10.3a)$$

$$\rho^{(1/2)} = -\frac{[\sigma^{(1/2)}]^2 - [\sigma^{(1)}]^2 - [\sigma^{(2)}]^2}{2\sigma^{(1)}\sigma^{(2)}}. \qquad (10.3b)$$

Note that three correlations can be found depending on which of the three vertices of the currency triangle is regarded as the common base currency. We could attempt to estimate the correlation between EURUSD and EURJPY, between EURUSD and USDJPY, or between EURJPY and USDJPY.

The extension of this to multiple spot rates is relatively straightforward, assuming that a common base currency can be found, e.g. USDJPY, AUDJPY, EURJPY. What is more complicated is trying to infer the correlation between two currency pairs that do *not* have a common base currency, e.g. EURUSD and AUDJPY. This is discussed in Section 14.3 of Hakala and Wystup (2002), where the currency triangle concept from earlier is extended to a currency tetrahedron. Clearly in order to do this, we need a graph structure with other links than just EURUSD and AUDJPY. Whereas in the currency triangle we have three vertices, three edges and three correlations, the currency tetrahedron has four vertices, six edges and 15 correlations.

In the same way as we obtained the spot rate for EURJPY by multiplying EURUSD by USDJPY, in the above algebra, we could obtain the spot rate for AUDJPY by multiplying AUDUSD and EURJPY, and dividing by EURUSD. This gives us a mechanism for inferring correlations given two currency pairs without a common base currency.

Figure 10.2   Currency tetrahedron

10.2   EXCHANGE OPTIONS

The first example of a multiasset option, in a way, is just an exchange option, or a Margrabe option – the right to exchange one risky asset for another at a prearranged strike. Margrabe (1978) was the first to consider this product and realised that one of the risky assets (asset two in his original paper, see footnote 6) can be used as numeraire. In the context of FX option pricing, this is quite natural. All currencies are simultaneously both risky and riskless, depending on one's frame of reference.

The payout at expiry, for an option to surrender one unit of currency 1 and receive one unit of currency 2 is

$$V_T = \max\left(S_T^{(2)} - S_T^{(1)}, 0\right).$$

By adopting currency 1 as numeraire, this can be viewed as a call on currency 2 and pricing proceeds as in Chapter 2. Rubinstein (1991) quotes the price for this as

$$V_0^{\text{exch}} = S_0^{(2)} e^{-r^{f;2}T} N(d_1) - S_0^{(1)} e^{-r^{f;1}T} N(d_2), \tag{10.4}$$

where

$$d_{1;2} = \frac{\ln\left(S_0^{(2)} e^{-r^{f;2}T} / (S_0^{(1)} e^{-r^{f;1}T})\right) \pm \frac{1}{2} [\sigma^{(2;1)}]^2 T}{\sigma^{(2;1)} \sqrt{T}}.$$

This can be written as

$$V_0^{\text{exch}} = S_0^{(1)} \left[\frac{S_0^{(2)}}{S_0^{(1)}} e^{-r^{f;2}T} N(d_1) - e^{-r^{f;1}T} N(d_2) \right] \tag{10.5}$$

and, of course, $S_0^{(2)}/S_0^{(1)}$ is just the FX cross $S_0^{(2;1)}$.

Obviously this can be priced in the currency 2 numeraire, where one prices the dual of this trade, i.e. a put on currency 1. The analysis is the same as in Section 2.9, 'The Law of One Price', and we have shown nothing more than the fact that *three* market participants agree on the price for this security: the two investors in the two 'foreign' economies who view this as a call and a put respectively, and the third investor in the 'domestic' economy who views this as an exchange option. There's still only one price. You've already seen it.

10.3   QUANTOS

Perhaps the simplest nontrivial multicurrency example one can really consider is that of an option which determines its value from a particular FX rate, but which pays that amount, not in the domestic currency, but in another currency. In other words, the value at expiry is determined by a formula that is generally thought of as having units of the domestic currency, but pays directly in a currency *other* than the domestic currency.

A particular limiting case of interest is the self-quanto option, which pays directly in the foreign currency. This is also known as a quadratic option, for reasons we see below.

Quantos are discussed in Reiner (1992), Section 13.6 of Hull (1997), Chapter 20 of Zhang (1998), Section 11.7 of Wilmott (1998), Chapter 8 of Hakala and Wystup (2002) and Section 4.5 of Baxter and Rennie (1996), and many other references can easily be found. The standard technique is to infer a quanto drift adjustment due to imposing an extra term in the expectation.

Counterintuitively, it is actually easiest to introduce this drift adjustment in the context of a one-dimensional model first.

10.3.1 Self-quanto option

Consider the case of a EURUSD call option. Ordinarily, this would have notional in euros, and the standard valuation methodology (be it under a Black–Scholes model, or other) would give us a USD price, i.e. a d/f price, as observed in (3.1). We could obviously obtain a euro price, i.e. a $\% f$ price, using $V_{\% f} = V_{d/f}/S_0$, or actual units of monetary price given notionals, i.e. $V_d = N_f \cdot V_{d/f}$ and $V_f = (1/S_0)N_f \cdot V_{d/f}$. This means that the payout at expiry of the standard European call option, in units of the domestic currency, is $N_f \cdot (S_T - K)^+$.

The self-quanto option, instead, has a payout at expiry in units of the *foreign* currency of $N_f \cdot (S_T - K)^+$. This means that, if we were to express the payout in units of the domestic currency, we have $V_T = S_T(S_T - K)^+$. Note that this is actually a quadratic, and hence the alternate terminology.

Following an approach similar to Section 2.8, we have

$$V_0 = e^{-r^d T} \mathbf{E}^d \left[S_T(S_T - K)^+ \right]$$

$$= e^{-r^d T} \mathbf{E}^d \left[S_T(S_T - K)\mathbf{1}_{\{S_T \geq K\}} \right]$$

$$= e^{-r^d T} \mathbf{E}^d \left[S_T^2 \mathbf{1}_{\{S_T \geq K\}} - K S_T \mathbf{1}_{\{S_T \geq K\}} \right]$$

$$= e^{-r^d T} \mathbf{E}^d \left[S_T^2 \mathbf{1}_{\{S_T \geq K\}} \right] - K e^{-r^d T} \mathbf{E}^d \left[S_T \mathbf{1}_{\{S_T \geq K\}} \right].$$

The second term in the above can be dealt with by changing from the domestic to the foreign risk-neutral measure, and we obtain

$$V_0 = e^{-r^d T} \mathbf{E}^d \left[S_T^2 \mathbf{1}_{\{S_T \geq K\}} \right] - K S_0 e^{-r^f T} \mathbf{P}^f \left[S_T \geq K \right].$$

As for the first term, this involves changing measure again, not from the domestic risk-neutral measure to the foreign risk-neutral measure (which regards S_t as the numeraire), but to a phantom *quadratic* risk-neutral measure $\mathbf{P}^{ff}$, which has S_t^2 as the numeraire.

Similarly to (2.53), we have

$$\frac{d\mathbf{P}^{ff}}{d\mathbf{P}^f} = \exp\left(\sigma W_T^f - \frac{1}{2}\sigma^2 T\right) \tag{10.6}$$

and thereby obtain

$$V_0 = S_0^2 e^{(r^d - 2r^f + \sigma^2)T} \mathbf{P}^{ff} \left[S_T \geq K \right] - K S_0 e^{-r^f T} \mathbf{P}^f \left[S_T \geq K \right],$$

which can be written as

$$V_0 = S_0^2 e^{(r^d - 2r^f + \sigma^2)T} N(d_0) - K S_0 e^{-r^f T} N(d_1), \tag{10.7}$$

obtaining d_0 and d_1 from (2.59), where d_1 is familiar from Chapter 2 and

$$d_0 = \frac{\ln(S_0/K) + \left(r^d - r^f + \frac{3}{2}\sigma^2\right)T}{\sigma\sqrt{T}}.$$

This is discussed particularly clearly in Mercurio (2003) and in Section 7.5 of Castagna (2010).

10.3.2 Self-quanto forward

Note that if the payout for this self-quanto product was $V_T = S_T(S_T - K)$, not $V_T = S_T(S_T - K)^+$, then the $N(d_0)$ and $N(d_1)$ terms in (10.7) vanish and we are left with

$$V_0 = S_0^2 e^{(r^d - 2r^f + \sigma^2)T} - K S_0 e^{-r^f T}. \tag{10.8}$$

In the manner of Section 2.8.1, we can solve for that value $\tilde{F}$ of K that makes $V_0 = 0$, thereby obtaining an expression for the self-quanto forward

$$\tilde{F} = S_0 e^{(r^d - r^f + \sigma^2)T}. \tag{10.9}$$

10.3.3 General quanto options

The three-currency quanto option, rather than paying the quantity $N_f \cdot (S_T - K)^+$ in either domestic or foreign currency units, pays it in a completely separate (though possibly correlated) *third* currency. For the rest of Section 10.3.3, therefore, we transform[5] our coordinate system so that the former 'domestic' currency is now the first foreign currency, and the 'quanto' currency is now the 'domestic currency'.

As a result, the payout will be something along the lines of

$$V_T = S_T^{(1)} \left(S_t^{(2;1)} - K \right)^+ \tag{10.10}$$

and we therefore need to construct the risk-neutral process for the cross rate in the risk-neutral measure for the (first) foreign currency.

Towards this end, we return to Section 10.1 and attempt to investigate the drift term we neglected earlier. We obtain

$$dS_t^{(2;1)}/S_t^{(2;1)} = \left[r^{f;1} - r^{f;2} + [\sigma^{(1)}]^2 - \rho_{12;d}\sigma^{(1)}\sigma^{(2)} \right] dt + \sigma^{(2;1)} dW_t^{(*;d)}$$

and the crucial thing to realise is that the quanto drift adjustment, as typically presented in the literature, is *not* with respect to $\rho_{12;d}$, the correlation between the two spot rates $S_t^{(1)}$ and $S_t^{(2)}$ as viewed from the ccy_0 perspective, but with respect to ρ_q, the correlation between the cross (on which the quanto is written) and the spot rate relating that cross to the currency in which payment is made, i.e. $S_t^{(2;1)}$ and $S_t^{(1)}$.

---

[5] We effectively take the currency triangle and flip it, applying a reflection along the line connecting vertex $f;2$ to the midpoint of the line opposite.

We obtain this by writing (10.2) in two ways:

$$[\sigma^{(2;1)}]^2 = [\sigma^{(1)}]^2 + [\sigma^{(2)}]^2 - 2\rho_{12;d}\sigma^{(1)}\sigma^{(2)}, \tag{10.11a}$$

$$[\sigma^{(2)}]^2 = [\sigma^{(2;1)}]^2 + [\sigma^{(1)}]^2 + 2\rho_q\sigma^{(2;1)}\sigma^{(2)}, \tag{10.11b}$$

where we take the domestic currency as the reference vertex in (10.11a) and the first foreign currency as the reference vertex in (10.11b). Note the sign change, because one of these spot rates (the one giving the price of the domestic currency in units of the first foreign currency, i.e. $\hat{S}_t^{(1)} = 1/S_t^{(1)}$) is anticorrelated in this analysis.

Adding (10.11a) to (10.11b) we immediately obtain

$$[\sigma^{(1)}]^2 - \rho_{12;d}\sigma^{(1)}\sigma^{(2)} = -\rho_q\sigma^{(2;1)}\sigma^{(2)}, \tag{10.12}$$

$$dS_t^{(2;1)}/S_t^{(2;1)} = \left[r^{f;1} - r^{f;2} + [\sigma^{(1)}]^2 - \rho_{12;d}\sigma^{(1)}\sigma^{(2)}\right]dt + \sigma^{(2;1)}\,dW_t^{(*;d)}$$

$$= \left[r^{f;1} - r^{f;2} - \rho_q\sigma^{(2;1)}\sigma^{(2)}\right]dt + \sigma^{(2;1)}\,dW_t^{(*;d)}. \tag{10.13}$$

Note the quanto correction introduced by requiring the $S_t^{(2;1)}$ process to be risk neutral in the domestic risk-neutral measure. If we were writing this process in the foreign risk-neutral measure corresponding to the first foreign currency as numeraire, we would instead have

$$dS_t^{(2;1)}/S_t^{(2;1)} = \left[r^{f;1} - r^{f;2}\right]dt + \sigma^{(2;1)}\,dW_t^{(2;f1)},$$

which can be integrated to give the forward for $S_T^{(2;1)}$ just as in Section 2.8.1, i.e.

$$F_{0,T}^{(2;1)} = S_0^{(2;1)}\exp((r^{f;1} - r^{f;2})T).$$

We therefore, by examination of (10.13), obtain the *quanto-adjusted forward*

$$\tilde{F}_{0,T}^{(2;1)} = F_{0,T}^{(2;1)}\exp(-\rho_q\sigma^{(2;1)}\sigma^{(1)}T) \tag{10.14}$$

required to price quanto products, depending on the $S_t^{(2;1)}$ cross rate, but which pay in units of the domestic currency.

Effectively, this just means introducing a drift correction from the point of view of the numerical methods discussed in Chapter 7, which is easily handled in well-designed option pricing libraries.

Quanto drift adjustments

It is quite common, instead of speaking of transforming coordinate systems, to speak of just transforming from domestic to quanto numeraire (though the effect of this is the same, we just end up transforming the coordinate system so that the payment is made in a separate currency, the quanto currency).

In this case, our original spot rates under consideration are no longer $S_t^{(2;1)}$ (the cross) and $S_t^{(1)}$ (the domestic currency with respect to the quanto currency) but $S_t^{(2;1)}$ and $1/S_t^{(1)}$ (the quanto currency with respect to the domestic currency).

We therefore have, in this representation,

$$S_t^{d/f} \equiv S_t^{(2;1)}, \tag{10.15a}$$

$$S_t^{d/q} \equiv 1/S_t^{(1)} = \hat{S}_t^{(1)}, \tag{10.15b}$$

$$S_t^{q/f} \equiv S_t^{(2)}, \tag{10.15c}$$

and a sign change for the correlation term above due to (10.15b), i.e. $\rho_{d/f;d/q} = -\rho_q$, since $\rho_q = \rho_{d/f;q/d}$. We can equivalently write

$$dS_t^{d/f} = (r^d - r^f)S_t^{d/f}\,dt + \sigma^{(2;1)}S_t^{d/f}\,dW_t^{(f;d)}, \tag{10.16a}$$

$$dS_t^{d/q} = (r^d - r^q)S_t^{d/q}\,dt + \sigma^{(1)}S_t^{d/q}\,dW_t^{(q;d)}. \tag{10.16b}$$

An interesting limiting case

The analysis above shows how an option that pays a certain number of units of domestic currency obtained in units of $S_0^{(2;1)}$ (the spot rate of the second foreign currency in units of the first) is affected by a quanto drift adjustment. If the currency triangle is degenerate, suppose that the second foreign currency and the domestic currency (i.e. the quanto currency) move in lockstep. This means that $S_t^{(2;1)}$ ($= S_t^{d/f}$) and $\hat{S}_t^{(1)}$ ($= S_t^{d/q}$) are perfectly correlated or, equivalently, that $S_t^{(2;1)}$ and $S_t^{(1)}$ are perfectly anticorrelated.

With $\rho_q = -1$, the risk neutral drift in (10.13) becomes $r^{f;1} - r^{f;2} + \sigma^{(2;1)}\sigma^{(2)}$ and we have

$$\tilde{F} = S_0 e^{(r^d - r^f + \sigma^2)T}, \tag{10.17}$$

which is equivalent to (10.9).

10.4   BEST-OFS AND WORST-OFS

These options allow one to take on a position that pays either the best or the worst performing of N assets. In this section we shall only be concerned with the example of two or three currencies, largely because this type of product is most useful for checking numerical implementations of two- and three-factor PDEs in the presence of large correlation terms.

Stulz (1982) and Johnson (1987) are the standard references. The payout for a best-of call is given, for the two- and three-factor cases, by

$$V_t = \max(S_T^{(1)} - K_1, S_T^{(2)} - K_2, 0), \tag{10.18a}$$

$$V_t = \max(S_T^{(1)} - K_1, S_T^{(2)} - K_2, S_T^{(3)} - K_3, 0). \tag{10.18b}$$

While these can be priced straightforwardly on either a two- or three-factor PDE or Monte Carlo engine, closed-form solutions only exist in the case where the strikes are all equal (see Zhang, 1998). Note that these solutions can be expressed in terms of multivariate normal distribution functions.

10.4.1   Two-asset best-of call

The algebra is not particularly difficult once armed with the change of measure apparatus. Consider the best-of-two European call, which has payout at expiry

$$V_T^{\text{Bof2C}} = \max\left(S_T^{(1)} - K, S_T^{(2)} - K, 0\right)$$

under the limitation that $K_1 = K_2 = K$. Here, in Section 10.4 only, we let X denote $S_T^{(1)}$ and Y denote $S_T^{(2)}$ in some of the moneyness and probability subscripts below, for conciseness – and Z will denote $S_T^{(3)}$ in due course.

We have $\sigma^{(2;1)}$ from (10.11a) and correlations as given in Section 21.3 of Zhang (1998):

$$\sigma^{(2;1)} = \sqrt{[\sigma^{(1)}]^2 - 2\rho_{12;d}\sigma^{(1)}\sigma^{(2)} + [\sigma^{(2)}]^2}, \tag{10.19a}$$

$$\rho_1 = \frac{\rho_{12;d}\sigma^{(2)} - \sigma^{(1)}}{\sigma^{(2;1)}}, \tag{10.19b}$$

$$\rho_2 = \frac{\rho_{12;d}\sigma^{(1)} - \sigma^{(2)}}{\sigma^{(2;1)}}. \tag{10.19c}$$

With this, risk-neutral probabilities in each of the three risk-neutral measures can be written, using the 'moneyness' terms, as

$$d_{\{X>K;d\}} = \frac{\log\left(S_0^{(1)}/K\right) + [r^d - r^{f;1} - \frac{1}{2}[\sigma^{(1)}]^2]T}{\sigma^{(1)}\sqrt{T}}, \tag{10.20a}$$

$$d_{\{Y>K;d\}} = \frac{\log\left(S_0^{(2)}/K\right) + [r^d - r^{f;2} - \frac{1}{2}[\sigma^{(2)}]^2]T}{\sigma^{(2)}\sqrt{T}}, \tag{10.20b}$$

$$d_{\{X>K;f1\}} = d_{\{X>K;d\}} + \sigma^{(1)}\sqrt{T}, \tag{10.20c}$$

$$d_{\{Y>X;f1\}} = \frac{\log\left(S_0^{(2)}/S_0^{(1)}\right) + [r^{f;1} - r^{f;2} - \frac{1}{2}[\sigma^{(2;1)}]^2]T}{\sigma^{(2;1)}\sqrt{T}}, \tag{10.20d}$$

$$d_{\{Y>K;f2\}} = d_{\{Y>K;d\}} + \sigma^{(2)}\sqrt{T} \tag{10.20e}$$

$$d_{\{X>Y;f2\}} = \frac{\log\left(S_0^{(1)}/S_0^{(2)}\right) + [r^{f;2} - r^{f;1} - \frac{1}{2}[\sigma^{(2;1)}]^2]T}{\sigma^{(2;1)}\sqrt{T}}. \tag{10.20f}$$

With this, we can compute the required risk-neutral probabilities using expressions for the univariate and bivariate normal distribution functions $N(x)$ and $N(x, y; \rho)$, where $N(x) = \mathbf{P}[\xi \leq x]$ and $N(x, y; \rho) = \mathbf{P}[\xi_1 \leq x \cap \xi_2 \leq y]$, where $\xi \sim N(0, 1)$ and (ξ_1, ξ_2) are distributed according to the bivariate normal distribution with means of 0 and covariance matrix of $\begin{pmatrix} 1 & \rho \\ \rho & 1 \end{pmatrix}$.

We obtain

$$\mathbf{P}^d[X_T > K] = N(d_{\{X > K;d\}}),$$

$$\mathbf{P}^d[Y_T > K] = N(d_{\{Y > K;d\}}),$$

$$\mathbf{P}^d[X_T > K \cap Y_T > K] = N(d_{\{X > K;d\}}, d_{\{Y > K;d\}}; \rho_{12;d}),$$

$$\mathbf{P}^d[X_T > K \cup Y_T > K] = \mathbf{P}^d[X_T > K] + \mathbf{P}^d[Y_T > K]$$
$$- \mathbf{P}^d[X_T > K \cap Y_T > K],$$

$$\mathbf{P}^{f1}[X_T > K] = N(d_{\{X > K;f1\}}),$$

$$\mathbf{P}^{f1}[X_T > K \cap Y_T > X_T] = N(d_{\{X > K;f1\}}, d_{\{Y > X;f1\}}; \rho_1),$$

$$\mathbf{P}^{f1}[X_T > K \cap X_T > Y_T] = N(d_{\{X > K;f1\}}) - \mathbf{P}^{f1}[X_T > K \cap Y_T > X_T],$$

$$\mathbf{P}^{f2}[Y_T > K] = N(d_{\{Y > K;fs\}}),$$

$$\mathbf{P}^{f2}[Y_T > K \cap X_T > Y_T] = N(d_{\{Y > K;f2\}}, d_{\{X > Y;f2\}}; \rho_1),$$

$$\mathbf{P}^{f2}[Y_T > K \cap Y_T > X_T] = \mathbf{P}^{f2}[Y_T > K] - \mathbf{P}^{f2}[Y_T > K \cap X_T > Y_T], \quad (10.21)$$

which we assemble into the price for a European best-of-two call:

$$V_0^{\text{Bof2C}} = S_0^{(1)} e^{-r^{f;1}T} \mathbf{P}^{f1}[X_T > K \cap X_T > Y_T]$$
$$+ S_0^{(2)} e^{-r^{f;2}T} \mathbf{P}^{f2}[Y_T > K \cap Y_T > X_T]$$
$$- K e^{-r^d T} \mathbf{P}^d[X_T > K \cup Y_T > K]. \quad (10.22)$$

Prices for other examples of two-dimensional multicurrency options can be found in the same manner, e.g.

$$V_T^{\text{Bof2P}} = \max(K - S_T^{(1)}, K - S_T^{(2)}, 0), \quad (10.23a)$$

$$V_T^{\text{BofCP}} = \max(S_T^{(1)} - K, K - S_T^{(2)}, 0), \quad (10.23b)$$

$$V_T^{\text{BofPC}} = \max(K - S_T^{(1)}, S_T^{(2)} - K, 0) \quad (10.23c)$$

have present values of

$$V_0^{\text{Bof2P}} = K e^{-r^d T} \mathbf{P}^d[X_T < K \cup Y_T < K]$$
$$- S_0^{(1)} e^{-r^{f;1}T} \mathbf{P}^{f1}[X_T < K \cap X_T < Y_T]$$
$$- S_0^{(2)} e^{-r^{f;2}T} \mathbf{P}^{f2}[Y_T < K \cap Y_T < X_T], \quad (10.24a)$$

$$V_0^{\text{BofCP}} = S_0^{(1)} e^{-r^{f;1}T} \mathbf{P}^{f1}[X_T > K \cap X_T + Y_T > 2K]$$
$$- S_0^{(2)} e^{-r^{f;2}T} \mathbf{P}^{f2}[Y_T < K \cap X_T + Y_T > 2K]$$
$$- K e^{-r^d T} \mathbf{P}^d[X_T > K \cup Y_T < K], \quad (10.24b)$$

$$V_0^{\text{BofPC}} = S_0^{(2)} e^{-r^{f;2}T} \mathbf{P}^{f2}[Y_T > K \cap X_T + Y_T < 2K]$$
$$- S_0^{(1)} e^{-r^{f;1}T} \mathbf{P}^{f1}[X_T < K \cap X_T + Y_T < 2K]$$
$$- K e^{-r^d T} \mathbf{P}^d[X_T < K \cup Y_T > K]. \quad (10.24c)$$

Note that in all the above cases, the event in $\mathbf{P}^d[\cdot]$ is the event that *one* of the options will be exercised, whereas $\mathbf{P}^f[\cdot]$ is the event that a *particular* option (perhaps a call on the first asset, perhaps a put on the second) will be exercised, the probability being assessed in the risk-neutral measure corresponding to that particular asset.

For example, in the case of the best-of-two put, consider $\mathbf{P}^{f1}[X_T < K \cap X_T < Y_T]$. This is the probability, in the risk-neutral measure corresponding to the first foreign currency, that $X_T < K$ is less than strike (and is therefore in-the-money) and $X_T < Y_T$ (and is therefore more in-the-money than the second risky asset).

The extension to three-dimensional multicurrency options proceeds in exactly the same manner. Of course, in this case the handling of correlation is even more complicated still. The actual events to be considered within $\mathbf{P}^d[\cdot]$ and $\mathbf{P}^f[\cdot]$ operations are easily obtained by Boolean algebra.

10.4.2 Three-asset best-of call

Let us suppose a three-currency Black–Scholes model, similar to (10.1), of the form

$$dS_t^{(1)} = [r^d - r^{f;1}]S_t^{(1)}\,dt + \sigma^{(1)}S_t^{(1)}\,dW_t^{(1;d)}, \tag{10.25a}$$

$$dS_t^{(2)} = [r^d - r^{f;2}]S_t^{(2)}\,dt + \sigma^{(2)}S_t^{(2)}\,dW_t^{(2;d)}, \tag{10.25b}$$

$$dS_t^{(3)} = [r^d - r^{f;3}]S_t^{(3)}\,dt + \sigma^{(3)}S_t^{(3)}\,dW_t^{(3;d)}, \tag{10.25c}$$

with correlations $\langle dW_t^{(i;d)}, dW_t^{(j;d)}\rangle = \rho_{ij;d}\,dt$ for $i \neq j$.

The best-of-three call with common strike K, with payout at expiry

$$V_t = \max\left(S_T^{(1)} - K, S_T^{(2)} - K, S_T^{(3)} - K, 0\right)$$

can then be priced in the same manner:

$$\sigma_{q;12} = \sqrt{[\sigma^{(1)}]^2 - 2\rho_{12;d}\sigma^{(1)}\sigma^{(2)} + [\sigma^{(2)}]^2}, \tag{10.26a}$$

$$\sigma_{q;13} = \sqrt{[\sigma^{(1)}]^2 - 2\rho_{13;d}\sigma^{(1)}\sigma^{(3)} + [\sigma^{(3)}]^2}, \tag{10.26b}$$

$$\sigma_{q;23} = \sqrt{[\sigma^{(2)}]^2 - 2\rho_{23;d}\sigma^{(2)}\sigma^{(3)} + [\sigma^{(3)}]^2}, \tag{10.26c}$$

$$\rho_{12;f1} = -\frac{\rho_{12}\sigma^{(2)} - \sigma^{(1)}}{\sigma_{q;12}}, \tag{10.26d}$$

$$\rho_{12;f2} = -\frac{\rho_{12}\sigma^{(1)} - \sigma^{(2)}}{\sigma_{q;12}}, \tag{10.26e}$$

$$\rho_{13;f1} = -\frac{\rho_{13}\sigma^{(3)} - \sigma^{(1)}}{\sigma_{q;13}}, \tag{10.26f}$$

$$\rho_{13;f3} = -\frac{\rho_{13}\sigma^{(1)} - \sigma^{(3)}}{\sigma_{q;13}}, \tag{10.26g}$$

$$\rho_{23;f2} = -\frac{\rho_{23}\sigma^{(3)} - \sigma^{(2)}}{\sigma_{q;23}}, \tag{10.26h}$$

$$\rho_{23;f3} = -\frac{\rho_{23}\sigma^{(2)} - \sigma^{(3)}}{\sigma_{q;23}}, \tag{10.26i}$$

$$\rho_{23;f1} = -\frac{\rho_{12}\sigma^{(1)}\sigma^{(2)} + \rho_{13}\sigma^{(1)}\sigma^{(3)} - \rho_{23}\sigma^{(2)}\sigma^{(3)} - [\sigma^{(1)}]^2}{\sigma_{q;12}\sigma_{q;13}}, \tag{10.26j}$$

$$\rho_{13;f2} = -\frac{\rho_{12}\sigma^{(1)}\sigma^{(2)} + \rho_{23}\sigma^{(2)}\sigma^{(3)} - \rho_{13}\sigma^{(1)}\sigma^{(3)} - [\sigma^{(2)}]^2}{\sigma_{q;12}\sigma_{q;23}}, \tag{10.26k}$$

$$\rho_{12;f3} = -\frac{\rho_{13}\sigma^{(1)}\sigma^{(3)} + \rho_{23}\sigma^{(2)}\sigma^{(3)} - \rho_{12}\sigma^{(1)}\sigma^{(2)} - [\sigma^{(3)}]^2}{\sigma_{q;13}\sigma_{q;23}}. \tag{10.26l}$$

Growing in boldness, we construct 'moneyness' terms in each of *four* numeraires:

$$d_{\{X>K;d\}} = \frac{\log\left(S_0^{(1)}/K\right) + [r^d - r^{f;1} - \frac{1}{2}[\sigma^{(1)}]^2]T}{\sigma^{(1)}\sqrt{T}}, \tag{10.27a}$$

$$d_{\{Y>K;d\}} = \frac{\log\left(S_0^{(2)}/K\right) + [r^d - r^{f;2} - \frac{1}{2}[\sigma^{(2)}]^2]T}{\sigma^{(2)}\sqrt{T}}, \tag{10.27b}$$

$$d_{\{Z>K;d\}} = \frac{\log\left(S_0^{(3)}/K\right) + [r^d - r^{f;3} - \frac{1}{2}[\sigma^{(3)}]^2]T}{\sigma^{(3)}\sqrt{T}}, \tag{10.27c}$$

$$d_{\{X>K;f1\}} = \frac{\log\left(S_0^{(1)}/K\right) + [r^d - r^{f;2} + \frac{1}{2}[\sigma^{(1)}]^2]T}{\sigma^{(1)}\sqrt{T}}, \tag{10.27d}$$

$$d_{\{X>Y;f1\}} = \frac{\log\left(S_0^{(1)}/S_0^{(2)}\right) + [r^{f;2} - r^{f;1} + \frac{1}{2}[\sigma_{q;12}]^2]T}{\sigma_{q;12}\sqrt{T}}, \tag{10.27e}$$

$$d_{\{X>Z;f1\}} = \frac{\log\left(S_0^{(1)}/S_0^{(3)}\right) + [r^{f;3} - r^{f;1} + \frac{1}{2}[\sigma_{q;13}]^2]T}{\sigma_{q;13}\sqrt{T}}, \tag{10.27f}$$

$$d_{\{Y>K;f2\}} = \frac{\log\left(S_0^{(2)}/K\right) + [r^d - r^{f;2} + \frac{1}{2}[\sigma^{(2)}]^2]T}{\sigma^{(2)}\sqrt{T}}, \tag{10.27g}$$

$$d_{\{Y>X;f2\}} = \frac{\log\left(S_0^{(2)}/S_0^{(1)}\right) + [r^{f;1} - r^{f;2} + \frac{1}{2}[\sigma_{q;12}]^2]T}{\sigma_{q;12}\sqrt{T}}, \tag{10.27h}$$

$$d_{\{Y>Z;f2\}} = \frac{\log\left(S_0^{(2)}/S_0^{(3)}\right) + [r^{f;3} - r^{f;2} + \frac{1}{2}[\sigma_{q;23}]^2]T}{\sigma_{q;23}\sqrt{T}}, \tag{10.27i}$$

$$d_{\{Z>K;f3\}} = \frac{\log\left(S_0^{(3)}/K\right) + [r^d - r^{f;3} + \frac{1}{2}[\sigma^{(3)}]^2]T}{\sigma^{(3)}\sqrt{T}}, \tag{10.27j}$$

$$d_{\{Z>X;f3\}} = \frac{\log\left(S_0^{(3)}/S_0^{(1)}\right) + [r^{f;1} - r^{f;3} + \frac{1}{2}[\sigma_{q;13}]^2]T}{\sigma_{q;13}\sqrt{T}}, \tag{10.27k}$$

$$d_{\{Z>Y;f3\}} = \frac{\log\left(S_0^{(3)}/S_0^{(2)}\right) + [r^{f;2} - r^{f;3} + \frac{1}{2}[\sigma_{q;23}]^2]T}{\sigma_{q;23}\sqrt{T}}, \tag{10.27l}$$

giving risk-neutral probabilities by use of the trivariate cumulative normal distribution function $N(x, y, z; \rho_{12;d}, \rho_{13;d}, \rho_{23;d})$:

$$\mathbf{P}^{f1}[X_T > K \cap X_T > Y_T \cap X_T > Z_T]$$

$$= N(d_{\{X>K;f1\}}, d_{\{X>Y;f1\}}, d_{\{X>Z;f1\}}; \rho_{12;f1}, \rho_{12;f1}, \rho_{12;f1}),$$

$$\mathbf{P}^{f2}[Y_T > K \cap Y_T > X_T \cap Y_T > Z_T]$$

$$= N(d_{\{Y>K;f2\}}, d_{\{Y>X;f2\}}, d_{\{Y>Z;f2\}}; \rho_{12;f2}, \rho_{23;f2}, \rho_{13;f2}),$$

$$\mathbf{P}^{f3}[Z_T > K \cap Z_T > X_T \cap Z_T > Y_T]$$

$$= N(d_{\{Z>K;f3\}}, d_{\{Z>X;f3\}}, d_{\{Z>Y;f3\}}; \rho_{12;f3}, \rho_{23;f3}, \rho_{13;f3}),$$

$$\mathbf{P}^{d}[X_T > K \cup Y_T > K \cup Z_T > K]$$

$$= 1 - N(-d_{\{X>K;d\}}; -d_{\{Y>K;d\}}, -d_{\{Z>K;d\}}; \rho_{12;d}, \rho_{13;d}, \rho_{23;d}), \qquad (10.28)$$

which we can similarly assemble into the price for a European best-of-three call

$$V_0^{\text{Bof3C}} = S_0^{(1)} e^{-r^{f;1}T} \mathbf{P}^{f1}[X_T > K \cap X_T > Y_T \cap X_T > Z_T]$$

$$+ S_0^{(2)} e^{-r^{f;2}T} \mathbf{P}^{f2}[Y_T > K \cap Y_T > X_T \cap Y_T > Z_T]$$

$$+ S_0^{(3)} e^{-r^{f;3}T} \mathbf{P}^{f3}[Z_T > K \cap Z_T > X_T \cap Z_T > Y_T]$$

$$- K e^{-r^d T} \mathbf{P}^{d}[X_T > K \cup Y_T > K \cup Z_T > K]. \qquad (10.29)$$

Note that $\mathbf{P}^{d}[X_T > K \cup Y_T > K \cup Z_T > K]$ represents the domestic risk-neutral probability that *one* of the options will be exercised (i.e. to buy asset 1, 2 or 3 at strike K), whereas each of the $\mathbf{P}^{f}[\cdot]$ terms represents a probability in a particular risk-neutral measure (the risk-neutral measure in which that asset is numeraire, to be exact) that the best-of option will be exercised in favour of that particular asset.

Once we have the correlation structure, the change of measure machinery is relatively straightforward. Decomposing the correlations into their pairwise representations, as viewed from the point of view of each vertex in the currency tetrahedron, is clearly the hard part.[6]

For numerical implementations of two- and three-dimensional multivariate normal distribution functions, Drezner and Wesolowski (1989) provide an algorithm for the bivariate normal distribution function, also described in Genz (2004). An algorithm for the trivariate normal distribution function is discussed in Drezner (1994).

Note also, as discussed in Rubinstein (1991), that best-of and worst-of options can be related to exchange options, since

$$\min(S_T^{(1)}, S_T^{(2)}) = S_T^{(2)} - \max(S_T^{(2)} - S_T^{(1)}, 0),$$

$$\max(S_T^{(1)}, S_T^{(2)}) = S_T^{(1)} + \max(S_T^{(2)} - S_T^{(1)}, 0).$$

---

[6] The extension to currency pentachorons, hexaterons and heptapetons for higher dimensional best-of options (Section 10.4.3) is left as an exercise for the reader.

10.4.3   N-asset best-of call

We can see some patterns emerging. In general, we have

$$V_0^{\text{BofNC}} = S_0^{(1)} e^{-r^{f;1}T} \mathbf{P}^{f1} \left[S_T^{(1)} > K \cap S_T^{(1)} = \max_i \{S_T^{(i)}\} \right]$$
$$+ \dots$$
$$+ S_0^{(N)} e^{-r^{f;N}T} \mathbf{P}^{fN} \left[S_T^{(N)} > K \cap S_T^{(N)} = \max_i \{S_T^{(i)}\} \right]$$
$$- K e^{-r^d T} \mathbf{P}^d \left[\max_i \{S_T^{(i)}\} > K \right]. \tag{10.30}$$

Given correlations from all reference points and suitable drift adjustments for the N foreign risk-neutral measures, the result would follow accordingly, precisely as in Sections 10.4.1 and 10.4.2.

10.5   BASKET OPTIONS

More generally, we often wish to construct baskets of several currencies, which has a natural economic rationale. A useful technique is to decompose such a basket into a synthetic long–short decomposition, where we effectively attempt to construct a synthetic asset that matches the moments of the basket. We detail this below, which extends to regular baskets as a limiting case.

Suppose we have a basket of $N + 1$ currencies (indexed $0, \dots, N$) and we consider the performance of N of these currencies against a common base currency, which without loss of generality we denote as currency ccy_0. Spot rates for the other currencies are quoted against this currency and are denoted $S_t^{i/0}$. Additionally, we choose one of these currencies as a notional currency and denote it by m. The price will be reported as a $\%ccy_m$ price. In the case where $m = 0$, this reverts to a standard basket performance option, and by control of the denominator flags below can be equated to a regular basket option as a limiting case.

We have weights $w_i \in \mathbb{R}$, which can be arbitrarily positive or negative, strikes $K_i \in \mathbb{R}^+$ and denominator flags D_i which control whether the performance term in the basket is specified either by a divide by spot or divide by strike quotient.

The composition of the basket is then given by

$$B_t = w_0 + \sum_{i=1}^N \frac{w_i (S_t^{i/0} - K_i)}{D_t S_t^{i/0} + (1 - D_i)K_i}. \tag{10.31}$$

Note that B_t is dimensionless. At expiry time T, the payout can be given by

$$V_T^{(m)} = N^{(m)} B_T, \tag{10.32}$$

from which we see that this is indeed a $\%ccy_m$ price.

We work in the Black–Scholes framework, extended to N risky assets. In units of the common base currency, express

$$dS_t^{i/0} = [r^{(0)} - r^{(i)}]S_t^{i/0}dt + \sigma^{i/0} S_t^{i/0} dW_t^{i/0},$$

where $< dW_t^{i/0}, dW_t^{j/0} > = \rho^{i/0;j/0} dt$ and $r^{(i)}$ is the interest rate in currency ccy_i.

These FX spot price processes are transformed in the ccy_m risk-neutral measure to

$$dS_t^{i/0} = [r^{(0)} - r^{(i)} + \rho^{i/0;j/0}\sigma^{i/0}\sigma^{j/0}]S_t^{i/0}\,dt + \sigma^{i/0}S_t^{i/0}\,d\hat{W}_t^{i/0},$$

where $d\hat{W}_t^{i/0}$ denotes differential increments in the driving Brownian motions in the ccy_m risk-neutral measure. We now compute, in the ccy_m risk-neutral measure, the expectation of the process $S_T^{i/0}$ at expiry, obtaining

$$\mathbf{E}^{(m)}[S_T^{i/0}] = F_T^{i/0}\exp(\rho^{i/0;j/0}\sigma^{i/0}\sigma^{j/0}),$$

where

$$F_T^{i/0} = \mathbf{E}^{(m)}[S_T^{i/0}] = S_0^{i/0}\exp\left(r^{(0)} - r^{(i)} - \frac{1}{2}[\sigma^{i/0}]^2\right).$$

Decompose the basket B_T into long and short components through appropriate choice of coefficients c_0, c_i and d_i (some of which will clearly be zero):

$$B_T = c_0 + \sum_{i=1}^{N} c_i S_T^{i/0} - \sum_{i=1}^{N} d_i/S_T^{i/0}.$$

Applying the long–short decomposition, we have

$$B_T = I_T - J_T,$$

where

$$I_T = a_0^+ + \sum_{i=1}^{N} a_i^+ S_T^{i/0} - \sum_{i=1}^{N} b_i^+/S_T^{i/0},$$
$$J_T = a_0^- + \sum_{i=1}^{N} a_i^- S_T^{i/0} - \sum_{i=1}^{N} b_i^-/S_T^{i/0}$$

denote the positive and negative constituents of the basket respectively. We can easily obtain $\mathbf{E}^{(m)}[S_T^{i/0}]$ and $\mathbf{Cov}^{(m)}[S_T^{i/0}, S_T^{j/0}]$. Without loss of generality, we assume that all b_i terms are zero (the extension is straightforward).

It is straightforward to compute first moments

$$\mathbf{E}^{(m)}[I_T] = a_0^+ + \sum_{i=1}^{N} a_i^+ \mathbf{E}^{(m)}[S_T^{i/0}],$$

$$\mathbf{E}^{(m)}[J_T] = a_0^- + \sum_{i=1}^{N} a_i^- \mathbf{E}^{(m)}[S_T^{i/0}].$$

Calculation of the second moments is a similar exercise. We have

$$\mathbf{E}^{(m)}[I_T^2] = \mathbf{E}^{(m)}\left[\left(a_0^+ + \sum_{i=1}^{N} a_i^+ S_T^{i/0}\right)\left(a_0^+ + \sum_{i=1}^{N} a_i^+ S_T^{i/0}\right)\right]$$

$$= [a_0^+]^2 + 2a_0^+ \sum_{i=1}^{N} a_i^+ \mathbf{E}^{(m)}[S_T^{i/0}] + \sum_{i=1}^{N} a_i^+ \sum_{j=1}^{N} a_j^+ \mathbf{E}^{(m)}[S_T^{i/0} S_T^{j/0}]$$

$$= [a_0^+]^2 + 2a_0^+ \sum_{i=1}^{N} a_i^+ \mathbf{E}^{(m)}[S_T^{i/0}]$$

$$+ \sum_{i=1}^{N} a_i^+ \sum_{j=1}^{N} a_j^+ \mathbf{E}^{(m)}[S_T^{i/0}]\mathbf{E}^{(m)}[S_T^{j/0}] \exp\left(\mathbf{Cov}^{(m)}[S_T^{i/0} S_T^{j/0}]\right)$$

and similarly for $\mathbf{E}^{(m)}[J_T^2]$ and $\mathbf{E}^{(m)}[I_T J_T]$.

The moment-matching technique involves approximating the joint distribution of I_T, J_T with $\hat{I}_T$, $\hat{J}_T$, where $\hat{I}_T = \exp(X)$, $\hat{J}_T = \exp(Y)$ and X and Y are jointly normal with parameters μ_X, μ_Y, σ_X^2, σ_Y^2 and ρ chosen to match the moments of I and J. We then use the parameters of the approximating distribution

$$\mathbf{E}[\exp(X)] = \exp\left(\mu_X + \frac{1}{2}\sigma_X^2\right),$$

$$\mathbf{E}[\exp(2X)] = \exp\left(2\mu_X + 2\sigma_X^2\right),$$

$$\mathbf{E}[\exp(X + Y)] = \exp\left(\mu_X + \mu_Y + (\sigma_X^2 + 2\rho\sigma_X\sigma_Y + \sigma_Y^2)/2\right),$$

making the equivalence

$$\mu_X = 2\ln(\mathbf{E}^{(m)}[I_T]) - \frac{1}{2}\ln(\mathbf{E}^{(m)}[I_T^2]),$$

$$\mu_Y = 2\ln(\mathbf{E}^{(m)}[J_T]) - \frac{1}{2}\ln(\mathbf{E}^{(m)}[J_T^2]),$$

$$\sigma_X^2 = \ln(\mathbf{E}^{(m)}[I_T^2]) - 2\ln(\mathbf{E}^{(m)}[I_T]),$$

$$\sigma_Y^2 = \ln(\mathbf{E}^{(m)}[J_T^2]) - 2\ln(\mathbf{E}^{(m)}[J_T]),$$

$$\rho = \frac{1}{\sigma_X\sigma_Y}\left(\ln(\mathbf{E}^{(m)}[I_T J_T]) - \mu_X - \mu_Y - \tfrac{1}{2}(\sigma_X^2 + \sigma_Y^2)\right).$$

This enables us to price the quanto basket by computing, given the approximating distribution $N(\mu_X, \mu_Y, \sigma_X^2, \sigma_Y^2, \rho)$, the expectation of the difference of $X - Y$ conditional on $X > Y$. Extension to quanto digital baskets is straightforward.

10.6 NUMERICAL METHODS

Clearly, we may well end up having to resort to Monte Carlo simulation for many of these multicurrency products. My objective in this chapter was to try to explain the various change of measure techniques that are employed when shifting the frame of reference in the coordinate system describing the various assets, depending on which is chosen as numeraire. Nevertheless, as we know from earlier chapters, there is only so much one can do with measure change and numerical methods must eventually come into play.

The general framework for an n-dimensional multicurrency model is

$$dS_t^{(i)} = [r^d - r^{f;i}]S_t^{(i)}dt + \sigma^{(i)}S_t^{(i)}\,dW_t^{(i;d)}$$

$$\vdots \tag{10.33}$$

$$dS_t^{(n)} = [r^d - r^{f;n}]S_t^{(n)}dt + \sigma^{(n)}S_t^{(n)}\,dW_t^{(n;d)}$$

with correlations $\langle dW_t^{(i;d)}, dW_t^{(j;d)}\rangle = \rho_{ij;d}\,dt$ for $i \neq j$.

Monte Carlo simulation of asset price processes in such a model is straightforward, the only complication factor being the Cholesky decomposition to obtain correlated random variables from independent draws from $N(0,1)$.

Finally, we certainly have a partial differential equation representation of the price of an option deriving its value from n tradeable securities:

$$\frac{\partial V}{\partial t} + \frac{1}{2}\sum_{i,j}\rho_{ij;d}\sigma^{(i)}\sigma^{(j)}S^{(i)}S^{(j)}\frac{\partial^2 V}{\partial S^{(i)}\partial S^{(j)}} + \sum_i(r^d - r^{f;i})S^{(i)}\frac{\partial V}{\partial S^{(i)}} - r^d V = 0$$

or, in logspot coordinates,

$$\frac{\partial V}{\partial t} + \frac{1}{2}\sum_{i,j}\rho_{ij;d}\sigma^{(i)}\sigma^{(j)}\frac{\partial^2 V}{\partial x^{(i)}\partial x^{(j)}} + \sum_i\left(r^d - r^{f;i} - \frac{1}{2}[\sigma^{(i)}]^2\right)\frac{\partial V}{\partial x^{(i)}} - r^d V = 0,$$

where obviously $\rho_{ii;\cdot} = 1$ on the diagonal.

In the case where $N \leq 3$, the algorithms from Chapter 7 may be employed to some effect, certainly with the potential for pricing barrier products such as the quadruple no-touch using Dirichlet boundary conditions, as described in Chapter 8, and possibly even using auxiliary state variables as described in Chapter 9 if the computational load is not too intense – e.g. an Asian option (arithmetic average, discrete fixings) with a continuous KO barrier on a second currency pair.

10.7   A NOTE ON MULTICURRENCY GREEKS

Note from Chapters 2 and 3 that we have a number of possible deltas, and this even more so in multicurrency options. One should, however, be aware that the definition of gamma is especially confusing in the world of multicurrency options. For example, many trading systems do not make it entirely clear what this means.

A typical gamma that is reported is a change in a delta, for a 1 % move in spot. Note that there are many different deltas for which this can be reported, as well as different spots in this case. For example, in the case of a USDJPY option we could have the change in USD delta for a 1 % change in USDJPY, the change in JPY delta for a 1 % change in USDJPY and even the change in the change in JPY delta for a 1 % change in EURJPY if the product was quantoed into euros.

Note that unlike the purely mathematical mixed partial derivative, real-world gammas are often *not* symmetric, depending on the way in which they are defined.

10.8   QUANTOING UNTRADEABLE FACTORS

In a general multicurrency setting, the extension to volatility smile modelling is nontrivial. One area that can be considered, however, is where the optionality is all in one currency pair and the actual payment is in a third separate currency, which the reader will remember from Section 10.3.

We can take a quanto call option under dynamics (10.16) and suppose that, as all the convexity is with respect to the $S_t^{d/f}$ spot rate, that we allow a stochastic volatility $\sigma_t^{(2;1)}$ to drive that particular spot process:

$$dS_t^{d/f} = (r^d - r^f)S_t^{d/f}\,dt + \sigma_t^{(2;1)}S_t^{d/f}\,dW_t^{(d/f;d)}, \tag{10.34a}$$

$$dS_t^{d/q} = (r^d - r^q)S_t^{d/q}\,dt + \sigma^{(1)}S_t^{d/q}\,dW_t^{(d/q;d)}, \tag{10.34b}$$

$$d\sigma_t^{(2;1)} = [\cdots]dt + [\cdots]dW_t^{(\sigma;d)}. \tag{10.34c}$$

For the purposes of this discussion, the exact nature of the stochastic volatility process is immaterial. Suppose that $W_t^{(\sigma;d)}$ and $W_t^{(d/q;d)}$ are completely uncorrelated, but $< dW_t^{(d/f;d)}, dW_t^{(\sigma,d)} >= \rho\,dt$, as is usual for one-asset stochastic volatility models, for some value of ρ.

We can then apply a Cholesky decomposition

$$W_t^{(\sigma,d)} = \rho W_t^{(d/f;d)} + \bar{\rho}W_t^{(d/f;d)\perp},$$

where $W_t^{(d/f;d)}$ and $W_t^{(d/f;d)\perp}$ are independent Brownian motions in the domestic risk-neutral measure.

The dynamics in the domestic risk-neutral measure are then described by three independent Brownian motions: $W_t^{(d/f;d)}$, $W_t^{(d/f;d)\perp}$ and $W_t^{(d/q;d)}$.

Upon translation into the quanto numeraire, after the manner of Section 10.3, we obtain

$$W_t^{(d/f;q)} = W_t^{(d/f;d)} - \rho_{d/f;d/q}\sigma^{(1)}t, \tag{10.35a}$$

$$W_t^{(d/f;q)\perp} = W_t^{(d/f;d)\perp}, \tag{10.35b}$$

$$W_t^{(d/q;q)} = W_t^{(d/q;d)} - \sigma^{(1)}t. \tag{10.35c}$$

Compare (10.35c) to (2.52) to check that the measure transformation between domestic and quanto numeraire is correct, at least with respect to the spot rate relating these two currencies. Note that it is the orthogonal components of the untradeable factor(s) that are unaffected by a change of numeraire.

Under this change of measure, we have

$$dS_t^{d/f} = (r^d - r^f + \rho_{d/f;d/q}\sigma^{(1)}\sigma_t^{(2;1)})S_t^{d/f}\,dt + \sigma_t^{(2;1)}S_t^{d/f}\,dW_t^{(d/f;q)}, \tag{10.36a}$$

$$dS_t^{d/q} = (r^d - r^q + [\sigma^{(1)}]^2)S_t^{d/q}\,dt + \sigma^{(1)}S_t^{d/q}\,dW_t^{(d/q;q)}, \tag{10.36b}$$

$$d\sigma_t^{(2;1)} = [\cdots]dt + [\cdots]dW_t^{(\sigma;q)}, \tag{10.36c}$$

where

$$
\begin{aligned}
W_t^{(\sigma;q)} &= \rho W_t^{(d/f;q)} + \bar{\rho} W_t^{(d/f;q)\perp} \\
&= \rho W_t^{(d/f;d)} - \rho \rho_{d/f;d/q} \sigma^{(1)} t + \bar{\rho} W_t^{(d/f;q)\perp} \\
&= W_t^{(\sigma;d)} - \rho \rho_{d/f;d/q} \sigma^{(1)} t.
\end{aligned}
\tag{10.37}
$$

As a result, we have the important observation that the drifts of untradeable factors such as stochastic volatility[7] are also affected by quanto adjustments, unless they are completely uncorrelated with market observables.

10.9   FURTHER READING

Langnau (2009, 2010) and Reghaï (2009), inspired by work on equity derivatives, have some interesting approaches involving extending the local volatility approach of Chapter 5 to multiple assets. Rombouts and Stentoft (2010) also have interesting work on multivariate option pricing including time-dependent volatility and correlation. Note that the numerical methods described briefly in Section 10.6 and more extensively in Chapter 7 are easily capable of handling term structures of volatility and correlation, and even local volatility/correlation, if provided with suitable drift/volatility coefficients or convection/diffusion/reaction terms.

---

[7] Or instantaneous short rates in a longdated FX model.

11

Longdated FX

There are two things I want to talk about in introducing this chapter – the growing importance of interest rate risk as FX option maturities increase and the fact that we've been using nontradeables as quasi-numeraires for much of this book. Both are of crucial importance for longdated FX option pricing.

Let $P^d(0, T)$ denote the price today (i.e. $P^d(t, T)$ with $t = 0$) of a domestic zero coupon bond with maturity T. We already know that the value of an ATMF option (see Figure 11.1) is approximately $0.04\sigma\sqrt{T}$, in a Black–Scholes world at least. Consequently, the vega is just $0.04\sqrt{T}$ and scales as the square root of T. In contrast, the interest rate risks, i.e. the rhos, scale linearly in T. One can verify this by setting $K = F$ in (2.67) and differentiating with respect to either r^d or r^f.

What this means is that for shortdated options, FX volatility, and volatility smile risk in particular, dominates, but for longer dated options, we are increasingly concerned with interest rate uncertainty.

Secondly, the attentive reader will remember that, in accordance with common FX practice, we have been slightly cavalier up to now with our choice of numeraire (I made an important footnote at the beginning of Chapter 3 to that effect). In Chapter 10, for example, we speak of using a JPY numeraire, currency 1 numeraire and S_t numeraire. As Baxter and Rennie (1996) would be the first to point out, and as mentioned in Chapter 2, it's not the spot rate itself that's a tradeable quantity, it is the product of that spot rate S_t and a foreign numeraire such as the foreign money market account B_t^f.

It is *only* in a deterministic interest rate world that one can assume discount factors to be deterministic, take them outside of the expectations and think of an FX spot rate S_t as a quasi-tradeable. Assuming that FX spot rate are tradeables is like assuming the world is flat for the purposes of navigation or that Newtonian physics provides an adequate model for reality. In many cases, the assumption is good enough for practical purposes.

For flying from London to Tokyo, observing the perihelion of Mercury or pricing longdated FX options, however, each of these assumptions are inadequate. A different world view is required.

This concluding chapter introduces typical instruments encountered in longdated FX and some methods for their valuation. Much of this chapter relies on underlying principles of interest rate derivative pricing, a subject on which many excellent books have been written and for which this chapter can serve as no substitute. We refer the reader, implying no particular ordering than chronological, to Musiela and Rutkowski (1997), Rebonato (1998, 2002), Hunt and Kennedy (2000), Pelsser (2000), Brigo and Mercurio (2006) and Andersen and Piterbarg (2010).

11.1 CURRENCY SWAPS

A currency swap is the typical longdated FX product. As described in Section 5.4 of Hull (1997), this enables a corporate to transform a loan in one currency (the funding currency)

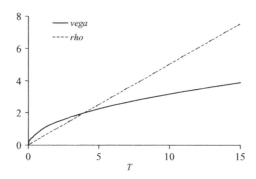

Figure 11.1   Vega and rho profiles for ATMF options

into a loan in another currency. In the same way as a mortgage holder can elect to take a fixed or a variable rate on their mortgage, each of these legs (in domestic and foreign currency respectively) can be fixed or floating. Not dissimilarly to FX options, we have a notional in each of the two currencies – domestic N^d and foreign N^f.

Let us suppose that we have a currency swap where the timepoints are fixed at $t_0, \ldots, t_i, t_{i+1}, \ldots, t_N$, with accrual fractions $\alpha_0, \ldots, \alpha_{N-1}$ denoting what proportion of an annualised coupon is paid in each interval. The accrual fraction α_i for the relevant time period depends on t_i and t_{i+1}, and on the day count convention for the currency in question.[1] Technically we should have different daycount fractions for the two currencies, so we can superscript these appropriately, obtaining α_i^d and α_i^f.

In the case of a fixed–fixed currency swap with coupons C^d and C^f respectively, cashflows of coupons $\alpha_i^d C^d N^d$ and $\alpha_i^f C^f N^f$ in domestic and foreign currencies take place on t_{i+1}, for i from 0 to $N - 1$.

In the case of floating coupons, one or both of these sequence of cashflow coupons becomes $\alpha_i^d L_{t_i,t_{i+1}}^d N_d$ and/or $\alpha_i^f L_{t_i,t_{i+1}}^f N_f$, where $L_{t_i,t_{i+1}}^{d;f}$ denotes the LIBOR (London interbank offered rate) for the domestic or foreign currency fixed at time t_i and applicable over the accrual period.

Note that most currency swaps involve an initial and a terminal exchange of principal amounts N^d and foreign N^f, in *addition* to the coupons described above – a pair of back-to-back transactions physically separated in time, which reverse out each other.

Figure 11.2(a) shows cashflows for a fixed–fixed cross-currency swap (the foreign payments, by convention, are depicted pointing upwards and the domestic payments point downwards), whereas Figure 11.2(b) shows typical cashflows for a floating–floating cross-currency swap. Equivalent cashflows for fixed–floating and floating–fixed cross-currency swaps follow in the obvious manner.

When viewed from the domestic investor's point of view, a fixed–fixed cross-currency swap is straightforward, as each pair of coupons can be valued in the domestic cash numeraire, in which case they are just $\alpha_i^d C^d N^d$ and $\alpha_i^f C^f N^f S_t$ respectively, for the fixed–fixed currency swap, which can be interpreted as a strip of domestic coupons and a strip of FX forwards. The terminal exchange similarly can be viewed in the same way.

The same, regrettably, is not true for floating–floating cross-currency swaps because of the basis risk.

---

[1] Common conventions are ACT/360, ACT/365, 30/360 and ACT/ACT; see Stigum and Robinson (1996) for details.

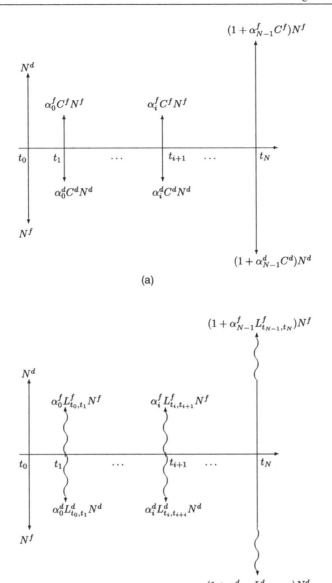

Figure 11.2   Cross-currency swaps: (a) fixed–fixed cross-currency swap; (b) floating–floating cross-currency swap

11.2   BASIS RISK

As well explained in Fruchard *et al.* (1995), Boenkost and Schmidt (2005) and Benhamou (2006), a basis swap is one where two streams of coupons, each consisting of floating rate payments (possibly in the same currency, e.g. 3M USD LIBOR versus 6M USD LIBOR, or possibly in separate currencies), are exchanged. A cross-currency swap in which floating rates of two different currencies are exchanged is therefore often known as a cross-currency basis swap. Such an instrument enables market participants to translate floating interest rate exposures from one currency into that of another currency. The market reflects in price terms both the relative supply and demand for floating coupons in various currencies, as well as concerns about the creditworthiness of the central bank in each of the two countries.

Creditworthiness is a major issue for basis swaps. Tuckman and Porfirio (2004) clearly make the point that since the time period between 3M floating USD LIBOR coupons is greater than that for 1M floating USD LIBOR coupons, 3M USD LIBOR should be adjusted with a spread to be fair against 1M USD LIBOR, for basis swap calculations. For LIBOR, which is calculated based on the interquartile mean of interbank rates offered by several (typically 8, 12 or 16) contributor banks, the creditworthiness of the banks is potentially as important, if not more, than the underlying sovereign risk for the country in question.

Tuckman and Porfirio (2004) take the standard interest rate parity argument, which relates the forward FX rate to today's spot rate plus the interest rate differential:

$$F_T = S_0 \frac{(1+y)^T}{(1+\tilde{y})^T}, \tag{11.1}$$

where y is the risk-free domestic interest rate applicable over T years but quoted annually and $\tilde{y}$ is the risk-free foreign interest rate (similarly applicable over T years but quoted annually).

Suppose we are working with 3M LIBOR payments in domestic and foreign respectively. Then (11.1) can be written as

$$F_T = S_0 \frac{(1+Y)^T}{(1+\tilde{Y})^T} \left[1 + X \frac{(1+Y)^T - 1}{R(1+Y)^T} \right], \tag{11.2}$$

where Y and $\tilde{Y}$ are the zero coupon swap rates in domestic and foreign economies respectively, R is the domestic par swap rate with quarterly fixed flows and X is a basis swap spread that makes 3M foreign LIBOR fair against coupons of 3M domestic LIBOR plus X.

This can be expressed as

$$F_T = S_0 \frac{(1+Y)^T \left[1 - b \dfrac{(1+Y)^T - 1}{R(1+Y)^T} \right]}{(1+\tilde{Y})^T \left[1 - \tilde{b} \dfrac{(1+\tilde{Y})^T - 1}{\tilde{R}(1+\tilde{Y})^T} \right]}, \tag{11.3}$$

where $\tilde{R}$ is the foreign par swap rate with quarterly fixed flows, b is the basis swap spread that ensures that a rolling position in the overnight domestic default-free rate plus b is fair against coupons of 3M domestic LIBOR and $\tilde{b}$ is the basis swap spread that ensures that a rolling position in the overnight foreign default-free rate plus $\tilde{b}$ is fair against coupons of 3M foreign LIBOR.

This provides a useful mechanism to relate the cross-currency basis swap spread X to the (single currency) basis swap spreads b and $\tilde{b}$ in each of the two issuance currencies.

Typical 5Y basis swap spreads as of September 2007 are shown in Table 11.1. Note that, even then, concerns about the strength of the Icelandic economy were clearly visible in the market. It should be noted that basis swap spreads are positive for AUD, NZD and CAD since the basis is between USD LIBOR and either bank bills (Australia or New Zealand) or banker's acceptances (Canada), which are collateralised and therefore less risky than LIBOR

Table 11.1 Typical basis swap spreads as of September 2007 (Source: Lehman Brothers)

EURUSD	−1.25 bp
GBPUSD	−2.25 bp
AUDUSD	+7.25 bp
NZDUSD	+5.25 bp
CADUSD	+6.00 bp
ISKUSD	−35 bp

style lending. The negative basis swaps for EUR, GBP and particularly ISK, however, showed definite concern about the banking systems in these economic areas as early as 2007.

The standard approach for dealing with basis swap adjustments in FX is the so-called 'two-curve approach', detailed in Chibane and Sheldon (2009), Section 2.1 of Boenkost and Schmidt (2005) and Bianchetti (2010), to which we refer the reader. Basically, this means that we use separate curves for discounting and forecasting.

11.3   FORWARD MEASURE

In shortdated FX, we typically adopt the domestic risk-neutral measure, which effectively means that we use $\mu_t = r_t^d - r_t^f$ as drift for the FX spot price process. This ensures that the continuously compounded foreign money market account, expressed in units of domestic currency, has the same expected appreciation as the continuously compounded domestic money market account, which we typically use as the numeraire.

The domestic money market account is not the only choice of domestic numeraire, of course. Another equally valid numeraire is the T-maturity domestic discount bond, which we denote as $P^d(t, T)$. Both cases are discussed thoroughly in Sections 7.4 and 7.5 of Rebonato (1996) respectively, in the case of interest rate derivatives.

Suppose we are attempting to price an equity derivative, in the domestic economy. As in Section 2.7.1, the domestic equity investor sees the equity S_t as the risky asset, driven by a $\mathbf{P}^d$ Brownian motion W_t, which at time t has the distribution

$$S_t = S_0 \exp\left(\sigma W_t + \left(\mu - \frac{1}{2}\sigma^2\right)t\right). \tag{11.4}$$

However, comparing this with the domestic discount bond $P^d(t, T)$, the risk-neutral investor expects the two assets to have the same expected returns. The ratio of these should therefore be a martingale. We have

$$Z_t^{(T;d)} = S_t / P^d(t, T),$$

where

$$S_t = S_0 \exp\left(\sigma W_t + \left(\mu - \frac{1}{2}\sigma^2\right)t\right)$$

and, consequently,

$$Z_t = S_0 \exp\left(\sigma W_t - \frac{1}{2}\sigma^2 t\right) \frac{\exp(\mu t)}{P^d(t, T)}.$$

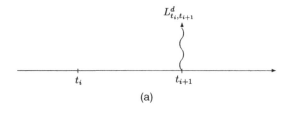

(a)

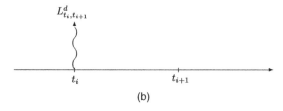

(b)

Figure 11.3 LIBOR floating cashflow diagrams: (a) standard LIBOR coupon; (b) LIBOR in arrears coupon

The Radon–Nikodym derivative relating the T-maturity forward measure to the domestic risk-neutral measure is therefore, as quoted in Section 4.1 of Pelsser (2000),

$$\frac{\mathrm{d}\mathbf{P}^{d;T}}{\mathrm{d}\mathbf{P}^d} = \frac{\exp\left(-\int_t^T r_s^d \, \mathrm{d}s\right)}{P^d(t, T)}. \tag{11.5}$$

11.4   LIBOR IN ARREARS

The uncertainty in interest rates requires models that describe stochastic discount factors over time intervals. By way of introduction to this, as a single currency example, we present the convexity correction required for valuation of a LIBOR in arrears swap. Even though this is a fixed income instrument rather than a foreign exchange instrument, the technique is one that should be familiar to longdated FX practitioners. Typically, LIBOR fixings are observed at the start of an interval and used to calculate the floating interest payments to be made at the *end* of the interval in question, as shown in Figure 11.3(a). However, as the quantity is known at the start of the interval, it could in fact be made earlier – at the start of the interval, as shown in Figure 11.3(b). This gives rise to the LIBOR in arrears swap, as discussed in Li and Raghavan (1996) and Section 14.3.3 of Hunt and Kennedy (2000). We consider only a single LIBOR in arrears coupon and extension to an entire swap follows naturally.

Suppose a sequence of increasing time points $t_0, \ldots, t_i, t_{i+1}, \ldots, t_N$ is provided and let us consider, without loss of generality, the time interval $[t_i, t_{i+1}]$. Let $L^d_{t_i, t_{i+1}}$ denote the (domestic) LIBOR rate fixed at time t_i and applicable over the time interval $[t_i, t_{i+1}]$. We also let α_i denote the daycount fraction over that time interval, which would be equal to $t_{i+1} - t_i$ were it not for the presence of calendar issues. Even though LIBOR rates for the $[t_i, t_{i+1}]$ interval are not determined until t_i, we denote the forward LIBOR rate observed at time $t \leq t_i$ by $L^d_{t_i, t_{i+1}}(t)$.

The forward LIBOR rates, being stochastic quantities, can be related using no-arbitrage arguments to stochastic discount factors. Suppose $P^d(t, t_i)$ denotes the price of the t_i maturity zero coupon bond at time t. Then we can either invest one unit of cash in a bond with maturity t_i, and roll it over at the prevailing LIBOR at t_i until t_{i+1}, or we can just invest the one unit of cash in a bond with maturity t_{i+1}.

Equating these two outcomes, we have

$$1/P^d(t, t_i)(1 + \alpha_i L^d_{t_i,t_{i+1}}(t)) = 1/P^d(t, t_{i+1}). \qquad (11.6)$$

Rearranging, we obtain

$$P^d(t, t_{i+1})(1 + \alpha_i L^d_{t_i,t_{i+1}}(t)) = P^d(t, t_i),$$

i.e.

$$P^d(t, t_{i+1}) + P^d(t, t_{i+1})\alpha_i L^d_{t_i,t_{i+1}}(t) = P^d(t, t_i),$$

which gives

$$L^d_{t_i,t_{i+1}}(t) = \frac{1}{\alpha_i}\frac{P^d(t, t_i) - P^d(t, t_{i+1})}{P^d(t, t_{i+1})}. \qquad (11.7)$$

Under the t_{i+1} forward measure $\mathbf{P}^{d;t_{i+1}}$, the forward LIBOR process $L^d_{t_i,t_{i+1}}(t)$ is a martingale, and hence the $\mathbf{P}^{d;t_{i+1}}$ expectation is just the value at time $t = 0$, i.e.

$$\mathbf{E}^{d;t_{i+1}}[L^d_{t_i,t_{i+1}}(t_i)] = L^d_{t_i,t_{i+1}}(0).$$

What this means is that

$$V^{LIB} = P^d(0, t_{i+1})\mathbf{E}^{d;t_{i+1}}[L^d_{t_i,t_{i+1}}(t_i)] = P^d(0, t_{i+1})L^d_{t_i,t_{i+1}}(0)$$

is the accurate price for a regular LIBOR coupon.

Consider now the LIBOR in arrears coupon. We have

$$V^{LIA} = P^d(0, t_i)\mathbf{E}^{d;t_i}[L^d_{t_i,t_{i+1}}(t_i)].$$

This necessitates a change of measure adjustment. We need

$$V^{LIA} = P^d(t, t_i)\mathbf{E}^{d;t_{i+1}}\left[\frac{d\mathbf{P}^{d;t_i}}{d\mathbf{P}^{d;t_{i+1}}}L^d_{t_i,t_{i+1}}(t_i)\right].$$

Construction of the Radon–Nikodym derivative $d\mathbf{P}^{d;t_i}/d\mathbf{P}^{d;t_{i+1}}$ proceeds along the following lines. Following Pelsser (2000), we have

$$\frac{d\mathbf{P}^{d;t_i}}{d\mathbf{P}^{d;t_{i+1}}} = \frac{P^d(t_i, t_i)}{P^d(t_i, t_{i+1})}\frac{P^d(0, t_{i+1})}{P^d(0, t_i)}.$$

Using (11.6), we have

$$1 + \alpha_i L^d_{t_i,t_{i+1}}(t) = \frac{P^d(t, t_i)}{P^d(t, t_{i+1})}$$

and therefore

$$\frac{d\mathbf{P}^{d;t_i}}{d\mathbf{P}^{d;t_{i+1}}} = \frac{P^d(0, t_{i+1})}{P^d(0, t_i)}\left[1 + \alpha_i L^d_{t_i,t_{i+1}}(t_i)\right].$$

We need to construct

$$V^{LIA} = P^d(0, t_i)\mathbf{E}^{d;t_{i+1}}\left[\frac{P^d(0, t_{i+1})}{P^d(0, t_i)}\left(1 + \alpha_i L^d_{t_i,t_{i+1}}(t_i)\right) L^d_{t_i,t_{i+1}}(t_i)\right]$$

$$= P^d(0, t_{i+1})\mathbf{E}^{d;t_{i+1}}\left[L^d_{t_i,t_{i+1}}(t_i) + \alpha_i[L^d_{t_i,t_{i+1}}]^2(t_i)\right].$$

We know from the analysis above that

$$\mathbf{E}^{d;t_{i+1}}[L^d_{t_i,t_{i+1}}(t_i)] = L^d_{t_i,t_{i+1}}(0)$$

so we have

$$V^{LIA} = P^d(0, t_{i+1})\left(L^d_{t_i,t_{i+1}}(0) + \alpha_i \mathbf{E}^{d;t_{i+1}}\left[[L^d_{t_i,t_{i+1}}(t_i)]^2\right]\right).$$

It remains to calculate the second term in the parenthetic expression above. If we suppose that forward LIBOR rates are lognormally distributed under the t_{i+1} forward measure $\mathbf{P}^{d;t_{i+1}}$, i.e.

$$dL^d_{t_i,t_{i+1}}(t) = \sigma L^d_{t_i,t_{i+1}}(t)\, dW_t^{\mathbf{P}^{d;t_{i+1}}},$$

then this has solution

$$L^d_{t_i,t_{i+1}}(t) = L^d_{t_i,t_{i+1}}(0)\exp\left(\sigma W_t^{\mathbf{P}^{d;t_{i+1}}} - \frac{1}{2}\sigma^2 t\right) \tag{11.8}$$

and, after immediately recognising this to be a $\mathbf{P}^{d;t_{i+1}}$ exponential martingale, it is clear that the martingale condition $\mathbf{E}^{d;t_{i+1}}[L^d_{t_i,t_{i+1}}(t)] = L^d_{t_i,t_{i+1}}(0)$ is satisfied.

Considering $\mathbf{E}^{d;t_{i+1}}[[L^d_{t_i,t_{i+1}}]^2(t)]$, we can write the square of (11.8) as

$$[L^d_{t_i,t_{i+1}}(t)]^2 = [L^d_{t_i,t_{i+1}}(0)]^2\exp\left(2\sigma W_t^{\mathbf{P}^{d;t_{i+1}}} - \sigma^2 t\right). \tag{11.9}$$

Let $\hat{\sigma} = 2\sigma$ and (11.9) simplifies to

$$[L^d_{t_i,t_{i+1}}(t)]^2 = [L^d_{t_i,t_{i+1}}(0)]^2\exp\left(\hat{\sigma} W_t^{\mathbf{P}^{d;t_{i+1}}} - \frac{1}{4}\hat{\sigma}^2 t\right)$$

$$= [L^d_{t_i,t_{i+1}}(0)]^2\exp\left(\hat{\sigma} W_t^{\mathbf{P}^{d;t_{i+1}}} - \frac{1}{2}\hat{\sigma}^2 t\right)\exp\left(\frac{1}{2}\hat{\sigma}^2 t\right). \tag{11.10}$$

Since $\exp\left(\frac{1}{2}\hat{\sigma}^2 t\right) = \exp(\sigma^2 t)$, this gives us

$$\mathbf{E}^{d;t_{i+1}}\left[(L^d_{t_i,t_{i+1}}(t_i))^2\right] = (L^d_{t_i,t_{i+1}}(0))^2\exp(\sigma^2 t_i).$$

We thereby obtain

$$V^{LIA} = P(0, t_i)\frac{1}{1 + \alpha_i L_{t_i,t_{i+1}}(0)}\left[L_{t_i,t_{i+1}}(0) + \alpha_i L^2_{t_i,t_{i+1}}(0)\exp(\sigma^2 t_i)\right]$$

$$= P(0, t_i)L_{t_i,t_{i+1}}(0)\frac{1 + \alpha_i L_{t_i,t_{i+1}}(0)\exp(\sigma^2 t_i)}{1 + \alpha_i L_{t_i,t_{i+1}}(0)}$$

$$= P(0, t_i)\tilde{L},$$

where

$$\tilde{L} = L_{t_i,t_{i+1}}(0)\frac{1 + \alpha_i L_{t_i,t_{i+1}}(0)\exp(\sigma^2 t_i)}{1 + \alpha_i L_{t_i,t_{i+1}}(0)}. \tag{11.11}$$

The quotient above is the convexity correction for the LIBOR in arrears swap, as required.

11.5   TYPICAL LONGDATED FX PRODUCTS

11.5.1   Power reverse dual currency notes

For some currency pairs such as USDJPY and AUDJPY, exchange rates in the future tend, once we actually get to those future dates, to be closer to current spot levels than the forward rates observed today would predict. This is discussed in Tang and Li (2007) and Tan (2010), and indicates a decoupling between forecasting models and arbitrage-free models, which structures such as the power reverse dual currency (PRDC) note attempt to exploit for the gain of the speculative investor. See Jeffrey (2003), Rule *et al.* (2004) and Sippel and Ohkoshi (2002) for further discussion of these yield enhancement structures.

These pay enhanced coupons to a domestic JPY investor in the event that future exchange rates S_{T_i} at times T_i are closer to current levels of spot S_0 rather than the forward $F_{T_i} = S_0 D_{T_i}^f(0)/D_{T_i}^d(0)$.

The exact structure is determined by a sequence of coupons $\{T_1, \ldots, T_N\}$, typically a 30-year strip with semi-annual coupons, each coupon being of the form

$$V_{T_i} = \alpha_i \max \left(N^d \left(\frac{S_{T_i}}{S_0} C^f - C^d \right), 0 \right) \qquad (11.12)$$

and with redemption of principal at maturity. Notationwise, α_i is the accrual factor, approximately $1/2$ as these structures invariably have semi-annual coupons, C^f is the coupon in the foreign currency and C^d is the coupon in the domestic currency. N^d is the notional in domestic currency. Note that the coupon rates are quite unrelated to actual money market interest rates. Typical values for the coupons might be $C^f \approx 15\%$ and $C^d \approx 10\%$ – and in fact if those numbers were, say, 7.5 % and 5 % then the structure would be identical, except with effectively half the notional. It is the ratio between the coupon that matters, not the absolute levels.

In fact, we can write (11.12) as

$$V_{T_i} = \alpha_i \frac{N^d C^f}{S_0} [S_{T_i} - K]^+, \quad \text{with } K = S_0 \frac{C^d}{C^f},$$

from which we see that a PRDC structure is, fundamentally, nothing more than a strip of USD call/JPY put longdated FX European options.

The coupons are often capped and floored, at levels $C^{\max}$ and $C^{\min}$, in which case we can write

$$V_{T_i} = \alpha_i N^d \max \left(\min \left(\frac{S_{T_i}}{S_0} C^f - C^d, C^{\max} \right), C^{\min} \right), \qquad (11.13)$$

where, even without a floor on coupons, we still require $C^{\min} = 0$ to preserve positivity of V_{T_i}. PRDCs are commonly found with either callability, trigger features, or both. We mention these briefly.

Callable PRDCs

A PRDC is typically issued by a financial and bought by retail Japanese investors. As the price can otherwise be quite expensive, the issuing bank often retains the right to call the structure, i.e. a cancellation feature is effective on a predefined set of cancellation dates.

Trigger PRDCs

Another way to make a PRDC less expensive is for it to have a knock-out feature, similar to those in Chapter 8, but with discrete barriers. Clearly, if a PRDC terminates early, either due to cancellation or triggering out, the principal is repaid at that date and the structure terminates therewith.

Chooser PRDCs

PRDCs take advantage of the retail investor being willing to bet, effectively, that the yen will not appreciate against the US dollar. If an investor is willing to take a stronger directional view, that the yen will not appreciate against two currencies (typically USD and AUD), then an improved coupon structure can be embedded in such a structure.

From the issuer's point of view, this means that they (not the PRDC holder, but the issuer) have the right to choose which of the exotic structured coupons to pay. Obviously they will choose the lesser, which is in their favour. As a result, we have

$$V_{T_i} = \alpha_i N^d \max \left(\min \left(\frac{S_{T_i}^{(1)}}{S_0^{(1)}} C^{f;1}, \frac{S_{T_i}^{(2)}}{S_0^{(2)}} C^{f;2} - C^d, C^{\max} \right), C^{\min} \right). \tag{11.14}$$

The first two of these features (KO and Bermudan features) can be handled using a three-factor PDE approach, such as presented in Chapter 7. The third requires extension to beyond a three-factor model and leaves little option but to resort to American style Monte Carlo techniques.

11.5.2 FX target redemption notes

Another frequently encountered longdated product is the FX target accrual reception note (FX-TARN). Whereas the PRDC is effectively a strip of FX options, which we see is basically analogous to a fixed–fixed cross-currency swap, the FX-TARN introduces linkage to floating rate benchmarks in the funding currency.

From the point of view of counterparty A, until the target level is attained (in which case the structure is said to 'tarn out'), they pay and receive P_i and R_i respectively:

$$P_i = \alpha_i N^d C_i, \tag{11.15a}$$

$$R_i = \alpha_{T_i}^d L_{T_i, T_{i+1}}^d + x, \tag{11.15b}$$

where the coupon payments are generally predetermined at an attractive level for an initial period such as the first coupon or the first year (e.g. $C_1 = 10\%$ and potentially $C_2 = 10\%$ also) and the subsequent structured coupons C_i, possibly involving a cap $C^{\max}$, take effect after the first fixing:

$$C_i = \min[C^d (S_{T_i} - K)^+, C^{\max}], \tag{11.15c}$$

where K is now specified exogenously, rather than inferred from foreign and domestic coupons.

If we denote the target level by Q, then the structure terminates immediately after the coupon N is paid for which $\sum_{i=1}^{N} C_i \geq Q$, and at that point the principal is repaid. Clearly there are two possibilities: one is the case where the entire final coupon P_i is paid, the other is the case where only that portion of P_i is paid that makes $\sum_{i=1}^{N} C_i = Q$. One should check the termsheet for the avoidance of doubt, but the case where the final coupon is paid in full is more commonplace – and, unfortunately, more difficult to handle using Q_t as an auxiliary state variable following the approach of Chapter 9, as Q_t is no longer capped at Q but can overshoot on the final coupon.

11.5.3   Effect on USDJPY volatility smile

The presence of these products in volume in the domestic Japanese market has an interesting effect, in that it creates a one-sided market for out-of-the-money USDJPY puts for banks to hedge the spot FX risk attached to these products. The demand for option protection on USDJPY falling to levels such as 80.00 and below is largely responsible for maintaining the steep volatility skews seen in currency pairs such as USDJPY and AUDJPY.

11.6   THE THREE-FACTOR MODEL

Section 11.4 above introduces the concept of valuation given uncertainty in the interest rate environment, but in foreign currency option pricing, as we have already seen, we have two interest rates to consider. This section introduces the valuation of longdated FX, where uncertainty in the interest rates must be considered as well as randomness in the FX spot process.

The model we consider below introduces Hull–White processes for the domestic and foreign short rate processes (Hull and White, 1993), together with a stochastic process for the spot FX process – either a term structure lognormal process or very possibly an instantaneous local volatility in order to permit FX skew (this is after all the *raison d'etre* for these yield enhancement products). Such three-factor models are described in the literature by Sippel and Ohkoshi (2002) and Piterbarg (2006b), but, as usual in the industry, the usage of such models predates their publication.

A standard three-factor model is one that combines one factor short rate processes for yield curves in domestic and foreign economies, with a lognormal process for the FX rate (quoted in domestic per foreign terms):

$$dS_t = (r_t^d - r_t^f)S_t \, dt + \sigma^{\text{fx}}(S_t, t)S_t \, dW_t^{(1;d)}, \tag{11.16a}$$

$$dr_t^d = (\theta_t^d - \kappa_t^d r_t^d) \, dt + \sigma_t^d \, dW_t^{(2;d)}, \tag{11.16b}$$

$$dr_t^f = (\theta_t^f - \kappa_t^f r_t^f) \, dt + \sigma_t^f \, dW_t^{(3;f)}. \tag{11.16c}$$

This system is clearly subject to three driving Brownian motions, but note that only the first two are driftless in the domestic risk-neutral measure – $W_t^{(3;f)}$ is driftless in the foreign risk-neutral measure, but not in the domestic risk-neutral measure. Consequently, even though r_t^f is untradeable from the longdated FX point of view, it still requires a quanto correction of the type introduced in Section 10.8, inferred using a similar Cholesky argument. We obtain

$$dW_t^{(1;f)} = dW_t^{(1;d)} - \rho_t^{fx;d} \sigma^{fx}(S_t, t) \, dt, \tag{11.17a}$$

$$dW_t^{(2;f)} = dW_t^{(2;d)} - \rho_t^{fx;d} \sigma^{fx}(S_t, t) \, dt, \tag{11.17b}$$

$$dW_t^{(3;f)} = dW_t^{(3;d)} - \rho_t^{fx;f} \sigma^{fx}(S_t, t) \, dt. \tag{11.17c}$$

Equation (11.17a) in particular is very reminiscent of (2.52).

We then have, as presented in Dang *et al.* (2010),

$$dS_t = (r_t^d - r_t^f) S_t \, dt + \sigma^{fx}(S_t, t) S_t \, dW_t^{(1;d)}, \tag{11.18a}$$

$$dr_t^d = (\theta_t^d - \kappa_t^d r_t^d) \, dt + \sigma_t^d \, dW_t^{(2;d)}, \tag{11.18b}$$

$$dr_t^f = \left[\theta_t^f - \kappa_t^f r_t^f - \rho_t^{fx,f} \sigma_t^f \sigma^{fx}(S_t, t) \right] dt + \sigma_t^f \, dW_t^{(3;d)}, \tag{11.18c}$$

where the Brownian motions are all with respect to the domestic risk-neutral measure, and are correlated with

$$< dW_t^{(1;d)}, dW_t^{(2;d)} > = \rho_t^{fx,d} \, dt,$$

$$< dW_t^{(1;d)}, dW_t^{(3;d)} > = \rho_t^{fx,f} \, dt, \tag{11.19}$$

$$< dW_t^{(2;d)}, dW_t^{(3;d)} > = \rho_t^{d,f} \, dt.$$

One can equivalently write (11.18a) in terms of logspot $x_t = \ln S_t$, using $\hat{\sigma}^{fx}(x, t) = \sigma^{fx}(e^x, t)$, as

$$dx_t = \left[r_t^d - r_t^f - \frac{1}{2} [\hat{\sigma}^{fx}(x, t)]^2 \right] dt + \hat{\sigma}^{fx}(x, t) \, dW_t^{(1;d)}. \tag{11.20}$$

Note that the FX volatility term $\sigma^{fx}(S_t, t)$, or equivalently $\hat{\sigma}^{fx}(x, t)$, permits either lognormal FX or local volatility, depending on whether this diffusion coefficient is homogeneous in the spatial coordinate or not.

The issue with models such as these is obtaining accurate levels for the mean reversion parameters and volatilities that suffice to reprice both the IR and FX markets respectively.

It is advantageous numerically to shift the mean reversion levels to zero by introducing offsets φ_t^d and φ_t^f, such that $r_t^d = y_t + \varphi_t^d$ and $r_t^f = z_t + \varphi_t^f$, having the desirable property that both y_t and z_t revert towards zero, i.e.

$$dy_t = -\kappa^d y_t \, dt + \sigma_t^d \, dW_t^{(2;d)}, \tag{11.21a}$$

$$dz_t = -\kappa^f z_t \, dt + \sigma_t^f \, dW_t^{(3;f)} \tag{11.21b}$$

or alternatively

$$dz_t = (-\kappa^f z_t - \rho_t^{\text{fx},f} \sigma_t^f \hat{\sigma}^{\text{fx}}(x, t)) \, dt + \sigma_t^f \, dW_t^{(3;d)}.$$ (11.21c)

We often presume that mean reversion rates are constant, though distinct for the two yield curve models. Generalising to time-dependent mean reversion rates is certainly feasible, though beyond the scope of this work – for this, we recommend a careful reading of Sections 17.3 and 17.4 of Hunt and Kennedy (2000), noting in particular that their SDE (17.10) permits an important representation of one-factor Vasicek–Hull–White interest rate dynamics in terms of driftless state variables M_{tT}, an approach that is very popular with interest rate practitioners. In general, we have

$$dx_t = \left[y_t - z_t + \varphi_t^d - \varphi_t^f - \frac{1}{2} [\sigma^{\text{fx}}(x_t, t)]^2 \right] dt + \sigma^{\text{fx}}(x_t, t) \, dW_t^{(1;d)},$$ (11.22a)

$$dy_t = -\kappa_t^d y_t \, dt + \sigma_t^d \, dW_t^{(2;d)},$$ (11.22b)

$$dz_t = \left[-\kappa_t^f z_t - \rho_t^{\text{fx},f} \sigma_t^f \sigma^{\text{fx}}(x_t, t) \right] dt + \sigma_t^f \, dW_t^{(3;d)},$$ (11.22c)

under the domestic risk neutral measure. Let us suppose that the domestic value of a derivative is given by $V(x, y, z, t)$. This admits the PDE representation

$$\frac{\partial V}{\partial t} + \left[\varphi_t^d + y - \varphi_t^f - z - \frac{1}{2} [\hat{\sigma}^{\text{fx}}(x, t)]^2 \right] \frac{\partial V}{\partial x} + \frac{1}{2} \left[\hat{\sigma}^{\text{fx}}(x, t) \right]^2 \frac{\partial^2 V}{\partial x^2}$$

$$- \kappa_t^d y \frac{\partial V}{\partial y} + \frac{1}{2} [\sigma_t^d]^2 \frac{\partial^2 V}{\partial y^2}$$

$$- \left[\kappa_t^f z + \rho_t^{\text{fx},f} \sigma_t^f \hat{\sigma}^{\text{fx}}(x, t) \right] \frac{\partial V}{\partial z} + \frac{1}{2} [\sigma_t^f]^2 \frac{\partial^2 V}{\partial z^2}$$

$$+ \rho_t^{\text{fx},d} \frac{\partial^2 V}{\partial x \partial y} + \rho_t^{\text{fx},f} \frac{\partial^2 V}{\partial x \partial z} + \rho_t^{d,f} \frac{\partial^2 V}{\partial y \partial z}$$

$$- (y + \varphi_t^d) V = 0.$$ (11.23)

11.7   INTEREST RATE CALIBRATION OF THE THREE-FACTOR MODEL

This proceeds in two parts: determination of the drifts required to recover zero coupon bond prices and the Hull–White volatilities required to match the prices of convex instruments in interest rate markets, such as caplets and swaptions.

11.7.1   Determination of drifts

Assuming constant mean reversion rates κ^d and κ^f, the drifts φ_t^d and φ_t^f can be obtained through no-arbitrage requirements, such as presented in the appendix of Tan (2010).

We require

$$P^d(0, T) = \mathbf{E}^d \left[\exp \left(- \int_0^T r_t^d \, dt \right) \right]$$

$$= \exp \left(- \int_0^T \varphi_t^d \, dt \right) \mathbf{E}^d \left[\exp \left(- \int_0^T \int_0^t \sigma_u^d e^{\kappa^d(u-t)} r_t^d \, dW_u^{(2;d)} \, dt \right) \right]$$

$$= \exp \left(- \int_0^T \varphi_t^d \, dt \right) \mathbf{E}^d \left[\exp \left(- \int_0^T \sigma_u^d \int_u^T e^{\kappa^d(u-t)} \, dt \, dW_u^{(2;d)} \right) \right]$$

$$= \exp \left(- \int_0^T \varphi_t^d \, dt \right) \mathbf{E}^d \left[\exp \left(- \int_0^T \frac{1}{\kappa^d} \sigma_u^d (1 - e^{\kappa^d(u-t)}) \, dW_u^{(2;d)} \right) \right]$$

$$= \exp \left(- \int_0^T \varphi_t^d \, dt + \frac{1}{2} \int_0^T \frac{1}{[\kappa^d]^2} (\sigma_u^d)^2 (1 - e^{\kappa^d(u-T)})^2 \, du \right).$$

This yields

$$\int_0^T \varphi_t^d \, dt = - \ln P^d(0, T) + \frac{1}{2} \int_0^T \frac{1}{[\kappa^d]^2} (\sigma_u^d)^2 (1 - e^{\kappa^d(u-T)})^2 \, du \qquad (11.24)$$

and hence

$$\varphi_t^d = - \frac{\partial}{\partial t} \left[\ln P^d(0, t) \right] + \int_0^t \frac{1}{\kappa^d} (\sigma_u^d)^2 (1 - e^{\kappa^d(u-t)}) e^{\kappa^d(u-t)} \, du. \qquad (11.25)$$

Similar analysis, which can be performed in the domestic risk-neutral measure with the quanto correction included, or natively in the foreign risk-neutral measure, yields

$$\varphi_t^f = - \frac{\partial}{\partial t} \left[\ln P^f(0, t) \right] + \int_0^t \frac{1}{\kappa^f} (\sigma_u^f)^2 (1 - e^{\kappa^f(u-t)}) e^{\kappa^f(u-t)} \, du. \qquad (11.26)$$

11.7.2 Determination of Hull–White volatilities

Note that while drift parameters φ_t^d and φ_t^f can be ascertained from the traded price of zero coupon bonds, the Hull–White volatilities σ_u^d and σ_u^f require calibration to interest rate instruments. This is a vast area of discussion and expertise in itself and well beyond the scope of this chapter; we refer the reader to the excellent books cited at the beginning of this chapter. We merely state for now that a common technique is calibration to coterminal swaptions, where one uses Itô's lemma to transform the short rate process r_t into one for discount bonds $P(t, T)$, construct the process for the swap rate from these discount bonds and employ a common 'drift freeze' technique, supposing that prices today for discount bonds to be valid for purposes of inference of swap volatilities. The argument, in the case of the domestic currency, is as follows.

For discount bonds, denoting $P(t, T) = P_d(t, T)$ in this section only, we know that

$$\frac{dP(t, T)}{P(t, T)} = - \frac{1}{\kappa^d} (1 - e^{\kappa^d(t-T)}) \, dy_t + [\cdots] \, dt, \qquad (11.27)$$

where we can neglect the drift term for now. Swap rates are defined by

$$S_t = \frac{P(t, T_0) - P(t, T_N)}{\sum_{i=1}^N \alpha_i^d P(t, T_i)}, \qquad (11.28)$$

which allows the differential to be expressed, using (11.27) as

$$
dS_t = \frac{dP(t, T_0) - dP(t, T_N)}{\sum_{i=1}^{N} \alpha_i^d P(t, T_i)} - \frac{P(t, T_0) - P(t, T_N)}{\left(\sum_{i=1}^{N} \alpha_i^d P(t, T_i)\right)^2} \sum_{i=1}^{N} \alpha_i^d dP(t, T_i) + [\cdots] dt
$$

$$
= \frac{\sigma_t^d}{\alpha_i^d P(t, T_i)} \left(-P(t, T_0)(1 - e^{\kappa^d(t-T_0)}) + P(t, T_N)(1 - e^{\kappa^d(t-T_0)}) \right.
$$

$$
\left. + S_t \sum_{i=1}^{N} \alpha_i^d P(t, T_i)(1 - e^{\kappa^d(t-T_i)}) \right) dW_t^{(2;d)} + [\cdots] dt.
$$

The drift freeze assumption involves replacing $P(t, T.)$ with $P(0, T.)$ in the above expression, obtaining

$$
dS_t \approx \frac{\sigma_t^d}{\alpha_i^d P(t, T_i)} \left(-P(0, T_0)(1 - e^{\kappa^d(t-T_0)}) + P(0, T_N)(1 - e^{\kappa^d(t-T_0)}) \right.
$$

$$
\left. + S_t \sum_{i=1}^{N} \alpha_i^d P(0, T_i)(1 - e^{\kappa^d(t-T_i)}) \right) dW_t^{(2;d)} + [\cdots] dt,
$$

which yields

$$
\sigma_{\mathcal{S}}^2 \approx \frac{1}{T} \int_0^T \left[\frac{\sigma_t^d}{\alpha_i^d P(t, T_i)} \left(-P(0, T_0)(1 - e^{\kappa^d(t-T_0)}) + P(0, T_N)(1 - e^{\kappa^d(t-T_0)}) \right. \right.
$$

$$
\left. \left. + S_t \sum_{i=1}^{N} \alpha_i^d P(0, T_i)(1 - e^{\kappa^d(t-T_i)}) \right) \right]^2 dt
$$

as an effective volatility that can be used in a typical Black swaption pricer, such as presented in Brace *et al.* (2001). The functional form for σ_t^d can be estimated using a bootstrapping technique, given a succession of swaptions for a calibration procedure.

11.8   SPOT FX CALIBRATION OF THE THREE-FACTOR MODEL

If we have knowledge of the interest rate volatilities, then we can attempt to determine values for the spot FX volatility $\sigma^{fx}(t)$ that are consistent with the term structure of implied volatility $\sigma_{3t}(t)$. In practice, we are generally able to access IR calibration parameters from other systems in the bank – we refer the reader to Chapter 17 of Hunt and Kennedy (2000) for a relevant discussion of how this might be realised.

Consequently, the calibration is just effectively a forward bootstrap – we assume that correlations in the three-factor model are provided and then for each implied volatility tenor t_i we attempt to construct $\sigma_{3t}^2(s)$, which recovers the implied volatility by constructing $\sigma_{fx}(t)$. One can think of this as the instantaneous spot FX volatility that is required, in conjunction with the interest rate uncertainty, to match the market prices (expressed in implied volatility terms) for FX Europeans.

11.8.1   FX vanillas with lognormal spot FX

The stochastic dynamics of discount bonds similarly can be expressed as

$$\frac{dP^d(t,T)}{P^d(t,T)} = r_t^d \, dt - \tilde{\sigma}_t^{d;T} \, dW_t^{(2;d)},$$
(11.29a)

$$\frac{dP^f(t,T)}{P^f(t,T)} = (r_t^f + \rho_t^{\mathrm{fx},f} \tilde{\sigma}_t^{f;T} \sigma^{\mathrm{fx}}(x_t,t)) \, dt - \tilde{\sigma}_t^{f;T} \, dW_t^{(3;d)},$$
(11.29b)

where we use $\tilde{\sigma}_t^{d;T}$ and $\tilde{\sigma}_t^{f;T}$ to denote domestic and foreign bond volatility respectively. Note the sign change of the Brownian motions, as positive increments in the short rate must lead to decreases in the prices of fixed income instruments such as discount bonds.

Recall from (2.67) the formula expressing the price of an FX European in terms of the forward, in the absence of any local volatility. We can use the forward measure approach to adapt this formula to price Europeans in the presence of interest rate uncertainty and correlation structure within the three-factor model when the FX volatility $\sigma^{\mathrm{fx}}(S_t, t) = \sigma^{\mathrm{fx}}(t)$ is presumed to be only time dependent. Use

$$F_T = S_t \frac{P^f(t,T)}{P^d(t,T)}$$

and note that we can use (11.29) to obtain

$$V_0 = \omega \Big(S_0 P^f(0,T) N(\omega d_1) - K P^d(0,T) N(\omega d_2) \Big),$$
(11.30)

where

$$d_{1,2} = \frac{\ln\left(\frac{S_0 P^f(0,T)}{K P^d(0,T)}\right) \pm \frac{1}{2} \int_0^T \sigma_{3f}^2(s) \, ds}{\sqrt{\int_0^T \sigma_{3f}^2(s) \, ds}}$$
(11.31)

using

$$\sigma_{3f}^2(t) = [\sigma^{\mathrm{fx}}(t)]^2 + [\tilde{\sigma}_t^{d;T}]^2 + [\tilde{\sigma}_t^{f;T}]^2 - 2\rho^{\mathrm{fx},d} \sigma^{\mathrm{fx}}(t) \tilde{\sigma}_t^{d;T}$$
$$+ 2\rho^{\mathrm{fx},f} \sigma^{\mathrm{fx}}(t) \tilde{\sigma}_t^{f;T} - 2\rho^{d,f} \sigma^d(t) \tilde{\sigma}_t^{d;T} \tilde{\sigma}_t^{f;T}.$$
(11.32)

Note that, even though bond volatilities $\tilde{\sigma}_t^{d;T}$ and $\tilde{\sigma}_t^{f;T}$ go to zero as $t \to T$ due to the 'pull to par', we have

$$\sigma_{3f}^2(t) > \sigma^{\mathrm{fx}}(t)$$

(and particularly so if t is large) due to the combined effects of spot FX volatility and interest rate volatility. This goes a long way to explaining the long end of the USDJPY volatility term structure, for example. It also provides some constraints on what sort of values for correlations $\{\rho^{\mathrm{fx},d}, \rho^{\mathrm{fx},f}, \rho^{d,f}\}$ are plausible.

Assume that the correlations between the Brownian motions are constant. In terms of implied parameters to expiry and the Hull–White model, we have

$$\log\left(\frac{S_T}{S_0}\right) = \int_0^T \left(r_t^d - r_t^f - \frac{1}{2}[\sigma^{\mathrm{fx}}(t)]^2\right)dt + \int_0^T \sigma^{\mathrm{fx}}(t)\,dW_t^{(1;d)}$$

$$= \int_0^T (\varphi_t^d - \varphi_t^f)\,dt + \int_0^T \frac{1}{\kappa^d}\sigma_t^d(1 - e^{\kappa^d(u-T)})\,dW_u^{(2;d)}$$

$$+ \rho_{\mathrm{fx},f}\int_0^T \frac{1}{\kappa^f}\sigma_t^f \sigma^{\mathrm{fx}}(u)(1 - e^{\kappa^f(u-T)})\,du$$

$$- \int_0^T \frac{1}{\kappa^f}\sigma_t^f(1 - e^{\kappa^f(u-T)})\,dW_u^{(3;d)}$$

$$- \frac{1}{2}\int_0^T [\sigma^{\mathrm{fx}}(u)]^2\,du + \int_0^T \sigma^{\mathrm{fx}}(u)\,dW_u^{(1;d)},$$

which upon examination of the quadratic variation, and taking into account the correlation structure of the Brownian motions, gives an equation for FX implied volatility $\sigma_{\mathrm{imp}}(T)$:

$$[\sigma_{\mathrm{imp}}(T)]^2 T = \int_0^T \left(\frac{1}{\kappa^d}\sigma_t^d(1 - e^{\kappa^d(u-T)})\right)^2 + \int_0^T \left(\frac{1}{\kappa^f}\sigma_t^f(1 - e^{\kappa^f(u-T)})\right)^2$$

$$- 2\rho^{d,f}\int_0^T \frac{\sigma_t^d \sigma_t^f}{\kappa^d \kappa^f}(1 - e^{\kappa^d(u-T)})(1 - e^{\kappa^f(u-T)})\,du$$

$$+ 2\rho^{\mathrm{fx},d}\int_0^T \frac{\sigma_t^d \sigma^{\mathrm{fx}}(u)}{\kappa^d}(1 - e^{\kappa^d(u-T)})\,du$$

$$- 2\rho^{\mathrm{fx},f}\int_0^T \frac{\sigma_t^f \sigma^{\mathrm{fx}}(u)}{\kappa^f}(1 - e^{\kappa^f(u-T)})\,du$$

$$+ \int_0^T [\sigma^{\mathrm{fx}}(u)]^2\,du$$

As $\sigma_{\mathrm{imp}}(T)$ values are known from the FX options market and the Hull–White parameters can be assumed to be known by calibration, the volatility $\sigma^{\mathrm{fx}}(u)$ for the spot FX process S_t can be obtained by bootstrapping.

11.8.2 FX vanillas with CEV local volatility

An important method commonly used for introducing local volatility into longdated FX models, presented by Piterbarg (2005a), presumes a CEV specification for local volatility, as in Section 5.8. With such a model, the $\sigma^{\mathrm{fx}}(S_t, t)$ in (11.18a) is expressible as

$$\sigma^{\mathrm{fx}}(S_t, t) = \sigma^{\mathrm{fx;atm}}(t)\left(\frac{S_t}{L_t}\right)^{\beta_t - 1} \tag{11.33}$$

for scale parameters L_t, which are related to the FX forward curve.

In the paper, a bootstrapping algorithm is presented, which enables construction of skew parameters β_t. We refer the reader to the original source for discussion of this method.

11.8.3   FX vanillas with Dupire local volatility

A fuller, but less numerically stable approach, is obtained by appealing to the forward induction approach seen in Chapter 6. Suppose, similarly to Section 2.11, that the present value of a call option with strike K and time to expiry T is given by

$$C(K, T) = \mathbf{E}^d \left[e^{-\int_0^T r_s^d \, ds} (S_T - K)^+ \right] = \mathbf{E}^d \left[C_T \right], \tag{11.34a}$$

where

$$C_T = e^{-\int_0^T r_s^d \, ds} (S_T - K)^+. \tag{11.34b}$$

Note that due to the stochasticity of the interest rates, we can no longer take the discount factor out of the expectation. Denote the (domestic) stochastic discount factor by

$$D_T^d = e^{-\int_0^T r_s^d \, ds}$$

so that $C_T = D_T^d (S_T - K)^+ = D_T^d V_T$ with $V_T = (S_T - K)^+$.

Consider the time evolution of the stochastic process C_t, depending on the spot rate S_t, the domestic short rate r_t^d (or alternatively the stochastic discount factor D_t^d) and, implicitly, the strike K, between $t = 0$ and $t = T$. We can write

$$\begin{aligned} dC_t &= d[D_t^d V_t] \\ &= V_t dD_t^d + D_t^d dV_t + < dD_t^d, dV_t >, \end{aligned}$$

from which it is clear, upon making the observation

$$dD_t^d = -r_t^d D_t^d \, dt,$$

$$dV_t = \mathbf{1}_{\{S_t \geq K\}} \, dS_t + \frac{1}{2} [\sigma^{\mathrm{fx}}(S_t, t)]^2 S_t^2 \delta_{\{S_t = K\}} \, dt.$$

that $< dD_t^d, dV_t > = 0$, leaving

$$\begin{aligned} dC_t &= d[D_t^d V_t] \\ &= V_t dD_t^d + D_t^d dV_t \\ &= V_t(-r_t^d D_t^d \, dt) + D_t^d \left[\mathbf{1}_{\{S_t \geq K\}} \, dS_t + \frac{1}{2} [\sigma^{\mathrm{fx}}(S_t, t)]^2 S_t^2 \delta_{\{S_t = K\}} \, dt \right] \\ &= -r_t^d D_t^d V_t \, dt + D_t^d \left[\mathbf{1}_{\{S_t \geq K\}} \left((r_t^d - r_t^f) S_t \, dt + \sigma^{\mathrm{fx}}(S_t, t) S_t \, dW_t^{(1;d)} \right) \right. \\ &\qquad\qquad \left. + \frac{1}{2} [\sigma^{\mathrm{fx}}(S_t, t)]^2 S_t^2 \delta_{\{S_t = K\}} \, dt \right] \\ &= -r_t^d D_t^d V_t \, dt + D_t^d \left[\mathbf{1}_{\{S_t \geq K\}} S_t \left((r_t^d - r_t^f) \, dt + \sigma^{\mathrm{fx}}(S_t, t) \, dW_t^{(1;d)} \right) \right. \\ &\qquad\qquad \left. + \frac{1}{2} [\sigma^{\mathrm{fx}}(S_t, t)]^2 S_t^2 \delta_{\{S_t = K\}} \, dt \right]. \end{aligned}$$

We now use the relation $[S_t - K]^+ = S_t \mathbf{1}_{\{S_t \geq K\}} - K \mathbf{1}_{\{S_t \geq K\}}$ to make the substitution

$$\mathbf{1}_{\{S_t \geq K\}} S_t = [S_t - K]^+ + K \mathbf{1}_{\{S_t \geq K\}} = V_t + K \mathbf{1}_{\{S_t \geq K\}},$$

thereby obtaining

$$dC_t = -r_t^d D_t^d V_t \, dt + D_t^d (V_t + K \mathbf{1}_{\{S_t \geq K\}})(r_t^d - r_t^f) \, dt$$

$$+ D_t^d \mathbf{1}_{\{S_t \geq K\}} S_t \sigma^{\mathrm{fx}}(S_t, t) \, dW_t^{(1;d)} + \frac{1}{2} D_t^d [\sigma^{\mathrm{fx}}(S_t, t)]^2 S_t^2 \delta_{\{S_t = K\}} \, dt$$

$$= D_t^d \left[-r_t^f V_t + K \mathbf{1}_{\{S_t \geq K\}}(r_t^d - r_t^f) + \frac{1}{2} [\sigma^{\mathrm{fx}}(S_t, t)]^2 S_t^2 \delta_{\{S_t = K\}} \right] dt$$

$$+ D_t^d \mathbf{1}_{\{S_t \geq K\}} S_t \sigma^{\mathrm{fx}}(S_t, t) \, dW_t^{(1;d)}.$$

Taking the expectation in the $\mathbf{P}^d$ measure, one obtains

$$\mathbf{E}^d[dC_t] = \mathbf{E}^d \left[D_t^d \left(-r_t^f V_t + (V_t + K \mathbf{1}_{\{S_t \geq K\}})(r_t^d - r_t^f) + \frac{1}{2} [\sigma^{\mathrm{fx}}(S_t, t)]^2 S_t^2 \delta_{\{S_t = K\}} \right) dt \right]$$

since the $dW_t^{(1;d)}$ term vanishes within the expectation of a stochastic integral.

We therefore have

$$d\mathbf{E}^d[C_t] = -\mathbf{E}^d[r_t^f D_t^d V_t] \, dt + K \mathbf{E}^d \left[D_t^d \mathbf{1}_{\{S_t \geq K\}}(r_t^d - r_t^f) \right] dt,$$

$$+ \frac{1}{2} \mathbf{E}^d \left[D_t^d [\sigma^{\mathrm{fx}}(S_t, t)]^2 S_t^2 \delta_{\{S_t = K\}} \right] dt.$$

which can be written, since $V_T = (S_T - K)^+$, as

$$\frac{\partial C(K, T)}{\partial T} = -\mathbf{E}^d[r_T^f D_T^d (S_T - K)^+] + K \mathbf{E}^d \left[D_T^d \mathbf{1}_{\{S_T \geq K\}}(r_T^d - r_T^f) \right]$$

$$+ \frac{1}{2} \mathbf{E}^d \left[D_T^d [\sigma^{\mathrm{fx}}(S_T, T)]^2 S_T^2 \delta_{\{S_T = K\}} \right]. \tag{11.35}$$

The final term in (11.35) admits the reduction

$$\mathbf{E}^d \left[D_T^d [\sigma^{\mathrm{fx}}(S_T, T)]^2 S_T^2 \delta_{\{S_T = K\}} \right] = [\sigma^{\mathrm{fx}}(K, T)]^2 K^2 \frac{\partial^2 C}{\partial K^2} \tag{11.36}$$

and direct substitution of (11.36) into (11.35) enables the effective local volatility to be expressed simply as

$$[\sigma^{\mathrm{fx}}(K, T)]^2 = \frac{\partial C / \partial T + \mathbf{E}^d[r_T^f D_T^d (S_T - K)^+] - K \mathbf{E}^d \left[D_T^d \mathbf{1}_{\{S_T \geq K\}}(r_T^d - r_T^f) \right]}{\frac{1}{2} K^2 \partial^2 C / \partial K^2}. \tag{11.37}$$

Note that if interest rates are deterministic, then (11.37) reduces to (5.28), as one would expect.

Inference of the spot FX local volatility $\sigma^{\mathrm{fx}}(S, t)$ proceeds analogously to the way we determined $A(S, t)$ in Section 6.8. Once again we take in as inputs the implied volatility structure for traded FX vanilla options and write the forward Fokker–Planck equation (this time in three state variables), which one can derive using the same technique as Section 6.8.2, similarly using the machinery from Section 5.2.2.

Having obtained such a Fokker–Planck equation and a numerical method to allow it to be solved forward in time, the final two terms in the numerator of (11.37) are obtained at each timeslice by integration against forward transition probabilities, which describe the joint distribution of the three state variables at forward times. In such a manner, we can attempt reconstruction of a spot FX local volatility surface which, in conjunction with Hull–White processes for domestic and foreign yield curves, recovers the prices of traded FX vanillas, including skew.

11.9   CONCLUSION

It is apt that this book finishes at the end of the longdated FX chapter. Having started with relatively few prerequisites on the part of the reader, we have covered a lot of ground.

Starting with standard material such as derivation of the Black–Scholes equation and obtaining the closed-form solution for European options by appealing to risk-neutral probabilities $\mathbf{P}^d(S_T \geq K)$ and $\mathbf{P}^f(S_T \geq K)$, I have tried to put this into an FX framework from the very beginning and introduce concepts of measure change relating domestic and foreign measures, in a way that extends to quantos, multicurrency options and even longdated FX options.

First and second generation products have been covered, together with the augmented state variable technique. Numerical methods for derivative pricing have been introduced, and I have given you some practical suggestions – nonuniform meshes for greater efficiency with PDEs, continuous barrier monitoring techniques for Monte Carlo, barrier bending, and so on.

Stochastic volatility has been introduced, together with the characteristic function technique that can be used as part of the calibration procedure, and a reasonably thorough discussion of the Feller condition and why it troubles FX quants so much.

We've discussed local volatility, which we saw is directly related to the Dupire formula, and can be used to obtain local volatility contributions for LSV models. Finally, the Dupire analysis from Chapter 5 and the Fokker–Planck bootstrap from Chapter 6 have come back into view right at the end of the book, where we've taken these ideas and extended them to describe a three-factor longdated FX model with skew.

I hope you agree that it was an interesting journey.

References

Andersen, L. B. G. (2007) Efficient Simulation of the Heston Stochastic Volatility Model (Version: 23 January 2007). http://ssrn.com/abstract=946405

Andersen, L. B. G. and Brotherton-Ratcliffe, R. (1998) The Equity Option Volatility Smile: An Implicit Finite-Difference Approach. *Journal of Computational Finance*, Vols 1–3, 1: 5–38.

Andersen, L. B. G. and Piterbarg, V. (2010) *Interest Rate Modeling*. Atlantic Financial Press, Vols 1–3.

Andersen, T. G., Bollerslev, T., Diebold, F. X. and Vega, C. (2003) Micro Effects of Macro Announcements: Real-Time Price Discovery in Foreign Exchange. *American Economic Review*, 93 (1): 38–62.

Antonov, A. and Misirpashaev, T. (2006) Markovian Projection onto a Displaced Diffusion: Generic Formulas with Applications. http://www.ssrn.com/abstract=937860

Bachelier, L. (1900) Théorie de la Spéculation. *Annales Scientifiques de l'École Normale Supérieure*, 3 (17): 21–86.

Badescu, A., Mekki, H. B., Gashaw, A. F., Hua, Y., Molyboga, M., Neoclous, T. and Petratchenko, Y. (2002) Price Pseudo-Variance, Pseudo-Covariance, Pseudo-Volatility and Pseudo-Correlation Swaps. In *Analytical Closed Forms*. Proceedings of the Sixth PIMS Industrial Problems Solving Workshop, Vancouver, PIMS University of British Columbia, 2002: pp. 27–37.

Bain, A. (2009) Stochastic Calculus (Version: 25 May 2009). http://www.chiark.greenend.org.uk/~alanb/

Bakshi, G., Cao, C. and Chen, Z. (1997) Empirical Performance of Alternative Option Pricing Models. *Journal of Finance*, 52: 2003–2049.

Bates, D. S. (1996) Jumps and Stochastic Volatility: Exchange Rate Processes Implicit in Deutsche Mark Options. *The Review of Financial Studies*, 9: 69–107.

Baxter, M. and Rennie, A. (1996) *Financial Calculus: An Introduction to Derivative Pricing*. Cambridge University Press, Cambridge.

Becker, C. and Wystup, U. (2005) On the Cost of Delayed Currency Fixing Announcements. HfB Working Paper, Center for Practical Quantitative Finance, vol. 3. www.frankfurt-school.de/dms/publications-cqf/CPQF_Arbeits3/CPQF_Arbeits3.pdf

Benaim, S., Friz, P. and Lee, R. (2008) On the Black–Scholes Implied Volatility at Extreme Strikes. http://www.math.uchicago.edu/~rl/BFL2008v5.pdf

Benhamou, E. (2006) Swaps: Basis Swaps. In P. Moles (ed.), *Encyclopedia of Financial Engineering and Risk Management*. Fitzroy Dearborn, London. http://www.ericbenhamou.net/documents/Encyclo/swaps%20basis%20swaps.pdf

Benhamou, E., Gobet, E. and Miri, M. (2009) Time Dependent Heston Model. http://www.ssrn.com/abstract=1367955

Bhansali, V. (1998) *Pricing and Managing Exotic and Hybrid Options*. McGraw-Hill, New York.

Bianchetti, M. (2010) Two Curves, One Price: Pricing and Hedging Interest Rate Derivatives Decoupling Forwarding and Discounting Curves (Version: 11 January 2010). http://www.ssrn.com/abstract=1334356.

Bingham, N. H. and Kiesel, R. (1998) *Risk-Neutral Valuation: Pricing and Hedging of Financial Derivatives*. Springer, London.

Black, F. (1976) The Pricing of Commodity Contracts. *Journal of Financial Economics*, 3: 167–179.

Black, F. and Scholes, M. (1973) The Pricing of Options and Corporate Liabilities. *Journal of Political Economy*, 81(3): 637–659.

Boenkost, W. and Schmidt, W. M. (2005) Cross Currency Swap Valuation, HfB Working Paper, Center for Practical Quantitative Finance, vol. 2. www.frankfurt-school.de/dms/publications-cqf/CPQF_Arbeits2/CPQF_Arbeits2.pdf

Brace, A., Dun, T. and Barton, G. (2001) Towards a Central Interest Rate Model. In E. Jouini, J. Cvitavic and M. Musiela (eds), *Option Pricing, Interest Rates and Risk Management* (Handbooks in Mathematical Finance). Cambridge University Press, Cambridge.

Breeden, D. T. and Litzenberger, R. H. (1978) Prices of State-Contingent Claims Implicit in Option Prices. *The Journal of Business*, 51(4), 621–651.

Brigo, D. and Mercurio, F. (2006) *Interest Rate Models: Theory and Practice: With Smile, Inflation and Credit*, 2nd edition. Springer, Berlin.

Broadie, M., Glasserman, P. and Kou, S. (1997) A continuity correction for discrete barrier options. *Mathematical Finance*, 7(4): 325–348.

Cai, F., Howorka, E. and Wongswan, J. (2006) Transmission of Volatility and Trading Activity in the Global Interdealer Foreign Exchange Market: Evidence from Electronic Broking Services (EBS) Data. Federal Reserve Board's International Finance Discussion Papers 863. http:www.federalreserve.gov/pubs/ifdp/2006/863/ifdp863.pdf

Castagna, A. (2010) *FX Options and Smile Risk*. John Wiley & Sons, Ltd, Chichester.

Chibane, M. and Sheldon, G. (2009) Building Curves on a Good Basis. Shinsei Bank Working Paper (Version: 24 April 2009). http://ssrn.com/abstract=1394267

Chu, C. C. and Kwok, Y. K. (2007) Target Redemption Note. *Journal of Futures Markets*, 27: 535–554.

Cont, R. and Tankov, P. (2004) *Financial Modelling with Jump Processes*. World Scientific, Singapore.

Cox, D. R. and Miller, H. D. (1965) *The Theory of Stochastic Processes*. Chapman & Hall, Boca Raton, Florida.

Cox, J. C. (1996) The Constant Elasticity of Variance Option Pricing Model. *The Journal of Portfolio Management*, 22(1): 15–17 (reprint of 1975 Working Paper from Stanford University).

Cox, J. C., Ingersoll, J. E. and Ross, S. A. (1985) A Theory of Term Structure of Interest Rates. *Econometrica*, 53: 385–467.

Cox, J. C. and Ross, S. A. (1976) The Valuation of Options for Alternative Stochastic Processes. *Journal of Financial Economics*, 3(1–2): 145–166.

Crack, T. F. (2001) *Heard on the Street: Quantitative Questions from Wall Street Job Interviews*. Timothy Crack (self-published), Bloomington, Indiana. http://www.investmentbankingjobinterviews.com/

Craig, I. J. D. and Sneyd, A. D. (1988) An Alternative Direction Implicit Scheme for Parabolic Equations with Mixed Derivatives. *Computers and Mathematics with Applications*, 16(4): 341–350.

Daglish, T., Hull, J. and Suo, W. (2007) Volatility Surface: Theory, Rules of Thumb, and Empirical Evidence. *Quantitative Finance*, 7(5): 507.

Dang, D. M., Christara, C. C., Jackson, K. R., and Lakhany, A. (2010) A PDE Pricing Framework for Cross-Currency Interest Rate Derivatives (Version: 1 May 2010). http://ssrn.com/abstract=1502302

Davydov, D. and Linetsky, V. (2001) Pricing and Hedging Path-Dependent Options under the CEV Process. *Management Science*, 47(7): 949–965.

DeGroot, M. H. (1986) *Probability and Statistics*, 2nd edition. Addison Wesley, Reading, Massachusetts.

Derman, E. and Kani, I. (1998) Stochastic Implied Trees: Arbitrage Pricing with Stochastic Term and Strike Structure. *International Journal of Theoretical and Applied Finance*, 1: 61–110.

Douglas, J. (1962) Alternating Direction Methods for Three Space Variables. *Numerische Mathematik*, 4: 41–63.

Douglas, J. and Rachford, H. H. (1956) On the Numerical Solution of Heat Conduction Problems in Two and Three Space Variables. *Transactions of the American Mathematical Society*, 82: 421–439.

Drăgulescu, A. A. and Yakovenko, V. M. (2002) Probability Distribution of Returns in the Heston Model with Stochastic Volatility. *Quantitative Finance*, 2: 43–453.

Drezner, Z. (1994) Computation of the Trivariate Normal Integral. *Mathematics of Computation*, 62: 289–294.

Drezner, Z. and Wesolowski, G. O. (1989) On the Computation of the Bivariate Normal Integral. *Journal of Statistical Computation and Simulation*, 35: 101–107.

Duffy, D. J. (2006) *Finite Difference Methods in Financial Engineering: A Partial Differential Equation Approach*. John Wiley & Sons, Ltd, Chichester.

Duffy, D. J. (2001) Robust and Accurate Finite Difference Methods in Option Pricing One Factor Models (Version: 1 May 2010). http://www.datasim-component.com.

Dupire, B. (1993) Pricing and Hedging with Smiles. In Proceedings of the AFFI Conference La Boule, June 1993.

Dupire, B. (1994) Pricing with a Smile. RISK, 7(1): 18–20.

Dupire, B. (1996) A Unified Theory of Volatility, Paribas Discussion Paper. In P. Carr (ed.). *Derivatives Pricing: The Classic Collection*, RISK Books, London.

Durrett, R. (1996) *Stochastic Calculus: A Practical Introduction*. CRC Press, Boca Raton, Florida.

Elices, A. (2008) Models with Time-Dependent Parameters Using Transform Methods: Application to Heston's Model. http://www.arxiv.org/abs/0708.2020v2

Feller, W. (1951) Two Singular Diffusion Problems. *Annals of Mathematics*, 54(1): 173–182.

French, D. (1984) The Weekend Effect on the Distribution of Stock Prices – Implications for Option Pricing. *Journal of Financial Economics*, 13(4): 547–559.

Fruchard, E., Zammouri, C. and Willems, E. (1995) Basis for Change. *RISK*, 8(10): 70–75.

Garman, M. B. and Kohlhagen, S. W. (1983) Foreign Currency Option Values. *Journal of International Money and Finance*, 2: 231–237.

Gao, C. and Wang, Y. (1996) A General Formulation of Peaceman and Rachford ADI Method for the *N*-dimensional Heat Diffusion Equation. *International Communications in Heat and Mass Transfer*, 23(6): 845–854.

Gatheral, J. (2006) *The Volatility Surface: A Practitioner's Guide*. Wiley Finance, Hoboken, New Jersey.

Genz, A. (2004) Numerical Computation of Rectangular Bivariate and Trivariate Normal and *t* Probabilities. *Statistics and Computing*, 14(3): 251–260.

Glasserman, P. (2004) *Monte Carlo Methods in Financial Engineering*. Springer, Berlin.

Gorovoi, V. and Linetsky, V. (2004) Black's Model of Interest Rates as Options, Eigenfunction Expansions and Japanese Interest Rates. *Mathematical Finance*, 14(1): 49–78.

Grigoriu, M. (2002) *Stochastic Calculus: Applications in Science and Engineering*. Birkhäuser, Boston.

Gyöngy, I. (1986) Mimicking the One-Dimensional Marginal Distributions of Processes Having an Itô Differential. *Probability Theory and Related Fields*, 71: 501–516.

Hagan, P. S. and West, G. (2006) Interpolation Methods for Curve Construction. *Applied Mathematical Finance*, 13(2): 89–129.

Hagan, P. S. and Woodward, D. E. (1999) Equivalent Black Volatilities. *Applied Mathematical Finance*, 6(2): 147–157.

Hagan, P. S., Kumar, D., Lesniewski, A. S. and Woodward, D. E. (2002) Managing Smile Risk. *Wilmott Magazine*, July: 84–108.

Hakala, J. and Wystup, U. (2002) *Foreign Exchange Risk*. Risk Publications, London.

Halai, J. (2008) *Extending the Heston Model to Time Dependent Parameters: An Application to Pricing and Calibration in FX*. MSc Dissertation, Imperial College, London.

Haug, E. (2007) *The Complete guide to Option Pricing Formulas*, 2nd edition. McGraw-Hill, New York.

Henry-Labordère, P. (2009) Calibration of Local Stochastic Volatility Models to Market Smiles. *RISK*, September: 112–117.

Heston, S. L. (1993) A Closed-Form Solution for Options with Stochastic Volatility with Applications to Bond and Currency Options. *The Review of Financial Studies*, 6(2): 327–343.

Heynen, R. C. and Kat, H. M. (1994) Partial Barrier Options. *Journal of Financial Engineering*, 2: 253–274.

Hicks, A. (2000) *Managing Currency Risk Using Foreign Exchange Options*. Woodhead, Abington, Cambridge.

Hildebrand, F. B. (1974) *Introduction to Numerical Analysis*. McGraw-Hill, New York.

Hull, J. (1997) *Options, Futures and Other Derivatives*, 3rd edition. Prentice Hall, Upper Saddle River, New Jersey.

Hull, J. and White, A. (1987) The Pricing of Options on Assets with Stochastic Volatilities. *Journal of Finance*, 42: 281–300.

Hull, J. and White, A. (1993) One Factor Interest Rate Models and the Valuation of Interest Rate Derivative Securities. *Journal of Financial and Quantitative Analysis*, 28(2): 235–254.

Hunt, P. J. and Kennedy, J. E. (2000) *Financial Derivatives in Theory and Practice*. John Wiley & Sons, Ltd, Chichester.

ICOM (1997) The 1997 International Currency Options Market (ICOM) Master Agreement Guide. `http://www.ny.frb.org/fmlg/icomgiu.pdf`

In t' Hout, K. J. and Foulon, S. (2010) ADI Finite Difference Schemes for Option Pricing in the Heston Model with Correlation. *International Journal of Numerical Analysis and Modeling*, 7(2): 303–320.

Jäckel, P. (2002) *Monte Carlo Methods in Finance*. John Wiley & Sons, Ltd, Chichester.

Jeffrey, C. (2003) The Problem with Power-Reverse Duals. *RISK*, 16(10): 20–22.

Jex, M., Henderson, R. and Wang, D. (1999) Pricing Exotics under the Smile. *RISK*, November: 72–75.

Johnson, H. E. (1987) Options on the Maximum or Minimum of Several Assets. *The Journal of Financial and Quantitative Analysis*, 22: 277–283.

Johnson, H. and Shanno, D. (1987) Option Pricing When the Variance is Changing. *The Journal of Financial and Quantitative Analysis*, 22: 143–151.

Jung, A. (1998) Improving the Performance of Low-Discrepancy Sequences. *Journal of Derivatives*, (Winter): 85–95.

Kammler, D. W. (2007) *A First Course in Fourier Analysis*, 2nd edition. Cambridge University Press, Cambridge.

Karatzas, I. and Shreve, R. (1991) *Brownian Motion and Stochastic Calculus*, 2nd edition. Springer, New York.

Kloeden, P. E. and Platen, E. (1992) *Numerical Solution of Stochastic Differential Equations*. Springer, Berlin.

Kohl-Landgraf, P. (2007) *PDE Valuation of Interest Rate Derivatives: From Theory to Implementation*. Peter Kohl-Landgraf (self-published), Norderstedt.

Langnau, A. (2009) Introduction into 'Local Correlation' Modelling (Version: 22 September 2009). `http://arxiv.org/abs/0909.3441`

Langnau, A. (2010) A Dynamic Model for Correlation. *RISK*, April: 92–96.

Lee, R. W. (2004) Implied Volatility: Statics, Dynamics and Probabilistic Interpretation. In R. Baeza-Yates, *et al.* (eds). *Recent Advances in Applied Probability*. Springer, New York: pp. 241–268.

Lewis, A. L. (2000) *Option Valuation under Stochastic Volatility with Mathematica Code*. Finance Press, Newport Beach, California.

Li, A. and Raghavan, V. R. (1996) LIBOR-in-Arrears Swaps. *Journal of Derivatives*, (Spring): 44–48.

Lipton, A. (2001) *Mathematical Methods for Foreign Exchange: A Financial Engineer's Approach*. World Scientific, Singapore.

Lipton, A. (2002) The Vol Smile Problem. *RISK*. February: 61–65.

Lipton, A. and McGhee, W. (2002) Universal Barriers. *RISK*, May: 81–85.

Lo, C. F., Yuen, P. H. and Hui, C. H. (2000) Constant Elasticity of Variance Option Pricing Model with Time-Dependent Parameters. *International Journal of Theoretical and Applied Finance*, 3(4): 661–674.

Longstaff, F. A. (1989) A Nonlinear General Equilibrium Model of the Term Structure of Interest Rates. *Journal of Financial Economics*, 23: 195–224.

Longstaff, F. A. and Schwartz, E. S. (2001) Valuing American Options by Simulation: A Simple Least-Squares Approach. *Review of Financial Studies*, 14: 113–147.

Lu, R. and Hsu, Y.-H. (2005) Valuation of Standard Options under the Constant Elasticity of Variance Model. *International Journal of Business and Economics*, 4(2): 157–165.

Lucic, V. (2008) Boundary Conditions for Computing Densities in Hybrid Models. `http://ssrn.com/abstract=1191962`

McKee, S. and Mitchell, A. R. (1970) Alternating Direction Methods for Parabolic Equations in Two Space Dimensions with a Mixed Derivative. *The Computer Journal*, 13: 81–86.

McLeish, D. L. (2005) *Monte Carlo Simulation and Finance*. John Wiley & Sons, Ltd, Chichester.

Malz, A. (1997) Estimating the Probability Distribution of the Future Exchange Rate from Option Prices. *Journal of Derivatives*, (Winter): 20–36.

Margrabe, W. (1978) The Value of an Option to Exchange One Asset for Another. *The Journal of Finance*, 33(1): 177–186.

Matsumoto, M. and Nishimura, T. (1998) Mersenne Twister: A 623-dimensionally Equidistributed Uniform Pseudo-random Number Generator. *ACM Transactions on Modeling and Computer Simulation*, 8(1): 3–30. `http://www.math.sci.hiroshima-u.ac.jp/~m-mat/MT/ARTICLES/mt.pdf`

Mercurio, F. (2003) *Pricing and Static Replication of FX Quanto Options*. Banca IMI Technical Document. http://www.fabiomercurio.it/FwdStartQuanto.pdf

Merton, R. (1976) Option Pricing when Underlying Stock Returns are Discontinuous. *Journal of Financial Economics*, 3: 125–144.

Morton, K. W. (1996) *Numerical Solution of Convection–Diffusion Problems*. Chapman & Hall, London.

Morton, K. W. and Mayers, D. F. (2005) *Numerical Solution of Partial Differential Equations*, 2nd edition. Cambridge University Press, Cambridge.

Musiela, M. and Rutkowski, M. (1997) *Martingale Methods in Financial Modelling*. Springer, Berlin.

Niederreiter, H. (1992) *Random Number Generation and Quasi-Monte Carlo Methods*. SIAM Press, Philadelphia, Pennsylvania.

Nocedal, J. and Wright, S. J. (2006) *Numerical Optimization*, 2nd edition. Springer, New York.

Øksendal, B. (1998) *Stochastic Differential Equations: An Introduction with Applications*, 5th edition. Springer, Berlin.

Peaceman, D. W. and Rachford, H. H. (1955) The Numerical Solution of Parabolic and Elliptic Differential Equations. *Journal of the Society of Industrial and Applied Mathematics*, 3: 28–41.

Pelsser, A. (2000) *Efficient Methods for Valuing Interest Rate Derivatives*. Springer, London.

Piterbarg, V. (2005a) A Multi-Currency Model with FX Volatility Skew (Version: 7 February 2005). http://ssrn.com/abstract=685084

Piterbarg, V. (2006a) Markovian Projection Method for Volatility Calibration (Version: 25 May 2006). http://ssrn.com/abstract=906473

Piterbarg, V. (2006b) Smiling Hybrids. *RISK*, May: 66–71.

Press, W. H., Teukolsky, S. A., Vetterling, W. T. and Flannery, B. P. (2002) *Numerical Recipes in C++*, 2nd edition. Cambridge University Press, Cambridge.

Rajabpour, M. A. (2009) Bessel Process and Conformal Quantum Mechanics. *Journal of Statistical Physics*, 136(4): 785–805.

Rannacher, R. (1984) Finite Element Solution of Diffusion Problems with Irregular Data. *Numerical Mathematics*, 43: 309–327.

Rebonato, R. (1996) *Interest-Rate Option Models: Understanding, Analysing and Using Models for Exotic Interest-Rate Options*, 2nd edition. John Wiley & Sons, Ltd, Chichester.

Rebonato, R. (2002) *Modern Pricing of Interest-Rate Derivatives: The LIBOR Market Model and Beyond*. Princeton, Princeton.

Reghaï, A. (2009) Using Local Correlation Models to Improve Option Hedging (Version: 30 October 2009). http://www.institutlouisbachelier.org/risk10/work/4823366.pdf

Reiner, E. (1992) Quanto Mechanics. *RISK*, March: 59–63.

Ren, Y., Madan, D. and Qian, M. Q. (2007) Calibrating and Pricing with Embedded Local Volatility Models. *RISK*, September: 138–143.

Rich, D. R. (1994) The Mathematical Foundation of Barrier Option-Pricing Theory. *Advances in Futures and Options Research*, 7: 267–311.

Risken, H. (1989) *The Fokker-Planck Equation: Methods of Solution and Applications*, 2nd edition. Springer, Berlin.

Rombouts, J. V. K. and Stentoft, L. (2010) Multivariate Option Pricing with Time Varying Volatility and Correlations (May 1, 2010). CIRANO, Scientific Publications 2010s-23. http://ssrn.com/abstract=1611793

Rubinstein, M. (1991) One for Another. *RISK*, 4(7): 30–31.

Rubinstein, M. and Reiner, E. (1991) Breaking down the Barriers. *RISK*, 4(8): 75–83.

Rule, D., Garratt, A. and Rummel, O. (2004) Structured Note Markets: Products, Participants and Links to Wholesale Derivatives Markets. *Financial Stability Review, Bank of England*, June: 98–117. http://giddy.org/sf/articles/structured_notes.pdf

Schmitz, K. E. (2010) Strong Taylor Schemes for Stochastic Volatility. http://www.performancetrading.it/Documents/KsStrong/KsS_Index.htm

Schöbel, R. and Zhu, J. (1999) Stochastic Volatility with an Ornstein–Uhlenbeck Process: An Extension. *European Finance Review*, 3: 23–46.

Schroder, M. (1989) Computing the Constant Elasticity of Variance Option Pricing Formula. *Journal of Finance*, 44(1): 211–219.

Scott, L. O. (1987) Option Pricing when the Variance Changes Randomly: Theory, Estimation and an Application. *Journal of Financial and Quantitative Analysis*, 22: 419–438.

Seydel, R. (2004) *Tools for Computational Finance*, 2nd edition. Springer, Berlin.

Sippel, J. and Ohkoshi, S. (2002) All Power to PRDC Notes. *RISK*, October: S31–S33.

Smith, G. D. (1985) *Numerical Solution of Partial Differential Equations: Finite Difference Methods.* Oxford University Press, Oxford.

Stein, E. M. and Stein, J. C. (1991) Stock Price Distributions with Stochastic Volatility: An Analytic Approach. *Review of Financial Studies*, 4(4): 727–752.

Stigum, M. and Robinson, F. L. (1996) *Money Market and Bond Calculations.* Richard D. Irwin, Chicago, Illinois.

Strikwerda, J. C. (1989) *Finite Difference Schemes and Partial Differential Equations.* Brooks/Cole, Pacific Grove.

Stulz, R. M. (1982) Options on the Minimum of the Maximum of Two Risky Assets: Analysis and Applications. *Journal of Financial Economics*, 10: 161–185.

Sundaram, R. K. (1997) Equivalent Martingale Measures and Risk-Neutral Pricing: An Expository Note. *The Journal of Derivatives*, Fall: 85–98.

Sundkvist, K. and Vikström, M. (2000) Intraday and Weekend Volatility Patterns – Implications for Option Pricing. Swedish School of Economics and Business Administration Working Paper 453. http://urn.fi/URN:ISBN:951-555-680-5

Taleb, N. (1997) *Dynamic Hedging: Managing Vanilla and Exotic Options.* John Wiley & Sons, Inc., New York.

Tan, C. C. (2010) *Demystifying Exotic Products: Interest Rates, Equities and Foreign Exchange.* John Wiley & Sons, Ltd, Chichester.

Tang, Y. and Li, B. (2007) *Quantitative Analysis, Derivatives Modeling and Trading Strategies.* World Scientific, Singapore.

Tavella, D. and Randall, C. (2000) *Pricing Financial Instruments: The Finite Difference Method.* John Wiley & Sons, Inc., New York.

Thomas, J. W. (1995) *Numerical Partial Differential Equations: Finite Difference Methods.* Springer, New York.

Topper, J. (2005) *Financial Engineering with Finite Elements.* John Wiley & Sons, Ltd, Chichester.

Tsuyuguchi, Y. and Wooldridge, P. D. (2008) The Evolution of Trading Activity in Asian Foreign Exchange Markets. *Emerging Markets Review*, 9(4): 231–246.

Tuckman, B. and Porfirio, P. (2004) *Interest Rate Parity, Money Market Basis Swaps, and Cross-Currency Basis Swaps.* Fixed Income Liquid Markets Research, LMR Quarterly, Vol. 2004-Q2, Lehman Brothers.

Wang, J. (2007) *Convexity of Option Prices in the Heston Model.* U.U.D.M. Project Report 2007:3. http://www.math.uu.se/research/pub/Wang1.pdf

Wesseling, P. (1992) *An Introduction to Multigrid Methods.* John Wiley & Sons, Ltd, Chichester.

Wilmott, P. (1998) *Derivatives: The Theory and Practice of Financial Engineering.* John Wiley & Sons, Inc., New York.

Wilmott, P., Dewynne, J. and Howison, S. (1993) *Option Pricing: Mathematical Models and Computation.* Oxford Financial Press, Oxford.

Wystup, U. (2006) *FX Options and Structured Products.* John Wiley & Sons, Ltd, Chichester.

Wystup, U. (2008) *FX Options and Structured Products: Solutions Manual.* http://www.mathfinance.com/FXOptions/Book/FXO-solution-manual.pdf

Zhang, P. G. (1998) *Exotic Options: A Guide to Second Generation Options*, 2nd edition. World Scientific, Singapore.

Zhu, J. (2000) *Modular Pricing of Options: An Application of Fourier Analysis.* Springer, Berlin.

Zhu, J. (2008) A Simple and Exact Simulation Approach to Heston Model (Version: 1 July 2008). http://ssrn.com/abstract=1153950

Zvan, R., Vetzal, K. R. and Forsyth, P. A. (2000) PDE methods for pricing barrier options. *Journal of Economic Dynamics and Control*, 24: 1563–1590.

Further Reading

Albrecher, H., Mayer, P., Schoutens, W. and Tistaert, J. (2006) The Little Heston Trap (Version: 11 September 2006). http://lirias.kuleuven.be/bitstream/123456789/138039/1/HestonTrap.pdf

Ball, C. A. and Roma, A. (1994) Stochastic volatility option pricing. *Journal of Financial and Quantitative Analysis*, 29: 581–607.

Bloch, D. and Nakashima, Y. (2008) Multi-Currency Local Volatility Model. Mizuho Securities Working Paper (Version: August 2008). http://ssrn.com/abstract=1153337

Borodin, A. N. and Salminen, P. (1996) *Handbook of Brownian Motion – Facts and Formulae*. Birkhäuser, Basel.

Breeden, D. T. and Litzenberger, R. H. (1978) Prices of State-Contingent Claims Implicit in Option Prices. *The Journal of Business*, 51(4): 621–651.

Briys, E., Bellalah, M. Mai, H. M. and de Varenne, F. (1998) *Options, Futures and Exotic Derivatives: Theory, Application and Practice*. John Wiley & Sons, Ltd, Chichester.

Burch, D. (2007) Girsanov's Theorem and Importance Sampling. http://www-math.mit.edu/~tkemp/18.177/Girsanov.Sampling.pdf

Carr, P. and Madan, D. B. (2005) A Note on Sufficient Conditions for No Arbitrage. *Finance Research Letters*, 2: 125–130.

Chibane, M. (2010) Modeling Long Dated Hybrid Structures, presented at ICBI Global Derivatives conference, Paris, 19 May 2010.

Christoffersen, P. and Mazzotta, S. (2004) The Informational Content of Over-The-Counter Currency Options, ECB Working Paper 366. http://www.ecb.europa.eu/pub/pdf/scpwps/ecbwp366.pdf

Eckhardt, R. (1987) Stan Ulam, John von Neumann, and the Monte Carlo Method. *Los Alamos Science*, Special Issue (15): 131–137.

Elices, A. and Fouque, J.P. (2010) Perturbed Copula: Introducing the skew effect in the co-dependence. (Version: 27 February 2010). http://arxiv.org/abs/1003.0041v1

Fouque, J. P., Papanicolaou, G. and Sircar, K. R. (2001) *Derivatives in Financial Markets with Stochastic Volatility*. Cambridge University Press, Cambridge.

Giles, M. and Carter, R. (2006) Convergence Analysis of Crank–Nicolson and Rannacher Time-Marching. *Computational Finance*, 9(4): 89–112.

Glasserman, P., Heidelberger, P. and Shahabuddin, P. (1999) Asymptotically Optimal Importance Sampling and Stratification for Pricing Path-Dependent Options. *Mathematical Finance*, 9(2): 117–162.

Guasoni, P. and Robertson, S. (2008) Optimal Importance Sampling with Explicit Formulas in Continuous Time. *Finance and Stochastics*, 12(1): 1–19. http://math.bu.edu/people/guasoni/papers/isbs.pdf

Kac, M. (1949) On Distributions of Certain Wiener Functionals. *Transactions of the American Mathematical Society*, 65(1): 1–13.

Kahl, C. and Jäckel, P. (2005) Not-so-Complex Logarithms in the Heston Model. *Wilmott Magazine*: 94–103.

Kloeden, P. E., Platen, E. and Schurz, H. (1997) *Numerical Solution of SDE Through Computer Experiments.* Springer, Berlin.

Kwok, Y.-K. (1998) *Mathematical Models of Financial Derivatives.* Springer, Singapore.

Kwok, Y.-K. (2009) Lattice Tree Methods for Strongly Path Dependent Options. `http://ssrn.com/abstract=1421736`

Lamberton, B. and Lapeyre, B. (1996) *Introduction to Stochastic Calculus Applied to Finance*, trans. N. Rabeau and F. Mantion. Chapman and Hall, London.

Lin, J. and Ritchken, P. (2006) On Pricing Derivatives in the Presence of Auxiliary State Variables. *Journal of Derivatives*, 14(2): 29–46.

McKee, S., Wall, D. P. and Wilson, S. K. (1996) An Alternating Direction Implicit Scheme for Parabolic Equations with Mixed Derivative and Convective Terms. *Journal of Computational Physics*, 126(2): 64–76.

Majmin, L. (2005) *Local and Stochastic Volatility Models: An Investigation into the Pricing of Exotic Equity Options.* MSc Dissertation, University of the Witwatersrand.

Mikhailov, S. and Nögel, U. (2003) Heston's Stochastic Volatility Model, Calibration and Some Extensions. *Wilmott Magazine*: 74–79.

Pelsser, A. (2001) Mathematical Foundation of Convexity Correction (Version: 18 April 2001). `http://ssrn.com/abstract=267995`

Piterbarg, V. (2005b) Time to Smile. *Wilmott Magazine*, (May): 71–75.

Reiswich, D. and Wystup, U. (2009) FX Volatility Smile Construction (Version: 8 September 2009). `http://www.mathfinance.com/wystup/papers/CPQF_Arbeits20.pdf`

Rebonato, R. (2004) *Volatility and Correlation*, 2nd edition. John Wiley & Sons, Ltd, Chichester.

Salmon, M. and Schleicher, C. (2006) Pricing Multivariate Currency Options with Copulas. University of Warwick Financial Econometrics Research Centre Working Paper WP06-21. `http://www2.warwick.ac.uk/fac/soc/wbs/research/wfri/rsrchcentres/ferc/wrkingpaprseries/fwp06-21.pdf`

Sheppard, R. (2007) *Pricing Equity Derivatives under Stochastic Volatility: A Partial Differential Equation Approach.* MSc Dissertation, University of the Witwatersrand.

Weithers, T. (2006) *Foreign Exchange: A Practical Guide to the FX Markets.* John Wiley & Sons, Ltd, Chichester.

Index

Index compiled by Terry Halliday

Printed and bound by CPI Group (UK) Ltd, Croydon, CR0 4YY

23/04/2025

14660969-0001